Library of
Exact Philosophy

Editor:
Mario Bunge, Montreal

Co-editors:
Sir Alfred Jules Ayer, Oxford
Herbert Feigl, Minneapolis, Minn.
Victor Kraft, Wien
Sir Karl Popper, Penn

Springer-Verlag New York Wien

Library of Exact Philosophy 11

Moritz Schlick

General Theory of Knowledge

Translated by Albert E. Blumberg

With an Introduction by
A. E. Blumberg and H. Feigl

Springer-Verlag New York Wien 1974

Translated from the 2nd German Edition of
Allgemeine Erkenntnislehre
(Naturwissenschaftliche Monographien und Lehrbücher, Band 1)
Berlin: Verlag von Julius Springer, 1925
Copyright 1925 by Julius Springer in Berlin

Printing type: Sabon Roman
Composed and printed by Herbert Hiessberger, Pottenstein
Binding work: Karl Scheibe, Wien
Design: Hans Joachim Böning, Wien

ISBN 0-387-81160-5 Springer-Verlag New York - Wien
ISBN 3-211-81160-5 Springer-Verlag Wien - New York

General Preface to the LEP

Exact philosophy can be described as the field of philosophy tilled with exact tools, i. e. logic and mathematics. Exactness concerns the methods or tools, not the subject. Regardless of its subject, a piece of philosophical investigation qualifies as exact as long as it involves a precise statement of the problems, a careful analysis of the key concepts and principles, and an attempt at systematization. If the outcome is a full fledged theory with a definite mathematical structure, and moreover a theory that solves some important philosophical problems, so much the better.

It is worth while, nay exciting and urgent, to try the exact method in every branch of philosophy — in semantics, epistemology, philosophy of science, value theory, ethics, legal philosophy, the history of philosophy, and perhaps even in aesthetics. The more exactly we proceed in handling genuine philosophical problems, the narrower should become the gap between the humanities on the one hand, and mathematics and science on the other. And the better we bridge this gap the lesser will be the chances that the anti-intellectualist trends will destroy contemporary culture.

Some great philosophers have worked in exact philosophy: not only Carnap and Russell but also Bolzano, Leibniz, and Aristotle. A whole school, the Vienna Circle, was devoted to the enterprise of reconstructing philosophy in an exact manner and in the light of the sciences. The Library of Exact Philosophy is a new link in this long thin chain. It was established in 1970 in order to stimulate the production and circulation of significant additions to *philosophia more geometrico*. The LEP has already made a contribution to that goal, and it is hoped that it will incorporate further works dealing in an exact way with interesting philosophical issues.

Zürich, April 1973

Mario Bunge

From the Preface to the First Edition

It may seem odd that a series of works devoted to the natural sciences should include — indeed begin with — a volume on philosophy. Today, of course, it is generally agreed that philosophy and natural science are perfectly compatible. But to grant the theory of knowledge such a prominent position implies not only that these two fields are compatible, but that there is a natural connection between them. Thus the inclusion of this book in the series can be justified only if such an intimate relation of mutual dependence and interpenetration really does exist.

Without anticipating what is to come, the author would like first to explain his point of view on the relationship between epistemology and the sciences, and in so doing make clear at the outset the method to be followed in this book.

It is my view — which I have already expressed elsewhere and which I never tire of repeating — that philosophy is not a separate science to be placed alongside of or above the individual disciplines. Rather, the philosophical element is present in all of the sciences; it is their true soul, and only by virtue of it are they sciences at all. Knowledge in any particular field presupposes a body of quite general principles into which it fits and without which it would not be knowledge. Philosophy is nothing other than the system of these principles, a system which branches out and penetrates the entire system of knowledge and thereby gives it stability. Hence philosophy has its home in all the sciences; and I am convinced that the only way one can reach philosophy is to seek it out in its homeland.

While philosophy has its residence deep within all the sciences, it does not reveal itself with the same readiness in every one of them. On the contrary, first principles will of necessity be found most easily in those disciplines that have already attained the highest level of generality. Clearly, the propositions that possess the most general validity for the real world are those of the natural sciences, in particular the exact sciences. It is only from their diggings that the philosopher can unearth the treasures he seeks. History is concerned with the destiny of a single species on a single planet, philology with the laws governing a quite specific activity of that species. In contrast, the validity of the laws discovered through the methods of the natural sciences is not confined to any individual domain of reality; it extends, in principle, to the entire universe, however distant in time and space. Therefore general epistemology is bound to take the scientific knowledge of nature as its point of departure.

This is not to say, however, that knowledge of nature is some special kind of knowledge. Knowledge everywhere is *one;* the most general principles are always the same, even in the humanities. The only difference is that in the humanities these principles, although just as operative there, appear as applied to much more specific and complicated matters and hence are much more difficult to perceive. Consider, for instance, how much easier it is to trace the workings of causality in a physical process than in an historical event.

It is pretty much in this fashion that the relationship between philosophic thought and the thinking characteristic of the individual sciences presents itself. Clearly the philosopher is called upon to address his full energies to the knowledge of nature. Conversely, the natural scientist finds that his most important problems strongly impel him toward the theory of knowledge; for these problems are of such extreme generality that his science, in dealing with them, continually impinges on the domain of the purely philosophical. He must indeed step over into that realm; otherwise he will not be able to understand fully the meaning of his own activity. The truly great scientist is always at the same time a philosopher. This close interrelationship of goals between epistemology and the natural sciences both permits and requires a close external association as well. It would be good if this were more clearly evident in the academies and universities, where it is still the custom to counterpose the philosophical and historical disciplines to the mathematical and scientific ones. Meanwhile, the interrelationship may find a modest expression in the way the present work is being published.

For these reasons, I was delighted to accept the publisher's proposal that this book appear in a series devoted to the "natural sciences".

I have constantly sought the simplest possible mode of presentation, one that builds slowly, so that the discussion can be understood without a special knowledge of philosophy. In a few places, it was necessary to include a detailed criticism of particular philosophical doctrines so that the author could characterize his own position more completely for the benefit of his colleagues. But these passages are easy to recognize, and they may be omitted without loss by the reader who is interested only in the general argument.

The pages that follow have been entitled *General Theory of Knowledge* because the inquiry is directed wholly to ultimate principles. If philosophical curiosity does not carry us to these most general principles, but comes to a halt, as it were, at the level before the last, then we shall find ourselves — if our point of departure has been natural science — in the province of the theory of natural knowledge, or the philosophy of science. Similarly, the road that leads from the science of history to general epistemology passes through the theory of historical knowledge, or the philosophy of history, that from mathematics through the philosophy of mathematics, and so on. We shall not be able, in what follows, to tarry at the level of these special epistemologies, although admittedly the substantiation of our results may seem incomplete at some points. But it would be quite impossible, if only for practical reasons, to go into the voluminous special studies in these areas. Thus the definitive completion of our argument as a whole must await a treatment of the special problems. This I hope to present later.

Preface to the Second Edition

This book has been out of print for more than two and a half years. The author feels that he should account to the reader for such a long delay in the appearance of a new edition, the more so since there has been a lively demand for the book in the meantime.

First of all, outside circumstances have kept the author occupied with tasks of an altogether different nature. But other factors, stemming from an awareness of certain deficiencies in the first edition, also have held back the start and progress of the revision. To overcome these deficiencies fully would have required a major development and expansion with regard to the logic of knowledge, and this would have meant reconstructing the entire work. So sweeping a change, however, could not be considered; for the book, thus transformed, would have lost its original character. It would no longer have been able to serve those needs the satisfaction of which has earned for it the particular place it holds in the philosophical literature. For the book to continue to occupy this place, it was necessary to retain the general design; for it to fulfill its role better than before, it was necessary to revise many details.

As a consequence, the revisions in the second edition had to be confined to corrections, small additions and deletions. And the important task of rounding out logically the epistemological ideas developed in the book had to be put over to a later comprehensive exposition of the principles of logic.

Convinced that correct ideas make their way best by virtue of the truth inherent in them, without their having to wage a long drawn out battle against error, I have eliminated all non-essential polemical excursions. The development of my own position has been tied in with a critique of opposing views only where the latter form a natural point of departure for positive considerations. Accordingly, the critical comments on the basic ideas of Kant and his school have had to be retained in the new edition. Indeed, it was necessary even to enlarge the important chapter on the "Critique of the Idea of Immanence", for although this chapter, in particular, had received widespread favorable attention, it seemed to me to be in need of some not insignificant supplementation and improvement.

I have devoted much care to reworking the chapters that deal with the psychophysical problem. It seems that the discussion of this topic, to which I attach a quite special systematic importance, has for the most part not been correctly understood. The experiences I have had in lectures and conversations permit me to hope that by means of the new formulations I have succeeded in avoiding the shortcomings of the earlier account.

Among other changes, I should like to mention the observations newly added as § 11, which make for a greater simplicity and compactness in the basic systematic outlook. Also, the exposition in the final section of the book is given in a still briefer outline than in the first edition. It had already become clear to me, while working on the first edition, that a satisfactory treatment of the questions raised in the section on inductive knowledge would actually require a separate volume. Since a more thorough handling of the problem was not possible within the existing limits, I have therefore chosen rather to shorten the chapter.

Despite numerous deletions and condensations, the book has grown in size, although not to a significant extent.

In response to many requests, a subject index has been added. For preparing this index, and another of authors, as well as for his extremely valuable help in correcting the proofs, I owe my warmest thanks to Herbert Feigl, student of philosophy.

Vienna, March, 1925

The Author

Contents

Introduction

By

Herbert Feigl and Albert E. Blumberg

An English translation of MORITZ SCHLICK's chief work, *Allgemeine Erkenntnislehre,* is long overdue. The book was first published in 1918; a second and revised edition appeared in 1925, a half century ago. It is this latter edition that is here translated into English under the title of *General Theory of Knowledge.*

I

Moritz Schlick (1882—1936) is best known as the founder and guiding genius of the "Vienna Circle of logical positivists". He was indeed the "center" of the famed Circle. And this notwithstanding the fact that, as an extraordinarily modest, self-effacing and kindly man, he chose in general to contribute to Circle discussions as a constructively critical "chairman" and "moderator" rather than as a protagonist. Only on rare occasions — in response, say, to some of Otto Neurath's challenging notions about a radical materialism or some of Felix Kaufmann's probing ideas about phenomenology — did Schlick allow his criticisms to take on any slight trace of sharpness or aggressiveness.

It is perhaps not universally known that Schlick obtained his doctorate in *physics.* His dissertation, completed at Berlin in 1904 under the supervision of the celebrated physicist Max Planck, dealt with the reflection of light in a non-homogeneous medium. It may also have escaped notice that before Schlick turned his full attention to problems of epistemology and the philosophy of science, he published in 1908 a remarkable little book called *Lebensweisheit* (*Wisdom of Life,* never translated), a somewhat romantic study in eudaimonism. It was reviewed quite favorably by WILHELM OSTWALD, editor of *Annalen der Naturphilosophie,* in the pages of his journal. Ostwald, basing himself solely on a reading of the book, described its author (then all of 24 or 25) as a "wise old doctor". In 1909, Schlick wrote an essay entitled "The Basic Problems of Aesthetics in the Light of Evolutionary History". As early as 1910, however, he began to publish papers on fundamental issues in the theory of knowledge and the philosophy of science.

It was not until 1927, and then only for a short period, that Schlick returned to the question of "the good life". In that year, he published a charming essay on "The Meaning of Life". There are also unpublished sequelae, partly unfinished, on a "Philosophy of Youth". His *Fragen der Ethik* (translated into English by DAVID RYNI as *Problems of Ethics,* Prentice-Hall, 1939) appeared in 1930.

Largely though not entirely independent of his epistemology, Schlick's philosophy of life is essentially a panegyric to the spirit of creative enthusiasm. By "youth" he means not an age group but a life of enthusiastic devotion to one's activities. Work (as for Friedrich Schiller) is to become "play" in the sense of something intrinsically enjoyable. Instead of pursuing questionable ends by even more questionable means, we should see to it that the means, by a sort of transfer of hedonic accent from the ends, themselves become ends.

Born of well-to-do parents, Schlick as a young man had never known poverty or severe distress. His life, on the whole, had been one of happiness and fulfillment. But his students, growing up in the depression and unemployment years of the twenties and thirties, found his optimistic, roseate outlook not too easy to understand. This may have contributed, perhaps, to motivating the mentally deranged student who, in June, 1936, approached Schlick on the stairway of the University of Vienna, and shot and fatally wounded him. The tragedy was a dreadful shock to his many friends and admirers, as well as to the philosophical and academic world as a whole.

Schlick in his early years had been sympathetic to the ideals of a pacifist socialism. But the rise of Nazism in Germany, among other factors, impelled him to modify his political outlook in a more conservative and individualistic direction. (I visited Schlick for the last time in 1935, a year before his death; my impression then was that he was deeply shaken by the events in Germany and that he no longer maintained as steadfastly as before his belief in "salvation" through human kindness — H. F.)

II

Schlick had an excellent background in mathematics and physics, and to a lesser extent in biology and psychology, Following Mach, Ostwald, Henri Poincaré and Bertrand Russell, he became one of the first informed, original and independent thinkers of the twentieth century to practice the newly interpreted discipline of *Naturphilosophie* in the sense of the modern philosophy (logic, methodology) of the sciences. Thus he was one of the first two professional philosophers (the other was C. D. Broad) to understand and write on Einstein's special and general theories of relativity. His paper "The Philosophical Significance of the Principle of Relativity" appeared in 1915, and his small book *Space and Time in Contemporary Physics* in 1917. Einstein himself, in a letter (December 9, 1919) to his friend the physicist Max Born, observed that "Schlick has a good head on him; we must try to get him a professorship. He is in desperate need of it", Einstein went on, "because of the devaluation of property. However, it will be difficult, as he does not belong to the philosophical established church of the Kantians." (*The Born-Einstein Letters*, Walker and Co., 1971, p. 18.) Schlick revered Einstein, and much of his early philosophical work reflects the great influence on him of Einstein's thought.

With his orientation toward science, it was therefore quite fitting that Schlick's *Allgemeine Erkenntnislehre* should appear as the *first* volume in the famous scientific series, *Naturwissenschaftliche Monographien und Lehrbücher,* published by the Verlag von Julius Springer, Berlin. As Schlick makes abundantly clear in the first chapter of the work, he regards the theory of knowledge, both of commonsense and of science, as an integral component of the entire cognitive endeavor. In his view, the philosophy of science concentrates on the conceptual and logical aspects of science. It is thus an indispensable supplement to the observational, mensurational, experimental and theoretical aspects. Here, as at many other points, Schlick's views were very close to those of the later Russell. At the same time, al-

though Schlick taught many excellent courses in modern logic, he
made scarcely any use of symbolic logic either in epistemology or
in the philosophy of science.

III

It is extremely important, historically and biographically, to bear
in mind that the *Allgemeine Erkenntnislehre* (1918, 1925) was written and published *before* the days of the Vienna Circle (1926—
1936), and thus before Schlick came under the tremendous influence
first of Rudolf Carnap and soon afterward of Ludwig Wittgenstein.
Though Wittgenstein never appeared in the Vienna Circle, Schlick
met privately with him on many occasions, at times with Friedrich
Waismann and Herbert Feigl, and for a while with Carnap. There
is no question that Schlick was profoundly impressed by the personality and the ideas of Wittgenstein. Indeed, the *Tractatus* was
read and subjected to close exegetical analysis in the Circle not only
in 1924/25 but once *again* in 1925/26.

Looking back from a later vantage point, historians of philosophy will perhaps deem it regrettable that Schlick abandoned the
"realism" for which he had argued so ably in the *Allgemeine Erkenntnislehre*. And they will no doubt charge this renunciation to
the "positivistic" influence of Carnap and Wittgenstein (two men
with diametrically opposed personalities and increasingly divergent
philosophical views). But we must also take special note that Schlick,
characteristically self-effacing, attributed to Wittgenstein certain
highly significant insights that he (Schlick) had *already* arrived at
long before he knew even of Wittgenstein's existence. Indeed, some
of the most crucial tenets of the *Tractatus* were anticipated in
Schlick's epistemology.

One example is the distinction between genuine knowledge-
claims and the mere having or living-through of immediate experience. (In Schlick, it is the distinction between *erkennen* and
erleben; in Wittgenstein, it is the distinction between what can be
said and what "only shows forth".) Other examples are: the symbolic and "structural" nature of concepts and propositions; the
sophisticated correspondence view of the meaning of 'truth', implicit in the *Tractatus* and made fully explicit and elaborated with

much greater logical precision in the later semantic analyses of Alfred Tarski; the analytic or tautological character of valid deductive inference, made more explicit by Wittgenstein with the aid of the truth tables used in sentential logic; the rather Humean and anti-Kantian empiricism, which corresponds to Wittgenstein's view of contingent as against necessary truth; the endorsement of the Frege-Russell view of mathematical truth, and in this connection the repudiation of psychologism (the one and only point on which Schlick agreed with Husserl).

We leave it to the historians of twentieth century philosophy to determine whether Russell may have served as a conduit through which some of Wittgenstein's ideas reached Schlick prior to the publication of the *Allgemeine Erkenntnislehre*. As far as we can now make out, however, Schlick could not have become acquainted with RUSSELL's "Philosophy of Logical Atomism" (*Monist,* 1918), until after the first edition of his own work had been completed.

Perhaps equally noteworthy, from an historical point of view, is the fact that Schlick anticipated Russell's solution (if it be a solution!) of the mind-body problem. Schlick had sketched his view in an article that appeared as early as 1916 in the *Vierteljahrsschrift für wissenschaftliche Philosophie,* Volume 40. At that time Russell, influenced by Wiliam James and Mach, still held to the position known as 'neutral monism'. This was an epistemological view very close to the phenomenalism of MACH's *Analysis of Sensations* and to the "radical empiricism" of JAMES (see his *Essays in Radical Empiricism,* edited by R. B. PERRY, 1912). Against these "philosophies of immanence" (see below §§ 25 and 26), Schlick offered a number of striking arguments, similar in part to those advanced by the influential psychologist and critical realist Oswald Külpe and by the sadly neglected Neo-Kantian Alois Riehl.

Influenced by Carnap and Wittgenstein (that is, Wittgenstein as understood by Schlick and most other members of the Vienna Circle), Schlick later came to look on the issue of realism versus phenomenalism as a metaphysical pseudo-problem. Much to the chagrin of, especially, Victor Kraft, Karl Popper, Edgar Zilsel and Herbert Feigl, he abandoned his realism in favor of a linguistically oriented "neutral" position. (This sort of view is contained in CARNAP's *Philosophical Foundations of Physics,* and echoes of it may be found in the writings of Schlick's pupil Bela Juhos.)

IV

Schlick's earlier epistemology, as presented in the *General Theory of Knowledge,* contains superb formulations of the causal theory of perception and of the "abstract"-symbolic-structural character of our "knowledge of the physical world", as well as a striking solution of the psycho-physical problem. He prepares the way with an incisive discussion of the subjectivity of (psychological) space and time, the phenomenal qualities of direct experience, and the purely structural (indirect) knowability of the "things-in-themselves".

The core of Schlick's solution of the mind-body problem (see §§ 31—35) is a form of what today is called the "identity theory", or, more precisely, a "psycho-neural" identity theory. It is fundamentally different from logical behaviorism and radical materialism (or "mindless" physicalism), as well as from pan-psychism. It anticipates by at least eleven years Russell's later views, first formulated in *Analysis of Matter* (1927), admirably reformulated in *Human Knowledge* (1948), and lucidly summarized in *Portraits from Memory* (1956, the chapter headed "Mind and Matter").

Schlick and Russell differed somewhat in their formulations, and in their modes of argumentation and logical construction as well. Nonetheless, they arrived at the *same* solution — and they did so, we believe, quite independently. Also neither, it seems, was acquainted at the time with the partially similar work of the American critical realists C. A. Strong (1903, and later) and Durant Drake (1925), or with the many materialist and near-materialist publications of the late Roy Wood Sellars.

A similar psycho-neural identity theory has been advanced by C. S. Pepper in his recent *Concept and Quality* (1966). His theory, influenced in part by FEIGL's *The 'Mental' and the 'Physical'* (1958, reprinted in book form in 1967, with a *Postscript after Ten Years*), has certain affinities with the more materialist Australian identity theories of U. T. Place, J. J. C. Smart and D. M. Armstrong. However, it is best characterized as a "pan-quality-ism" (as Pepper has remarked in conversation). It is particularly interesting that Pepper, despite his anti-positivist outlook, has formulated a solution of the mind-body problem that in many essential respects resembles Schlick's earlier position.

We stress these relationships not only because thus far they have not been widely noticed, but because we believe that the ideas expressed in §§ 31—35 of the *General Theory of Knowledge* (which coincide basically with the later views of Russell) constitute perhaps the most original contribution made by Schlick to — we need not hesitate to say it — *metaphysics*. It seems likely that Schlick's ideas on the mind-body problem were stimulated by Riehl and by the involved but highly ingenious writings of Richard Avenarius. It was probably Riehl who drew Schlick's attention to a passage in the *Critique of Pure Reason* in which the usually voluble Kant devotes but a half page, in very obscure language, to the "notorious" problem of the relationship between mind and body, and suggests a solution that foreshadows the later philosophical monism of Riehl, Schlick and Russell.

This beautiful solution can, with generous allowances, be traced back to the metaphysical doctrines of Spinoza and Leibniz. Of course it contains some quite venturesome conjectures about matters of fact in the areas of psychophysiology, neurology, and the like, and it depends obviously on the adequacy of the logical analysis of the concepts of the "mental" and the "physical". Hence it is bound to remain controversial — perhaps indefinitely. Yet the logical ingenuity and scientific plausibility of the solution and the progress made on related issues, such as the free will problem, may stimulate the reader to search further in this direction. He will be encouraged to avoid indeterminist-emergentist or interactionist-dualist solutions, and at the same time to reject any temptation to pronounce the ancient problem unsolvable *("ignoramus et ignorabimus")*.

There is one serious lacuna in Schlick's acount of the "mental". Following tradition, he equated the mental with conscious direct awareness, or acquaintance. Despite the Vienna *Zeitgeist* that surrounded him, Schlick ignored completely Freud's psychoanalytic theory of the unconscious. No doubt he would have regarded psychoanalytic concepts as only (poorly defined) place-holders for concepts to be introduced at a later stage in the development of neurophysiology. (Indeed, Freud himself was inclined to this view; yet he also affirmed the enormous heuristic value of psychoanalytic concepts and hypotheses.)

V

Several other highlights of SCHLICK's *General Theory of Knowledge* should be noted, if briefly. One is his account of *implicit defini-*

tions, for which he drew inspiration from David Hilbert's studies in the axiomatization of geometry and other disciplines in pure and applied mathematics. (Schlick does not mention J. D. Gergonne, who introduced the term and the idea.)

Another feature is the reliance that Schlick, in essence following Hume and Kant, placed on the distinction between analytic and synthetic propositions. This distinction later came under fire from the brilliant American logician W. V. Quine. But Schlick himself took this distinction as sufficiently well established, and with its aid presented a devastating criticism of the Kantian and Neo-Kantian doctrine of the synthetic *a priori.*

Schlick felt far less confident about an overall solution to the problem of induction. That, in fact, is why he dealt with this issue more briefly and more cautiously in the second edition of the *General Theory of Knowledge* than in the first. He would surely have followed the later work on this problem by Hans Reichenbach, Carnap, Popper and others with the greatest interest. And he would have been among the first to agree that no stable solution has yet been reached.

His treatment of the unity of consciousness (see § 17) also left him somewhat uneasy (as he indicated in conversations in the twenties — H. F.). Perhaps he felt that on this basic question, if nowhere else, he had proceeded in too Kantian a manner. But do we have a better answer today?

Schlick's discussion of the relationship between the logical and the psychological (see § 18) anticipated in embryonic form some of the later philosophic concerns with the abilities and competencies of "thinking machines".

On a broader plane, Schlick's general analysis of the nature of scientific knowledge paved the way for the detailed logical reconstructions — elaborated in diverse ways by Reichenbach, Popper, Carl Hempel, Wolfgang Stegmüller and many others — of such central scientific notions as the hypothetico-inferential method and of probability theory.

VI

In his London lectures on "Form and Content" in 1932 (cf. *Gesammelte Aufsätze,* Gerold, Vienna, 1938) Schlick came dangerously close, as he himself well knew, to a "metaphysics of the ineffable".

Only logical form or structure is communicable in intersubjective discourse; the experienced *qualia* remain inexpressible. Schlick in this period, reflecting the positivist influence of Carnap and Wittgenstein, insisted on the verifiability criterion of factual meaningfulness. And he formulated it, unhappily, in the notorious slogan "The meaning of a sentence is the method of its verification" — a slogan that is typical of the phobia of positivists from Hume through Mach to Wittgenstein. In 1918—1925, Schlick did not hesitate to reconstruct reasoning about other persons' minds and mental contents as reasoning by analogy. But in his later phase, he came to regard the (not directly verifiable) conclusions of such inferences as "bad metaphysics". In our opinion, his views of 1918—1925 may well be the sounder, though they of course require some revising.

At all events, history will record Schlick as a trailblazer in the theory of knowledge and the philosophy of science. No other thinker was so well prepared to give new impetus to the philosophical questings of the younger generation. Though many of his students and successors have attained a higher degree of exactitude and adequacy in their logical analyses of problems in the theory of knowledge, Schlick had an unsurpassed sense for what is essential in philosophical issues. From his "Olympian" point of view, much that is being published today in epistemology might well have appeared as idle quibbling. His was a truly seminal mind, and his work will remain a milestone in the development of a new empiricism and naturalism.

Notes and References

Among the posthumously published works of Schlick, mention should be made of his slender book *Natur und Kultur* (edited by J. RAUSCHER), Humboldt-Verlag, Wien—Stuttgart 1952, which contains many stimulating ideas. For readers interested in Schlick as a person as well as a philosopher, there is a small book, *Aphorismen*, in the Selbstverlag von Blanche Hardy Schlick, Wien 1962. Also the *Vienna Circle Collection* published by D. Reidel, Dordrecht, Holland, will include some of Schlick's essays, both early and later ones, published and unpublished, and some biographical material.

Schlick as man and philosopher is dealt with in HERBERT FEIGL's memorial essay in *Erkenntnis,* Vol. VI, pp. 393—419, 1939 (written in 1936). A very fine essay on Schlick's philosophical outlook, both pre-Wittgenstein and post-Wittgenstein, is F. WAISMANN's *Vorwort* in MORITZ SCHLICK, *Gesammelte Aufsätze,* Gerold & Co., Vienna 1938.

The story of the Vienna Circle is well told in VICTOR KRAFT's *Der Wiener Kreis* (English translation by A. PAP, Philosophical Library, New York 1953), and in a second slightly revised and expanded edition (Springer, Wien 1968).

See also: J. JØRGENSON, The Development of Logical Empiricism, in: *International Encyclopedia of Unified Science,* University of Chicago Press, 1951;

H. FEIGL, The Wiener Kreis in America, in: D. FLEMING and B. BAYLIN, eds., *The Intellectual Migration, Europe and America, 1930—1960,* Harvard University Press, Cambridge, Mass., 1969;

H. FEIGL, The Origin and Spirit of Logical Positivsm, in: S. F. BARKER and PETER ACHINSTEIN, eds., *The Legacy of Logical Positivism,* The Johns Hopkins Press, 1969.

Logical Positivism, a valuable collection of essays including some of Schlick's in English translation, with a lucid and informative introduction by its editor A. J. AYER, was published by the Free Press, New York 1959.

Finally, there is a long chapter on the Vienna Circle in WOLFGANG STEGMÜLLER, *Hauptströmungen der Gegenwartsphilosophie,* 4th edition (translated into English by ALBERT E. BLUMBERG as *Main Currents in Contemporary German, British and American Philosophy,* D. Reidel, 1969).

Part One

The Nature of Knowledge

§ 1. The Meaning of the Theory of Knowledge

There was once a time when philosophers marvelled that man could move his limbs even though he was not familiar with the nerve and muscle processes on which such movements depended. They even went so far as to conclude that man was quite incapable of moving his body by himself. Whenever he wished to perform some movement, they believed, a higher power had to come to his aid and do it for him.

The danger of coming to a conclusion of this sort is even greater when we consider the wondrous human activity we call knowing. How *does* the process of cognition take place? How is it that our mind is able to master nature, to comprehend and predict the most distant happenings in the world? At first glance this seems every bit as mysterious as the processes whereby, when we so wish, our hand picks up a stone and flings it. For this reason, skeptics have argued time and time again that since we do not understand how knowing is possible, we do not really possess any knowledge, that it is a delusion to suppose that we can ever lay hold of the truth, that in reality we do not know anything.

But just as man has continued to move and to act regardless of whether the scholars were able to explain to him the "how" and the "whereby", so too the sciences have gone about their business untroubled by what the philosophers might think concerning the possibility and explanation of knowledge. There is no doubt that we do possess sciences, and sciences are bodies of knowledge. How can anyone deny that they exist? At most, a skeptic may refuse to *call* the findings of science knowledge. But he does not thereby abolish them; he has merely said that to him they do not appear to conform to the requirements that he believes must be imposed on knowledge. Scientific findings may not, indeed, fulfill the hopes initially cherished by the philosopher. This, however, does not deter the scientist, who goes right on working in the domain of his particular science. For him, the findings remain knowledge — goals achieved by his science. He determines upon goals and reaches them; he sets himself problems and solves them. These solution do constitute knowledge; they are real phenomena, which the philosopher encounters as surely as he encounters movements of the human body.

To move our limbs we need not be acquainted with the physiological processes necessary for the movement to occur. Nor is an investigation of cognition necessary in order to gain knowledge in science. In other words, just as behavior does not require a familiarity with physiology, so scientific knowledge does not in principle depend for its existence on the theory of knowledge. The interest displayed by physiology in nerve and muscle processes is purely theoretical, and so is the interest manifested by epistemology in the process of scientific advance. A mastery of physiology does not create the capacity for performing bodily movements; it merely enables us to explain them and to understand how they are possible. Likewise, epistemology can never issue decrees that lay down what is or what is not to count as scientific knowledge; on the contrary, its task is only to clarify and interpret that knowledge.

This is not to deny, of course, that under certain circumstances the findings of epistemology may be of benefit in the work of the individual sciences, just as a knowledge of the physiology of nerves and muscles may in certain instances have some practical bearing on the capacity to move one's limbs — for example, when that capacity has been impaired by pathological changes and the problem is to restore it. The process of acquiring scientific knowledge also is one that does not always unfold normally. Pathological phenomena — we call them antinomies or paradoxes — may appear at times, and their elimination may enlist the services of epistemology. But this is not its primary task. The theory of knowledge is independent of the immediate problems of the individual scientific disciplines and is to that extent separable from them.

Here a word of caution is necessary, lest our comparison of cognition with the physiological processes of innervation give rise to a fundamental misunderstanding. Since the factors that lead to it will be operative time and again in the course of our inquiry and might generate false conceptions, we must get rid of this misunderstanding at the very outset. Specifically, one might suppose that just as physiology seeks to analyze innervation processes, so epistemology studies the psychological processes by which scientific thinking occurs. Taken in this way, however, the analogy is altogether false. For such a study would of course be purely a task for psychology. While the carrying out of this task might to a certain extent be important for the epistemologist, it could never constitute his real goal — if for no other reason than that psychological knowledge itself is a problem for him. His goal lies beyond, and in quite another direction. He inquires into the universal grounds on which valid knowledge in general is possible — an inquiry that clearly differs basically from one that addresses itself to the mental processes by which knowledge develops over time in one or another individual. Only in the course of our study will this basic difference emerge with full clarity. For the present, the point has been merely to sound a preliminary warning against a likely error and to distinguish the theory of knowledge from research in the sciences, psychology included, as something that stands on its own feet and is in principle independent.

We can carry on our work quite well in the sciences without providing them with epistemological foundations, but unless we do so, we shall never *understand* them in all their depth. An understanding of this kind is a peculiarly philosophical need, and the theory of knowledge is philosophy.

There are innumerable roads to philosophy. Indeed, as Helmholtz stressed, *any* scientific problem will lead us to philosophy if only we pursue the problem far enough. When a person gains knowledge in some particular science (and thus learns the causes of one phenomenon or another) and when the inquiring mind asks in turn for the causes of these causes (that is, for the more general truths from which the knowedge he has gained may be derived), he soon reaches a point where he can go no further with the means furnished by his science. He must look for enlightenment to some more general, more comprehensive discipline. For the sciences form, as it were, a system of nested receptacles, where the more general contains the more specific and supplies it with a foundation. For example, chemistry deals with only a limited range of natural phenomena; but physics embraces them *all*. Hence when the chemist undertakes to establish his most general laws, such as those relating to the periodic table of elements, valence, and the like, he must turn to physics. And the most general domain, into which the advancing processes of explanation must all finally flow, is that of philosophy, the theory of knowledge. For the ultimate basic concepts of the most general sciences — the concepts, say, of consciousness in psychology, of axiom and number in mathematics, of space and time in physics — admit in the end only of a philosophical or epistemological clarification.

But they not only admit of it. They demand it, at least for anyone who is unwilling to call an arbitrary halt to the philosophical impulse from which in the last analysis the sciences, too, arise.

§ 2. Knowing in Everyday Life

Before a discipline can begin its work, it must form a definite concept of the subject matter it intends to investigate. Any inquiry must be preceded by some kind of definition of the area that is to be studied. For we must be quite clear at the outset as to what we are going to deal with, what questions we hope to answer. Hence the first thing we must ask ourselves is: What actually is knowledge?

It seems quite obvious that this question must be the starting-point. It is all the more strange, therefore, how seldom the question has been treated in the proper place and with the proper attention. Very few authors, in fact, have given it a clear, positive and serviceable answer. The reason of course is that to most people the meaning of the word 'knowledge' seems so obvious that there is no need for a more detailed, careful elucidation. It simply does not occur to them that a rigorous and exact definition might be required. Now there are certainly many concepts that are so familiar and are used in such a way that a special definition would indeed be superfluous. Thus it may appear that when I say "I know something", my words have just as commonplace a meaning as when I say "I see something" or "I hear something". And in many instances this is quite true. Everyone knows what is meant when a physician says that he *knows* the cause of an illness to be bacteria of a certain sort, or a chemist says that he *knows* a gas to be helium. Here no one feels any need for further elaboration.

But circumstances may arise in which a more exact definition and elucidation of the word 'know' become absolutely necessary, where many who suppose themselves quite clear about its meaning would be altogether in error. As a matter of fact, we shall soon see that the concept of cognition tacitly assumed by most thinkers is not a reliable guide in philosophy. Each of us associates with the words 'see' and 'hear' meanings that are sufficiently precise for the purposes of everyday life; yet for the study of visual and auditory perception these meanings must be made far more exact. In the same way, the theory of knowledge must first determine once and for all just what specific process the term 'knowledge' is to designate.

Now it might be thought that a complete and satisfactory definition of knowledge can be secured only at a later stage of the inquiry or even at its conclusion, that to obtain such a definition is in fact the principal task of epistemology. But were we to accept this view, the boundaries of our field of research, as well as the correct point of entry, would be left in obscurity.

"Should a definition of the subject-matter come at the beginning of a science or at its conclusion?" It is rather amusing to see how often this question is raised and treated as a profound problem in philosophical works, especially in the introductions (see, for example, KANT's Critique of Pure Reason, Kehrbach edition, p. 560). The answer, of course, is that every discipline must rest upon an implicit, if not avowed, delimitation of its field. The insights eventually arrived at enable the discipline to bring out the subject-matter in sharp relief by displaying its manifold relationships and so to provide a "definition" of it in a new sense. But this in no way obviates the need to start with some conceptual determination of the subject-matter. In optics, for example, the finding that light consists of electrical waves of a specified length may ultimately count as a definition of light; but it is clear that at the inception of optical research the concept of light had to be defined, and actually was defined, in an entirely different way, namely, as something of which our eyes make us aware through certain sensations. By the same token, whatever may be said about knowledge in a finished philosophical system, it must be possible independently of that system to lay down an adequate definition. This must be so in the case of any concept that finds a clear application whether in everyday thinking or in science. And it also holds without further ado for the concept of knowledge. For, as indicated in the preceding section, there is no doubt that in the sciences we really do possess both knowledge and advances in knowledge. This implies that the sciences have at their disposal a sure criterion for deciding when genuine knowledge is at hand, and in what it consists. Thus the sciences must already contain implicitly a full definition of the concept; all we need do is infer it from the research, read it off from any undeniable advance in knowledge. Then, with this definition as a firm starting-point, we can begin our deliberations.

It is extremely important that we assure ourselves of such a starting-point, with which we can maintain close contact in the course of the inquiry and thus determine at any time just where we are and where we want to go. Only in this way do we avoid a series of pseudo-problems, which have often confused philosophical thought and which could have been eliminated merely by reflecting on the nature of cognition itself. We have blindly wished for knowledge without knowing exactly what we wanted. We have asked such questions as "Can man know the infinite?" or "Is man capable of knowing how an effect results from a cause?". We have made such statements as: "The essence of force is unknowable" or "Physical happenings can be regarded as known only if they are reduced to the pressure and impact of masses in motion." Questions and statements like these have been voiced precisely because the word 'know' has been used in an unthinking manner. In the same category is that formidable question which has bulked so large in the history of philosophy: "Can we know things as they are in themselves independently of how they appear to our human apprehension?" Such problems cease to be problems once we make clear to ourselves just what the word 'know' can mean in these cases; for it becomes immediately evident either that the question is badly put or that the way is open to a precise, if perhaps unanticipated, answer.

Before we seek to determine by an examination of scientific thought just what 'knowing' has to mean in that context, it is helpful first to trace the word in its everyday usage. For this term does stem from ordinary life, as do indeed the most technical of terms — except that these latter had *their* origin in the everyday life of the Greeks and Romans.

Consider a simple case in which the word 'know' is employed in a natural way. I become aware, while walking home, of a brown object moving in the distance. By its movements, size and other characteristics I *know* that it is an animal. The distance diminishes and eventually a moment arrives when I *know* for certain that the animal is a dog. He comes closer, and soon I *know* that this is not just some strange dog I have never seen before, but a familiar one, my own dog Tyras, or whatever his name may be.

In this account the word 'know' occurs three times. What was known the first time was only that the object is an animal and not, say, some lifeless thing. Now what does this statement signify? Plainly, that the moving object is not something totally unfamiliar to me which has never appeared within the circle of my experience, but that it belongs to a class of objects that I have had frequent occasion to perceive and that I had already as a child learned to designate by the name 'animal'. I have *re-cognized (wiedererkannt)* in that brown thing the characteristics (especially the property of auto-motion) that an object must have if it is to be designated an animal. I can thus say (the formulation is vulnerable psychologically and we use it with the proviso that it will be improved upon later): "In the perception of that brown thing, I have rediscovered the mental image or idea that corresponds to the name 'animal'." The object has become something familiar, and I can call it by its right name.

Next, what I do mean when, on coming closer to the object, I say: "Now I know the animal to be a dog?" Plainly I mean (again using a provisional formulation to be made more exact later) that the appearance of the object fits not only the idea I have of animals in general, but also the idea I have of a quite definite class of animals, which we designate in English by the word 'dog'. To say that I have recognized the animal means once again that I am able to designate it by its right name, 'dog'; and we call this name the right one precisely because it is used generally for the class of animals to which this animal in fact belongs. Here too there is a rediscovery of something familiar.

The situation is no different when we come to the third stage of this act of cognition. Knowing the dog to be mine signifies here, too, that I *re*-cognize it (I know it *again*). That is, I determine that the animal I see before me is identical with the dog I am used to having about me every day. And what makes this possible is again the fact that I have a more or less exact image of what my dog looks like, and that this image is the same as the one conveyed to me by the sight of the approaching animal. The shape, the color, the size, perhaps also the sound of the bark, all coincide with the picture that memory gives me of my dog. Up to this point, the only names with which I could correctly designate the object were names of classes — 'animal', 'dog'. But now I call it by a name that belongs to just one individual in all the world. I say that this is "my dog Tyras", and thus the animal is uniquely designated as an individual.

What is common to all three stages of this act of knowing is the fact that an object is re-cognized, that something old is rediscovered in something new and can now be designated by a familiar name. And the process terminates when the name is found that belongs to the object known and to no other. In ordinary life, to know a thing means no more than to give it its right name.

This is all so simple and obvious that it seems almost silly to make such a to-do about it. Yet philosophy often derives much benefit precisely from a careful examination of the ordinary and the insignificant. What we find in the simplest situations recurs not infrequently in the most complicated problems, but in such an intricate disguise that had we not first beheld it so clearly in our everyday experience we should never have been able to detect it.

Furthermore, from the standpoint of psychology, even so plain a process as knowing or recognizing a dog is by no means a simple and obvious matter. Indeed, it is a mystery how we can claim that any image is one with which we are already acquainted. How do we know that the same perceptual image was present once before in consciousness? As a matter of fact, what was present previously was not the exact same image but at most a similar one. Psychologists have argued a great deal about how we should conceive the process of recognition, and the question is still open. But this psychological question is none of our affair and we may leave it aside entirely. At the same time, we do have here a clear example of the difference between the psychological and the epistemological approach, of which we spoke in the preceding section. The epistemologist is not concerned with the psychological laws that govern the process of recognition and render it intelligible. What is of moment to him is only the fact *that* under certain circumstances recognition does occur. And this fact stands no matter how psychology may eventually resolve questions about the mental processes through which recognition occurs.

§ 3. Knowing in Science

A deeper and more prestigious meaning seems to attach to the term 'know' in scientific research than in everyday life. The word is, as it were, pronounced with a totally different stress. Yet we shall soon see that 'know' does not take on a new, special meaning in science, that knowing in science and knowing in ordinary life are essentially the same. The only difference is that in science and philosophy the loftier aim and subject-matter of the cognitive process lend it a greater dignity.

To maximize the contrast with the example used above, let us consider an illustration drawn from a completely rigorous science, the most exact of all, physics. The history of that discipline is full of instances where, in the unanimous opinion of the experts, knowledge has made notable advances. An examination of any such instance ought to yield the answer to our question about the nature of knowledge. For we should then be able to read off the tacitly assumed definition of knowledge.

For example, physics has succeeded in explaining, or understanding, or knowing — all of these words signify one and the same thing — the nature of the phenomenon of light. What has physics explained light to be? As far back as the 17th century, Huyghens put forward the undulatory theory of light, according to which light consists in the propagation of a state in wave form. Later, following the experiments of Fresnel and Young, it was established beyond doubt that the properties and laws of the transmission of light are identical with the properties and laws of the propagation of waves under certain conditions. Both can be represented by the same mathematical formulas. In brief, the relationships exhibited by the phenomena of light were *re-cognized* to be the same as those that occur generally in the propagation of waves, and hence they were already familiar. (This is precisely how I knew the animal to be a dog. I re-cognized in it the features already familiar to me as characteristic of dogs.)

At that time, however, the only waves known to man were those consisting of the mechanical motion of a medium — water waves, air waves or other vibrations of an elastic body. It was therefore taken for granted that in the case of light, too, what were involved were mechanical vibrations, waves arising from the movements of particles of the medium about an equilibrium position. Later, as a result in particular of the work of Heinrich Hertz, electromagnetic waves became known and their laws were set forth in rigorous mathematical form. It was then noticed that the laws governing electrical waves could be found again in the laws for optical phenomena, and in fact fitted these phenomena more perfectly than did the laws for mechanical vibrations. That is, certain peculiarities in the behavior of light that were not accounted for by the mechanical theory could now be re-cognized and thereby understood; to cite but one, the velocity of propagation of electrical waves was found to be the same as that of light, whereas no waves in elastic media were known to have this velocity. On the basis of such acts of recognition, it was now possible to say: light is an electromagnetic phenomenon. Light had been called by its right name.

Here we have a bit of knowledge acquired in two stages: first, light was explained as a vibration phenomenon, as the propagation of a wave; then, through a second act of discovery, these vibrations and waves were determined to be electrical in nature. The situation in the case of the dog was quite similar: at first I was able to call it only by the more general name 'animal'; but after re-cognizing more of its properties, I designated it as a dog.

However, there is a significant difference that should be noted. In the example drawn from everyday life, I established directly the agreement or sameness between the two experiences, a perception and a mental image. In the illustration taken from science, on the other hand, two terms related by the act of cognition have as their common element a "law", something that cannot be perceived directly but can be obtained only in a roundabout way. Whether or not the "sameness" of laws can in turn be verified only through the "sameness" of two perceptions or other experiences we shall not inquire into here. This is a problem that belongs to the general theory of scientific methodology, and we are not required to solve it in order simply to define the concept of knowledge. In any event, the main point is that in cognition the two members are ascertained to be "one and the same". Thus what is involved is a sameness that can pass over into identity. If, as in the above instance, the common element is a *law,* then the sameness we find will be an *identity;* for a law is a conceptual creation, and we know that so far as concepts are concerned, sameness and identity coincide. The distinction touched on here has, for the moment, no further interest for us; our concern has been to establish only that when we speak of "knowl-

edge" in science, we are referring once again to a rediscovery of
what is the same.

Had we considered any other example from any other science,
we should still have come to the same result. Everywhere the core
of the knowledge process turns out to be a rediscovery. When we
ascertain, for example, that Aristotle wrote the manuscript on the
Athenian state — a determination that is an instance of *historical*
knowledge — what we do is to identify the author of this writing
with the philosopher who is well known to us on other grounds.
Thus we re-cognize the latter in the former. When in philology we
come to know the kinship of two words from different languages,
this means that we have confirmed the *sameness* of the roots from
which the two words originate. And this is true of any example we
may imagine. But there is no need to undertake further analyses of
this kind. They always yield the same result — knowing in science,
as in ordinary life, signifies a rediscovery of one thing in another.

From this simple principle we may already draw some important
conclusions regarding the aim and method of scientific knowledge.

To begin with, we remark that knowing requires only that, of
two previously separate phenomena, one be reduced to the other.
Hence it is not necessary (as is often supposed) that we be better
acquainted with the explaining member than with the member to
be explained. It is not true that knowledge is acquired only where
the familiar is rediscovered in the unfamiliar. This can easily be
shown by examples from scientific research. When modern physics,
say, manages to reduce the laws of mechanics to those of electromagnetism, this is just as much an explanation, an advance in knowledge, as if the long-pursued opposite course — finding a mechanical explanation of electricity — had proved successful. And this
holds even though we have been acquainted for a much longer
time with the laws of mechanics and they are much more familiar
to the human mind than are the laws of electromagnetism. Similarly,
the discovery of a new language on earth might very well furnish
the connecting link and explanatory ground that enable us to understand the features of the most familiar languages.

We also frequently encounter the formulation that to know is
"to reduce that with which we are not acquainted to that with
which we are". But this is absurd. The item to be explained must
always be something with which we are acquainted. For why should
we want to explain anything with which we are totally un-

acquainted? There is a confusion here between *being acquainted with (Kennen)* and *knowing (Erkennen)* or *understanding,* and this confusion, as we shall see later, can have the most serious consequences for philosophy (see § 12, below). But even if we correct this error and insert "the unknown" in place of "that with which we are unacquainted", the formula will still not be correct. For the explanatory factor to which we reduce the unknown does not have to be something with which we were previously acquainted; it may be something new, something that we have assumed expressly for this particular piece of knowledge. This occurs whenever, in order to explain a set of facts, we construct a new concept or a new hypothesis, which must then of course be confirmed on other grounds before we can regard the explanation as successful. But where a happily conceived hypothesis makes certain facts intelligible for the first time, the knowledge thereby acquired consists in reducing something with which we are acquainted to something with which we previously were not acquainted, which is just the opposite of the formula above. Moreover, the explanatory factor that makes the knowledge possible need not itself be something known; it may be something ultimate, which we cannot yet reduce to other factors. Thus for the formula to be correct it must be generalized into the less specific principle that knowledge is the reduction of one thing to another.

That this reduction does capture in full the essence of knowing has been perceived and acknowledged by many philosophers. But none of them has put this insight into practice and drawn from it all of its consequences. All great questions of principle take us back in the end to the nature of the cognitive process. We are bound to attack all philosophical problems, and the philosophical aspect of all problems, with the same weapons. There are two questions that we must always ask: First, what are the factors to which we can reduce that which is to be known? Second, what path must we take in order to effect this reduction?

The individual sciences raise these questions automatically in the course of solving their special problems, and it is easy to study their method. In some cases the path of reduction is marked out in advance. The task then is to locate the explanatory factors, and it often requires no little courage to contemplate without flinching what we encounter along the way. This is how physics, for instance, arrived at the modern hypothesis of quanta and the theory of relativity.

In other cases the explanatory factors are at hand, and the task is to seek out the *path* of explanation. This is the usual situation. Examples are the attempts to explain the movements of the planets by means of Newton's Law of Gravitation; to account for meteorological phenomena by the laws of thermodynamics, or of biological phenomena by the laws of physics and chemistry; to derive the causes of some historical event from antecedent happenings. True, we are often mistaken as to which factors must be invoked as explanatory principles, and so are led astray by some will-o'-the-wisp. An instance is the once prevalent view, mentioned above, that all physical phenomena must admit of explanation as mechanical processes.

There are also cases, however, where we lack both the path *and* the principle of explanation, both compass and goal. Then the best thing to do is let the problem rest (for under these conditions it cannot even be regarded as a well-formulated problem) until we are led back to it later along different paths and thus obtain clues to its solution.

Even at this early stage of the inquiry we are already able to form some idea of the *ultimate goal* of all knowledge.

We need only notice that understanding advances from stage to stage by first rediscovering something in another thing, then in that something rediscovering still another something, and so on. How far does the whole process go and what is its outcome? This much, at least, is clear: if we proceed in the fashion described, the number of phenomena explained by one and the same principle becomes ever greater, and hence the number of principles needed to explain the totality of phenomena becomes ever smaller. For since one thing is continually being reduced to something else, the set of things not yet reduced (i. e., the set of things to be explained that are not yet explained) steadily diminishes. Consequently, the number of explanatory principles used may serve as a measure of the level of knowledge attained, the highest level being that which gets along with the fewest explanatory principles that are not themselves susceptible of further explanation. Thus the ultimate task of knowing is to make this minimum as small as possible.

It would be premature to try to say anything more definite about just how far we can push this diminution in the number of final

principles. But one thing is certain: the endeavors of those philosophers who would derive the totality of being, the whole richness
of the world, from a *single* principle deserve no more than a tolerant
smile. On the other hand, we cannot but have the highest admiration
for the results already achieved by the sciences in reducing the number of principles and, in recent times, literally decimating them in
a mighty assault. The progress can best be observed and measured
in physics where, within a few decades, there has been an extra-
ordinary decrease in the number of basic laws serving to explain
all the others. Mechanics, optics, heat and electricity were once
distinct domains, each with its own laws. Now the physicist recognizes fundamentally only mechanics and electrodynamics as separate
parts of his discipline, all the others having already been reduced to
these two. And even these show at various points that the possibility
of a mutual reduction and unification cannot be ruled out.

Furthermore, we can now see what constitutes the real difficulty
in explanation, in obtaining ultimate knowledge: we are called upon
to employ a minimum of explanatory principles, and at the same
time to determine completely with their aid every single phenomenon in the world. In other words, the individual entity is to be
designated uniquely with the help only of the most general names,
and yet to be designated uniquely — a requirement that at first
glance seems almost self-contradictory.

In the case of the dog, we did obtain a unique designation. But
this was thanks to the use of an individual name ('my dog Tyras')
and for that reason the designation was not a piece of scientific
knowledge. Conversely, it is very easy to designate an individual
by means of an appropriate general name, which, however, does
not determine that individual with full uniqueness. This does not
constitute scientific knowledge either, only its semblance; for there
is no difficulty in finding or constructing general concepts that can
be rediscovered in all the phenomena of the world. Thales, for example, thought he recognized the same substance, water, in all
things. But this did not represent any acquisition of genuine knowledge, since the notion was of no use to him in completely and
unambiguously determining, say, the individual differences between
a piece of marble and a piece of wood. And the situation is not
essentially different when, for instance, modern metaphysics advances the thesis that all that exists is *mind*. Despite more comprehensive argumentation and the most refined dialectic, such

modern formulations are basically still on a par with that of Thales (*cf.* below, § 35).

The untutored person is scarcely conscious of this distinction between "erudition" *(Wissen)* and knowledge *(Erkenntnis)*. His mind is set at rest as soon as *some name or other* is assigned to each thing or phenomenon. How clever the gardner fancies himself because he can tell us the Latin names of all his plants! How often do we hear people priding themselves on their storehouse of names, phrases and numbers, which they would pass off as knowledge[1].

Later we shall see that there is in fact only one method that can yield scientific knowledge in the strictest, genuinely valid sense and thus satisfy the *two* conditions under discussion: to determine the individual completely and to achieve this determination by a reduction to that which is most general. This is the method of the mathematical sciences. But there is still much ground to cover before we get to that point. Our present purpose has been merely to indicate in passing some of the vistas already opened up by the position we have reached. Before we proceed to enlarge these vistas, we wish first to create the means for distinguishing more clearly what they will show us.

To this end we return to the analysis of the cognitive process in order to round out and make more precise our as yet incompletely formulated results.

§ 4. Knowing by Means of Images

To know is to re-cognize *(Wiedererkennen)* or rediscover *(Wiederfinden)*. And to rediscover is to equate *what* is known with *that as which* it is known. We must now clarify this act of equating if we are to deepen our insight into the nature of knowing.

Equating presupposes comparing. In acquiring knowledge, what do we compare with what?

It is easy enough to answer this question for the knowledge processes of ordinary life where, in general, what are compared are

---

1 *Cf.* LOTZE's comments in Mikrokosmos, 5th edition, Vol. II, pp. 249 ff.; also VAIHINGER, Die Philosophie des Als Ob, 2nd edition, p. 318.

images or ideas. We recall from our earlier example that I know the
perceived animal to be a dog because the perceptual image I have
of the animal agrees in a certain way with the memory image
I have of dogs generally. It thus agrees with one of the images that
come to mind when I hear the words 'Spitz', 'Bulldog', 'Newfound-
land' or the like. Psychologically what takes place, perhaps, is that
when the perception occurs, the memory image that serves for comparison purposes is evoked by association, images may merge, a
specific "familiarity-quality" may appear. These are matters of psychology with which we are not concerned. Behind them, however,
lies concealed an epistemological problem, the consideration of
which will quickly take us a good deal further along our way.

We put aside for the moment the fundamental question — which
the reader is apt to think of first — as to how images are related
to the reality represented in them. For the time being, we leave
entirely open even the question of the existence, apart from images,
of any reality at all outside of consciousness. The problem we have
now to consider is quite independent of these matters, and in any
event must be solved first.

The point is that when we undertake to compare images, as is
required in cognition, we run into a serious difficulty. If we are to
locate and verify sameness in images, it would seem necessary that
images be sharply defined and clearly determined structures. For if
they are vague or unclear, how can we establish with certainty that
two images are the same? How can we be sure that we are not
overlooking minor or even important differences? Yet, as we all
know from experience, memory images are in fact extremely hazy
and fleeting structures that dissolve like mist. When I try to visualize
some familiar object, say a house on the other side of the street,
I may think that I can do so with great accuracy. But as soon as
I ask myself about particulars — the number of windows, the shape
of the roof and the like — I find that I am not able to supply with
certainty any precise information about the details of my memory
images. No picture stands out more clearly in our mind's eye than
the faces of our immediate family whom we see daily; yet closer
consideration shows that even such images have very little clarity
or definiteness. A person presents a wholly different picture depending on the side from which he is viewed, the posture he assumes,
the mood he is in, or the clothes he is wearing. From these in-
numerably many views, the memory image singles out only a few

details, and even these but dimly. We can easily convince ourselves of this by asking someone, as an experiment, to describe the color of the eyes, the shape of the nose, the part in the hair, of their closest relatives and friends. As a matter of fact, what do remain fixed in our memory of an object are not just random aspects or particulars but certain characteristics that belong to the object as a whole and are called "Gestalt-qualities" by the psychologist.

Our images, then, are quite vague and blurred. One would therefore suppose that a cognitive process that rests on comparing such structures and verifying their sameness would be at best highly uncertain and open to question. And at that, visual images — the only ones involved in our examples — are far clearer than any others.

Nevertheless, experience shows that re-cognition and knowing do take place in everyday life with an accuracy and certainty that suffice for ordinary needs. This may be explained psychologically by the fact that the perceptual image of an object, on entering consciousness, perhaps evokes the memory image of that object with greater sharpness than if no external stimulus were present, and that the two images then merge. But again the question is only of psychological interest. What is significant for the epistemologist is the *fact that* knowing does take place in this manner in ordinary life and that it possesses certainty enough for all practical purposes. In point of fact, no one would regard it as possible for me, through error or false recognition, to mistake a strange dog for my own, or to fail to recognize my father on sufficiently close view. (We assume, of course, that neither my dog nor my father had meanwhile undergone such changes, say as the result of age, that the perceptual image would in fact be totally different from the memory image. And in the latter event, the object to be known would not really have remained the same but would have become a different one.)

Theoretically, of course, — and this is what we must hold to from the standpoint of philosophy — there always remains the possibility either that my memory is not reliable and has altogether distorted the memory image (which actually happens in the case of the mentally ill) or that a remembered object and a perceived one resemble each other so closely that what seemed to be knowledge was really an error. For in principle it would be possible for a strange dog to be the "living image" of my own dog and to be indistinguishable from it even on the most careful inspection.

But these are only theoretical possibilities, of no importance in real life. (The *Comedy of Errors* could take place only in Shakespeare's imagination, not in the real world.) The situation is quite different if the cognitive process involves not individual images, as in the example cited above, but what are called 'general images'. This expression refers to images that, in our thinking, represent a whole class of objects at once rather than a single, individual object. An instance is the image that corresponds to the word 'dog'. What sort of visual picture comes to mind when I hear this word, when I think of dogs in general? A variety of mental processes occur. What usually happens is that a vague picture takes form in my consciousness of a dog belonging to some particular breed, a Saint Bernard perhaps. At the same time, a secondary thought arises to the effect that not only this kind of dog but all other kinds are to be taken into account. The secondary thought may, in turn, make itself felt in my consciousness through the emergence, dimly and for a moment, of faintly indicated images of other breeds, such as terriers and the like. Be that as it may, one thing is certain: it is absolutely impossible for me to form an intuitive image of an animal that is just a dog in general. It is impossible to imagine a triangle in general, a triangle that is neither scalene nor isosceles nor equilateral, a triangle that possesses all and only the properties that *every* triangle has and yet is without specific properties. As soon as one imagines a triangle, it is already a specific triangle, for in the image its sides and angles must be of some magnitude or other.

Thus there are no such things as general images — so long as we do not alter the meaning of the word 'image' but continue to understand by it just that structure given us intuitively in sense-perception and memory. It was Berkeley who first enunciated this proposition with full clarity and it has since become one of the permanent possessions of philosophy.

When we operate in thought with general concepts, such as "man" or "metal" or "plant", what occurs for the most part is this: there appears before the mind's eye, in the manner indicated above, a faint individual image of a sample of the species in question and, linked with it, the consciousness that the individual image is to count solely as a *representative* of the entire species. So much for the psychological facts.

As can readily be seen, this situation gives rise to important epistemological difficulties. Since all images are vague, identification and re-cognition can never be regarded as completely certain, even if the images are individual ones. What then of acts of cognition by means of which an individual is determined as belonging to a particular class? As we have seen, in order to gain such knowledge we would have to compare the perceptual image, through which the individual is given to us, with the image of the class as a whole and then find that the two are the same. But it is impossible to have an image of a species as a whole; at most, the species can be *re-presented* by an individual memory image. How then can we compare the two and find them the same?

Here again experience shows that this is in fact possible, and with a degree of certainty that nearly always suffices for real life situations, although it leads now and again to error. In general, I quite correctly recognize a dog *as* a dog because the perceptual image agrees closely enough with the ideas or images of animals I have already seen and learned to designate as dogs. But doubtful cases may also occur. Thus some dogs resemble wolves so closely that under certain circumstances the two can be confused. In other cases it may be quite impossible for an inexperienced observer to compare images with certainty, as when he is called upon to tell whether a motionless animal is alive or dead, or whether two pieces of writing are by the same hand.

These considerations indicate that the identification and re-cognition of mere images or ideas is generally satisfactory for the cognitive processes of everyday life (and of large areas of science). But they also prove beyond contradiction that it is impossible, in this manner, to set up a rigorous and exact concept of knowledge, one that is fully serviceable from the scientific standpoint. The kind of knowledge that meets the needs of pre-scientific thought and practical life cannot find legitimate employment in a science that demands at all times the greatest possible rigor and the highest degree of certitude.

How then does science set about obtaining the sort of knowledge that conforms to its own requirements for rigor and certainty?

Since images are vague and incapable of precise identification, science seeks to replace them with something else, something clearly determined, something that has fixed bounds and can always be identified with complete assurance. This something, which is meant to take the place of images, is the *concept*.

§ 5. Knowing by Means of Concepts

What is a concept? A concept is to be distinguished from an intuitive image above all by the fact that it is completely determined
and has nothing uncertain about it. One might be tempted to say
— and many logicians have indeed said — that a concept is simply
an image with a strictly fixed content. As we have seen, however,
there are no such entities in psychological reality because all images
are to one degree or another vague. One might of course suppose
that images with fixed content are at least *possible;* but this supposition would still be limited to individual images. It would not
apply at all in the case of general ideas or images, and these are
what we need for knowing; for, as we have just made clear, general
images cannot possibly exist as real mental entities.

Thus a concept is not an image. It is not a real mental structure
of any sort. Indeed it is not real at all, but imaginary — something
that we assume in place of images with strictly determined content.
We operate with concepts as if they were images with exactly
delineated properties that can always be re-cognized with absolute
certainty. These properties are called the *characteristics* or *features
(Merkmale)* of the concept, and are laid down by means of specific
stipulations which in their totality constitute the *definition* of the
concept. In logic, the totality of the characteristics of a concept is
called its "intension" (or "content"); the set of objects denoted by
the concept is called its "extension".

Thus it is through definitions that we seek to obtain what we
never find in the world of images but must have for scientific knowledge: absolute constancy and determinateness. No longer is the
object to be known compared with vague images; instead we investigate whether or not the object possesses certain properties fixed
by definition. In this way, it becomes possible to know the object,
that is, to designate it by its right name. For the definition specifies
the common name we are to apply to all objects that possess the
characteristics set forth in the definition. Or, to use the traditional
language of logic, every definition is a nominal definition.

Accordingly, a concept plays the role of a *sign* or *symbol* for
all those objects whose properties include the various defining
characteristics of that concept.

It need scarcely be emphasized that the words 'object' and 'property' are to be taken in the widest possible sense. An object is simply

anything we can think of and designate or symbolize: not only "things" but also processes, relations, arbitrary fictions (hence concepts, too), and the like. The same holds for 'property'. It is to stand for anything that in any way characterizes and can help determine an object, whether it be something tangible, a relation, something imaginary, or anything else.

Since concepts are unreal, they have to be represented in acts of thought by some mental reality; for thinking as such is, of course, a real mental process. In the case of non-verbal thought, as we have already pointed out, what often serve as signs are intuitive ideas or images in which some, at least, of the defining characteristics of the concept are approximately realized. In speech, concepts are designated by words or names; and these, in turn, can be fixed and represented for the purposes of communication by written signs. In the language of science, however, all words as far as possible are intended to designate concepts. That is why some contemporary logicians reverse matters and wish to define concepts as "meanings of words".

It does not matter if a concept is represented in actual thought by intuitive images, despite their vagueness, provided we realize that this is a question merely of representation and take care not to regard all the properties of an image as characteristics features of the concept. Thinking that proceeds by means of intuitive images can be called pictorial, and in this sense all of our thinking is more or less pictorial. But this need not prevent us from arriving at correct results, so long as (1) we keep in mind that the intuitive images serve only as stand-ins and (2) we remain constantly aware of just *what* they replace. This is not always so easy, however. Indeed, the use of images as proxies for concepts has probably been the most prolific source of error in philosophic thinking in general. Thought takes flight without testing the load capacity of its wings, without determining whether the images that carry it correctly fulfill their conceptual function. Now this can be established only by going back again and again to the definitions. But often serviceable definitions are altogether lacking, and the philosopher ventures the flight with images that are not sustained by a firm conceptual framework. The consequences are error and an early crash.

We note that today investigators are more and more emphasizing — and seeking experimental confirmation for — the view that thinking is not always *purely* pictorial or intuitive in nature. This view is no doubt sound. But we should not suppose that non-intuitive thinking is thinking in pure concepts, with concepts exhibiting themselves *realiter* as do images in intuitive thinking. Rather, non-intuitive thinking consists in certain real conscious processes — best termed "acts" — the close study of which lies in the province of the psychologist. These "acts" are vague and fleeting in character, whereas concepts are meant to be absolutely determined and clear. Like the ideas or images in pictorial thinking, such "acts" can only represent concepts; they cannot themselves be the concepts. Just *which* particular mental states or processes represent concepts in actual thinking, whether these states are intuitive images or something else, is a purely psychological question and is not our concern. Also, it is perfectly true, as has been pointed out[2], that the pictorial images representing a concept do not make up its "meaning". A concept is not the representative of images; quite the contrary, it is represented by them.

Concepts are not real. They are neither real structures in the consciousness of the thinker nor are they, as medieval "realism" held, some kind of actual thing within the real object that is designated by means of them. Strictly speaking, concepts do not exist at all. What does exist is a *conceptual function*. And this function, depending on the circumstances, can be performed on the one hand by images or various mental acts and on the other by names or written signs. Anyone who speaks of concepts as if they were images, as if they were real occurrences in consciousness, creates thereby a fiction in Vaihinger's sense (Die Philosophie des Als-Ob, 2nd edition, pp. 53, 399). But if we do not confuse the two, if, instead of ascribing real being to concepts we regard only conceptual functions as real, then we do not make any consciously false assumptions. Hence it is a mistake to describe concepts in general as fictions.

In the thinker's consciousness, thinking of a concept takes place by means of a special experience that belongs to the class of contents of consciousness which modern psychology in the main calls "intentional". This term is applied to experiences that not only are there in consciousness but also contain a reference to something outside themselves. Consider, for instance, my present memory of a song heard yesterday. Not only is a mental image of the sounds present in my consciousness; I am also aware that it is the image

---

2 E. HUSSERL, Logische Untersuchungen, II, pp. 61 ff.

of sounds perceived yesterday. And this awareness — the fact that the sounds *mean* or *intend* the object of the ideas or images, their being directed toward it, their "intention" toward it — is something different from the image itself. It is a mental act, a psychical function. Not only is it something other than an intuitive image; according to Stumpf, it is not even bound to it[3]. The insight that these functions are of basic significance in understanding mental life is an important achievement of modern research. Here we are indebted especially to Stumpf, who sees as the prime task of psychology the study of precisely these functions. Husserl, and Külpe and his school, also deserve great credit for contributing to a proper appreciation of "acts". One such "act" or function is thinking of a concept, being directed toward it. It is thus the conceptual function that is real, not the concept itself.

But these are merely incidental remarks aimed at clarifying the psychological circumstances. Epistemologically, the import of the conceptual function consists precisely in *signifying* or *designating*. Here, however, to signify means nothing more than to *coordinate* or *associate (Zuordnen)* that is, to place in a one-one or at most a many-one correspondence *("Zuordnung")*. To say that objects fall under a certain concept is to say only that we have coordinated or associated them with this concept[4].

In this connection, we take note of recent efforts to evaluate logically and epistemologically the ambiguity of the terms 'sign' and 'signify' or 'designate'. It is necessary to distinguish between *designate* in the sense merely of "announce" or "advertise" and *designate* in the sense of *express, represent, denote, mean,* and perhaps many similar verbs; and to all of these different meanings there may correspond different "acts" or modes of consciousness[5]. Common to all of them, however, is the fact that they involve a *coordination* or *correspondence,* and this alone is essential for the theory of knowledge. The differences, whatever else one might want to say about them, are chiefly psychological in character. That they are irrelevant to epistemology is born out by the fact that only the aspect of

---

3 C. STUMPF, Erscheinungen und psychische Funktionen, in: Abhandlungen der Berl. Akad. d. Wiss., 1906.

4 O. KÜLPE, in his Die Realisierung (Vol. I, p. 226), presented the same view of the nature of concepts: "For objective science, concepts are *'fixed coordinations'* between signs and signified objects." (Transl. AEB.)

5 E. HUSSERL, *op. cit.,* pp. 23—61.

coordination — which is in no way affected by these differences — is of importance in solving the problem of the nature of knowledge. It is a great error to believe that the solution of problems in the theory of knowledge requires that we first distinguish all the various modes of consciousness and "acts". If that were the case, we should never be able to answer any epistemological question. For the number of modes of consciousness is unlimited and inexhaustible; no single experience, strictly speaking, is exactly the same as any other. The method of "phenomenological analysis", so widely prized and practiced today, undertakes to make just such differentiations. Hence the more thoroughly it is carried out, the farther it takes us into a realm without limits. This method does not yield real knowledge; it only prepares the way for knowledge. For it does not reduce one thing to another; on the contrary, it seeks to separate or distinguish things as much as possible.

But these are merely comments in passing. We return to our discussion of the nature of concepts.

The view adopted above — that concepts do not actually exist, that to talk of concepts is simply to use a kind of shorthand, that in reality there are only conceptual *functions* — has encountered widespread opposition. It has been argued that entire sciences exist, such as mathematics and pure logic, whose subject matter consists exclusively of concepts and their relationships. Thus it seems that we cannot deny existence to concepts without being led to absurdities of the sort Lorenz Oken expressed so well when he said "Mathematics is based on Nothingness *(Nichts)* and hence arises from Nothingness". For this reason, we generally prefer to say: concepts *do* exist, they have a kind of being just as sense objects, for example, do; but it is an *ideal* being rather than a *real* one. Granted that the concepts of triangle, of the number five, of the syllogism, and the like have no real existence. Yet they are not just nothing, since we can make various valid statements about them. Therefore we must ascribe to them a kind of being, and this we call ideal being to distinguish it from real being.

There is no objection to this form of expression, of course, so long as the question is purely one of terminology. But such talk of ideal objects leads all too easily to unclear and erroneous views, views that point in the direction of the Platonic metaphysics on which these linguistic formulations lean. Almost without noticing it, we come to counterpose to the real world another world *indepen-*

dent of it, a world of ideal being, a realm of ideas, a realm of values and truths, of that which is valid — in short, a timeless world of concepts. This second world appears as a fixed, self-subsistent one, in which concepts and truths are everlastingly enthroned and which would be there even if there were no realm of real being. For two times two, so it is claimed, would equal four even if nothing real existed at all. The question then arises of the relationship between the two realms, of the connection between the real and the ideal, with the consequence that philosophic thought is burdened with numerous pseudo-problems. It is supposed that ideal objects are somehow apprehended or comprehended through real processes: concepts by means of ideas or images, truths by means of acts of judgment, and so forth. A special term has been coined for this act of apprehending — 'ideation'. Thus the relationship that was to be clarified actually becomes ever less clear, especially if one is reluctant to take the final step toward a complete hypostatization of concepts and an unadulterated Platonic Theory of Forms (see below, II, § 18).

We avoid all these entanglements if from the outset we make clear to ourselves that the ideal "being" under discussion cannot in any way be compared or counterposed to real being. It is neither akin to it nor capable of entering into any sort of real relationship with it. In particular, it makes no sense to attribute to the realm of ideas an existence *independent* of the real world — as if truths and concepts could somehow exist independently of creatures that judge and comprehend. The nature of truths and concepts consists in their being signs; hence they always presuppose someone who wishes to signify or designate, someone who desires to set up co-ordinations or correspondences. The conceptual function has its locus only in the referring or relating consciousness, and it is there-fore nonsense to impute to concepts an existence independent of conscious beings. It is equally wrong, of course, to view concepts as a part or an aspect of a specific conscious process; this would be to regard them as mental realities, whereas the whole point is that they are not real at all.

Medieval realism has long been outmoded. Yet people still commit many errors by conceiving the relationship between a con-cept and the objects that fall under it not merely as one of designa-tion but as something closer or more intimate. An illustration is the theory of *abstraction,* understood as implying that a concept can, so to speak, be *generated* from things by abstracting from their individual properties. If this theory were true, it would then follow conversely that by adding certain characteristics to a concept we would be able to transform it back into a real thing. This too is nonsense, of course. No matter how many specific features we add, a concept can at most become the concept of an individual thing; it can never become the thing itself. Notwithstanding, the question of the so-called *principium individuationis* — the principle through which an individual object supposedly grew out of a general concept — did play a large role in medieval scholasticism. And the strange doctrine arose of the *"haecceitas"*, that characteristic which, when joined to a general concept, converts it into an individual reality.

It is equally impossible for an *image* or *idea* to grow out of a concept by the addition of characteristics to the concept. For an idea also is something real; it is a form of mental reality. Just as real things or ideas cannot be built up out of mere concepts, so too concepts cannot be *generated* from things and ideas by the omission of certain properties.

In general, we cannot "think away" a property from a thing, and leave the other properties unaltered. For example, I cannot form the concept of a mathematical sphere by first imagining a real sphere and then abstracting from all of its properties, such as color and the like. I can, of course, visualize a sphere of any given color, but not a sphere of no color at all. We do not arrive at concepts by *omitting* certain features of things or ideas. As the example of the sphere shows, we cannot simply leave out features without providing a substitute. Quite the contrary, the way we arrive at concepts is by distinguishing the various features from one another and giving each a designation. But as Hume already saw[6], this differentiation is made possible by the fact that the individual characters can vary *independently* of one another. Thus in the case of the sphere, I am able to separate shape and color as particular features because on the one hand I can imagine bodies with any arbitrary shape but of the same color and, on the other, bodies of any arbitrary color but with the same shape.

This brief account will suffice, I hope, to furnish some initial clarity concerning the nature of concepts and to warn against any

---

6 D. HUME, Treatise on Human Nature, Book I, Part I, near the end of section VII.

and all reification of them. Concepts are simply imaginary things *(Gedankendinge)*, intended to make possible an exact designation of objects for the purpose of cognition. Concepts may be likened to the lines of latitude and longitude, which span the earth and permit us to designate unambiguously any position on its surface.

§ 6. The Limits of Definition

Have we, by taking the steps described above, attained the desired goal of absolute certainty and precision in knowing? Unquestionably, we have made considerable progress. By using defined concepts, scientific knowledge raises itself far above the level of knowing in everyday life. Whenever we have at our disposal suitably defined concepts, knowledge becomes possible in a form practically free from doubt.

Consider an example. If someone hands me a piece of metal, I won't know whether it is pure silver or not, so long as I am restricted to the perceptions obtained merely from seeing or touching the metal. My memory images of silver are not sharp enough for me to distinguish them clearly from images of similar metals, such as tin or certain alloys. But the situation is entirely different if I make use of the scientific *concept* of silver. Then silver is defined as a substance with the specific gravity of 10.5, an atomic weight of 108, a certain electrical conductivity, and so on. I need only see if the substance possesses these properties in order to determine, to within any desired degree of accuracy, whether what has been given me is silver or some other metal. I satisfy myself of the presence or absence of the required properties — and there is no other way of doing so — by carrying out such experiments as weighing, chemical analyses, and the like, the outcome of which I ascertain by observation.

In the final analysis, however, sensory observation, such as the reading of a scale, always involves the re-cognition of a perceptual image, and the latter, as we have made clear, is ever subject to an essential uncertainty. The position of a pointer on an instrument, for example, can never be determined with absolute precision. Every reading contains an error of some size.

Hence we face the very same difficulty that we encountered at the beginning. Once again what is required is the re-cognition of intuitive structures, the comparison of perceptual images with memory images. The only difference is that the images are not of the object to be known but of its properties. The characteristic features into which a definition resolves the concept of a real object must, in the end, be intuitive in nature. The presence of these features in a given object can be ascertained only by intuition; for whatever is given, is given us ultimately through intuition. The sole exceptions are non-intuitive experiences of consciousness, or "acts". But these, as we have emphasized, are no whit less vague and uncertain than intuitions.

So the difficulty that was to have been overcome by the introduction of concepts has in reality not been disposed of; it has only been pushed back. Yet in the process something has been obtained that is of great benefit to knowledge. The gain lies in the fact that now it is possible, by appropriate definitions, to shift the difficulty to the most favorable locations, where error can be excluded with a degree of certainty that suffices for the purposes of the individual sciences. For instance, if the concept of fish includes the features that it lays eggs and breathes through gills, then we can never make the mistake of taking a whale for a fish. The whale brings living young into the world and possesses lungs; these are characters with regard to whose presence exact observation and investigation cannot possibly deceive us. Likewise, the features characteristic of the concept "silver" — the example used above — are so chosen that their recognition can be guaranteed with sufficient accuracy for all practical as well as scientific purposes, even though re-cognition itself comes about only with the aid of sensory images. And the same holds for all other cases.

Yet no matter how fully this procedure may satisfy the demands of practical life and the sciences, it does not meet the requirements of the theory of knowledge. From the viewpoint of the latter, the difficulty continues to exist in principle however far back it may be pushed. The question for epistemology is whether this difficulty admits of being eliminated altogether. Only if this is so does it appear possible for there to be absolutely certain knowledge. It is therefore on this question that the theory of knowledge centers its attention.

An answer, it seems, is readily forthcoming with a moment's reflection. To define a concept is to specify its characteristics. But these latter, if they are to be precisely determined, must in turn be defined; that is, they must be resolved into further characteristics, and so forth. Now if it were both possible and necessary to continue this series of subdefinitions without end, the resulting infinite regress would of course render all defining illusory. The fact is, however, that very soon we come upon features that simply do not admit of being further defined. The meaning of words that designate these ultimate characteristics can be demonstrated only through intuition, or immediate experience. We cannot learn what "blue" or "pleasure" is by definition, but only by intuiting something blue or experiencing pleasure. With this we appear, however, to have answered our question definitely and in the negative: an eventual return to what is immediately given, to intuition and experience, is unavoidable. And since the immediately given is in principle always marked by a certain haziness, it seems altogether impossible to obtain *absolutely* precise concepts. Must we not then concede that skepticism is right in denying the existence of indisputably certain knowledge?

At this point, an important observation needs to be inserted. When we say that intuitive structures are indistinct, we do not mean to deny that mental events are completely determined down to the last detail. As actual processes, they are determined in every respect; indeed, anything that is real is uniquely what it is and not something else. Yet the blurredness of which we speak is always present. For although these processes are at each moment fully determined, nevertheless they differ from moment to moment. They are fleeting and variable; our recollection in the very next moment cannot even reproduce the preceding moment with perfect accuracy. We cannot distinguish between two nearly identical colors, between two tones of almost the same pitch; nor can we tell for certain whether two nearly parallel lines form an angle. In short, although intuitions as actual structures cannot properly speaking be described as being undetermined in themselves, they nonetheless give rise to indeterminacy and uncertainty as soon as we try to make judgments about them. For in order to make judgments, we must hold these intuitions fixed in memory, something which their transitory nature resists. In what follows, we shall express this fact in abbreviated form by saying that all intuition or other experience lacks full sharpness and exactness.

Until quite recently logic generally had not been too disturbed over this situation. It had declared that the ultimate concepts at which the process of defining must come to a halt not only are incapable of definition but do not *need* definition. The passion for defining everything was viewed as unnecessary hair-splitting, which hinders rather than promotes the advance of science. The content of the simplest concepts is exhibited in intuition (the pitch of the note "a", for example, by sounding a tuningfork). And this demonstration accomplished roughly what Aristotle had in mind as the task of a so-called real definition: to specify the "essence" of the object designated by a concept. This definition by ostension has also been called "concrete" or "psychological" definition, in contrast to logical definition proper, from which, of course, it differs *toto genere*.

Now the declaration that definitions may be dispensed with for the simplest concepts may mean two very different things.

In the first place, it may mean that intuition *is* able to endow certain concepts with a perfectly clear and definite content. In that event, our contention that all intuition is blurred (in the sense explained above) would have to be challenged and corrected.

In the second place, however, it may mean that we do not ever require absolutely accurate and theoretically perfect knowledge. The assumption then would be that only approximate or probable knowledge can be attained in any domain, so that to desire absolute certainty would not make sense.

The second alternative in its full form has been defended by only a very few philosophers. An example that might be cited is the doctrine of the Sophist Gorgias; the radical empiricism of John Stuart Mill — if carried out with thoroughgoing consistency — results in the same view. According to this philosophy, absolute certainty cannot be claimed for any knowledge, not even for so-called pure conceptual truths, such as the propositions of arithmetic. Our knowledge that, say, 3 times 4 equals 12 is obtained ultimately only through real mental processes, and these share the blurredness of anything that is given. The epistemological problem we encounter in reflecting on this viewpoint will have to be dealt with later. Then the attitude we must adopt toward the second of the two alternatives will be apparent at once. For the present we turn to the first alternative.

Here what is at issue is saving the certainty and rigor of knowledge in the face of the fact that cognition comes about through fleeting, blurred experiences. Now this can be done only if we assume that experiences are *not* indistinct in every respect, but that there is something quite constant or clearly determined about them which becomes evident under certain circumstances. What is given at any moment is undoubtedly transitory in nature. Thus what is constant can only be the *law* that governs the given and provides it with its form.

Possibilities now open up that may enable us to make our way out of the Heraclitian flux of experiences onto solid ground. To be sure, it seems that a basic doubt must always remain: even if our intuitive ideas are ruled somehow by absolutely rigorous laws (and this is surely the case), the question still arises as to what we then *know* of these laws. Doesn't such knowledge also consist, in the final analysis, of fleeting experiences? And if this is true, wouldn't the entire question come up again and again, without end?

This is not yet the place to decide how far the basic doubt is justified, to determine whether we do indeed lose the assurance of absolute rigor as soon as we go back to the intuitive meaning of concepts. But regardless of what the decision may be, the theory of knowledge must be prepared against an unfavorable outcome. Hence it is of prime importance for epistemology that it investigate whether the content of all concepts is to be found ultimately only in intuition, or whether under some circumstances it may make sense to speak of the meaning of a concept without reducing it to intuitive ideas. The determinateness of such concepts could then be guaranteed independently of the degree of sharpness that characterizes our intuitions. We would no longer have to be dismayed by the fact that our experiences are in eternal flux; rigorously exact thought could still exist.

The sense in which something of this sort can be maintained will be indicated in the next section.

§ 7. Implicit Definitions

Although logic from the beginning was able to perceive the above-mentioned problem, the impetus for its definitive solution came from another quarter. It came from research in a particular science, to whose needs logic, in this instance as in most others, did not adapt itself until later. In the nature of the case, the only science that could forge ahead to a rigorous formulation of our problem was one so constituted that absolute certainty had to be guaranteed for its every step. This science was mathematics. The remaining sciences, not only because of inadequate definitions but on other grounds as well, were unable to raise such lofty claims to rigor; hence they had no occasion to formulate their problems in so basic a manner. Nevertheless, the significance of the studies we are about to report is by no means confined to mathematics. On the contrary, they are in principle just as valid for scientific concepts generally as they are for those of mathematics. It is simply a matter of convenience that we take mathematical concepts as a paradigm on which to base our considerations.

When mathematicians discovered that the most elementary geometrical concepts, such as point or straight line, are not really definable (that is, they are not resolvable into still simpler concepts), they first took comfort in the notion that the meanings of these concepts are given so clearly in intuition that from them the validity of the geometrical axioms seemingly could be read off at once with perfect certainty. Modern mathematics, however, was not satisfied with this resort to intuition. Addressing itself to the basic questions, it set out in search not only of new geometrical theorems, but also of the grounds for the validity of *all* geometrical truths. Mathematical proof, the derivation of new propositions from those already known, gained in rigor as mathematicians strove to avoid any appeal to intuition. All conclusions were to be derived not from intuition but from explicitly formulated propositions using purely logical means alone. Phrases such as "It follows from a consideration of the figure . . ." or "It can be seen from the drawing . . ." were henceforth banned. In particular, there would no longer be any *tacit* recourse in geometrical proofs to properties whose presence could be established only by observing the figure. Instead, the existence of these properties would have to be deduced in a purely logical manner from the assumptions and axioms, or if that turned out to be impossible, specifically stated in new axioms.

At this juncture, it seemed intolerable that the ultimate principles — the axioms of geometry, which underlie all proofs and therefore are not themselves provable — should still owe their validity to intuition alone. This was the very same intuition which mathematicians sought to eliminate from proof procedures because, instructed especially by the development of views about the parallel postulate, they had come to suspect its reliability. If the meaning of basic mathematical concepts, such as "point", "line" or "plane", could be exhibited only by means of intuition, then the axioms that hold for them also could be obtained only from intuition. Yet it is the legitimacy of precisely such proof that is at issue.

In order to escape from this uncertainty, mathematicians struck out on a path that is of the greatest significance for epistemology. Building on the preparatory work of others[7], David Hilbert undertook to construct geometry on a foundation whose absolute certainty would not be placed in jeopardy at any point by an appeal to intuition[8]. Whether Hilbert was successful in every particular or whether his solution still needs to be completed and perfected does not concern us here. Our interest is solely in the principle, not the execution and elaboration.

The principle itself is amazingly simple. The task was to introduce the basic concepts, which are in the usual sense indefinable, in such a fashion that the validity of the axioms that treat of these concepts is strictly guaranteed. And Hilbert's solution was simply to stipulate that the basic or primitive concepts are to be *defined* just by the fact that they satisfy the axioms.

This is what is known as definition by axioms, or definition by postulates, or implicit definition.

It is important that we be quite clear as to what this kind of definition means and provides, and wherein it differs from the ordinary sort. In science generally the purpose of definitions is to create concepts as clearly determined signs, by means of which the work of knowledge can go forward with full confidence. Definitions build concepts out of all the characteristics that are needed for just this work. Now the *intellectual* labor of science — we shall soon have to examine its nature more closely — consists in *inferring*, that is, in deducing new judgments from old ones. Inference can proceed only from judgments or statements. Hence when we utilize a concept in the business of thought, we employ none of its properties save the property that certain judgments hold with respect to the concept — for example, that the axioms hold for the primitive concepts of geometry. It follows that for a rigorous science, which en-

---

7 Special mentions should be made of M. PASCH's Vorlesungen über neuere Geometrie, 1882.

8 D. HILBERT, Grundlagen der Geometrie, 4th edition, 1913. (English translation of first edition by E. J. TOWNSEND, 1902: The Foundations of Geometry.)

gages in series of inferences, a concept is indeed nothing more than that concerning which certain judgments can be expressed. Consequently, this is also how the concept is to be defined.

Modern mathematics, in electing to define the basic concepts of geometry in this manner, is not really creating something entirely new and exceptional. It is merely uncovering the role that these concepts actually play and have always played in mathematical deduction. That is to say, when we deduce mathematical truths from one another, the *intuitive* meaning of the basic concepts is of no consequence whatsoever. In so far as the validity and interconnection of mathematical propositions are concerned, it makes no difference whether, for example, we understand by the word 'plane' the familiar intuitive figure everyone thinks of when he hears the word, or any other figure. What matters is only that the word means something for which a particular set of statements (the axioms) holds. And exactly the same thing is true of the remaining concepts that occur in these axioms. They too are defined solely by the fact that they stand in certain relations to the other concepts.

Thus Hilbert's geometry begins with a system of propositions in which a number of terms occur (such as 'point', 'straight line', 'plane', 'between', 'outside of', and the like) that, to begin with, have no meaning or content. These terms acquire meaning only by virtue of the axiom system, and possess only the content that it bestows upon them. They stand for entities whose whole being is to be bearers of the relations laid down by the system. This presents no special problem, since concepts are not real things at all. Even if the being of a real, intuitive thing cannot be regarded as consisting merely in its standing in certain relations to another thing, even if we are obliged to think of the bearer of relations as being endowed with some nature of its own — this would by no means hold for concepts.

Still, experience shows that it is very difficult for a beginner to grasp the notion of concepts that are defined by a system of postulates and are devoid of any actual "content". We instinctively assume that a concept must have a sense that can be represented as such; and it is even more difficult to disregard the intuitive sense of the relations that exist between concepts. Take, for example, the sentence "The point C lies between points A and B on the straight line a". We are to associate with the words 'between' and 'lie upon' only the meaning that they signify certain specific relations among certain objects *A*, *B* and *C* — but they need not designate precisely *those* relations that we usually associate with those words. Anyone who is not acquainted with this extremely important notion will do well to familiarize himself with it by considering a variety of examples.

Naturally it is mathematics that furnishes such examples in their purest form. This discipline makes frequent use of the fact that the mutual relations of geometrical concepts can be studied as such quite independently of their intuitive meanings. For instance, consider the family of the infinitely many spherical surfaces passing through a particular point in space, and imagine this point itself as having been removed from the space. Now take the theorems of ordinary Euclidean geometry; wherever the word 'plane' occurs let it signify one of the spherical surfaces, let the word 'point' signify a point and the words 'straight line' a great circle on a spherical surface, reinterpret the word 'parallel' in an analogous manner, and so forth. As can easily be seen, we then obtain a set of propositions all of which hold for the system of spheres. Hence in this instance exactly the same relations exist among the spheres, great circles and the like, as among the planes, straight lines, etc., in ordinary space (from which no point is thought of as having been removed). But our intuitive picture is, of course, entirely different in the two cases. Here we have an example of structures that differ in intuitive appearance from the straight lines and planes of ordinary geometry, yet stand in the same relations to one another and obey the same axioms. It is an easy matter for a mathematician to devise *arbitrarily* many other structures that accomplish the same thing.

Let us take another example. The theorems of the Riemannian geometry of the plane are completely identical with those of the Euclidean geometry of the sphere, provided we understand by a straight line of the former a great circle of the latter, and so forth. Similarly, the theorems of projective geometry preserve their truth under an interchange of the words 'point' and 'straight line'. And yet how different are the intuitive structures that we commonly designate by these words.

Such examples can be multiplied at will. Theoretical physics also offers an abundance of them. It is a familiar fact that essentially different phenomena may nevertheless obey the same formal laws. The same equation may represent quite different natural phenomena depending on the physical meanings we assign to the quantities that occur in it. A very simple case, familiar to all, in which the mutual relations of concepts appear wholly disengaged from their intuitive content is found in the formulas commonly used to elucidate the Aristotelian modes of inference. When we infer "All *S* are *P*" from the two premisses "All *M* are *P*" and "All *S* are *M*", the logical relationship holds quite independently of what the symbols '*S*', '*M*' and '*P*' may mean. All that matters is that the concepts stand to one another in the relations specified in the premisses. The symbol '*S*' can equally well designate men, or ship's propellers, or logarithms. It is thus easy to see that the introduction of any *ambiguous* symbol initiates a separation of content from the purely logical form, a separation which, pursued consistently, leads eventually to the determination of concepts by means of implicit definitions.

We conclude that a strictly deductive construction of a scientific theory, as found, say, in mathematics, has nothing to do with the intuitive picture we form of the primitive concepts. Such a construction takes into consideration only what is laid down in the implicit definitions, that is, the mutual relations of the primitive concepts as expressed in the axioms. From the standpoint of mathematics as a fixed structure of interconnected propositions, the intuitive ideas we associate with the words 'plane', 'point', and the like, count only as illustrative examples. And these, as we have seen, can be replaced by entirely different examples. It is true that, in the cases cited above, what we substituted for the usual meanings of the primitive concepts were in turn spatial figures familiar to us from ordinary geometry. But in principle nothing prevents us from using non-spatial objects, such as feelings or sounds, or for that matter wholly non-intuitive objects. In analytic geometry, for instance. the word 'point' strictly speaking means nothing more than *number-triple*. The fact that we can assign the intuitive meaning of spatial coordinates to these numbers does not affect their mutual relations or the calculations we make with them.

Thus geometry as a solid edifice of rigorously exact truths is not truly a science of space. The spatial figures serve simply as intuitive examples in which the relations set up *in abstracto* by the geometrical propositions are realized. As to the converse — whether geometry in so far as it does aim to be a science of space can be regarded as a firmly joined structure of absolutely rigorous truths — this is a question for the epistemology of mathematics. We shall not try to resolve it here, since our concern for the present is only with the general problems of knowledge. However, it should be clear enough from what has been said that we cannot take for granted that the answer is in the affirmative, as one might otherwise suppose. For it was precisely the misgivings about the absolute rigor of propositions dealing with intuitive spatial forms that led to defining concepts not through intuition but through systems of postulates.

The meaning and effect of implicit definitions and how they differ from ordinary definitions ought now be more clear. In the case of ordinary definitions, the defining process terminates when the ultimate indefinable concepts are in some way exhibited in intuition (concrete definition, *cf.* § 6). This involves pointing to something real, something that has individual existence. Thus we explain the concept of *point* by indicating a grain of sand, the concept of *straight line* by a taut string, that of *fairness* by pointing to certain feelings that the person being instructed finds present in the reality of his own consciousness. In short, it is through concrete definitions that we set up the connection between concepts and reality. Concrete definitions exhibit in intuitive or experienced reality that which henceforth is to be designated by a concept. On the other hand, implicit definitions have no association or connection with reality at all; specifically and in principle they reject such association; they remain in the domain of concepts. A system of truths created with the aid of implicit definitions does not at any point rest on the ground of reality. On the contrary, it floats freely, so to speak, and like the solar system bears within itself the guarantee of its own stability. None of the concepts that occur in the theory designate anything real; rather, they designate one another in such fashion that the meaning of one concept consists in a particular constellation of a number of the remaining concepts.

Accordingly, the construction of a strict deductive science has only the significance of a game with symbols. In such an abstract science as number theory, for example, we erect the edifice for the sake of the pleasure obtained from the play of concepts. But in geometry, and even more in the empirical sciences, the motive for putting together the network of concepts is above all our interest in certain intuitive or real objects. Here the interest attaches not so much to the abstract interconnections as to the examples that run parallel to the conceptual relations. In general, we concern ourselves

with the abstract only in order to apply it to the intuitive. But —
and it is to this point that our consideration returns again and
again — the moment we carry over a conceptual relation to intuitive examples, we are no longer assured of complete rigor. When
real objects are given us, how can we know with absolute certainty
that they stand in just the relations to one another that are laid down
in the postulates through which we are able to define the concepts?

Kant believed that immediate self-evidence assures us that in
geometry and natural science we can make apodictically certain
judgments about intuitive and real objects. For him the only problem was to explain how such judgments come about, not to prove
that they exist. But we who have come to doubt this belief find ourselves in an altogether different situation. All that we are justified
in saying is that the Kantian explanation might indeed be suited to
rendering intelligible an *existing* apodictic knowledge of reality; but
that it exists is not something that we may assert, at least not at
this stage of our inquiry. Nor can we even see at this point how a
proof of its existence might be obtained.

It is therefore all the more important that in *implicit definition*
we have found an instrument that enables us to determine concepts
completely and thus to attain strict precision in thinking. To achieve
this end, however, we have had to effect a radical separation between concept and intuition, thought and reality. While we do relate
the two spheres to one another, they seem not to be joined together
at all. The bridges between them are down.

Even though the price may seem very high, it must for the time
being be paid. We cannot begin our work with the preconceived
notion of preserving, under any and all circumstances, the rigor
and validity of our knowledge of reality. Our task is solely to gain
a knowledge of knowledge. And we have made considerable progress toward our goal through the insight that it is possible to
divorce completely the two realms of concepts and reality. The more
definitely and firmly we carry out this divorce, the more clearly
we shall grasp the relations into which these two realms enter in
the act of cognition.

As a supplementary remark and to avoid misunderstandings, we
stress that not every arbitrary set of postulates may be conceived
of as the implicit definition of a group of concepts. The defining
axioms must fulfill certain conditions, for example, that they do
not contain a *contradiction*. If the set of postulates is inconsistent,

then no concept will satisfy all of its members. Hence if the aim is to construct a deductive theory on the basis of certain axioms, the latter must be shown to be consistent. Often this is a very difficult task. But it is an internal affair of the theory in question, and we may think of it as solved so far as our theoretical discussion of implicit definitions is concerned.

We should also note that the expression 'implicit definition' is here used in a wider sense than is customary in present-day mathematics. There by an *explicit* definition we mean one that expresses a concept by means of a combination of other concepts in such a way that the combination may be put in place of the concept wherever it occurs; and we speak of an *implicit* definition when such a combination cannot be specified. I retain the usage employed in this section because it has gained a certain citizenship in philosophical literature since the first edition of this book appeared and because there is no danger of any misunderstanding.

§ 8. The Nature of Judgments

From the considerations set forth in the preceding section, we learn that a full insight into the nature of concepts can be obtained only if we first explore the nature of *judgments*. For, implicit definitions determine concepts by virtue of the fact that certain axioms — which themselves are judgments — hold with regard to these concepts; thus such definitions make concepts depend on judgments. All other types of definitions likewise consist of judgments. At the same time, concepts appear in all judgments, so that judgments in turn seem to be composed of and to presuppose concepts. Concepts and judgments are thus correlative. They imply one another; the one cannot exist without the other.

Clearly, concepts exist only so that judgments can be made. When people designate objects by means of concepts and concepts by means of words, they do so only in order to think and speak about these objects, that is, to make judgments about them.

What then is a judgment?

Here we are not concerned with the psychological character of the act of judging anymore than we were with the nature of the mental processes that represent concepts in the reality of consciousness. Moreover, the nature of judging as a psychical act does not admit of adequate description. As in the case of any other mental phenomenon, we can become acquainted with it only by experiencing it when we ourselves perform an act of judgment. Characterizations of the act of judging can be no more than metaphorical paraphrases, as when someone declares it to be a "joining" or a "separating" of ideas, or a "putting together" of several ideas into one (Sigwart) or a "breaking apart" of one idea into several (Wundt). The fact of the matter is that we can think of ideas as "bound together" or as "taken apart" *without* thereby making a judgment, as Leibniz noted against Locke, who described a judgment as a "joining or separating of ideas". John Stuart Mill stated quite emphatically that a mere combining of ideas in no way constitutes a judgment; that something else must be added; but that the question of just what is this something else is "one of the most intricate of metaphysical problems"[9]. Many philosophers believe that the essence of the judgment is to be found in the attitude of the judger, which is either one of affirmation and acknowledgement or (in the case of negative judgments) one of denial and rejection. But surely this does not suffice to describe what is peculiar to the process of judgment as against mere supposing, two basic mental phenomena that are more and more widely recognized as being very different.

But our inquiry is not addressed to the psychological nature of judging. Our concern is with the epistemological significance of the judgment, and this we may hope to determine without too much difficulty if we recall what we have already learned about the nature of concepts.

The essence of the concept, we saw, consists simply in its being a sign that we coordinate in thought to the objects of which we are thinking. It is therefore natural to suppose that a judgment also is nothing other than a sign. But *what* does it designate? In the preceding section we showed that axioms, which are judgments, lay down *relations* among concepts. Now since concepts are signs for objects, it may be presumed that judgments are signs for relations among objects. We must now examine whether this presumption is generally valid and what further explanation or qualification it may need. These matters are best determined if we consider an example.

Let us take a simple illustration, the judgment "The snow is cold". The words 'snow' and 'cold' (the subject and predicate of

---

9   J. S. MILL, Logic, Book I, Chapter V, § 1.

the sentence) designate concepts whose meaning is well known to us from intuition. Plainly, the judgment does designate a relation between the snow and coldness — a connection familiar to us as the thing-property relationship. To carry our analysis forward, let us assume that the judgment was made by a child whose previous acquaintance with snow had been confined to visual perception. His concept of snow is then constituted of such characteristics as *white, flaky, floating-down-from-the sky*. When for the first time he touches snow with his hand, he finds that this white, flaky thing is also a cold thing. The sensation experienced through his fingers is familiar to the child. He has learned to designate it by the name 'cold', and now, by the judgment "The snow is cold", he attributes this name to the snow. Hence, in accord with what was said in § 3, we have here an instance of *knowledge:* on the basis of an act of re-cognition, the object "snow" is invested with the correct name 'cold'. If we go back to the content of the subject-concept — in this case, a white thing falling from the sky in flakes — we see that our judgment designates the circumstance that bound up with these features is the feature of being cold. Where the former occur, so does the latter. Nothing of course has as yet been said as to whether this holds only for the snow just touched or is true quite generally.

Here we see that the judgment designates a coexistence of characteristics (in particular, a spatial and temporal coexistence, since the coldness is found at the same time and place as the snow). Accordingly, we must modify somewhat our earlier statement in the following way: a judgment designates not merely a relation between objects, but the *existence* of this relation, that is, the fact that the relation obtains between them. That the two formulations are not the same is quite obvious. The mere designating of a relation does not require a judgment; a concept suffices for that. When we declared that a concept is a sign for objects, we stated explicitly that the term 'object' is to be taken in its widest sense so as to include relations as well. For instance, "simultaneity" and "difference" are concepts of relations; but that various objects are in fact simultaneous or different can be expressed only by means of a judgment. John Stuart Mill called particular attention to this distinction in the following passage (in which the concept of an order among sensations or ideas appears in place of what we here have called relations among objects): " . . . it is necessary to distinguish between the mere sug-

gestion to the mind of a certain order among sensations or ideas . . .
and the indication that this order is an actual fact . . .[10]."

Judgments then are signs for *facts*. Whenever we make a judgment, what we intend thereby is to designate a set of facts. The
facts may be real or conceptual; for we are to understand by a set
of facts not only the relationship of real objects, but also the existence of relations among concepts. It is a fact that the snow is cold;
it is also a fact that 2 times 2 equals 4.

It is no paradox that concepts alone do not suffice to designate
what there is in the world, and that we require still another kind
of sign. If concepts are to designate objects, then in order to designate the *existence* of relations among these objects we need new
signs that are not concepts. I can, of course, embrace both the objects and the relation holding between them in a *single* concept.
Thus I can form the concept of the coldness of the snow or of the
equality of 2×2 and 4. But this is something entirely different from
making the judgments "The snow is cold" or "$2 \times 2 = 4$". It is only
the judgments, and not the concepts, that designate sets of facts.

A judgment always presupposes a set of facts, a factual existence, a being at hand or "being the case" of that which is stated
in the judgment. It is this correct insight that underlies FRANZ BREN-
TANO's theory of judgment (*cf.* his Psychologie, Book 2, Chapter 7).
I say underlies, because the formulation in which Brentano em-
bedded the sound kernel of his theory seems to me to be misleading. He held that the existential proposition (a statement such as
"God exists" or "There are airships") is the original form of the
judgment, to which all other forms are to be reduced. The proposition "Some man is sick" means "A sick man exists" or "There is
a sick man"; the proposition "All men are mortal" means "An
immortal man does not exist" (*loc. cit.*, p. 283). According to this,
the proposition "Light is an oscillatory process" would actually
have to read "There is no light that is not an electrical oscillatory
process". It is evident that on this theory the so-called universal
affirmative judgments of logic would in reality be negative existential propositions. This is surely an artificial construction which
turns the natural state of affairs upside down. That the formulation is unsuitable is revealed even more clearly by a conclusion that

---

10 J. S. MILL in a footnote to J. MILL, Analysis of the Phenomena
of the Human Mind, 2nd edition, I, p. 162, note 48.

seems to follow from the theory, namely, that a judgment need not always designate the existence of a relation, that its subject-matter can just as well be constituted by a single, simple object. The sense of the judgment would then consist merely in the "acknowledging" of this object; nothing would have to be said about any relations. The situation with respect to negative judgments would be the same, except that "rejection" would take the place of acknowledgment.

But it is obvious that acknowledgment and rejection can at most characterize judging as a psychological act. They do not reach its epistemological and logical significance and this is what is at issue in our inquiry into the nature of judgments. The logical side of Brentano's theory — the claim that basically every judgment is one-termed — is an error that can lead to serious philosophical mistakes, in particular to the attempt to detach "things" from the relations existing among them (of which we shall speak at another place). We expose the error best if we simply verify that not even those judgments that are avowedly existential propositions can be looked upon as one-termed or free of relations. For instance, one might wish to regard the judgment "The world *is*" as one-termed, in contrast, for example, to the plainly two-termed judgment "The world is large", since only the one concept "world" occurs in the first proposition while the second contains the two concepts "world" and "large". This, however, would be to confuse two quite different meanings of the word 'is'. In the second proposition it serves as the copula, whereas in the first it carries the meaning of 'has existence' or 'is real'. Thus in the first proposition, in addition to the concept of the world there appears also the concept of existence or reality; indeed, every existential proposition has the sense of asserting that the object designated by its subject-concept is a *real* object (in contrast, say, to a mere concept). These judgments thus designate a specific *relation* between a concept and reality. The (extra-logical) question whether reality as such is to be understood only as a system of relations[11] need to be taken up here. It will be discussed later in our study in a quite different context.

The term 'existence' has a different sense in judgments about purely conceptual facts than in judgments about reality. When a

---

11 It is from this aspect that existential statements have been treated by C. SIGWART, Logik, 3rd edition, 1904, pp. 93 ff.; and J. COHN, Voraussetzungen und Ziele des Erkennens, pp. 78 ff.

judgment asserts that a concept exists, all that this means is that the concept does not contain a contradiction. The mathematician has proved the "existence" of a mathematical object once he has shown that it is defined without contradiction. The mathematical concept possesses no other "being" than this. The same thing is true of all pure concepts, and is a consequence of the considerations presented in the preceding section. That is to say, "pure" concepts are those that are determined by means of implicit definitions, and the only condition to which they are subject is that they be free of contradiction. But a contradiction, of course, is nothing but a *relation* between judgments; it consists in the fact that two opposing claims have been put forward concerning the same object. In the case of concepts, therefore, it is especially clear that "existence" means the existence of a relation, that is, a relation among the defining judgments. (In mathematics today attempts are occasionally made to distinguish between consistency and existence; but this has no bearing in the present context since it does not touch the decisive point — tracing matters back to relations among several terms.)

Hence, although we acknowledge the correct point of departure of Brentano's theory, we shall consider it as established that judgments, as signs for the existence of relations, possess more than one term.

There is one further remark to be made. Those who would support the claim that many judgments are one-termed by pointing to the so-called *impersonalia* (propositions such as "It is snowing", "It is raining", and the like), make the mistake of confusing linguistic relationships with logical ones. For despite their simple form, it is obvious that these short sentences invariably designate a state of affairs with several elements (e. g., "It is snowing" means "Flakes are falling"). It is always possible for language, of course, to express even the most complicated relations in abbreviated form by means of a *single* word.

Every judgment is thus a sign for a fact, and a fact always comprises at least two objects and a relation holding between them. If there are more objects, it may be possible to break down the total state of affairs into simple relations existing between two objects. This question, however, we leave open. What we call a set of facts in ordinary life or in science is in any event always something complex, from which several aspects may be singled out.

For us to be able to tell from a judgment what set of facts it is coordinated to, the judgment must contain specific signs for the elements distinguished in the set of facts and for the relations between these elements. Accordingly, at least two concepts must appear in the judgment as representatives of the two terms of the relation, and in addition there must be a third sign to indicate the relation itself. This is not to say, of course, that these three parts of the judgment are always represented by the three parts of the sentence: subject, predicate und copula. The coordination does not have to be that simple; as a matter of fact, the situation is generally more complicated. For the present, we need not be concerned with the particular means by which the various aspects of a set of facts are designated in a judgment. The main thing is that a judgment as a whole is coordinated to a fact as a whole. Nor shall we at this point seek to determine which variations in the judgments correspond to variations in the relations, and whether all kinds of relations can perhaps be reduced to a single kind. In so far as an answer to these questions requires an examination of the formal properties of judgments, the theory of knowledge can leave this to pure logic; and to the extent that the answer presupposes a study and classification of relations, this cannot be undertaken until later when we come to consider the objects themselves. For the moment we have to do not with making judgments about objects, but solely with making judgments about judgments. In addition, what has been said here concerning the nature of judgments will in the sequel be very much amplified.

Judgments and concepts stand in a peculiar interrelationship. Concepts are linked together by means of judgments, since every judgment designates a joining of two concepts. But it is also true that judgments are linked with one another by means of concepts: one and the same concept appears in a number of judgments and thus sets up a relation between them. Now a concept must occur in several different judgments if it is to have any sense and meaning at all. Suppose that a concept was present in only a single judgment; then the statement expressing that judgment would of necessity be the definition of the concept; else the concept would have to be defined by other judgments, and by assumption there are no other judgments in which it occurs. But it would be perfectly absurd to define a concept that otherwise played no role whatever in thought. There is no point in creating a concept of that sort, and no one in fact does. Objects of which we cannot assert anything, we simply do not designate.

Thus a concept constitutes, as it were, a point at which a series of judgments meet, namely, all those in which the concept occurs. It is a link that holds them all together. Our scientific systems form a network in which concepts represent the nodes, and judgments the threads that connect them. In actual thinking, the sense of concepts consists entirely in their being centers of relations of judgments. It is only as junction points of judgments and *in* judgments that concepts lead a life within living thought.

The definitions of a concept are those judgments that, so to speak, put it in touch with the concepts nearest it. The concept can be looked upon as a brief expression of these connections, a situation which A. Riehl described as follows: "Concept and definition differ in general only as what is potential differs from what is actual[12]." But it is for precisely this reason that we, in contrast to Riehl, must count definitions as genuine judgments. In a completely self-contained, deductively connected scientific system, genuine judgments can be distinguished from definitions only in a practical or psychological sense, not in a purely logical or epistemological one. This we see very clearly in the case of the fixed, rigorous systems of judgments offered most notably by mathematics. There we can, under certain assumptions, select arbitrary theorems, treat them as definitions, and derive from them as consequences those judgments that serve ordinarily as the definitions of the concepts. In such purely conceptual systems the distinction between definition and judgment is thus a relative one. Which properties of a concept I had best employ in defining it depends only on considerations of expediency. At one time, mathematicians regarded as axioms those propositions that seemed especially self-evident; today we do not hesitate in principle to derive such "axioms" partly from less obvious propositions and to look upon these as the axioms (and hence as the definitions of the primitive concepts), if by doing so we can achieve a simplification in the construction and compactness of the system[13].

---

12 Beiträge zur Logik, 2nd edition, 1911, pp. 13 f.

13 *Cf.*, for example, L. Couturat, Die philosophischen Prinzipien der Mathematik, 1908, pp. 7 f. (German translation of Les principes des mathématiques, 1905.)

When we carry such considerations over to the factual sciences, we must be mindful that these sciences are never strictly self-contained. On the contrary, as we study real objects, we constantly become acquainted with new properties, so that the concepts of these objects acquire in time an ever richer content. Thus concepts change, whereas the words with which we designate them still remain the same. The word stands for the real object in the full abundance of its properties and relations; the concept stands only for whatever as allotted to it by definition. For this reason, definitions and genuine judgments are strictly separated from one another in the thinking of the factual sciences; yet one and the same sentence may, depending on the particular state of the inquiry, serve either as a definition or as an instance of knowledge. Hence so far as the linguistic formulations are concerned — and ultimately it is only in these that judgments can be fixed — in the factual sciences too the difference in kinds of judgments is a relative one. The concept of an object is always defined initially by means of those properties or relations through which the object was originally discovered. As science advances, it happens not infrequently that a concept of the *same* object is later defined in an entirely different manner so that the judgments asserting the existence of the properties first discovered now appear as derived judgments. Consider, for instance, the word and the concept "electricity". At the earliest stage it was defined by the effect exercised on a small body by a piece of rubbed amber. Today, at the highest level of theoretical physics, the concept belonging to that word is most conveniently defined by means of the relations expressed in the fundamental equations of electrodynamics, from which the phenomena first discovered are then deduced as particular consequences.

Every judgment places a concept in relation to other concepts and designates the fact that this relation exists. If the concept in question is already familiar and defined, then we have an ordinary judgment. If this is not the case, then the concept is to be regarded as having been created by the judgment. The latter thus becomes the definition, which constructs the concept out of its characteristics. It therefore seems quite proper to grant the status of judgments to definitions as well; theoretically, definitions do not occupy a special position. Thus we unify the picture we must make of the great connected structure of judgments and concepts that constitute science. It is this interconnection that is the essence of *knowledge*.

The possibility of such an interconnection rests on the fact that concepts are joined together by judgments. Only in judging is there knowledge.

§ 9. Judging and Knowing

With this we return to the analysis of the cognitive process. For we have now gone far enough in our study of the means required for knowing — concepts and judgments — to be able to penetrate more deeply into the nature of knowledge itself.

To know an object is to discover or find again another object in it. When we say "in it", the word 'in', which signifies first of all a spatial relation, can in this instance have only a metaphorical sense. In order to understand this sense correctly, we must examine more closely the relationship between two concepts where one designates the known object and the other the object as which it is known.

To say "I know *A* as *B*" or, equivalently, "I know that *A* is *B*", is to say that the concepts *A* and *B* designate one and the same object. Thus when I say "I know that light is an oscillatory process", I assert that the same phenomenon can be designated just as well by the concept of light as by the concept of an oscillatory process. Accordingly, we need to determine under what circumstances two concepts designate the same object.

We shall leave aside the trivial case where the two concepts are identical in every respect, having the same origin, definition and name. Here the result is merely an empty tautology, such as "Waves are waves" or "light is light". This case apart, there are several possibilities to consider. The first is that the two concepts initially became signs for the same object in virtue of some arbitrary stipulation. An example would be the first time anyone voiced the sentence "The reason why two substances combine violently with one another is because of their strong chemical affinity" or the sentence "The cause of the attractive action of amber is electricity". When first uttered, these judgments did not contain any knowledge; they were merely definitions. For the sense of the first sentence was simply that the concepts "cause of the violent reaction" and "strong chemical affinity" are to be taken as designating one and the same thing; the concept of chemical affinity had not been otherwise defined and was not already familiar from other utterances. This is also true in the example of the amber, and indeed wherever anyone has attempted to explain some fact or phenomenon by means of a *"qualitas occulta"*. All that has happened is that the same object has been designated in two different ways, the first time as a specific "quality" and the second as the "cause" of some particular observed behavior. What has been imparted is not knowledge, but merely a definition, an explanation of a newly introduced word.

On the other hand, we do have genuine knowledge whenever two concepts designate the same object not merely by virtue of the definitions of the concepts but on the strength of various cross correlations. If two concepts are defined in altogether different ways, and we find later that among the objects designated by the one concept (in virtue of its definition) there are also objects that fall under the second concept, then the one is known by means of the other. Specifically, discovery takes place either through observation and experience, in which what is obtained is knowledge of *real* correlations or connections; or it results from an analysis of concepts, in which case what is afforded is the disclosure of hitherto unnoticed *conceptual* relationships. An example of knowledge of the latter kind is the solution of a mathematical problem.

To know is to discover a relation between objects. Thus when we express a cognition, we designate a relation; and in designating a relation, we make a judgment. Every judgment that is not a patent tautology or a definition contains knowledge, provided that the judgment does not happen to be *false*. What this last means will be investigated in the next section.

We had occasion in the preceding section to point out that the distinction between definitions and other judgments is only relative. Since this is so, it follows that a cognition, expressed in language, is something that is relative to the definitions. Although this conclusion may seem paradoxical at first glance, it is nonetheless true. For whether or not a judgment contains knowledge depends on what we knew beforehand. If previously we had been acquainted with an object, which we designate by the word 'A', only through the properties a and b, and if later we ascertain that A also has the properties c and d, then the judgment "A has the properties c and d" conveys some knowledge. But this same judgment would be no more than a definition if A has always been given to us by means of properties c and d, without our being aware of any other of its attributes. We must notice, however, that at the outset the word 'A' signifies *different* concepts in the two cases; only afterwards does it turn out that the concepts designate one and the same object. For example, a child might conceivably have first become acquainted with snow on a dark night through the sense of touch. The property "cold" would then be part of his definition of the concept "snow"; but the judgment "The snow is white", made when day came, would contain a piece of knowledge.

Once a science has developed into a rounded-out more or less closed structure, what is to count in its systematic exposition as definition and what as knowledge is no longer determined by the accidental sequence of human experiences. Rather, those judgments will be taken as definitions that resolve a concept into the characteristics from which one can construct the greatest possible number (possibly all) of the concepts of the given science in the simplest possible manner. Clearly, it is this procedure that best suits the ultimate purposes of knowledge, for in this fashion the concepts of all objects in the world may most easily be reduced to the fewest possible elementary concepts.

After this necessary digression, we return to our task of determining more exactly the mutual relationship of the objects that are joined together in the act of cognition. A while back we satisfied ourselves, and have just again recalled, that every cognition signifies a certain equating. The object is set equal to that as which it is known — the author of the manuscript on the Athenian state to Aristotle, light to certain oscillatory processes of a definite kind, snow to something cold, and so forth. Corresponding to the equating of objects which takes place in knowledge is a certain identifying of concepts that is consummated in the judgment. We can therefore understand how a number of thinkers (Lotze, Riehl, Münsterberg, among others) came to accept the theory that the essence of a judgment consists in general in positing an identity. This theory stemmed from entirely correct ideas; only where it is wrongly formulated or misunderstood is it incapable of withstanding the objections of its opponents. These objections reduce to the following: if judgments really did assert perfect identities, they would all be degraded to mere tautologies. "Outside of formal logic, no one is so foolish as to state empty identities[14]." Consequently we must be quite clear

---

14   J. COHN, Voraussetzungen und Ziele des Erkennens, p. 87.

as to how the identification effected in real knowledge differs from a mere tautology.

   In order for a child to make the judgment "The snow is cold", two specific acts of knowledge must have taken place in his consciousness. One, he has been given a certain visual impression; after this is processed or apperceived, there arises the judgment (to be sure, unuttered) "This is something white and flaky", a judgment which then immediately changes to "This is snow", where the word 'snow' simply appears in place of the words 'white' and 'flaky' and means exactly the same thing they mean. Two, the child has experienced a certain cutaneous sensation; and in a second act of apperception this sensation is recognized as one to which the name 'cold' belongs. Formulated explicitly, this piece of knowledge reads "This is cold". Now, does the subject of the two judgments, the "this", designate the same object in both instances? At the outset, it would seem that it does not. The first time it stands for the visual sensation, the second time for the cutaneous sensation. The first judgment asserts not that the cold thing is white, but that the white thing is white; and the second judgment asserts not that the white thing is cold (the cutaneous sense obviously can have nothing to do with a sensation of white), but that the cold thing is cold. Hence the "this" each time is something different. We can now see why H. Lotze reached the conclusion that the judgment "S is P" is really impossible and breaks down into the judgments "S is S" and "P is P" [15].

   But Lotze undoubtedly goes much too far. Even the judgments "This is white" and "This is cold" are not perfect identities and tautologies. They do not simply identify certain contents of consciousness with the meanings of the words 'cold' and 'white'. Rather, they place these contents in the classes of objects designated by the words. The object designated by the subject term is identified with only *one* of the infinitely many objects that fall under the predicate concept. What occurs, in other words, is a subsumption or a classification. The insight that something of this sort takes place in every judgment has led to the formulation of the subsumption theory of judgments. It, too, like the identity theory, is based on a thoroughly correct idea. But we should not exaggerate this idea — as a radical "extensional logic" is inclined to do — into the claim

---

15 Logik, p. 54.

that the only way to do justice to the real, innermost sense of a judgment is to regard it as an assertion about the membership of an object in a class. Counterposed to the subsumption theory is the classification theory. According to the latter, it is the *content* (or *intension*) of concepts alone that matters, and what a judgment does is to arrange one concept under another in accordance with the content. Erdmann formulates this as follows: "A judgment is the . . . classifying of an object within the content of another . . . based on the equality of content of their material components[16]." Since the content (intension) and extension of a concept necessarily correspond, there is no difference between the two theories from the standpoint of pure formal logic.

Before we go on to consider the relationship of the two terms in cognition, let us attempt to answer the question raised above: What is involved in equating the objects designated by the demonstrative pronoun in the two sentences "This is snow" and "This is cold"? The particular content of consciousness that was designated as *white* is certainly not identical with the one that was called *cold*. Obviously we can affirm an identity only if we think of these contents of consciousness as being related to an object distinct from them, only if we interpret these adjectives as naming properties of an object and specifically of one and the same object. Thus it seems that we can justify and understand the import of a judgment only if we take as a basis the thing-property or substance-attribute relationship. These, however, are metaphysical concepts which conceal many difficulties. One need only think of Herbart's formulation of the problem of the thing. White and cold, he would say, are not the same. How then can the white thing at the same time be the cold thing? This is why Lotze was right when he said that for the sort of problem under study here, recourse to metaphysical relationships is neither permissible nor useful[17].

Nor is it required. In the preceding section, we already analyzed the judgment used here as a paradigm, and to ascertain its real meaning we need only go back to that analysis. We saw that the judgment simply asserts a certain connection among the characteristics *white*, *flaky* and *cold*. These are joined together into an aggregate, and this joining can take place quite independently of the notions of thing

---

16 Logik, I, 2nd edition, p. 359.

17 *Loc. cit.*, § 53.

and property. The basis for forming the aggregate is the fact that these qualities are found in the same place and at the same time. Thus the identity actually affirmed in the judgment turns out in this case provisionally to be the identity of a space-time point. The concept of an objective spatial position ascribed to the "snow" can itself be defined by means of the sum total of the subjective space positions of the *white* in visual space and the *cold* in the space of touch. Hence no concepts occur that cannot be justified by empirical psychology.

But it is important that we understand how something that is a mere spatio-temporal identity can still become for us the identity of an object.

We may not, of course, simply take as identical any elements that are found together regularly in the same place and at the same time. We do have the right, however, to combine them into a unity, to regard this unity as an object, to designate it with a concept and a name, and then to speak of the elements included as attributes or properties or states of that object. For theoretically we are of course free to combine in thought quite arbitrary elements, even those that lie arbitrarily far apart in time and space, by stipulating that to their totality there shall be coordinated a *single* concept. But in general such a combination makes no sense unless there is some special reason for it, a reason without which it would not be possible to apply the newly formed concept. And the strongest reason is always to be found in constant spatio-temporal coincidence. In material reality, space and time are the great uniters and dividers. In the end, all the determinations by which we mark off an object of the external world and distinguish it as an individual thing from other individual things consist of specifications of time and place. Suppose the several distinguishable elements *a*, *b* and *c* always appear together in such fashion that *a* is never observed without *b* and *c* being found in the same place at the same time, while *b* and *c* may often be encountered without *a*. Then since *a* in no case appears in isolation from *b* and *c*, the totality *a b c* will immediately be conceived of as a unit, as an object; for the spatio-temporal determinations, by which alone in the final analysis we normally distinguish individual things from one another, are the same for all three elements, and so far as we are concerned it will therefore seem that only one *single* individual is there. To us *a* will stand forth as the essential element of the object; *b* and *c*, on the other hand, will appear as properties that the object has in common with other things deb, fbc, and the like.

The analysis suggested here should be clearly distinguished from the positivistic dissolution of a body into a complex of "elements" (Ernst Mach). In the first place, the object under discussion need not of course be a body; it might just as well be a process, a state, and so forth. In the second place, we have been using the word 'element' in a far wider sense (in fact, almost in the same sense as 'object' itself). In the third place, we do not claim that a material object *is* nothing but a complex of the elements we distinguish in it. Rather, the question of the relationship of an object to its properties (or whatever else they may be called) remains entirely open for the time being. Here we meant only to indicate our undoubted right to designate collectively by means of a *single* concept things that always appear together, and to point out the reason that leads us to do so.

Thus we see how it comes about that we designate the cold object and the white object as one and the same snow. But it still remains correct that on stricter analysis the identity of the object seems to disappear, and to dissolve into the identity of a space-time point.

A similar analysis can be given for any other judgment containing knowledge of the world of sense-objects. For everything in the external world is in a specific place at a specific time. We can therefore say, to begin with, that finding one thing again in another means assigning both to the same place at the same time. Historical knowledge, too, can be viewed this way, for it is surely a task of history — if it is not its ultimate goal — to locate in space and time as precisely as possible all that happens to all mankind. In most historical judgments, the kind of identification carried out consists in equating the performer of a particular historical deed with a certain person who also appears elsewhere in history. Historical happenings are connected primarily through the personalities of the actors in historical events. For history, these individuals represent the law-like interconnection the discovery of which in their own particular domains constitutes the most essential task of the more exact sciences.

In the exact disciplines, and generally where knowledge penetrates more deeply, the identification we obtain is not merely that of a space-time position or of an individual object that remains approximately the same in the course of time. It is a more significant, a richer identification — in the final analysis, that of a shared *regularity*. Heat is known to be molecular motion because its behavior can be described by identically the same laws as the behavior of a swarm of agitated particles. The will is explained as a particular sequence of images and feelings once we succeed in showing that the laws governing the processes of volition are precisely the ones that govern certain sets of feelings and images. In the example of heat, the existence of the regularity is still based ultimately on the identification of points in space and time. In the second example, which does not deal with knowledge of the external world, spatial determinations are entirely absent; but as in all knowledge of reality, identification of points of time remains essential: the process of volition is of course simultaneous with the series of feelings of which it consists.

There are various possible ways in which one object may be identified with another (the two are then naturally one). Most important and absolutely basic to the whole edifice of knowledge is the case where an object is given by means of the *relations* in which it stands to other objects. Here cognition means the finding anew of one and the same object as a term in different relations. Expressed schematically, we have an object O defined by its relation R_1 to a familiar object A_1; we then find that the very same object bears the relation R_2 to another object A_2. In the special case when O designates an immediate experience of consciousness, it can be given us directly, rather than through relations; and it becomes *known* by virtue of our finding that this identical O is also at the same time a term in a relation R to a certain A.

On closer inspection, it turns out that every genuine cognition that leads to full identification is of the sort just described. At least one of the two terms equated in the act of knowledge is defined by means of a relation (or a complex of relations). We may verify this for all of the examples discussed earlier.

In the judgment "A light ray is a beam of electrical waves", the expression 'light ray' does not, as might be supposed, designate something given in immediate experience. No one can see or hear a light ray. It is observed only because bodies placed in its path (for example, motes in a sunbeam) are illuminated and because an eye on which the ray impinges experiences a sensation of light. Only through its relation to the illumination is the light ray defined at all; that is, it is conceived of as the cause of the illumination. Here we use the word 'cause' simply as the name for a certain relation; the precise nature of this relation is at this point quite irrelevant to our general discussion. Clearly, there is nothing to prevent the full identification with each other of the two objects "cause of the illumination" and "electrical wave". For, an object that has a particular relation to one thing can of course stand in an entirely different relation to other things, or in general have any other properties whatsoever, or be defined in any other way that is desired. The same point B can lie to the right of A and to the left of C.

To avoid fundamental errors, we emphasize that an object A that stands to another object B in a quite definite complex of relations K cannot also stand in just the same complex of relations to a third object C. In other words, given the three things A, B and C, any two of them always uniquely determine the third. The relation "greater than", for instance, may indeed hold between the numbers a and b and at the same time between the numbers a and c. The words 'greater than', however, do not completely designate a quite definite relation, but rather a whole class of relations. If we express this relation with absolute exactness — for instance, by writing 'greater by the amount d than' — then b and c would be the same identical number. Müller can stand in the relation "father of" to both Max and Fritz. But the physical process of procreation, which is the basis of the particular relationship designated in brief by the expression 'father of', is obviously an individually different one in the two cases. A thing can have the same relation to different things only so long as these relations are not specified to the last detail, that is, so long as they are not individually determined.

Applying all of this to our paradigm, we may say, roughly speaking, that the snow is the cause of both the sensation of cold and the sensation of white. In a strict sense, however, the causal relation cannot be the same in both instances. As a matter of fact, physics and psychology teach us that the causes of the two sensations are to be sought in different natural processes. Consequently, these causes may not be identified with one another, and this confirms the fact that the judgment "The snow is white" does not set up an identity of objects in the same sense as the scientific judgment "Light consist of electrical waves".

In the latter judgment, one of the concepts was defined by means of a causal relation. We now want to stress that this is not merely something that occurs by chance in a particular example; it is typical of all scientific explanation. When I say "Heat is molecular motion", for instance, the object "heat" is thought of only as the cause of a heat sensation or of a thermometer reading. Now we have already determined (§ 9) that the concepts of electricity and of chemical affinity were initially formed in just this manner. And a similar conclusion holds generally. In all empirical research, the object under investigation can be described by means of causal relations, and usually this is the most natural way to specify it. Thus the view held by many thinkers that a scientific explanation must be a causal explanation is justified. Whether this sort of formulation is epistemologically the most finished one, whether on closer analysis it may appear desirable to replace the causal concept by other more general ones — these are questions that we are not yet ready to examine.

The nature of the equating or identification effected in knowledge is most easily understood in the case of judgments that refer to *pure concepts*. All purely conceptual knowledge consists in showing that a concept defined by means of certain relations (the axioms) likewise occurs as a term in certain other relations. It may be that the concept itself is already uniquely defined by each of two complexes of relations. In that case, we have a total identity (such as $2 \times 2 = 2 + 2$). But if one of the complexes does not suffice for a complete determination, then we have a partial identification, also called subsumption ($2 = \sqrt{4}$ is an example, since the concept $\sqrt{4}$ contains in addition the concept -2). Every mathematical problem the solution of which truly presents some conceptual knowledge is nothing other than a demand that a concept given by certain relations be expressed with the help of *other* relations. Thus to find the roots of an equation in one unknown is to represent the numbers defined by that equation as a sum of integers and fractions (a sum which may of course, under certain circumstances, have infinitely many members).

In scientific cognition, the act of finding two things the same results in either a partial or a complete identification. Since the concern of the exact empirical sciences is centered so strongly on what is general, subsumptions or partial identifications are for them the most important thing; and a complete identification, extending all the way to the individual natural process itself, counts not as a genuine advance in knowledge, but as something whose use is always possible. Thus the judgment "Light consists of electrical waves" contains some of the essential knowledge for which physics strives; yet what it expresses is only a subsumption, since not every electrical wave is a light wave. On the other hand, the judgment "Yellow light of the color of the D lines in the spectrum is an electrical wave with a frequency of approximately 509 billion kilocycles per second" expresses a full identity, and this is easy to recognize because the judgment remains valid under conversion (interchange of subject and predicate terms). Clearly the second judgment expresses a fact that is, so to speak, more accidental and less fundamental than the one expressed by the first judgment.

But the goal of the exact sciences is still to push knowledge so far forward that means will be at hand to make a complete identification possible in any particular case, and thereby to determine completely that which is individual in the world. To go back to our example: the scientific judgment describing a light ray can be made to approximate the affirmation of a perfect identity as closely as we please by including in the predicate an exact specification of place and time, direction, intensity, and the like.

The predicate concept is formed by the intersecting of a number of general concepts. By means of the judgment, the subject is subsumed under each of these general concepts and is thus determined as that which is designated by them all, that which partakes of them all conjointly.

We can now see how the great task of knowledge (*cf.* § 3) — that of designating individual or particular objects with the aid of general concepts — is solved. The intersection of the general concepts serves to mark off a region in which there is no room for anything but the object, which then becomes known.

As one of our examples shows, in the rigorous sciences this ever more exact circumscribing of the conceptual location to which the known object belongs is effected with the help of quantitative determinations. Nothing is so well suited for cutting off and bounding the domains of concepts as *numbers*. But the immeasurable significance of the number concept for exact knowledge is not rooted in this alone; it lies even deeper, as will appear in the course of our study.

Let us now review briefly the relationship between judging and knowing.

Every judgment serves to designate a set of facts. If the judgment coordinates a *new* sign to this set of facts (that is, if in the judgment a concept appears that was devised solely for the purpose of designating these facts), then the judgment represents a *definition*. But if it uses only concepts employed on other occasions, then on precisely this account it constitutes a piece of *knowledge*. For an object is designated by means of concepts already coordinated to other objects only if that object has previously been found anew in those objects, and it is just this that makes up the essence of cognition. The concept that corresponds with or is coordinated to the known object stands in certain relations of subsumption to the concepts through which the object becomes known, and the existence of these relations is precisely the fact which the judgment serves to designate.

§ 10. What is Truth?

What is our purpose in coordinating concepts to objects? The answer has already been given: to be able to make judgments about objects. But why do we make judgments about objects, why do we coordinate judgments as signs to facts? To answer this, we need only make clear to ourselves what end is served generally by the use of signs.

The task of a sign is to be a representative of that which is designated, to act in its place in some respect or other. Wherever it is impossible or inconvenient to operate with the objects themselves, we replace them with signs which can be manipulated more easily and as desired. If I want to take a book out of a library, I can look for the volume by going up and down the book-shelves. But this is usually a laborious and time-consuming procedure; so I do better to consult the catalogue, which is simply an ordered collection of signs each of which corresponds to a volume in the library. Since the catalogue is smaller and more conveniently arranged (the authors' names in alphabetical sequence, for example), I can find my way about in it more easily than in the library itself. We act on a similar principle whenever we number objects, whether it be in order to ticket garments in a theater cloak-room or to differentiate between two sovereigns bearing the same name who rule the same state at different times. Writing or calculating or speaking, like numbering, is working with symbols, and so is thinking. To say that in thought we are masters of the world is to say that we are masters of the thoughts and judgments that serve us as signs for all the objects and facts of the world.

We carry out these coordinations all the time in ordinary life. But if they are to reach their goal of making symbols authentic representatives of that which is designated, the coordinations must satisfy one essential condition: they must be *unique,* they must tell us exactly which object belongs to a particular sign. The same sign must never mean different objects. (The converse is not absolutely necessary; there is no harm in having several different signs correspond to the same object, provided we know for sure that these signs do have the same meaning, and are constantly aware that they may be exchanged or substituted for one another at will.)

Now this also holds with regard to the correspondence of judgments with facts. And a judgment that *uniquely designates* a set of facts is called *true.*

The problem of the nature of truth has always attracted philosophical attention, most especially in recent years. But it has shared the fate of numerous problems whose solutions were not immediately perceived and accepted by everyone only because they had been sought at too great a depth. The account that will be offered here of the essential nature of truth is modest and unpretentious; yet we shall quickly see that it is indeed able to do justice to all the properties ascribed to truth both in science and in ordinary life, from the plainest to the most exalted — those that make truth one of the highest human goods.

Formerly, the concept of truth was almost always defined as an agreement between thought and its object — or, better, between judgment and what is judged (for truth is ascribed not to the psychological acts of judging but to judgments as ideal or conceptual structures). There is no doubt that this definition expresses a correct conception. But which conception?

It is certain that true judgments in some sense fit the facts, are somehow in keeping with them or "agree" with them, whereas false judgments do not conform to the facts, are not in accord with them, do not "agree" with them. But the word 'agree' only pins a label on the question, it does not answer it. In ordinary discourse, agreement simply means likeness or sameness. Two tones, two colors, two sizes, two opinions are in agreement if they are the same. Obviously the word 'agree' is not to be taken in that sense here, for a judgment is something entirely different from that which is judged and to which it is coordinated; it is not the same as what is judged, and this can be disputed only by those strange metaphysical systems which equate thought and being altogether and on which we need waste no words here.

If agreement does not mean sameness, perhaps what is intended is similarity. Are our judgments in some sense similar to facts? In this context, similarity has to mean much the same thing as partial sameness; hence it should be possible to find certain aspects of the judgments that are exhibited in the facts themselves. In the case of purely conceptual truths, where the objects judged, like the judgments themselves, consist merely of ideal structures, the same thing might, under certain circumstances, be found in both the "facts" and the judgment. But this cannot be the essential feature of truth, since propositions about real things also make truth claims — indeed, it is here that the nature of truth first becomes a problem — and in these we shall seek in vain for any such similar aspects. The concepts occurring in a judgment are surely not the same kind of thing as the real objects which they designate. Nor are relations among concepts the same as relations among real things; for temporal aspects always enter into the latter, and usually spatial aspects as well, whereas conceptual relations are non-temporal and non-spatial. In the judgment "The chair is to the right of the table", the concept "chair" is not placed to the right of the concept "table".

So the notion of agreement, in so far as it is to mean sameness or similarity, melts away under the rays of analysis, and what is left is only unique coordination. It is in this latter that the relationship of true judgments consists, and all those naive theories according to which our judgments and concepts are able in some fashion to "picture" reality are completely demolished. No other sense remains for the word 'agreement' than that of unique coordination or correspondence. We must dismiss from our minds altogether the notion that a judgment can be *more* than a sign in relationship to a set of facts, that the connection between the two can be anything more intimate than mere correspondence, that a judgment is in a position somehow to describe, express or portray adequately a set of facts. Nothing of the sort is the case. A judgment pictures the nature of what is judged as little as a musical note pictures a tone, or the name of a man pictures his personality.

The one essential virtue of a coordination is its uniqueness, and since truth is the sole virtue of judgments, then truth must consist in the uniqueness of the designation for which the judgment is to be used.

If this analysis is correct, then a false judgment can only be one that is guilty of an ambiguity in correspondence. This can be confirmed very easily. To return to our old example, take the false judgment "A light ray consists of a stream of rapidly moving particles". (This sentence, as we know, corresponds to the Newtonian theory of the emission of light.) By examining all the facts taught us by physical research, we soon become aware that this judgment does not provide a unique designation of the facts. That is to say, we find that two different classes of facts are coordinated to the same judgments, that therefore an ambiguity is present. On the one hand, we have the facts that actually do involve moving corpuscles, as in the case of cathode rays; on the other hand, we have a different set of facts, those concerning the propagation of light, designated by the very same symbols. Moreover, at the same time, *different* signs are coordinated to two identical series of facts, namely, those of the propagation of light and those of wave propagation. Uniqueness is forfeited, and the proof that this is so is also the proof that the judgment is false. We shall not be occupied with the question of proof, or the criterion of truth, until later; but we can already clearly perceive that what has been said is correct. In science, a proof is nearly always conducted as follows: from the judgments we have, we derive new judgments that designate *future* events (and are thus predictions); and if, instead of the anticipated facts, we are confronted with facts that must be designated by judgments other than those we derived, then contradiction and ambiguity are present and we call the judgments we began with false. Were we to permit our prediction, which is a sign for an expected set of facts foreseen in imagination, to be a sign also for the set of facts that actually appeared, then the same judgment would mean two different events — and were we to hear it expressed later, we should not know which event was intended.

It is because of such intolerable ambiguities that we find the false and the untrue so hateful. The disorder generated by a false assertion, the evil of the lie, originate in confusions that follow from ambiguity. Anyone who pictures these relationships to himself with full clarity will see that the whole point of the distinction between true and false judgments is indeed to safeguard the uniqueness of linguistic and intellectual expression. This is a necessary precondition for any understanding, and without it all designation and expression become purposeless and idle.

There is an obvious objection (and I have heard it made) to the effect that we cannot speak of ambiguity in the case of a false judgment, since what correspond to a false judgment are not several sets of facts but no facts at all. Such a view would lead to a definition of truth something like the one formulated by J. L. Kreibig[18]: "Truth is the characteristic of a judgment that asserts the particular set of facts that is present in the domain of the judged objects." Although this vague definition certainly can not be regarded as satisfactory without a more precise interpretation, the correct thought which it seeks to express turns out to be quite compatible with our account. It is indeed true that a false judgment does not "fit" any existing set of facts; that is, we find no fact to which we can coordinate the judgment, assuming that we observe all the definitions and the rules of logic. But the falsity of the judgment consists precisely in the circumstance that the maker of the judgment nevertheless does use it to designate a specific set of facts. If this designation is accepted, then ambiguity appears as described above in our illustration. The rules of coordination, which are meant to safeguard uniqueness, are violated, and confusion and contradiction are instituted. It is as a result of this ambiguity that we first *recognize* that the set of facts to which the false judgment could justly be coordinated does not exist at all. It is therefore quite proper to take ambiguity as the distinguishing mark of falsity. Hence our conception seems preferable; but the two views do not contradict one another[19].

In order to express that a given judgment "S is P" is false, that is, that the judgment does not designate a fact uniquely, we make use of *negation,* and we say "S is not P". Thus the sense of a negative judgment is in the first instance simply to reject the corresponding positive judgment, to brand it as an ambiguous sign unsuited

---

18 Die intellektuellen Funktionen, Vienna and Leipzig, 1909, p. 142.

19 That there is essential agreement is confirmed by KREIBIG (Zeitschrift für Psychologie, Vol. 61, 1912, p. 281) in connection with a discussion of my paper "Das Wesen der Wahrheit" (Vierteljahrsschrift für wissenschaftliche Philosophie, 1910, Vol. 34).

to the judged set of facts. This conclusion we may express in a more learned style by saying that the category of negation reduces to that of plurality.

A negative judgment means simply the rejection of an affirmative statement. Such a judgment necessarily presupposes that someone intended or tried to make, or actually made, a false affirmative judgment. It is therefore obvious that the occurrence of negative judgments depends on the occurrence of false judgments. And since false statements are grounded only in the psychological imperfection of our mind, negation occurs solely because of our faulty makeup. Consequently, it must be possible to do logic and science without taking negative judgments into account. Strictly speaking, such judgments ought never to have found a place in pure logic, which as a conceptual science is not concerned with the practical conditions of thought nor with its psychological limitations. Negative judgments are only of practical or psychological use; they have no theoretical or logical value. The edifice of science consists exclusively of positive statements. In those cases where the concept of negation seems indispensable in designating certain sets of facts, it can be replaced completely by the concept of *difference*. The judgments "*A* is not *B*" and "*A* is different from *B*" have exactly the same meaning. The further question as to whether a logic can be constructed without the concept of difference is not our concern at the moment; nor can we now enter into a discussion of certain related issues of importance to logic.

The negative judgment "*S* is not *P*" thus designates the fact that the affirmative proposition "*S* is *P*" is false. This we can express by saying that if the judgment "*S* is not *P*" is true, the judgment "*S* is *P*" is false, and vice versa. In this statement we have the celebrated principles of *contradiction* and of *the excluded middle*. As we see, they follow immediately from the nature of negation, and may be looked upon as its definition. Most logicians today have concluded that the sense of these two principles is merely to determine the nature of negation; thus neither do they contain some alleged truth of metaphysical significance nor do they represent a barrier to human thought that perhaps would not exist for creatures with a different mental constitution (*cf.* § 36 below). The boundaries of the meaning and applications of the two principles are the same as those of negation.

We must still clear up one or two important points and bring some familiar properties of truth into harmony with our definition.

A first question is: If truth is uniqueness of designation, why is it then that only judgments can be true whereas concepts, which also are signs, cannot?

The difference is that a judgment is not merely a sign. For in a judgment we always think of a designation as having actually been carried out, a coordination as having been consummated. This we stated above when we said that a judgment designates not merely a relation, but the *existence* of a relation. If I utter the word 'water' and call to mind an image of water as representing the concept, there is nothing in this process that can be either true or false, univocal or ambiguous. But if on uttering the word I point to a colorless liquid, then my action at once becomes tantamount to a judgment; I indicate by my action that I intend to execute a coordination, and this coordination can indeed be correct or incorrect. If I pronounce the judgment "This liquid is water", the meaning is exactly the same as if I utter the word 'water' in connection with the gesture of pointing. I coordinate the judgment to the precise fact that the liquid possesses the properties of water. And the judgment is false if it turns out that the liquid, instead of behaving like water, exhibits the behavior that serves to define the concept, say, of alcohol. Not only is the judgment as a whole coordinated to the fact as a whole, but, as follows from the nature of judgments, concepts are thereby also coordinated to objects; and the uniqueness of the first coordination is conditioned on the uniqueness of the second.

This brings us to a question that must be clarified if we are to obtain a full understanding of the nature of truth. Through what means does a particular judgment become a sign for a particular fact? In other words, how do I know what fact a given judgment designates?

If we wish to coordinate a system of signs to a system of objects, it is obvious that we must in all cases begin by arbitrarily selecting certain symbols for certain things. The designating of numbers by numerals and of tones by letters are conventions of precisely this sort. They are adopted in various forms by various peoples. Another example is the use of flags to designate nations. Only someone who is acquainted with the conventions can interpret these symbols; he must learn by heart which sign belongs to a particular fact or to a particular object. Learning a language is nothing more than making such a sign system one's own. Sometimes memorizing can be avoided and can be replaced by certain physical acts. Thus a hotel porter does not try to remember which pair of boots belongs to which guest; he simply marks the room number on the soles, that is, he attaches to the boots a visual symbol that resembles the one on the door of the appropriate room and that can be determined at any time by sense perception. Most objects of knowledge, however, are not of the kind to which numbers can be affixed and they must be designated in other ways.

It would do no good, however, to designate all the things in the world simply by inventing individual signs for each of them, and then committing to memory the meaning of each sign. Theoretically, of course, it would be quite possible to carry out an unambiguous coordination in this manner; and since truth consists merely in the uniqueness of the coordination, it would in principle be child's play to arrive at perfect truth. Now if knowledge were simply identical with truth, the sciences would have a very easy task indeed. But this is most emphatically not the case. Knowledge is more — much more — than mere truth. Truth requires nothing but uniqueness of co-ordination; as far as truth is concerned, it does not matter what sign is used for that purpose. Knowledge, on the other hand, means unique coordination with the help of certain definite symbols, name-ly, those that have already found application elsewhere. If a physi-cist were to discover a new kind of rays and to name them Y-rays, then the judgment "The rays discovered by the physicist are Y-rays" would of course be true. But this would not mean any advance in knowledge, since the new object would have been designated simply by the use of a new word. The judgment "Abracadabra is abra-cadabra" is always true no matter what 'abracadabra' may mean. The coordination it effects is of a symbol to itself, and such a co-ordination is by its very nature unique. But it is certainly not knowl-edge. Hence if we were to coordinate a special sign to each fact and each object in the world, we should have nothing but isolated truths, each of which would have to be learned separately. This, of course, would be impossible in practice because of the enormous number. There would be no way of deriving some of these truths from others, any more than we could draw conclusions about the appearance of the Italian flag from having observed the German and American flags. Our truths would be nothing but discrete points, so to speak; they would not form a coherent system. Yet it is only in such a system that knowledge is possible, since the finding anew of one thing in another presupposes a pervasive interconnection.

Thus our use of judgments to designate sets of facts must, so far as judgments contain knowledge, be of a different sort. We do not need to learn separately which fact is designated by a particular judgment; we can tell this from the judgment itself. A cognitive judgment is a *new* combination made up exclusively of *old* concepts. The latter occur in innumerable other judgments, some of which (for example, the definitions of these concepts) must have been known to us already. Such concepts form the connecting links by means of which what is new is incorporated into the great system of known judgments that constitutes the stock in hand of ordinary experience and of science. By virtue of the interconnection of judgments a new truth receives a specific place in the circle of truths; the fact corresponding to this new truth is thereby assigned to the place that, by virtue of the interconnection of facts, it occupies in the domain of reality. And it is precisely because a judgment points this place out to us that the object or fact becomes *known*. Hence it is the structural connectedness of our system of judgments that produces the unique coordination and conditions its truth. And it is the position occupied by a proposition in our system of judgments that alone informs us which facts the proposition designates.

Only the primitive concepts and judgments — those to which knowledge reduces all the others — depend on conventions and have to be learned as arbitrary signs. Of course, language uses *separate* signs to designate not only the fundamental concepts but also the more complicated ones — those that arise from the intersection of elementary concepts — and all these words must be memorized. (A philosophy and science of language that attains ideal perfection, though, would also be able in principle to discover the words used by various peoples to designate particular concepts; for the reasons that lead to the acceptance of particular conventions are themselves facts that can be designated and known.) Language, for its part, operates in a fashion similar to the cognitive process. It forms new words not through new sounds but through new combinations of a relatively small number of basic linguistic sounds. The most highly developed language is the one that is able to express

5*

the entire wealth of thought with a minimum number of different forms, and yet to do so briefly. A true "humanism" is apt to find the rich yet concise idiom of many modern languages more suited to the purposes of philosophy than the tortuous loquacity of Greek. The passion for inventing new words is characteristic of the smaller minds among philosophers; a man like Hume, whose ideas laid new foundations, was content to clothe his thoughts in the plainest of terms.

The merit of the theory unfolded here seems to me to lie in the fact that it rests solely on the relation of pure coordination or correspondence, which is the simplest and most general of all relations. We become truly aware of the advantage thus gained if we compare our theory with a theory of truth built up entirely out of differences that characterize various kinds of relations, an example being the ingenious view found in BERTRAND RUSSELL's The Problems of Philosophy (Chapter XII).

The objection is sometimes heard that the coordination or correspondence theory of truth is too formalistic, that the decisive factors in the case of truth are the *objective* relations between judged objects, and that the correct portrayal of these relations by means of judgments is basic. This criticism, however, overlooks the fact that our theory does accord full justice to objective or material relations. They too, of course, are among the facts that get designated by judgments, and no coordination would be possible at all without taking them fully into account. The ascertaining of factual connections is an integral part of the "finding anew" that is a necessary precondition for a cognitive coordination. Unambiguous coordination means that the same sign is always to correspond to the "same" object, and this is possible only if each object is distinguished from all the others and is re-cognized each time as the same. Thus there is no coordination without re-cognition. Cognition of the most primitive sort, however, does not yield a system; on the contrary, what it produces is initially only a collection of independent single coordinations. There are as many signs as distinguishable objects, and their number can be reduced only if another condition is fulfilled, namely, that it be understood that cognitive objects are not predetermined, strictly bounded units. Modern psychology uses the term "Gestalt-quality" — coined by Christian Ehrenfels — to denote the fact that the contents of our consciousness combine into certain complexes that we experience as "units". The *Gestalten* play an absolutely fundamental role in the description of the immediately given. There is present at the same time what we call "interconnection" or "coherence": the same element may belong to different objects. Finally, if we choose a suitable standpoint, it is possible to discover the *same* very few elements repeated in all objects of a particular domain. Thus coordination, finding-the-same-again, and interconnection are all indissolubly linked: the theory of truth offered here would appear to give a complete account of their interrelationship.

§ 11. Definitions, Conventions and Empirical Judgments

Every judgment we make is either definitional or cognitive. This distinction, as we noted above (§ 8), has only a relative significance in the conceptual or "ideal" sciences. It emerges all the more sharply, however, in the empirical or "real" sciences. In these sciences it has a fundamental importance; and a prime task of epistemology is to make use of this distinction in order to clarify the kinds of validity possessed by various judgments.

In line with the conclusions we have reached thus far, we may say the following about this question.

The factual sciences, as a system, constitute a network of judgments the individual meshes of which are coordinated to individual facts. This coordination is obtained by means of definition and knowledge. Of the two kinds of definitions with which we have become acquainted — the concrete and the implicit — only the former, of course, is involved initially in the case of concepts of real objects. A concrete definition is a quite arbitrary stipulation, and consists in introducing a particular name for an object that has been singled out in one fashion or another. If we again encounter an object so designated (that is, if we have again the same experiences we had at the time the object was concretely defined) we call this *experience* in the sense of coming-to-know. Now experience exhibits the same object in the most diverse relations. As a consequence, we are able to make a large number of judgments that form a connected net inasmuch as they contain the same concepts and therefore concern the same objects. Where we require a new experience to establish each individual judgment, where we achieve a unique coordination only by means of a new direct connection with reality, the cognitive network consists of a class of judgments that can be termed *descriptive* or *historical*. The descriptive and historical disciplines, as well as the narratives and reports of daily life, are composed for the most part of truths of this kind.

Now the remarkable thing is that for a suitable choice of objects (singled out by means of concrete definitions), we can find implicit definitions such that the concepts defined by them may be used to designate uniquely those same real objects. That is, the concepts will then be connected to one another by a system of judgments coinciding fully with the network of judgments that on the basis of experience had been uniquely coordinated to the system of facts. Whereas we had to obtain this network of judgments empirically mesh by mesh through laborious single acts of knowledge, the system of judgments that coincides with the network can be derived *in toto* by pure logic from the implicit definitions of its basic concepts.

Thus once we succeed in discovering these implicit definitions, we have the whole network of judgments at one fell swoop, without having to resort in each instance to new individual experiences. Such, in fact, is the procedure in the exact sciences, which apply to the world the implicitly defined conceptual system of mathematics. Indeed, this is the only conceivable path along which there can be a solution to the task for which science was invented: to make assertions even about those real facts, such as future events, concerning which there is as yet no experience. For example, astronomy can report purely descriptively the positions of the planets at various times and thus describe events in the solar system by means of an immense number of historical judgments. But it can also designate the planets by means of the concept of bodies that move in accordance with certain equations, which amounts to an implicit definition. From these basic equations of astronomy we can then obtain purely deductively all the desired assertions about the past and future locations of the bodies that make up the solar system.

Obviously, to suppose that the world is intelligible is to assume the existence of a system of implicit definitions that corresponds exactly to the system of empirical judgments. And our knowledge of reality would be best off if we knew with absolute certainty that concepts always exist which are generated by implicit definitions and which guarantee a strictly unambiguous designation of the world of facts. But on this point we have already had to adopt a skeptical attitude (see § 7), and we shall not go beyond it in the course of our study. Thus the claim that a particular conceptual system provides perfect knowledge in the sense described — or even the claim that such a system exists — cannot itself be proved to be a true judgment. Rather, it is an *hypothesis,* and for precisely this reason every judgment about real facts that is neither a definition nor a purely descriptive judgment bears the character of an hypothesis.

While we are thus never certain whether a complete conceptual system really is in a position to furnish an unambiguous designation of the facts, there is still the possibility at least of arranging certain individual concepts in such a way as to fit reality under all circumstances, so that the objects they designate can always be found again in reality. To define a concept implicitly is to determine it by means of its relations to other concepts. But to apply such a concept to reality is to choose, out of the infinite wealth of relations in the world, a certain complex or grouping and to embrace this complex as a unit by designating it with a name. By a suitable choice it is always possible under certain circumstances to obtain an unambiguous designation of the real by means of the concept. Conceptual definitions and coordinations that come into being in this fashion we call *conventions* (using this term in the narrower sense, since in the broader sense, of course, all definitions are agreements). It was Henri Poincaré who introduced the term 'convention' in this narrower sense into natural philosophy; and one of the most important tasks of that discipline is to investigate the nature and meaning of the various conventions found in natural science.

As for a general theory of conventions, we simply note here that the conditions that make conventions possible are present wherever nature offers an unbroken, continuous manifold of homogeneous relations, since then we can always select from such a manifold any desired complex of relations. Spatio-temporal relations, in particular, are of this kind; hence they form the true domain of conventions. In fact, the best known typical instances of conventions are judgments that assert an equality of time or space intervals. Within broad limits one can define the equality of times and spaces arbitrarily and still be certain of finding spaces and times in nature that are equal according to the definition.

The easiest way to clarify the special character of conventions and the manner in which they differ from concrete definitions is by using the example of *time measurement*. When we stipulate that the periods of rotation of the earth about its axis (sidereal days) are equal and are to be taken as a basis for the measurement of time, what we have in essence is a concrete definition, since our stipulation refers to a concrete process that involves a unique cosmic body. Theoretically it would be just as possible for us to consider the pulse beats of the Dalai Lama as marking off equal periods of time and to base our temporal measurements on them. The only objection is that this sort of time measurement would be quite impractical and not at all suitable for regulating clocks. For the rate at which the processes of nature run their course would then depend on the health of the Dalai Lama; for example, if he had a fever and a faster pulse beat, we would have to ascribe a slower pace to natural processes, and the laws of nature would take on an extremely complicated form. If we choose the rotation of the earth as the measure of time, these laws appear in a very simple form, and indeed this is why we make that choice. Yet, for the most exact description of the astronomical facts, it turns out that to stipulate the absolute equality of sidereal days does not yield the best possible definition of time. It is more practical to assert that, as a consequence of friction due to the ebb and flow of the tides, the rotation of the earth gradually slows down and hence sidereal days grow longer. Were we not to accept this, we would have to ascribe a gradual acceleration to all other natural processes and the laws of nature would no longer assume the simplest form. Thus maximizing the simplicity of nature's laws is the criterion that determines the *final* choice of a definition of time. And it is only at that stage that the unit of time acquires the character of a convention in our sense. For then it is no longer tied to one or another concrete process, but is determined by the general precept that the basic equations of physics should appear in their simplest form. In the pure abstract system of science these equations are to be understood as implicit definitions of the basic physical concepts.

Once a certain number of concepts are fixed by convention, the relations that hold between the objects so designated are not conventional. They must be determined through experience. Only experience can see to it that uniqueness of coordination is preserved for the whole conceptual system of science.

We now describe in more detail the two great classes of judgments out of which every system of factual science is constructed.

First, we have the definitions used by exact cognition in its effort to substitute implicitly determined concepts for all concretely determined ones. Prominent among these definitions are conventions, which safeguard the substitution in advance by means of an appropriate stipulation. Second, we have the cognitive judgments, which either designate observed facts on the basis of acts of re-cognition and are called *historical* judgments, or claim to hold also for facts not observed and then bear the name of *hypotheses*. Note, however, that the distinction between hypotheses and historical judgments, important though it may be for research, in principle cannot be maintained strictly and absolutely. For the class of historical judgments dwindles to zero if we consider that strictly speaking it can embrace only such facts as are immediately experienced in the present moment. Uttered a moment later, such judgments already contain a hypothetical element. All past facts without exception, even those that have just been observed, can basically only be inferred; theoretically, it may be merely a dream or an illusion that they were ever observed. When examined closely, historical judgments too take on the character of hypotheses, and thus we conclude that all judgments in science are either definitions or hypotheses.

In the class of definitions in the wider sense, we include also those propositions that can be derived by pure logic from definitions. Epistemologically, such derived propositions are the same as definitions, since by what was said above (§ 8) they are interchangeable with them. From this standpoint purely conceptual sciences, such as arithmetic, actually consist exclusively of definitions; they tell us nothing that is in principle new, nothing that goes beyond the axioms. In return, however, all of their assertions are absolutely true. On the other hand, the principal content of the factual sciences is made up of genuine cognitive judgments in the narrower sense. But in the final analysis these remain only hypotheses; their truth is not absolutely guaranteed. We must be content if the probability (whatever it may be) of our having attained a unique correlation assumes an extremely high value.

Philosophy has been most reluctant to acquiesce in this view, and from time immemorial there has been no dearth of attempts to preserve absolute certainty for at least part of our knowledge of reality. Every rationalistic system may be regarded as just such an endeavor. But the sole undertaking of this sort that still merits discussion today is the philosophy of Kant, which we have remarked on above (see § 7). According to him, besides the two classes of judgments we have described — definitions in the widest sense (Kant calls them analytic judgments) and empirical judgments or hypotheses (these he calls synthetic judgments *a posteriori*) — there is a third class, the so-called synthetic judgments *a priori*. In the case of this third class, unique coordination and hence truth is attained neither by definition nor by experience, but by something else, namely, a special faculty of the reason, a "pure intuition" and a "pure reason". Now Kant was very well aware that we never know any single fact of reality except through experience. Consequently, he felt the full weight of the great paradox contained in the notion of "synthetic judgments *a priori*": that we are supposedly able to make absolutely true judgments about real facts that have not yet been given to us in experience. And the entire *Critique of Pure Reason* is devoted basically to the problem posed by the possibility of such judgments.

Later we shall take a look at the solution which Kant thought he had discovered. Here it suffices to note that what led him to this incorrect formulation of the whole problem was the fact that he never entertained the least doubt about the actual presence of synthetic judgments *a priori* in the exact sciences. Otherwise he would certainly not have considered them possible and hence would not have sought an explanation for their possibility. The fact of the matter is that no one has as yet succeeded in exhibiting a synthetic judgment *a priori* in any science. That Kant and his followers nevertheless believed in their existence may be explained quite naturally by the fact that among both the definitions and the empirical propositions of the exact sciences we find statements that are deceptively similar to synthetic judgments *a priori*. In the class of definitions, which by their very nature possess a validity independent of experience and thus are *a priori*, there are a great many conventions that, viewed superficially, seem not to be derivable from definitions and hence to be synthetic. Their true character as conventions is revealed only by a most painstaking analysis. An example would be the axioms of the science of space. In the class of empirical judgments, which are clearly synthetic since their validity for reality does not follow from the definitions, there are many propositions (for example, the principle of causality) of such seemingly unconditional validity that in the absence of a more penetrating examination it is easy to mistake them for *a priori* judgments.

Once we demonstrate, as we shall do later, that the judgments held to be synthetic and *a priori* are in fact either not synthetic or not *a priori,* there is no reason whatever to suppose that judgments of this strange sort might yet exist in some obscure corner of the sciences. And this is sufficient ground for us to try in what follows to explain all knowledge of reality as a system built up exclusively of judgments belonging to the two classes described above.

Since terminology is a not unimportant element in understanding, let us at this point summarize some definitional stipulations.

By "analytic" judgments we are to understand those that ascribe to a subject a predicate that is already contained in the concept of the subject. Here 'contained' can mean only that the predicate is part of the definition of the subject. Thus the set of facts designated by an analytic judgment is always given in a definition. The ground for the truth of an analytic judgment always lies solely in the concept of the subject, in its definition, and not in some experience. Analytic judgments are therefore *a priori.* To use Kant's classic example, if we define the concept *body* in such a way that spatial extension is one of its features, then the judgment "All bodies are extended" is analytic. By the same token, it is also *a priori:* it is not based on any experience, since no experience can ever reveal bodies that are *not* extended. Were I to encounter in experience something unextended I could not designate it as a body, for if I did I would be *contradicting* the definition of a body. Thus we may say with Kant that analytic judgments rest on the principle of contradiction; that is, they are derivable from definitions with the help of this principle.

The opposite of an analytic judgment is a *synthetic* judgment. A judgment is synthetic if it asserts of an object a predicate that is not already contained by definition in the concept of the object. Such a judgment goes beyond the concept; it is ampliative, whereas analytic judgments are only explicative. To use another of Kant's examples, the proposition "All bodies are heavy" is synthetic, since the characteristic of being heavy, of mutual attraction, is not part of the definition of the concept body, as commonly used. Had the property of being heavy been included in the definition of "body" (in which case a weightless object in nature, if experience should exhibit any such, would not be a body), then the judgment of course would be analytic.

Accordingly, we might be tempted to think that the distinction between analytic and synthetic judgments cannot be drawn sharply, since one and the same judgment may be synthetic or analytic depending on what we include in the subject concept. But this opinion ignores the fact that the judgment is really *not* the same in the two cases. In the first case, we define the concept *body* in "All bodies are heavy" so that being heavy is one of its features; in the second case, we do not. True, the sentence contains the same *words* each time, but they designate different judgments, for the word 'body' has a different meaning in each. We explained above (§ 8) that one and the same (linguistic) sentence can express both a definition and a piece of knowledge. It all depends on what concepts we connect to the words. The partitioning of judgments into analytic and synthetic is thus something quite well defined and objectively valid, and does not depend, say, on the subjective standpoint or mode of comprehension of the one who judges. The point is so evident that I would not have mentioned it were not certain misunderstandings about it present in the literature[20]. These may be explained by the fact that some authors do not hold firmly enough to the position that the nature and content of a concept are to be regarded as determined solely by the features it includes.

Since the point, although obvious enough, is important, we emphasize once again that definitions are to be reckoned among analytic judgments. They give us only the features that already belong to a concept. In a sense, of course, we are justified in saying that a definition effects a synthesis in that it puts various features together into a concept. But a definition is not thereby transformed into a synthetic judgment, since it does not endow the concept with any features over and above those it already possesses. A synthetic judgment, we may say, designates the uniting of objects to form

---

20   An example is E. Dürr (Erkenntnistheorie, p. 81), who rejects the distinction in question "because one and the same judgment can often be made in two ways: the subject concept may be thought of as containing the predicate concept or it may be thought of without the predicate concept." But anyone who thinks of the predicate concept as being contained in the subject concept is thinking of a *different* subject concept from the one thought of without the predicate concept. The concept is different in the two cases even if the object designated by means of it is the same. T. Ziehen also attempts to treat the logical distinction psychologically (Erkenntnistheorie, 1913, pp. 408 ff., 559 ff.).

a set of facts, while a definition designates the uniting of features to form a concept.

Nearly all the judgments that in daily life make up the content of our speech and thought are synthetic. Obviously, "Gaul was conquered by the Romans" or "There is fish for lunch today" or "My friend lives in Berlin" or "The melting point of lead is lower than that of iron" are all synthetic propositions. To be sure, it may be very difficult to obtain unanimity on the definitions of many of the concepts, such as "Gaul" or "lead", that appear in these judgments. But it follows unequivocally from the entire context in which we utter sentences of this sort that their predicates are not among the features that belong to the subject concepts, and this by itself is enough for us to decide the nature of the judgments.

We also see that the judgments used here as examples designate various empirical facts. The basis for their validity lies in experience; they are *a posteriori*.

Besides the analytic judgments, which *eo ipso* are *a priori,* and the synthetic judgments *a posteriori*, it is possible to conceive of a third class of judgments — the synthetic *a priori*. These, if they existed, would assert that an object possesses a certain predicate *not* contained in the concept of that object even though the ground for this assertion is not to be found in experience. In other words, the fact designated by such a judgment is that certain objects, not united by definition, — for example, an event and its cause — are correlated, yet it is not experience that certifies this correlation to be a fact.

Kant was properly astonished that synthetic judgments could apparently be made *a priori*. For if the objects under consideration are themselves given only in intuitive experience, what could possibly inform us of their correlations except experience?

A priori judgments alone provide rigorous, universally valid knowlege (*a posteriori* judgments hold solely for the individual facts of experience that they designate). Analytic judgments tell us only about conceptual relationship, not about reality. It follows that the question of the existence of synthetic judgments *a priori* is equivalent to the question of the existence of apodictic knowledge of real objects. The consideration of analytic judgments is a problem of pure thought, for they rest entirely on the mutual relations of concepts. In contrast, the investigation of synthetic judgments, which rest on the interrelations of real objects, is a problem of reality, and must be reserved for a later part of this work[21].

The system of definitions and cognitive judgments, which constitutes any real science, is brought into congruence at individual points with the system of reality, and is so constructed that congruence then follows automatically at all remaining points. Those propositions in the system of judgments by virtue of which the system rests directly on real facts we may call *fundamental* judgments. They are definitions, in the narrower sense, and historical judgments. With them as a basis the whole system is erected step by step, the individual building blocks being obtained by a purely logical, deductive procedure. One such procedure is the syllogistic method, which consists in combining two judgments into a third by the elimination of a concept (the so-called middle term). If the whole edifice is correctly built, then a set of real facts corresponds not only to each of the starting-points — the fundamental judgments — but also to each member of the system generated deductively. Every individual judgment in the entire structure is uniquely coordinated to a set of real facts.

Individual sciences differ in character essentially in the way they arrive at a complete uniqueness of coordination. Disciplines that use a more descriptive method — the most striking examples are the *historical* sciences — are able to obtain complete congruence of the two systems (of judgments and of reality) only through the acceptance, almost exclusively, of fundamental judgments without building further on them. They stick to the given facts, as it were, for to rise above them in a free construction of thought would immediately risk uniqueness of coordination. In these sciences we are usually required to learn by heart which concepts and judgments are coordinated to the individual facts. We cannot derive the date of Napoleon's death from the date of his birth; we must memorize both. No one can deduce the succession of Roman emperors and the years of their rule from other historical data. Historical judgments by and large lack the interconnections and common elements that can serve as middle terms in inferences. This deficiency must be compensated for by an enormous variety of independent judgments

---

21 KANT puts it this way: "In an analytic judgment, the predicate goes to the concept, in a synthetic judgment it goes to the object of the concept, because the predicate is not contained in the concept."

if unique designation is still to be attainable. Disciplines of this kind are material-rich and knowledge-poor. Historical events are never so perfectly grasped that they can be deduced from the circumstances without loss. That is why historians cannot predict the future.

The exact sciences use an altogether different method. They do not secure unique coordination of judgment system and reality through maximizing the number of fundamental judgments. On the contrary, they strive to make this number as small as possible, and leave it to the necessary workings of logical interconnection to bring the two systems into unambiguous agreement. An astronomer who has observed the positions of a comet at only three different points of time can predict its position at any abitrary moment. A physicist with the help of a small number of equations (due to Maxwell) can coordinate suitable judgments to the entire domain of electromagnetic phenomena; with the help of a very few laws of motion he can do the same for the whole realm of mechanical processes. He does not have to formulate and learn a separate law for each individual phenomenon. Thus the exact sciences may be likened not to a mole's burrow winding its way through the soil of facts, but to an Eiffel Tower which, supported at only a few points, rises freely to the lofty heights of the most general concepts from which to command more perfectly the individual facts. The fewer the fundamental judgments which lie at the base of a science, the smaller the number of elementary concepts it needs to designate the world and hence the higher the level of knowledge to which it raises us.

Thus all the sciences, in providing us with knowledge (some more, some less), are engaged in creating a great network of judgments designed to capture the system of facts. But the first and most important condition, without which the whole enterprise would make no sense, is that each member of the judgment structure be coordinated uniquely with a member of the fact structure. And if this condition is fulfilled, the judgment is *true*.

§ 12. What Knowledge is Not

Anyone who looks at the findings obtained thus far concerning the nature of knowledge will perhaps fall prey to a certain feeling

of disappointment[22]. Is knowledge nothing more than a mere designating? If so, does the human mind not remain forever a stranger
to and remote from the things, processes and relations it wishes to
know? Can it never effect a more intimate union with the objects
of this world, of which it too is a member?

Our answer is that it can indeed. But in so far as it does so, it
is not engaging in *cognitive* behavior. The essence of knowing
absolutely requires that he who would practice it must betake himself far away from things and to a height far above them, from
which he can then view their relations to all other things. Whoever
comes close to things and participates in their ways and works,
in engaged in living, not in knowing; to him, things display their
value aspect, not their nature.

But is knowing not also a function of life? Certainly, but it
holds such a special position (we shall discuss it in the next section)
in relation to all other vital functions that we must continually
warn against mistaking its true nature, against conflating it with
other functions. It therefore seems desirable to buttress from two
directions the results thus far obtained. First, we want to show
negatively that under no circumstances can the concept of knowledge be given a meaning other than the one set forth in the investigations above, that no other function of the human mind is able to
fulfill the tasks assigned to cognition. Second, we want to prove
positively that all the hopes man justifiably places in knowledge can
actually be fulfilled by carrying out the process described, that of
finding one thing again in another, and of designating by means
of judgments and concepts. It does seem remarkable that there should
reside in such a simple and unpretentious procedure the mighty power
we know inheres in knowledge. It is truly astonishing that such a
modest process should yield one of the most glorious flowers of
human culture — a flower whose intoxicating fragrance creates an
ecstasy that many men have preferred to any other pleasure, as
witness the fact that they have dedicated their lives to knowledge.
And yet this is the case. All efforts to confer the rank of cognition
on any process other than that of simply comparing, finding again

---

22 A typical expression of this appears in the following words from
a review of the first edition of this book: "It is incomprehensible to this
reviewer how anyone who has ever struggled to obtain an insight can be
satisfied with this point of view" (Jahrbücher über die Fortschritte der
Mathematik, 1923).

and coordinating finally fail miserably at the decisive points, even though they may often succeed for a time in deceiving us as a result of misleading appearances[23].

The closest conceivable relation between two objects is that of complete identity, so that in reality they are not two but one. There has been no dearth of philosophers who profess not to be happy with any lesser concept of knowledge than that of a complete union of the knower with the known; according to medieval mystics this was how a knowledge of God in particular was supposed to have been secured. If such ideas were abandoned in the wake of scientific philosophy, it was because people became convinced that a union of the knowing consciousness with objects does not take place and indeed is not possible. But the doctrine ought to have been rejected first of all on the ground that even if such a union were possible, it would not in any event constitute *knowledge*. The failure to attend to this important point has become a major source of philosophical errors. We shall return to the matter shortly.

If fusion or full identity with things is not possible, there still seems to be a process that sets up an exceptionally close relation between subject and object, namely, *intuition (die Anschauung)*. Through this process, the known entity appears to move into the knowing consciousness, as it were. When I gaze at a red surface, the red is a part of the contents of my consciousness; I experience it, and only in this experience of immediate intuition, never through concepts, can I know what red is. Hearing a sound is an intuitive experience; I can know what the note *A* is only if someone actually sounds the note for me to hear. Only intuition teaches me what pleasure is, or pain, or cold, or heat. Are we not then fully justified in saying that intuition is knowledge?

As a matter of fact, the majority of philosophers are convinced that intuition provides us with immediate knowledge. Indeed, in the most vigorous currents of contemporary philosophy the opinion prevails that only intuition is true knowledge — that the method of science (operating with concepts) can furnish only a surrogate, not genuine knowledge of the nature of things.

---

23 In connection with what follows, see my article "Gibt es intuitive Erkenntnis?", Vierteljahresschrift für wissenschaftliche Philosophie und Soziologie *37* (1913), pp. 472—488.

Let us examine first the doctrine of those who champion this extreme view. They counterpose conceptual and intuitive knowledge, concede the former to the exact sciences especially, and then lay claim to the latter in the name of philosophy. "To philosophize is to place oneself within the object by the exercise of intuition[24]." They bid us acknowledge that "a properly philosophical intuition ... serves to open up an endless field of work together with a science that, without any symbolizing or mathematicizing methods, without an apparatus of inferences and proofs, nevertheless obtains a wealth of knowledge quite rigorous and decisive for *all* further philosophy"[25].

These conceptions stand out in sharpest conflict with all the results of our previous deliberations. They label as knowing a mental activity totally different from the process of comparing, finding again and designating, which revealed itself to us as the true essence of cognition. Now it might be said that perhaps the question is one merely of terminology: we are free to give the name knowledge to intuition as well. We would then distinguish between two kinds of knowing — conceptual or discursive, and intuitive. But the prophets of intuition also claim the right to give it the name knowledge on the contention that immediate intuition provides in a more perfect way *that* which symbolizing cognition tries to supply through the inadequate instrumentality of concepts.

But here they are very much mistaken. Intuition and conceptual knowledge do not at all strive for the same goal; rather, they move in opposite directions. In knowing there are always two terms: *something* that is known and *that as which* it is known. In the case of intuition, on the other hand, we do not put two objects into relation with one another; we confront just one object, the one intuited. Thus an essentially different process is involved; intuition has no similarity whatever to cognition. When I give myself fully to an intuitive content of my consciousness, say a red patch I see before me, or when in behaving I submerge myself fully in the feeling of activity, I experience through intuition the red or the activity. But have I really come to know the essence of the red or of the activity? Not at all. If I had arranged the red in some order through

---

24 H. Bergson, Einführung in die Metaphysik, Jena 1901, p. 26.

25 E. Husserl, Philosophie als strenge Wissenschaft, Logos I, (1910/11), p. 341.

a comparison with other colors and thereby correctly designated its shade and intensity, if I had analyzed the feeling of activity psychologically and discovered in it, for example, sensations of tension, feelings of pleasure, and so on — *then* I could assert that I had come to know to a certain degree the nature of the red I experienced or of the feeling of activity. So long as an object is not compared with anything, is not incorporated in some way into a conceptual system, just so long is it not known. In intuition objects are only *given,* not *understood.* Intuition is mere experience, but cognition is something quite different, something more. Intuitive knowledge is a *contradictio in adjecto.* Even if there were an intuition by means of which we could insert ourselves into things or things into us, it would still not constitute knowledge. Uncivilized men, and animals as well, probably intuit the world in a more complete way than we do. They are much more absorbed in it; they live in it more intensively, since their senses are sharper and more alert. Yet they do not know nature better than we do; they do not know it at all. We understand and explain nothing through intuition. What we obtain by that means is an acquaintance with things, but never an understanding of things. It is the latter alone that we aim at when we search for knowledge in science and in philosophy.

Here we uncover the great error committed by the philosophy of intuition: the confusing of acquaintance *(Kennen)* with knowledge *(Erkennen).* We become *acquainted with* things through intuition, since everything that is given to us from the world is given to us in intuition. But we come to know things only through thinking, for the ordering and coordinating needed for cognition is precisely what we designate as thinking. Science does not make us acquainted with objects; it teaches us to understand or comprehend what we are already acquainted with, and that means to know. Acquaintance and knowledge are such fundamentally different concepts that even ordinary discourse has two different words for them. And yet they are hopelessly conflated by the majority of philosophers, with only too few laudable exceptions[26].

---

26 Among these I cite A. RIEHL, who contrasts immediate acquaintance with understanding (Der philosophische Kritizismus, II, i, p. 221), and B. RUSSELL, who distinguishes quite correctly between "knowledge of things" *(Kennen)* and "knowledge of truths" *(Erkennen).* For this, see The Problems of Philosophy, p. 69. Also see E. VON ASTER, Prinzipien der Erkenntnislehre, 1913, pp. 6 ff.

For many metaphysicians the error has been disastrous. It will be worth our while to demonstrate this with the aid of some particularly clear examples.

Even though we cannot in general through intuition put things into ourselves or ourselves into things, this is not true of our own Ego. We stand to it in just the relationship that the mystics so greatly desired for cognition, that of full identity. We are, in the strict sense, completely acquainted with it. Hence anyone who ignores the distinction between acquaintance and knowledge will have to believe that we possess absolutely perfect knowledge of the nature of the self, and in fact this is a widely held view. Numerous metaphysical thinkers would subscribe to the proposition that has been formulated in our day as follows: "In so far as the Ego grasps itself in self-consciousness, it knows something real as it is in itself . . .[27]." Now this proposition is false no matter how often or in what form it is expressed. For psychological data, of which we become aware in consciousness, are not thereby known in the least; they are merely given or posited. Consciousness experiences them, they participate in it. Consciousness becomes acquainted with them in experience, it does not know them. They can become known in the proper sense of the term only through a scientific psychology, one that classifies and constructs concepts. Indeed, if the contents of consciousness could be known fully through mere intuition, we could dispense with all psychology.

In the proposition quoted just above, knowing was termed a "grasping". This is an idiom that very few thinkers have managed to avoid in their investigations of the nature of knowing. Time and again we read that cognition is a "spiritual grasping". But this of course is not a definition of the cognitive process; it is only a comparison of that process to the physical act of seizing, touching, feeling — a not particularly happy comparison in fact. When I grasp an object with my hand, all that I do is set up a relation between that object and myself, whereas in cognition the essential element is precisely the establishment by the knower of a relation among *several* objects. Thus to talk of knowing as a grasping is in general to use a misleading figure of speech; such talk is justified only if it is

---

27 F. PAULSEN in P. HINNEBERG'S volume Systematische Philosophie, 1907, p. 397.

interpreted to mean the capture or inclusion of the known object by *concepts* that assign it a unique place in their midst.

The error (and its consequences) contained in the pseudo-concept of intuitive knowledge is nowhere so clearly evident as in the philosophy of Descartes. His thesis is that we have intuitive insight into the existence of our own self (or, to put it in more modern terms, into the existence of the contents of our consciousness) and that this insight constitutes knowledge, indeed knowledge of basic significance. All of this seems to be an altogether irrefutable truth. It appears to be certified by the fact that we experience the contents of consciousness without any conceptual elaboration, any comparing and finding again, having to take place. What is this if not genuine knowledge?

Our answer is that this is of course an intuition, but despite everything it is not *knowledge*.

Certainly the judgment *"cogito, ergo sum"* (after all necessary corrections are made) does express an incontrovertible truth, namely, that contents of consciousness exist. But we saw some time back that not every truth need be knowledge; truth is the broader concept, knowledge the narrower one. Truth is uniqueness of designation, and uniqueness can be obtained not only through knowledge, but also through definition. And that is the case here. Descartes' thesis is a concealed definition; it is an improper definition of the concept *existence* — what we earlier called a "concrete definition". What we have is simply a stipulation that experience, or the being of contents of consciousness, is to be designated by the words 'ego sum' or 'the contents of consciousness exist'. If the concept of being or existence were already known to us from other applications and we now found on closer examination of the processes of our consciousness that they exhibited all the features of that concept, and if we could only utter the sentence "The contents of consciousness *exist*" on the basis of this finding-again — then and only then would Descartes' thesis constitute knowledge. But in that case, it would no longer be intuitive knowledge; on the contrary, it would fall entirely under the concept of knowledge that we have developed thus far. This, of course, was not the view of the great French metaphysician, and it would be foolish to interpret his thesis in this fashion. Rather, the thesis was intended only to point out the undeniable fact that the contents of consciousness are given; it was intended to serve as the foundation for all further philosophizing;

no other knowledge was supposed to precede it. As a matter of fact, the experience of conscious states (we return to this question in the third part of the book) is the original and sole source of the concept of existence; thus it is not an instance to which a concept already at hand is subsequently applied. The "I am" is simply a fact, not knowledge[28].

Having erred on this point, Descartes inevitably made further mistakes. Since he took his fundamental thesis to constitute knowledge, he then had to inquire about the criterion that ensures the validity of this thesis. He considered that he had found the criterion in *self-evidence* (or, as he put it, in the clearness and distinctness of the insight). But the only guarantee he could find for the infallibility of self-evidence lay in the veracity of God. Thus he was forever trapped in a circle. For the existence of the entity that assured him of the reliability of self-evidence was itself guaranteed only by self-evidence.

Anyone who holds that the Cartesian thesis constitutes knowledge will inevitably be drawn into a similar circle. The thesis can be interpreted only as a definition, as a designation of a fundamental set of facts. The *"ego sum"*, the existence of the contents of consciousness, needs no foundation. It is not knowledge but a set of facts; and facts merely exist, they require no certification through self-evidence, they are neither certain nor uncertain, they simply *are*. It makes no sense to seek a guarantee of their existence.

In recent times the Cartesian error has been elevated into a principle of philosophy in the form of the Psychology of Self-Evidence, founded by Franz Brentano. According to him, every mental act is accompanied by a cognition directed to this act[29]. He says: "We think or we crave something and we know that we do this. But knowledge is had only in a judgment[30]." Therefore, he reasons, a judgment is contained in every mental act! "Hence with every mental act", he continues, "there is bound up a two-fold inner consciousness — one is an idea or representation related to the act and the other a judgment related to it, the so-called inner percep-

---

28 The same truth lies at the base of the somewhat involved comment that KANT makes on the Cartesian thesis, Kritik der reinen Vernunft, KEHRBACH edition, p. 696.

29 F. BRENTANO, Psychologie vom empirischen Standpunkt, 1874, p. 185.

30 *Ibid.*, p. 181.

tion which constitutes immediately self-evident knowledge of the act[31]." In Brentano's view, every perception counts as a judgment "whether it be a cognition or a (possibly erroneous) perceiving"[32]. Yet one would expect a psychology developed "from an empirical standpoint" to exhibit a judgment as an experienced element in every mental act before asserting the presence of the judgment in the act. Instead, the *inference* is made that since perception is cognition, it must therefore contain a judgment. But the correct inference, obviously, would be: since experience shows that perception does not contain judgments, therefore perception is not knowledge[33]. The conflating of knowing and being-acquainted-with is all too clear in the passages cited.

Pure unelaborated perception or sensation is mere acquaintance *(Kennen)*. If this is what one has in mind, it is entirely wrong to speak of a "perceptual knowledge". Sensation gives us no knowledge whatsoever of things, but only an acquaintance with them. Now as we know, isolated pure perceptions almost never occur in a developed consciousness; what happens is that a so-called apperception process is associated with the sensation, that is, the sensation or complex of sensations immediately merges with related ideas into a total structure, which presents itself in consciousness as something with which we were previously acquainted. For example, the black-white sensations I have when I look at the paper lying in front of me at once become a perception of letters. Here of course is knowledge, even if of the most primitive kind. For I am not left with a mere sense impression; on the contrary, the latter is at once incorporated into the range of my previous experiences, re-cognized as being of such and such a sort. Consequently, if we restrict the expression 'perception' to apperceived sense impression, then indeed, but only then, may we speak of perceptual knowledge. If we wish to distinguish such knowledge — so long as it is not yet clothed in imagined or spoken words — from verbally formulated knowledge by de-

---

31 *Ibid.,* p. 188.

32 *Ibid.,* p. 277.

33 L. NELSON draws the opposite conclusion (Die Unmöglichkeit der Erkenntnistheorie, Abhandlungen der Friesschen Schule, III, 1912, p. 598). He argues that since a perception is knowledge but is not a judgment, therefore not every cognition need be a judgment. In doing so, he adopts the mistaken view of "immediate self-evidence" which we seek to refute here. He says that perception is "immediate knowledge" *(op. cit.,* p. 599).

signating the former as 'intuitive', then naturally there can be no objection[34]. We need scarcely mention that this concept of intuitive knowledge has not the least connection with the one found in Bergson and Husserl, which we discussed above and rejected.

Kant did not perceive the full weight of the truth that without apperceptive or conceptual elaboration there is no knowledge. Hence he expressed it only incompletely in his famous words: "Intuitions without concepts are blind." Notice how he begins the *Critique of Pure Reason:* "No matter in what way and through what means a piece of knowledge may relate to objects, *intuition* is that through which it is immediately related to them and to which all thought as a means is aimed." Here it is evident that Kant still saw as an essential factor in knowledge the inner connection set up by intuition between the object and the intuiting person. This also prevented him from unmasking the problem of the knowledge of things in themselves as a pseudo-problem. That is, Kant believed that such knowledge had to be an intuition of the kind that "represents things as they are in themselves", and this he declared to be impossible because things "cannot make their way over into my faculty of representation". But now we know that even if this were possible, even if things were to become one with our consciousness, then although we would be *experiencing* things, that would be something altogether different from a *knowledge* of things. "Knowledge of things in themselves" is simply a *contradictio in adjecto* so long as we understand by knowing some sort of intuiting or intuitive representation; for this would involve us in the absurdity of representing things as they are independently of any representation. Thus the question of the possibility of such knowledge cannot be raised at all.

How do matters stand with this question once we are clear about the true nature of knowledge? If everyone had always been aware and kept in mind that knowledge comes about through a mere coordinating of signs to objects, it would never have occurred to anyone to ask whether it is possible to have knowledge of things as they are in themselves. What led to this problem was only

---

34 This is what B. ERDMANN does in his fine monograph Erkennen und Verstehen, Sitzungsberichte der königlichen preussischen Akademie der Wissenschaft 53, p. 1251, where he invariably uses the expression 'perceiving knowledge' in the one acceptable sense explained above.

the view that cognition is a kind of intuitive representation that *pictures* or *portrays* things in consciousness. Only on this assumption could we ask whether the pictures or images exhibit the same attributes as the things themselves.

Whoever holds cognition to be an intuitive representation, by means of which we "grasp" things or "receive them into our mind" or the like, must repeatedly find cause to complain about the inadequacy and futility of the cognitive process. For a cognitive process so constituted would still not be able to carry its object over into consciousness without altering the object more or less basically. Thus it would always fail of its ultimate aim, namely, to behold things unchanged exactly as they are in themselves.

The correct concept of knowledge, as it has now been unfolded to us, does not have any unsatisfactory features. Knowing consists in an act — that of merely designating — which in fact does leave things untouched or unaltered. A picture or image can never fulfill its task perfectly, for then it would have to be a duplicate of the original. But a sign can supply all that is demanded of it, namely, uniqueness of coordination. An object can never be depicted as it is in itself; for every picture must be taken from a certain position and by some picturing agent. Hence it can offer only a subjective and, as it were, perspectival view of the object. Designation, on the other hand, leaves every object as it is. The signs employed and the methods of coordination do of course bear a subjective character imprinted upon them by the knower; but the coordination achieved shows no trace of this character. By its very nature, coordination is independent of standpoint and agent.

It is for this reason that we can say with confidence that *every* cognition does in fact give us knowledge of objects as they are in themselves. For no matter what the *designatum* may be, whether phenomenon or thing in itself (what this distinction means and whether it is justified will be considered later), still what is designated is just the thing itself as it is. Assume for the moment that our acquaintance extends only to "phenomena", behind which there are things in themselves with which we are *not* acquainted. Then these things would also be *known* to us along with the phenomena. For our concepts are coordinated to the phenomena and the phenomena are assumed to be coordinated to the things; hence our concepts would also designate the things, since a sign of a sign is at the same time a sign of the *designatum* itself.

We now turn to another point which can perhaps help clarify for us the advantages of the concept of knowledge worked out above, and show how easy it is to resolve a question that has often presented annoying difficulties — the question of the possibility of a theory of knowledge. The objections raised against this possibility are familiar. If knowing is supposed to know itself, if it is supposed to decide its own validity, then the watchman has been set to watch himself, and we may ask with Henry Sidgwick: *"Quis custodiet custodem?"* The project of investigating cognition before using and relying on it was ridiculed by Hegel who compared it with wanting to learn to swim before going into the water. Herbart thought the objection cogent, and Lotze believed the only way out was to ground epistemology in metaphysics. How in fact can the cognitive process be applicable to itself? *Feeling* is not felt, *hearing* is not heard, *seeing* is not seen. If knowing were analogous to these intuitional processes, then it would indeed be badly off in respect of its theory. But knowing is not that sort of thing at all; it is a process of coordinating. And such a process admits of being applied to itself without any difficulty: designating can itself be designated through an act of coordination. Even Leonard Nelson's famous proof of the impossibility of epistemology can be refuted on the basis of our insight into the nature of knowing. His proof contains the following reasoning: Suppose that the criterion of the objective validity of knowledge is itself a piece of knowledge. "Then in order for it to serve in the solution of the problem it must itself be *known (bekannt)*, that is, it must be capable of being an *object* of knowledge *(Erkenntnis)*. But whether this knowledge *(Erkenntnis)* whose object is the criterion in question is valid must already have been decided if the criterion is to be applicable[35]." But for something to be known *(bekannt)* it need *not* have been an object of knowledge *(Erkenntnis)*, and with this the chain of inference is broken.

Thus we see how mistaken we would be if we felt disappointed at the proof that the cognitive act is not an intimate marriage of subject and object, not a grasping or penetration or intuiting, but simply a process (governed, of course, by quite special laws) of designating the object. This proof does not mean a renunciation or a degrading of knowledge. We must not think that the activity of comparing, ordering and designating is merely a makeshift for some more

---

35 Abhandlungen der Friesschen Schule, II, p. 444.

perfect kind of knowing, forever denied us but perhaps possible for creatures differently constituted. This is entirely out of the question. Every act of finding anew, comparing and designating — as knowing has shown itself to be — supplies absolutely all that we require of cognition in ordinary life and in science. No other process, no "intellectual intuition", no becoming-one-with-things, could do the same. It is singular that even today there are some who believe that knowledge — indeed, a whole science — can come into being through mere intuition prior to any comparing or ordering. After all, the truth we are defending here was formulated many years ago most precisely in the proposition with which a celebrated logician began his chief work: "Science arises from the discovery of Identity amidst Diversity [36]."

The thesis that every cognition presupposes the establishment of a sameness has been objected to on the ground that sameness is simply one relation among many, and that the discovery of any other relation is just as much knowledge as is the determination of sameness. To this we answer that knowledge is certainly at hand when we determine anywhere the presence of a particular relation. But what does this determination consist in? It consists precisely in the fact that the relation is designated as this or that particular one, as a causal relation, as succession, and so on. But in order for us to be able to give it a name, we must establish that the relation before us is the *same* as another one that I had earlier come to know as a causal relation, a succession, and so on. This case simply confirms our general thesis. Sameness must be accorded a position distinct from all other relations; it is more fundamental and absolutely conditions all knowing.

This objection, however, can be generalized, and in its broadened form seems less easy to refute. Generalized, the objection reads: Must we not say that knowledge is constituted not merely by the establishment of a relation but quite generally by the determination of the presence of any new object, even if that object is not yet in any way incorporated, named, designated, judged? An example will serve to illustrate the sort of case that comes to mind. A psychologist who is analyzing some conscious process — say, a volition — finds that several factors may be distinguished in what was initially held to be an absolutely simple datum of consciousness. These fac-

36 S. JEVONS, The Principle of Science, 1874.

tors had not been observed before, and no names exist for them. Here it seems as if we cannot talk of finding the same again, for these factors have just been uncovered for the first time; the psychologist is obliged to invent special names for them. Yet who would want to deny that this is a case of genuine knowledge? Undoubtedly, no one. But in what exactly does this knowledge consist? Clearly in the fact that the structure of the conscious process under investigation, here the volition, has been more exactly determined; initially regarded as something simple, it has become known through the analysis as something composite, something made up of a number of factors. But this is a piece of knowledge according to our normal schema: the object is subsumed under the class of "composite data of consciousness". The individual factors that make it up, however, are not thereby known for themselves; they are only distinguished and counted.

In sum, the mere process of becoming *acquainted with* certain data, the mere intuiting of them, is an experiencing of these data, not a knowing of them. It does, however, provide a foundation for knowledge of the total experience that is built up out of these data. To be sure, this latter knowledge is of the most primitive kind. That is, it consists only in the fact that the whole becomes known as something that is not simple but composite. As soon as we attempt to go beyond this scanty result and ask *of what* the whole is composed, we find that merely to have experienced the partial aspects no longer provides a sufficient answer. These aspects must be recognized and named, incorporated into some context or other. Not until then can we express in judgments the nature of the object to be known.

This insight is important if we are to evaluate correctly the claims made in behalf of a philosophical method that is widely propagated today and is known as phenomenology. This method consists in imagining or bringing into experience, through intuition (of essences) or "Wesensschau", the objects to be known in all their aspects. But so long as the result of phenomenological analysis ends here, *nothing* is gained so far as knowledge is concerned. Our insight is not enriched, only our experience; what has been obtained is only *raw material* for cognition. But the work of cognition first begins when the material is ordered through the processes of comparing and finding again. The mere experiencing of an object as being there is not knowledge; it is only the precondition for knowledge. At most, intuition or *Wesensschau* can procure the stuff of which knowledge is made and in that way contribute important services to knowledge. But it must not be confused with it.

In the philosophy of science, the concept of knowledge developed here has fortunately come to prevail almost universally. It was Gustav Kirchhoff who set it forth with the greatest clarity in his celebrated definition of mechanics. The task of mechanics, he declared, is merely "to describe completely and in the *simplest* way the movements that take place in nature"[37]. By 'describe' is to be understood of course exactly what we have called a coordinating of signs. The words 'in the simplest way' mean that in connection with this coordination we should use a minimum number of elementary concepts[38]. And 'completely'signifies that through this coordination an absolutely unambiguous designation of every detail must be attained. Many epistemologists, building on this foundation, hold that Kirchhoff determined the task of science to be description, not explanation. But this is obviously wrong. For his contribution consists precisely in the discovery that explanation or knowledge in science is nothing other than a special kind of description. To be sure, he himself occasions the error by seeming to regard his definition as imposing a *restriction* on the task of mechanics[39]. He counterposes description to the discovery of causes[40]. We shall have to inquire later whether the concept of cause may applied in such a way that its use becomes legitimate in connection with designating natural objects.

The same school of epistemology is responsible for another distorted conception of the nature of knowledge on which we shall comment in the next section.

In closing we repeat that the discovery of the true nature of cognition as a kind of describing or designating does not mean a depreciation or disparagement of knowlege. For the value of the cognitive process lies not in what it consists of but in what it is

---

37   Vorlesungen über Mechanik, 4th edition, 1897, p. 1.

38   Avenarius too understood by "simplest" description the one that employs the smallest possible number of concepts. See F. RAAB, Die Philosophie des AVENARIUS, 1912, p. 146.

39   *Ibid.*, Preface, p. v.

40   *Ibid.*

capable of. How great this capability is we see from the sciences, especially the natural sciences, and their applications. And how great it may still become we can scarcely imagine.

§ 13. On the Value of Knowledge

It is now appropriate to ask why men really seek knowledge. Why do we devote our lives to this curious occupation of constantly searching out sameness in difference? Why do we strive to designate the rich manifold of the universe by means of only those concepts that are built up from a minimum number of elementary concepts?

There is no doubt about the ultimate answer: the reduction of one thing to another affords us pleasure. And to say that we have within us a *drive* for knowledge which demands satisfaction is only to give the same answer in other words. But obviously our question has a further purpose. We want to learn *why* it is that such a pursuit can afford us pleasure; we want to know how a drive could evolve that has as its goal mere cognition and that appears to be so remote from all the other goals of life.

The explanation of this riddle will indicate the place occupied by cognition in relation to other human activities. At the same time, it may also shed new light on the nature of knowledge.

The line of reasoning that will lead us to a solution of the problem must of necessity lie in the province of biology. For what gives a person pleasure and the sort of drives that develop in him depend solely on the conditions of his life and how he is constituted.

All theories of biological development agree that as living creatures evolve, their impulse toward activities favoring the preservation of the individual and the species must intensify, while tendencies toward activities inimical to life and the species must atrophy and disappear. The drive for knowledge undoubtedly falls under this principle. In its origin, thinking is only a tool for the self-maintenance of the individual and the species, like eating and drinking, fighting and courting.

We must assume that every animal that has a consciousness is also capable of acts of re-cognition. An animal must perceive prey as prey, an enemy as an enemy; otherwise it cannot adapt its behavior to the environment and must perish. Surely what we have here is, at the very least, the most primitive kind of cognition, that of perceiving. We must think of it as a process of apperception, with which the animal's movements of defense and attack are associated. The more complicated the creature's needs and the conditions essential for his life, the more complicated must be the processes of association. And clearly this increasing degree of complication is nothing other than the development of what we call understanding, or the ability to reason. For however much genuine acts of judgment differ in their epistemological *status* from mere associations of ideas, yet as psychological operations the processes of judgment (acts of thought in the narrower sense) grow out of the processes of apperception and association. There is a very close kinship between them[41].

The mechanism of judging and inferring makes possible a much more extensive adaptation to the environment than automatic association can ever attain. Association is focussed only on typical cases. An animal lunges at something to eat even where this action in no way favors the preservation of its life, for example, when the prey has been placed in a trap as bait. Man, however, is able to recognize ambush and danger even when it is camouflaged; he can set traps and outwit not only wild animals but also the invisible small creatures that threaten his body from within. In order to hold his ground in nature he must gain mastery over it, and this he can do only if throughout nature he finds again that with which he is acquainted. Were this not possible, he would not be able to dissolve what is new and unfamiliar into that with which he is acquainted. And so only too often he would stand helpless before nature. He would act falsely, fail to reach his goals, because he did not correctly foresee the consequences both of his own behavior and of other events. To know an object is to find-again other objects in it. Hence knowledge (provided practical obstacles do not stand in the way) enables us to constitute an object in a really creative way by combining the other objects, or to predict its structure from the observed appearance together of the elements and to take measures either to defend ourselves against it or to put it to use. Any behavior that looks to the future is therefore impossible without knowledge.

That all knowledge originally served only practical purposes is an indubitable, much emphasized truth. It is a well-known fact,

---

41 J. SCHULTZ brings this out very nicely in Die drei Welten der Erkenntnistheorie, Göttingen 1907, pp. 32 ff. and 76 ff.

embodied in the name itself, that geometry grew out of the need to measure land; the first astronomical observations were used for soothsaying; the first studies in chemistry had as their objective the making of gold; and the same thing is true in general of other disciplines. Today, as well, science and practice, pure knowledge and the activities of everyday life, are most intimately related. Practice constantly offers new stimulus to pure research and presents it with new problems, so that in our time too we may say that new sciences arise directly from the demands of life. But the converse effect is incomparably greater: pure science reveals an astonishing profusion of new paths in the struggle for the preservation and enhancement of existence. Indeed, it is knowledge that does not originate in practical demands that has come to be of greatest use for the objectives of life. The whole of modern culture has been nourished by discoveries made at a time when no one could foresee their applicability. Volta and Faraday had no thought of any such thing as electrical engineering. The pioneering investigations of Pasteur were addressed to the possibility of spontaneous generation, a theoretical question, and not to matters of hygiene and therapy, for which they were to assume such enormous importance. At the time radium was discovered no one knew that its rays would one day be used in the treatment of cancer ... but it is not necessary to add further examples of such patent truths.

This close tie between knowledge and practical use has led many writers to maintain that the value of cognition, now as earlier, consists altogether in just such use. Science, they say, serves only the needs of practical foresight, the mastery of nature; this alone is its point and value. The call to seek knowledge for its own sake, without thought to its application in life, is alleged to flow from a misconceived idealism and to be tantamount in fact to a debasement of science[42]. Yet these writers concede that the scientist, in pursuing his cognitive goals, fares better if he does not think of practical applications and does not take as the aim of his endeavors the discovery of only practically applicable truths; he should therefore set to work *as if* truth itself were the final goal. As experience teaches, this is the only way to make the great advances that subsequently prove so fruitful; if when we began we had in mind only

42 See W. Ostwald, Grundrisse der Naturphilosophie, 1908, p. 22.

what was useful to man, we would never have arrived at such knowledge. But even though it is thus useful for humanity to pretend that truth and pure knowledge constitute the ultimate aim of science, the real goal of cognition nevertheless is actually practical use, which alone provides the struggle for truth with its reason for being. The striving for knowledge "for its own sake" is merely a game, an unworthy waste of time.

This view overlooks certain points that are most important especially for an appreciation of the intellectual development of mankind. As certain as it is that the human understanding originally was only an instrument for the maintenance of life, so is it equally certain today that the understanding is in itself a source of pleasure and not a mere instrument. What brings about this metamorphosis is a natural process that also operates elsewhere: the transformation of means into ends. Activities that are a necessary means for the attainment of certain ends, but the performance of which is not at first directly connected with pleasure, gradually grow so familiar to us through habituation that they come to be an integrating component of life. Eventually we indulge in these activities "for their own sake" without associating them with any goal or using them to attain any objective. It is the carrying out itself that affords pleasure; what once were means have now become ends. Formerly they had value only as means; now they are valuable in their own right. There is hardly an activity whose role in life could not undergo such a change. And all of us have reason to rejoice in this. Speech, at first a means of communication, becomes song; walking, originally a means of getting about, grows into dance; seeing turns into looking-at, hearing into listening-to, work into play. At the apex are those activities connected with play. They alone satisfy immediately, while all behavior that serves simply as means directed to ends — work — acquires value only in relation to the results obtained.

The metamorphosis of means into ends is a process that constantly enriches life [43]. It inspires new drives in us and thus gives rise to new possibilities of pleasure, since the satisfying of a drive is only another name for pleasure. It creates the drive for beauty, from which art springs — pictures to look at, music to listen to. It is

---

43 I have sought to evaluate the significance of this process in a nontechnical book Lebensweisheit, Munich 1908. See also W. WUNDT's Prinzip der Heterogonie der Zwecke.

likewise the creator of the drive for knowledge, which in turn begets science and constructs the edifice of truth for its own satisfaction and not merely as a dwelling-place for material culture. That the latter nevertheless generally finds the dwelling habitable is not of the least concern to the knowledge drive. The same means-end transformation has been well described by Hans Vaihinger, who says of the world picture created by knowledge: "Science goes on to convert these structures into ends in themselves, and where it does so, where it no longer serves merely for the development of means, it is strictly speaking a luxury, a passion. But everything that is noble in man has a similar source[44]." Anyone who would deny that knowledge is the ultimate goal of scientific effort must then also condemn art; if we listened to him, life would be robbed of all content, all richness. The fact is that life in itself does not possess value; it becomes valuable only by virtue of its content, the abundance of its pleasure. Knowledge, together with art and a thousand other things, constitutes just this sort of content, a veritable horn of plenty overflowing with pleasure. It is a means not only for preserving life but also for fulfilling it. While most cognitive acts have some utility, some sort of end beyond themselves, pure science exists only where it is its own end; all other knowing is practical wisdom or applied science. Certainly we live life for its content; and just as certainly Herbert Spencer's dictum — "Science is for Life, not Life for Science" — is not the whole truth.

An insufficiently penetrating biological view of the drive for knowledge has often led to unclear notions about the meaning of science, even when the aim of science is not taken to be merely the maintenance of life. Consider, for example, the "principle of the economy of thought", so designated by Ernst Mach. The sense of this principle may also be found in Avenarius and others, and it has played a prominent role among many representatives of contemporary positivist philosophy. Now the originators of the principle did not intend to claim that all thinking serves only the practical, economic ends of life, and that science too is therefore only a means to such ends. True, Mach's own utterances about the real nature of the principle are quite vague, so that the sharp censure it has sometimes received, from Max Planck for example, seems not unjusti-

---

44 Die Philosophie des Als Ob, 2nd edition, 1911, p. 95.

fied[45]. But the principle is generally described as one that guides the psychological process of thinking in such a way that its goal is reached with the least possible exertion and along the least encumbered path; and the task of science is to find the shortest and easiest paths along which thought can effect a summary of all knowledge in the simplest possible formulas, so that thought may be spared any unnecessary labor.

Understood in this manner, the principle of economy is of course not a correct expression of the essence of science. Yet it does contain a kernel of truth, and the reader of the preceding sections will have no doubt as to where to look for it. Knowing consists in designating the things of the world completely and uniquely by means of a minimum number of concepts. To achieve this designation with the smallest possible number of concepts — *this* is the economy of science. No pains are too great for the scientist who pursues this goal, and to reach it he must travel the most laborious of paths. How absurd to believe that the goal of knowledge is to make our thought processes less arduous, to spare us intellectual effort, when in fact labor of the greatest intensity is demanded. True economy of thought (the principle that the number of concepts be a minimum) is a *logical* principle; it refers to the interrelationships of concepts. But the Mach-Avenarius principle is a biologico-psychological one and deals with our ideational and volitional processes. It is a principle of convenience, of taking the easy path; the other is a principle of unity.

Although, as we know, the method of science came into being originally in response to biological necessities, it entails not a saving of intellectual energy but rather a copious expenditure of it. To require that our thought designate everything in the world by means of a minimum number of concepts is to assign it not an easy task but an extremely difficult one. We have seen, of course, that reducing one thing to another is, up to a certain point, necessary to maintain life or alleviate its condition. But beyond this point reduction becomes very difficult. It is an undertaking that demands patience and love and for which as yet only a minority of mankind has developed a taste; the number of those who are inspired by a strong

---

45 M. PLANCK, Zur Machschen Theorie der physikalischen Erkenntnis, Vierteljahresschrift für wissenschaftliche Philosophie *34* (1910), pp. 499 ff.

desire for knowledge is still not very great. The human mind seems to operate with less trouble and to find its way about in the world more easily if it employs a relatively large stock of ideas, even though these ideas, when replaced by concepts, can be logically connected, derived from one another, and thus simplified. To work with a large number of ideas requires only memory, but to achieve the same results with *fewer* elementary ideas demands ingenuity. And while we know that our fellowman's memory may often prove unreliable, yet we sooner trust his memory than his capacity for logical reflection. This point is demonstrated quite clearly by the whole practice of instruction and training in ordinary life. Which sciences do the majority of people deem the most difficult? Obviously the mathematical sciences — even though these exhibit logical economy in its most fully developed form, since their concepts are all constructed out of a very few fundamental ones. Most mathematics students are better at memorizing formulas than at deriving them from other formulas.

In short, it is training, habit and association that facilitate or ease the thought process — just the opposite of logical connection, on which the method of science rests.

We see how easily we are led, by laxness in thought and expression, to confuse things that are diametrically opposed to each other. Mach's dictum — "Science itself may therefore be equated with the minimum task of presenting the facts as completely as possible with *the least expenditure of thought*" — is correct if the phrase 'the least expenditure of thought' is interpreted logically to mean designation by a minimum number of concepts [46]. But it is incorrect if these same words are understood psychologically to mean the shortest and easiest possible way of representing or imagining the facts. The two are not the same; in fact, to a certain degree, they are mutually exclusive.

Thus knowledge, so far as it is science, does not serve any other of life's functions. It is not addressed to the practical mastery of nature, although it may often be useful later for that purpose. It is an independent function, whose exercise affords us *immediate* satisfaction, a unique road to pleasure comparable to no other. And its

---

46 E. MACH, Die Mechanik in ihrer Entwicklung, 3rd edition, 1907, p. 480.

value lies precisely in the pleasure with which the drive for knowledge fills the life of the scholar.

From time to time an attempt has been made to heighten still further the grandeur of knowledge by maintaining that it is a value "in itself", regardless of the pleasure it may afford us, and that we would have to strive for it even if it gave us no joy. Truth, it is said, is an "absolute" value.

A critique of this doctrine would go beyond the bounds of our task. Consequently, I shall simply express without proof my own firm conviction that the assertion of values in themselves totally unconnected to pleasure or aversion seems to me one of the most erroneous doctrines in all philosophy. For it has its source in certain deeply ingrained prejudices. Such a doctrine lifts the concept of value into the rarefied atmosphere of metaphysics and believes that it thereby enhances it, whereas actually this serves only to dissolve the concept and to convert it into a mere word.

All moral philosophers to the contrary notwithstanding, the good is good not because it has "a value in itself", but because it gives joy. So too the value of knowledge consists quite simply in the fact that we enjoy it.

Part Two

Problems of Thought

§ 14. The Interconnectedness of Knowledge

Science is a system of truths, not a mere collection.

This follows from the very concept of knowledge. For when we reduce two terms to one another by finding a third term again in each of them, we thereby create a connection between them.

It is important to keep in mind what is meant here by the word 'connection', which to begin with is of course a metaphorical expression. Two judgments are said to be connected if one and the same concept occurs in both. Each of the two judgments designates a fact and the two together designate a complex set of facts. This latter often admits of being designated by means of a new judgment in which the concept common to the first two judgments does not appear. We then say that the new proposition has been *derived* from the other two, and we call it the conclusion and the other two propositions the premises. In their totality the three judgments make up the familiar structure known since Aristotle's time as a *syllogism*.

The theory of inference, of the interconnection of judgments, can be presented in various forms. Modern logic (anticipated by Leibniz) is in the process of creating a much more serviceable symbolism than the one fashioned by Aristotle. However, in the discussion that follows, we shall base ourselves on the latter, because it is the one that is most familiar and because in my opinion it *still* provides a means of presenting all logical relationships, and in particular the interconnections of judgments found in syllogistic inference. Whether this form of inference is the most natural is not at issue in a purely theoretical treatment.

Scholastic logic, as we know, listed 19 different moods of the syllogism, distributed among four 'figures', and these 19 valid moods were regarded as a selection from among 64 possible moods, 45 of which were invalid, that is, they did not permit any conclusion to be inferred even though the two premisses exhibited a common term. From its own standpoint, scholastic logic was quite right in making all of these determinations. Our own situation, however, is appreciably simpler, since for our purposes we need take into account only those judgments that are fully valid scientifically.

In short, we shall be concerned in this part of our study only with problems that arise from a consideration of the interconnections of judgments *among themselves*. Our concern is thus solely with the relations of signs to one another, without any regard at first for what they designate. Our interest is only in the mutual relationship of truths, not their meaning, not their original source. Hence we assume we have a scientific system not in its genesis but in a perfected state; and what we consider is not the more or less accidental path along which we have been able to establish the individual judgments but the dependences that exist among them in the finished system of truths. This assumption we join to our earlier insight that *negative* judgments are to be assigned only a secondary significance (see § 10), since they owe their existence only to the imperfection of our thought and hence have no place in the completed portions of a science. Consequently, we may also exclude negative judgments from our account and thus omit moods of the syllogism that contain such judgments. These judgments do of course play a partial role in the practical pursuit of knowledge, since we arrive at truth only through error; but they are not required in the domain of truths obtained. Moods that contain negative judgments are twelve in number, so of the 19 we began with, seven remain.

What holds for negative judgments, however, also holds for particular judgments, that is, judgments of the form "*Some S are P*". Important as they are in practice, for science they have only a provisional significance, as it were, and hence do not belong in a rigorous system. These judgments subsume under a concept only a part of the objects correlated with a given concept, and do so in such a way as to leave undetermined *which* part of the whole set of objects is intended. In actuality, it is possible to establish a par-

ticular judgment only when we in fact are acquainted with certain
S's that are P. Even in practice, the truth of a particular judgment
invariably has its source in an acquaintance with certain quite definite S's and must be traceable back to it. Thus a particular judgment
is only an imperfect abbreviation for the judgment "S_1 and S_2 and S_3
and so on are P." And wherever the S's cannot be specified individually (where, for instance, we have forgotten them or rely on the
statements of others) the judgment is uncertain. In order to be sure
of its truth we must go back to the individual objects that make
up the subject concept "some S", and when we do so we replace the
particular judgment with a general one. In place, say, of the judgment "Some metals are lighter than water" there appears "Potas-
sium, sodium and lithium are lighter than water". And it is only the
latter judgment that meets the standards of science.

For our purposes, then, particular judgments may likewise be
eliminated. Since six of the remaining seven valid moods contain
particular judgments, only a single syllogistic mood is left. Upon it
devolves the important office of setting up the mutual interconnection of strict truths and to it alone we confine our examination.
This is the mood "Barbara", which is of the form

$$\text{All } M \text{ are } P$$
$$\underline{\text{All } S \text{ are } M}$$
$$\text{All } S \text{ are } P$$

The essence of this mode of inference may be said to lie in the
fact that it subsumes a special case under a general proposition.
That is, the truth expressed by the major premiss about *all M* is
applied by means of our syllogism to those M's that are S.

The principle according to which the inference proceeds is the
so-called *dictum de omni;* it states that a character possessed by *all*
M belongs to *each M*. JOHN STUART MILL recognized quite correctly
(Logic, Book II, Chapter 2, § 2) that this dictum is nothing more
than a definition of the concept *"omnis"* (or of the concept of class).

That the interconnection of truths in rigorous scientific systems
can indeed be represented by means of this form of inference is
shown by any inquiry into such systems. The only reason an
investigation is needed to confirm this fact is that scientific deductions are almost always presented in abbreviated rather than pure
syllogistic form. In particular, the minor premisses for the most part

are not stated separately, since they can easily be gathered from the sense, and the trained thinker usually hurries by them. The prime example of a tightly interconnected system of scientific truths that comes naturally to mind is mathematics. Here individual propositions are linked together by those processes we call proofs and calculations. These are nothing other than sequences of syllogisms in the mood *Barbara*. In principle, all demonstrations proceed according to the same schema, in the form illustrated by the following example:

Every right triangle is endowed with such and such properties.
The figure *ABC* is a right triangle.

ABC is endowed with such and such properties.

The major premiss states a general rule (proved, in turn, from still more general propositions), under which the syllogism subsumes the particular subject of the minor premiss. The correctness of the latter, however, rests either directly on definition (or, in the language of geometry, construction) or indirectly on a proof that takes the proposition back to the fundamental definitions (axioms) of geometry.

Geometrical demonstrations are of this kind. Sigwart is right when he objects to taking as the paradigm of mathematical inference a simple syllogism such as: A parallelogram is a quadrilateral; a square is a parallelogram; hence a square is a quadrilateral[1]. He is wrong, however, when he concludes further that the major premisses of geometrical inferences cannot in general be conceived of as subsumption judgments and that they only seem to have the form of the mood *Barbara*[2]. Specifically, his view is that geometry does not deal only with the subsumption relationship of concepts. Rather, it "always goes beyond mere conceptual judgments"; it derives its propositions "with the aid of law-like relations taken from somewhere or other" (this "somewhere or other" must obviously be intuition), relations not contained in the definitions. To counter this view, we need only recall some of our earlier discussion (Part I, § 7). We saw that a modern rigorous system of geometry uses just those relations that *are* contained in the definitions. Indeed, the

---

1 Logik, 3rd edition, Tübingen 1904, p. 482.
2 *Ibid.*, p. 483.

definition of the basic concepts of the system takes place precisely through these relations, and that is why the laws governing the relations may be represented as subsumption relationships of concepts, and conversely. Sigwart, still the captive of older views on the nature of mathematical thought, overlooked this point when he insisted that mathematical reduction proceeds not on the basis of subsumption relationships of concepts but on the basis of relationships of relations. But from a purely logical and mathematical standpoint, the two are one and the same, since strict, pure concepts are simply nodal points of relations.

What is true of geometry is true in similar fashion of arithmetic and algebra. "Calculation" is nothing but inference based on general theorems[3]. Fundamentally it consists in the following: the highest principles, which are the axioms or definitions of arithmetic and which are valid for *all* numbers, are applied in turn to various specific numbers (every arithmetical expression being ultimately nothing other than a more complicated sign for a number). And the propositions thus obtained are then applied again to arbitrary numerical expressions, and so on. The logical schema of calculation (which in practice of course is never given in complete form) would therefore look something like this: a certain proposition holds for all numbers; $a, b, \ldots$ are numbers; the proposition holds for $a, b, \ldots$. Consider a concrete example. We obtain the value of the expression $(a + b + c)^2$ by regarding it as a special case of the expression $(x + c)^2$, where the number x has the form $a + b$. All calculation is a substitution; but substitution is subsumption. The terms that are substituted for one another in calculating are, for the most part, completely equal, that is, they are only different terms for the same concept; such substitution is then a subsumption in which both concepts have the same extension.

It thus becomes clear that the most rigorous systems of knowledge can be rendered by means of the mood *Barbara*. From the standpoint of pure logic, there is no distinction between the rigorous inferences of any arbitrary science and those of mathematics; for in treating inferences, we consider only the relationship of concepts to one another, without regard to the various intuitive

---

3 See, for instance, O. Hölder, Die Arithmetik in strenger Begründung (Programmabhandlung der Philosophischen Fakultät zu Leipzig, 1914, p. 7).

objects that are designated by means of these concepts. Hence all truths that have precise logical interconnection (that is, that admit of being deduced from one another) can be represented as far as their mutual linkage is concerned by means of syllogisms, specifically in the mood *Barbara*.

The Aristotelian theory of inference needs no modification or extension in order to be applicable to modern science. What is necessary is only that the theory of concepts be deepened, and this has already taken place, as indicated in part of the preceding discussion. Modern logic, in the form developed by Bertrand Russell, for example, no doubt offers a much more useful set of inference procedures than the syllogistic. Beyond this, however, all the arguments advanced against the dominion of the syllogism prove only that the actual thought of man does not proceed in regular syllogisms — and this is an undeniable psychological fact. But they fail to refute the thesis that presentation of an absolutely rigorous system of truth, so far as the presentation is meant to be absolutely exact and complete, can always take place in syllogistic form. And it is only this thesis that must be maintained here. It is quite obvious, for example, that the actual discovery of geometrical truths need by no means follow the pattern of *Barbara*. The process of discovery may involve the use, say, of negative judgments (as in so-called indirect proof). But this does not affect the inner ties which necessarily connect the individual propositions and on which our examination is centered.

§ 15. The Analytic Character of Rigorous Inference

The more important and comprehensive the role played by the syllogistic form in rigorous inference, the more sensitive does pure thought become to any criticism that attacks the actual import and usefulness of this kind of inference. This, perhaps, is what motivates the efforts, referred to just above, of those who do not wish to see the exact inferences in the sciences come under the jurisdiction of the syllogism. For it is a well-known fact that philosophy long ago passed a very harsh judgment on the value of syllogistic inference for human knowledge.

Indeed, precisely the same considerations that have just demonstrated to us that particular judgments are useless for a rigorous scientific system and that the mood *Barbara* is the sole principle of unification guaranteeing the absolutely certain linkage of truths among one another — these same considerations also teach us that the conclusion of a syllogism never contains knowledge that is not already assumed as valid in the major premiss or, perhaps, in both premisses of the inference. A particular judgment can be asserted only on the basis of certain universal judgments, for which it constitutes only an indeterminate abbreviation. Similarly, the major premiss of a syllogism necessarily presupposes for its validity the truth of that judgment which appears as the conclusion. In short, the whole thing is a vicious circle. Consider the inference: All M are P, all S are M, therefore all S are P. We are certain that the major premiss is correct only if we are convinced that all M without exception really are P. But by virtue of the minor premiss, all S are among these M, so that we must already know that they are P before we may assert the truth of the major premiss. Thus in order to establish the major premiss we must already know that all S can be designated by the concept P. Therefore the conclusion, which designates S by means of P, does not offer any new mode of designation and accordingly does not provide any knowledge whatsoever with regard to the major premiss.

This proves that although the syllogism binds together the individual truths of a completed system, it is not an instrument by which *new* knowledge can be procured. Its function in the realm of cognition is solely to connect and to order, not to create.

The ancient skeptics knew this, and we would scarcely have had to linger over the point were it not for the fact that even today the process of exact inference is often credited with making a greater contribution than is within its power. But a clear insight into its true capacity is so important for the further course of our inquiry that we are justified in examining carefully the principles used in defending the syllogism against the attacks of the skeptics.

Many philosophers defend the syllogism by showing how significant and absolutely necessary it is for practical affairs[4]. They are entirely correct. But so far as their arguments relate only to the practical value of inference and fail to consider the absolute character of its validity, they do not bear on our question. When we ask whether the syllogism can furnish us with new knowledge, what

---

4 WUNDT, Logik I, 2nd edition, p. 322.

we want to know of course is whether this mode of inference contains a guarantee of that new knowledge. This is the point at issue in any formulation of the epistemological problem. As a matter of fact, in ordinary life and in empirical science the syllogism is not generally charged with the task of deriving from absolutely valid truths new ones that are fully certain. Rather, its most useful applications are found where the truth of at least one of the premisses remains to be established. This premiss usually is a "hypothesis", while the conclusion consists of an empirically verifiable judgment. If the judgment is actually confirmed by experience, then this is seen as a verification of the hypothesis, since it is an indication that at least in the case examined the correlation sought by means of the hypothesis is in fact unique. For example, in proving the wave character of Roentgen rays we set up the following syllogism (in which the hypothesis to be verified is the minor premiss):

> The propagation of waves is attended under certain circumstances by the phenomena of diffraction and interference.
>
> Roentgen rays are propagated as waves.
>
> Therefore, Roentgen rays under certain circumstances exhibit the phenomena of diffraction and interference.

This is the schema of inference by which all experimental science proceeds. Here the syllogism is used not to derive a new truth from valid propositions, but solely to guide the search for empirical instances that will provide support for the validity of a proposition.

The situation is different in the case of the familiar textbook example where the proposition "All men are mortal" is applied to an individual who is still alive. Here the point in carrying out a syllogistic inference is to reach a certain conclusion. This is what we do over and over again in ordinary life — whenever we give thought to and prepare ourselves for the death of a human being. But a bit of thought shows that in this case knowledge of the mortality of someone who is still alive is not first obtained through the syllogism, since the major premiss obviously presupposes the validity of the conclusion. (As a matter of fact, the textbook example cited above is often used to clarify this very point.) The real cognitive advance lies solely in the transition from the proposition "All men who died previously were mortal" to the proposition "All men are mortal", and this transition is made before the major premiss is set up. Our inference merely makes use of the bridge already erected from the particular to the universal in order to move back over it in the opposite direction. Whether passing from some instances to all instances is legitimate or not constitutes the well-known problem of induction. However, this is a problem that has to do not merely with the relationships of concepts but with the realities designated by the concepts.

Similarly, nothing is gained if we try to rescue the cognitive value of the syllogism by declaring that it still can provide a basis for new knowledge in *those* cases where the major premiss is to be understood as asserting not the *universality of the number* of instances but the *necessity* in each individual instance of connecting the predicate with the subject[5]. For example, suppose the major premiss of a syllogism reads: "Every event has a cause." This assertion, so it is argued, states not merely that whenever an event takes place a cause is present, but that each event has a cause *necessarily*.

Yet even if we grant that this is so, we must still note two things.

First, the argument assumes that we are *acquainted with* sentences of this sort whose validity for us is absolute. Hence we must possess in our consciousness independently of experience some kind of guarantee of the truth of such universal propositions; for experience itself can never provide this assurance, since it teaches us only what *is,* not what *must be*[6]. Thus the argument assumes the existence of truths that, following Kant, we designated above (Part I, § 11) as "synthetic judgments *a priori*". But we have seen that this assumption must be regarded with the greatest skepticism. The whole question will have to be dealt with definitively later; but it is already clear that as far as we are concerned any argument founded on the existence of such judgments can carry no weight.

Second, even if we were to grant that there are such truths, closer consideration would show that then the cognitive advance would be due in reality not to the syllogism but to the mental faculty that assures us of the validity of the major premiss, which is already complete when it enters into the syllogism. This faculty would have to supply exactly what, in the instance discussed above, induction is intended to provide. (Indeed, it would have to do more, since it supplies *certainty,* whereas induction, as is generally acknowledged, furnishes only probability.) The incontrovertible fact

---

5 SIGWART, Logik I, 3rd edition, p. 479.
6 KANT, Prolegomena to Any Future Metaphysics, § 14.

remains: the conclusion of a syllogism never in any way goes beyond the range of the truths embraced in the major premiss. The major premiss always tells us *more than* (and in the limiting case, as much as) the conclusion. What the conclusion asserts of any particular case, the major premiss expresses as a *universal* truth.

Syllogistic inference can indeed make clear to us what is contained in the major premiss. But it can never yield knowledge that is *not* contained in the premiss and that goes beyond it. Consider, for example, what occurs when we apply to a particular happening the proposition that every event has a cause, and affirm that this happening too is causally conditioned. The resulting knowledge does not seem at all new or surprising to us, even though the event may be of an entirely new and unforeseen kind. We simply incorporate the new event, without fanfare, into the causal network.

There may of course be cases where the conclusions of syllogistic procedures, say the results of some calculation, do astonish us and present us with unexpected findings. But this shows merely that psychologically the final outcome was not conceived of along with the major premiss. It does not mean that the end result is not contained logically in the major premiss — and this is all that matters here. We are asking not about what this or that person knows or conceives of, but solely about the way in which judgments in the domain of truths are linked with or follow from one another.

In few areas is the difference between the logico-epistemological and the psychological viewpoint so often ignored as in the question of the value of deductive inference. It would not occur to anyone to doubt its psychological value. Obviously we can arrive by means of syllogisms at truths with which we were not previously acquainted; but the fact that we were not explicitly conscious of such truths does not prevent them from being contained logically in the premisses. The truth that 113 is a prime number may be something new for a student, something of which hitherto he was not aware. Yet this truth can without doubt be derived purely syllogistically from the definitions of the concepts "prime number" and "113", and, logically, is given with them. What are involved here are only ideal relations among judgments and not connections among the acts of judgment which represent the judgments in consciousness and which are of course real processes.

The difference between the two viewpoints on this matter becomes even clearer when we turn to the most weighty arguments advanced in support of the value of deductive inference. A number of writers (Bradley, Riehl, Störring) cite a class of inferences that have the following form: *a* is larger than *b*, *b* is larger than *c*, therefore *a* is larger than *c*. Again, *A* is to the right of *B*, *C* is to the left of *B*, therefore *A* is to the right of *C*; and the like. Here, says one of these writers, the conclusion contains a truth "that is given in *neither* of the two assertions made by the premisses ... It is a *new* determination and is produced by thought"[7]. For in asserting (in the first premiss) that *a* is larger than *b*, we do not appear to have said anything about *c*, and in the second premiss *a* does not occur at all. The conclusion, which makes an assertion about the relationship between *a* and *c*, is therefore evidently something quite new.

But when we analyze such inferences more closely, it turns out that this argument cannot be sustained. The logical structure of the inferences is more complicated than appears at first glance. It has been said that these inferences are not syllogisms, that they lack a middle term (since "to the right of" and "to the left of", the predicates in the example, are different concepts), that they are simpler in form than syllogistic inferences[8]. But clearly this class of inferences owes its special character to the peculiar nature of the ordinal concepts — "larger than", "smaller than", "to the right of", "to the left of" — that occur in these inferences. And any judgment about the essence of these inferences must be regarded as premature so long as it does not take into account the special features of those relations.

The truth is that the inferences in question can be viewed as abbreviated formulations of normal syllogisms that are composite in character. That is, the conclusions do not follow immediately and directly from the premisses. In drawing the conclusions, we rely on certain principles that are not explicitly stated but that enter in intuitive garb into the process of representation and thus remain unnoticed. These principles are furnished by the definitions of the ordinal concepts used in the inferences.

For purposes of illustration, we may take the relation "greater than" as a paradigm, since the other inferences of this sort are reducible to this schema. (For example, '*A* is to the right of *B*' means

---

7 STÖRRING, Erkenntnistheorie, 1920, p. 250.

8 A. RIEHL, Beiträge zur Logik, 2nd edition, p. 53.

that, given a vertical axis Y with A and B on the positive side, the distance from A to Y is greater than the distance from B to Y.)

In order to judge whether the content of a conclusion goes beyond that of the premises or whether its truth is fully contained in them, we must disregard completely all intuitive or actual objects for which the inference may hold. Otherwise, we run the risk of taking for a purely logical derivation something that in reality is read off from intuition. According to what was said earlier, however, this means that we must go back to the implicit definitions of the concepts that appear in the inferences. These implicitly defined concepts, between which the relation of "greater than" obtains, are called *numbers;* indeed, inferences of the form in question are applicable to reality only where we have enumerable or measurable magnitudes. Thus the definitions with which we have to do here are no other than those that make up the axiom system of number theory or arithmetic.

Now the question of the complete consistency of the axiom system of arithmetic has not yet been definitively settled. Hence in this instance an appeal to the established results of mathematics is rendered more difficult. But usually the relation "greater than" in such a system is simply *defined* with the aid of the property of "transitivity". A relation R is said to be transitive if when it holds between a and b and between b and c, it also holds between a and c. (This is the way BERTRAND RUSSELL puts it in the Principles of Mathematics, Cambridge, 1903). We see at once that under these circumstances the claim can no longer be made that the inferences in question lead to new knowledge. On the contrary, they express quite trivially only what is contained by definition in the concepts used. Moreover, as we may easily verify, those inferences can be presented, if in a somewhat cumbersome fashion, in the form of ordinary syllogisms in *Barbara,* with the proposition "The relation *greater than* is transitive" as one of the premises.

If the relation *greater than* is defined in terms of other properties, then the axiom system must be so constituted that transitivity can be deduced purely logically from those other properties. In any event, due to the wealth of relations latent in the implicit definitions, the proposition "a is greater than b" contains much more than appears at first glance. By virtue of the properties possessed by numbers and by the relation *greater than,* the proposition also asserts that a is greater than any number that is smaller than b. The second premiss, "b is greater than c", which according to the definitions of the concepts *greater than* and *smaller than* is identical with the judgment "c is smaller than b", picks out c from among those infinitely many numbers. Thus here too the conclusion states nothing new; in fact, it says something less than the first premiss[9]. Thus the judgment "a is greater than c" is actually only a part of the truth embraced by the proposition "a is greater than b".

Of course in the actual practice of thought, logical considerations of this type are altogether absent; we simply read off everything from intuition. Nor is there anything surprising about this. Our definitions are all so constituted that they run parallel to the intuitive representation, since they are intended to designate the intuitive by means of concepts. But since our concern here is for absolute rigor, we may look for the essence of concepts only in the relations in which they stand to one another. Accordingly, we consider concepts independently of their purposes, independently of intuition. Then the inference form under discussion, which is immediately evident in intuition, becomes an ordinary syllogistic structure, an inference from general propositions. As these propositions are merely the definitions of the concepts that occur in the "premisses", they are actually the *major premisses from which* the conclusion is inferred, and cannot be regarded (as Riehl supposes[10]), as *principles according to which* the inference takes place.

It then follows strictly that in every inference the conclusion is already contained in the premisses and hence does not signify new knowledge. The set of facts designated by the conclusion is completely contained in the set of facts correlated with the major premiss; and the minor premiss simply selects from the major premiss what is relevant with respect to the conclusion, directs our attention

---

9 E. Dürr, who incidentally treats this class of inferences in a similar fashion, came close to this view (Erkenntnistheorie, Leipzig 1910, pp. 68 ff.). He did not reach it fully because he overlooked the fact that these inferences hold strictly only for *number concepts*. He says (*op. cit.*, p. 69): "The concept of B does not contain the fact that C is located to its right." Of course not. But the concept of a definite number (which gives the empirically observed position of B) does contain the fact that the number is larger than a certain other number (which has been shown by experience to be the number that determines the position of the object C).

10 A. Riehl, Beiträge zur Logik, 2nd edition, p. 53.

to what was perhaps unnoticed before, and in so doing bestows psychological value upon the inference.

It has been necessary here to defend our view in considerable detail against philosophical attacks. Yet from what we know about the true nature of judgments and concepts, our conclusion is perfectly natural and comes as no surprise. For how could anything result from the combining of judgments except what is already in them? Concepts and judgments are not real things; they are not plastic structures, able to expand and develop and bring forth something new. They are fixed signs, which have no properties other than those assigned to them by definition. No matter how we combine and arrange concepts and judgments, all that we obtain will be new concepts, never new knowledge[11].

Thus pure thought — inference that rests exclusively on the mutual relationships of concepts and does not take intuitive realities into account — can never be a source of real knowledge. Its contribution consists solely in making explicit what the major premisses contain, in breaking down what is comprised in them. That is why we say that all strictly deductive inference is *analytic* in nature.

Wherever science proceeds in a purely deductive manner, it does no more than develop analytically whatever is contained in its general propositions. The source of these propositions varies with the discipline. In the pure conceptual sciences, such as arithmetic, the universal propositions have the character of definitions. In the factual or empirical sciences, however, the universal propositions must include empirical propositions. Of course, deduction or strict inference requires no appeal to experience; only the major premises are needed in order to obtain the conclusion. The conclusion lies concealed in them, and all that is necessary is to fetch it out by means of analysis. Thus analysis, by its very nature, is *a priori;* that is, it is logically independent of experience.

Deductive, syllogistic inference stands in contrast to *inductive* inference. The latter is not analytic but synthetic. However, it is not rigorous inference; it does not possess apodictic validity. We cannot at this point determine anything about its relationship to experience, for, as noted above, the investigation of induction is a problem not of thought but of reality (Part III).

---

11 For example, the discovery of "new" fields of pure mathematics means simply the formation of new combinations of concepts.

§ 16. A Skeptical Consideration of Analysis

The results yielded by analytic judgment and inference have apodictic validity. The conclusion of a syllogism is derived from the premisses, an analytic judgment from the definition of the subject term.
And to the extent that the derivation takes place in conformity with
the simple rules of formal logic, the outcome is absolutely correct,
that is, it is in accordance with the assumptions from which it is
inferred. It has to be correct for the simple reason that it says nothing different from what these assumptions assert; it says the *same
thing* that is already contained in them.

This is why analytic judgments and inferences, *as such,* are not
an epistemological problem. The results of analysis seem to belong
to that small realm of the absolutely certain, which is completely
secure against any doubt and which contains the firm bases without
which any philosophy would float unsupported in mid-air.

But a skepticism prepared to go to any lengths can, even in
analytic procedures, discover points where it can attack with some
hope of success. Such a skepticism will argue as follows:

Whatever the relationship among them may be, judgments and
concepts are merely fictions or ideal structures, not realities that
can be exhibited in consciousness. In the final analysis, real processes of consciousness are all that we are acquainted with or that
are given to us. Conceptual relationships are accessible to us only
in so far as they are represented by conscious processes. No matter
how certain and well-defined these relationships may be, of what
use is this to us unless the same is true of the real processes that
are supposed to run parallel to these relationships and that alone
are known to us?

Thus, while deduction itself is not open to skeptical doubt, we
can doubt the sequence of mental processes by which deductions are
represented in thought, and in practice, of course, this amounts to
the same thing. For we are real beings, not concepts.

There are no perfectly defined processes in our consciousness,
any more than there is a perfect spherical body in nature. And in
theory it may be doubted whether such blurred processes do lead
to absolutely exact results. Can we carry out the analysis that occurs
in deduction in such a way that it is fully proof against objection?
The idiot or the untrained child is unable to test the validity of a
logical principle or to solve the simplest arithmetical problem. Yet

there are no sharp differentiations, but only gradual transitions, between a mature man, a child and an idiot. The most intelligent person is subject to error in carrying out even very short deductions; the most brilliant mathematician cannot guarantee that he won't make a mistake in addition. It is true that everything must hold necessarily of a concept that is ascribed to it by virtue of its definition. But are we sure that we can retain that definition in memory even for a short time without a new concept — due to some diabolic trick of our consciousness — slipping in unnoticed during the brief interval required for an analysis and replacing the concept we intended to analyze? We all know that this sort of thing does happen. But do we also know with absolute certainty that there are any cases in which such a substitution or alteration is totally excluded? It seems that any guarantee that can be given would itself be uncertain, in however small a measure. We have said that an analytically obtained result is apodictically certain, for it contains only what is in the premises from which it is deduced. But it is not enough that the content *be* the same; we must also *re-cognize* it as the same. And acts of re-cognition are in principle not immune to all doubt, since they require us to retain and compare representations or images, and in consciousness these constantly fluctuate and are not sharply bounded.

In practice, it is by recourse to procedures of *verification* that we ensure ourselves against mistakes that might arise through faulty functioning of the mental apparatus. For example, when we solve an arithmetical problem, we test the result, or we repeat the calculation, or we have someone else repeat it; and if the result agrees with the one first obtained, we are satisfied and regard it as correct. In so doing, we rightly assume that just because mental processes are not uniform, exactly the same error will not be committed in every test or repetition. That is why we regard the absence of deviations as confirmation of correctness. Now this is all quite plausible. But whence do we derive the *certainty* that this is the way things are?

Thus we *can* doubt all certainty. But this does not mean that we actually *do* so. As a matter of fact, we know that no one seriously harbors this sort of doubt, and even the philosopher who occasionally voices it, does not really believe it in the innermost recesses of his heart. But for us it makes no difference whether anyone really cherishes this sort of doubt. All that matters is that there is the *possibility* of doubting; this is what we must acknowledge and take into account. It is not idle curiosity that impels us to examine such doubts, nor a fondness for paradoxical and extreme positions. Nor is it for the sake of doubting that we doubt, but because we hope thereby to gain an insight into the depths of human consciousness and thus be helped in solving the great problems of knowledge. Descartes made use of methodical doubt for this very reason; Hume proceeded in a like manner when on occasion he indulged in reflections similar to those above[12].

When we stand with such thoughts on the highest peak of skepticism, a shudder of intellectual anxiety comes over us. We are seized with dizziness, for we glimpse an abyss that seems bottomless. This is a point at which the paths of the theory of knowledge, of psychology and — as I hope I may add — of metaphysics intersect and suddenly break off. We cannot be satisfied, once we have looked into the abyss of doubt and uncertainty and have drawn back from the brink, merely to return unmoved to the land of common sense. We cannot comfort ourselves with the thought that such doubts are fruitless and that despite them the sciences enjoy a firmly grounded existence. We do not want to ascend once more into the light of science until we have taken full measure of the depths of the knowing consciousness. Epistemology is not as fortunately situated as the individual sciences, which can leave the verification of their foundations to a more general discipline; the theory of knowledge is concerned precisely with the ultimate presuppositions of *all* certainty. We can hope to overcome universal doubt only if we strip the difficulty of its wrappings and face it calmly.

Most philosophers cut through the troublesome Gordian knot with the sword of "self-evidence". They reason somewhat as follows: Suppose I have gained knowledge of some truth; for example, I have calculated that two times three is six. Then the correctness of each and every step in the calculation, on close examination, is guaranteed for me by an immediately experienced *self-evidence*. I know, to use the language of Descartes, *clare et distincte*, that I have made no mistake, and this holds *despite* the comparative haziness that attaches to all mental processes. Either I must rely on this self-evidence or I cease to think altogether.

---

12 Treatise of Human Nature, Book I, Part IV, Section I.

While many writers have given the problem this particular twist, we cannot, it seems to me, be content with it. Spoken of in this way, self-evidence is merely another word for the demand that doubt end at this point. The term only strikes down misgivings, it does not resolve them. Just because our thought processes are imperfect, it often happens that we think we have made a judgment on the basis of self-evidence only to have that judgment turn out later to be false. It is in such cases that the theory of self-evidence reveals its impotence; it cannot defend itself against the attacks of a vigorous skepticism. We shall return to the theory of self-evidence.

Instead of explaining away the discomforts of doubt simply by means of a word, we prefer rather to try to bring to light all the various presuppositions that must tacitly be made in any analytic procedure. Consider a rather long deduction, say a proof in mathematics. This sort of deduction comes about when a conclusion that has just been drawn serves in turn as a premiss for the next inference, and so on. It is not possible to conduct the entire proof in a single instant; the narrow limits of consciousness prevent the human mind from grasping so many syllogisms all at once. The whole process takes time, and the results obtained in the course of the deduction must be retained in memory from one step to the next. Thus what is involved here is our faculty of memory, and that is a psychological capacity whose unreliability has often enough been the subject of complaint.

How little we may rely on memory is acknowledged by the fact that in such deduction we almost always resort to writing things down. Indeed, otherwise we would be unable for the most part to carry out deductions, since the average person, as we know, can do only fairly simple problems in his head. Of course, it should not be supposed that the possibility of writing down the deduction can contribute in the least to doing away with our fundamental doubt. Even though paper may preserve what is entrusted to it far better than does human memory, we cannot possibly accept as one of the ultimate presuppositions of the theory of knowledge the notion that written characters in manuscripts and books possess any very great permanence. For this is a matter of general physical conditions, and the situation with respect to our knowledge of physical objects still remains to be investigated by the theory of knowledge. Moreover, we would also have to assume that no mistake or error could possibly be made in writing down the characters and in making them out. This too is questionable; for when we read, it is our sensory capacities that come into play, and when we write, it is our motor capacities. And we cannot of course make any assumptions about the trustworthiness of these physiological faculties when our problem is to combat extreme doubt. We have no assurance that we do not err in some particular way in writing or reading, nor any guarantee, when we close a book or turn our eyes away from it for a moment, that a change is not wrought in the printed symbols as a result of some mysterious influence. In any case, we may completely disregard the support that writing gives to memory; theoretically it is of no help at all.

It is therefore a necessary presupposition of deduction, and ultimately of every simple analytic judgment, that our consciousness be able to retain the ideas needed for the derivation process at least as long as the process itself lasts. This capacity of consciousness we call *memory*.

Descartes, the originator of the notion of methodical doubt, had already called attention to this point. His aim, as we know, was to found his philosophy on fundamental truths that *intuitively* are of absolute certainty. But such truths do not comprise all that is fully certain. Rather, "... there are a great many things that, without being evident by themselves, nevertheless bear the character of certainty provided that they are deduced from true and unchallenged principles by a *continuous and uninterrupted movement of thought* and with a distinct intuition of each thing ..." [13]; thus, he continues, "deduction ... in one way or another borrows all of its certainty from *memory*" (all emphasis Schlick's). It is worth noting that Descartes was not at all disturbed by this finding; he trusted memory without question, and saw nothing problematic in the fact that memory must play a part in obtaining any knowledge that is certain. Only in passing did he remark that we can reduce the influence of memory to a minimum by frequent repetition of the chain of inferences. We add that the brief comments Locke devoted to our problem are entirely inadequate [14].

---

13 DESCARTES, Règles pour la direction de l'esprit, Commentary on the third rule.

14 An Essay Concerning Human Understanding, Book IV, Chapter I, § 9.

Recent discussions of the matter, it seems to me, have not advanced the question in any essential. This is true regardless of whether it is assumed, with Meinong, that judgments grounded upon memory are to be ascribed a special kind of immediate self-evidence which, to be sure, is only the "self-evidence of a presumption" [15]; or whether, as Volkelt maintains, there is no difference between the certainty of recollection and the *cogito-ergo-sum* certainty of consciousness. The latter says: "For me the certainty of *having experienced* this or that content of consciousness has exactly the same immediacy and indubitability, the same self-evidence, as the certainty of *just now experiencing* a particular content of consciousness [16]." Here we find the Cartesian delusion we have already had occasion to point out (§ 12 above). The existence of a present content of consciousness does not become *certain* to us through self-evidence; it is a *fact*. It makes no sense to apply the terms 'certain' and 'uncertain' to a fact; a fact simply *is*. That I *believe* I have had particular experiences is likewise simply a fact. But the *question* is whether these experiences were indeed facts, and of this, it seems to me, I can never be certain.

One person who has faced the difficulty squarely is Störring. In his search for an answer, he points out that certainty of recall may vary widely in degree, and that in the cases in question it is the highest degree of certainty that is involved. This degree of certainty can be recognized objectively by the fact that what is recalled is verified at *every* check point, that every test yields a favorable result. He concludes: "Therefore, the principle of verification, however much we may resist acknowledging its claims, must be vigorously supported as the ultimate principle of certainty even in complex deductive reasoning [17]." Here it is openly admitted that we cannot avoid accepting the purely practical criterion of verification as the *last* resort, for there is no theoretical answer to the question of why this criterion could not deceive us.

The problem is also raised by E. Becher, who states that in the final analysis the reliability of memory cannot be demonstrated.

---

15 A. MEINONG, Zur erkenntnistheoretischen Würdigung des Gedächtnisses, Vierteljahrsschrift für wissenschaftliche Philosophie *10* (1886), p. 30.

16 J. VOLKELT, Die Quellen der menschlichen Gewißheit, Munich 1906, p. 16.

17 STÖRRING, Einführung in die Erkenntnistheorie, pp. 97 ff.

Like many other presuppositions of knowledge, it rests purely on
faith, "on the natural faith in common sense" [18].

It follows undoubtedly that the reliability of recall, at least for
certain small intervals of time, represents a necessary presupposition
without which our consciousness — even in the case of merely
analytic reasoning — cannot with certainty make the slightest step
forward.

We shall soon become acquainted with another necessary presupposition, still more general and more obvious. As a preliminary,
however, we resume discussion of the findings obtained thus far.

§ 17. The Unity of Consciousness

Is there, despite everything, a way out of doubt? Is there perhaps
some assurance that the presupposition we have acknowledged as
necessary is actually fulfilled? It would be vain to hope for any
"proof" of this; proofs would only offer new points for radical
skepticism to attack. No. The only thing that can help us is to present something that is exempt in advance from any doubt, that is,
a fact. If there is such a fact, then the skepticism that put us on its
track was not fruitless; it will have served to bring to light certain
basic data of consciousness whose immeasurable significance might
otherwise not have been correctly recognized and turned to account.

Now it appears that there actually is a fact on which we can
rely here. It is more primitive than any doubt, more primitive than
any thought. It lies at the base of all mental processes, it is directly
given, it is a presupposition always fulfilled in consciousness. It is
the plain, ordinary fact which we designate as the *unity of consciousness*.

What is to be understood by it cannot be expressed in a definition or description. We can only *hint*, by suitable phrases, at something that everyone finds present in his own consciousness. We are
accustomed to say — and this is only metaphorical — that whatever
I imagine or feel or sense is "in" my consciousness. The word 'in'
has only a figurative meaning; for it is certain that consciousness is
not a receptacle — nor is it indeed comparable to a receptacle, which

---

18 E. BECHER, Naturphilosophie, p. 108 (Kultur der Gegenwart, Part
III, Division 7, Volume I, 1914).

in itself always remains the same and which can be filled by ever changing "contents". The term *'consciousness'*, as well as the term *'soul'*, is reserved for the totality of "contents" or mental processes that at the time are joined into a unified whole. I apprehend all the ideas or feelings or acts that exist together and follow one another as belonging together, as forming together a *single* whole, an *"I"*. But this *"I"*, this consciousness, is not merely the sum of the individual ideas, not merely a bundle or collection of perceptions, as Hume supposed[19]. The mere being together of the perceptions is not enough to make them components or states of one and the same consciousness. Something more must be added, and this is precisely the *unity* of consciousness.

As we have said, it is impossible to describe more closely this something that needs to be added. Its presence is simply a fact. We can make this fact stand out more clearly if we try to imagine what a bundle of psychical data looks like where this unity is *missing*.

If I have a feeling or sensation at a certain point in time and someone else has a feeling or sensation at the same time[20] — say, I shake hands with a person and we simultaneously experience certain sensations of touch as our hands meet — there is then a co-existence or sum of mental data. These data, however, lack that connectedness which cannot be more closely described but can only be experienced. We express this lack by the judgment that these psychical processes belong not to the same consciousness but to different ones. Moreover, the continuity of a consciousness does not consist merely in an uninterrupted sequence of experiences; on the contrary, experiences must be united by a quite special kind of connection if they are to count as the experience of one and the same consciousness. To appreciate the truth of this remark we need only imagine the sensations that make up an unbroken sequence as being distributed among different individuals[21].

---

19 A Treatise of Human Nature, Book I, Part IV, Section VI.

20 Here we disregard the question as to whether it is at all possible to define a "same" point of time for different consciousnesses.

21 I am happy to say that these statements, as well as some of the developments that follow respecting the same problem, although independent in conception, agree with ideas expressed by H. CORNELIUS in his Einleitung in die Philosophie, 2nd edition, 1911, § 23.

The peculiar situation that exists in general regarding the continuity of consciousness can best be pictured in the following manner. Suppose an isolated sensation turns up for a short time — I deliberately do not say "in consciousness". Suppose it turns up and then disappears without leaving a trace. A new sensation then arises (the same or a different one, but which of these it is cannot be decided if we assume that both sensations are completely isolated), and after that one sensation follows another, either at intervals or immediately, but always in such a way that each new element makes its appearance as if the preceding ones had not been there. Now we ask: Would it make sense to say of these elements, which have merely the relationship of sequence to one another, that they belong to one and the same consciousness? Obviously, there is no basis or justification for anything of the sort, since these elements have nothing in common with each other. There is no real connection or relation between them. Instead, we would say that there are as many consciousnesses as there are elements we distinguish. Whenever a new element appeared, a new consciousness would begin, which would have nothing to do with the ones that preceded it and the ones that followed. What would be missing would be precisely the fact that constitutes the *unity* of consciousness.

We can go a step further. Up to now we have assumed that each of the individual elements of sensation or feeling has a certain duration and that during this interval we may speak of a *single* continuous consciousness. But we can think of each such sensation as broken down into sensations of shorter duration that succeed one another immediately, and these in turn into sensations of even shorter duration, and so on. What was true previously of the original sensation is now true of its parts: if there is no relation between them but that of mere temporal sequence, if each part is so much a thing by itself that it seems as if there are no neighbors preceding or following it, then we have no right to assert of these parts that they belong to *one* consciousness. The beginning and end of each such tiny interval of sensation will signify the appearance or disappearance of a new consciousness. Thus for even the briefest and most fleeting element of consciousness, if it can be said to be an element of consciousness at all, there must be a wholly unique connection or fusion of its momentary parts. A mere continuous sequence of such parts does not join them into that unity without which they cannot be counted as elements of the same consciousness.

Now all of this holds true even when one thinks of the process of temporal division as being continued further and further, and the duration of each part as continually shrinking; that is, it holds true even if the duration falls below any assignable limit. In other words, when we think of the successive momentary parts of a content of consciousness as separate, independent entities, we do not think of that content as the content of a *single* consciousness. Rather, we think of a consciousness coming into being and ceasing to exist at each instant — a consciousness that has nothing in common with and does not merge into the moments of consciousness that precede or follow it. But what then are we thinking of? A consciousness that is extinguished the instant it comes into being, a consciousness without duration? But this is something entirely different from what we usually call consciousness; indeed we ought not use the same name for it. What we are thinking of in this case is differentiated from consciousness precisely by the lack of "unity", by the absence of that characteristic continuity which, as real connectedness, is something altogether different from the continuum in the mathematical sense.

Thus we see that where the unity of consciousness is missing, the fact of consciousness itself is also absent. In short, where there is consciousness at all, there is also unity of consciousness[22].

And where there is unity of consciousness, the individual moments of consciousness then exist not for themselves but, as it were, for each other. That is, they cannot be considered independently of their neighbours. Torn from their interconnection with them, they would no longer be the same; the interconnection is of their *essence*. Every attempt to re-cognize this altogether peculiar connection of unity — to find in it again perhaps some other interconnection already familiar to us — fails under any and all circumstances. Even Hume erred on this point when he thought that he could reduce the unity of the self to the *causal* relation (together with the relation of similarity, which we can disregard here)[23]. In his view, when we imagine a human consciousness what we really picture is a system of different sensations or different existences that are linked to one

---

22 Wundt also remarks that a momentary consciousness would have to be called an "unconscious" one. See his System der Philosophie, 8th edition, Vol. II, 1907, p. 147.

23 Treatise of Human Nature, Book I, Part IV, Section VI.

another by the relation of cause and effect, and that reciprocally produce, destroy, influence and modify each other. According to our account, this in no way suffices to characterize the essence of the connectedness of consciousness. What is missing is precisely the most important thing of all. For the interconnections described here by Hume could exist just as well between the elements of *different* consciousnesses. The laws of nature could be such — indeed in a certain sense and to a certain degree they actually are such — that the states of consciousness of an individual are causally connected to those of one or of several other individuals and thus follow, produce, destroy or modify one another in a definite way. But this would not result in the different consciousnesses merging into one; on the contrary, each individual would possess a consciousness of his own. Thus it is not the continuous temporal succession or causal chain of the single elements that makes for their belonging to one and the same consciousness, but rather a quite specific interconnection, which must be accepted as an ultimate fact.

This indescribable interconnection contains within itself — and this is the important thing for us — what we designate as *memory*. The extending of each momentary content of consciousness beyond itself into the next moment, which binds these moments into a unity, is equivalent to just that retention and preservation contributed by memory in the form of immediate recall. In fact, as is quite commonly remarked, it is this very recall that holds together the widely separated experiences of an individual in such a way that they can be reckoned as part of a continuing consciousness and so provide a basis for the unity of the personality. This conception is unequivocally confirmed by familiar examples found in psychopathological observations[24]. Thus there are cases where one and the same physical individual is the seat (we use this expression for brevity's sake) of two or more personalities, entirely different from one another, that take turns, as it were, in inhabiting the same body. Someone in a pathological condition may in one state have an unpleasant character, be uneducated, unskilled, melancholy, and in another state good-natured, happy, educated and endowed with many skills. And while he is in one state, he has absolutely no recollection of having been in the other state, so that the two personalities that make up his being know nothing of one another. What we then

---

24 For example, see T. Ribot, Les Maladies de la personalité, 1901.

have is not one consciousness but several, and these are entirely separated from one another precisely because the bond of recollection between them is completely severed. Taine draws the happy comparison of the relationship between the consciousness of a caterpillar and that of a butterfly [25].

The connectedness that constitutes the unity of a consciousness may thus be called a connectedness of recall. If we do not fear a paradoxical expression, we may also say that the connection comes into being because memory enables us to experience temporally adjacent elements of consciousness not merely as succeeding one another but also as being simultaneous. This appears to be contradictory only if we fail to bear in mind that we are engaging in abstraction when we equate the "present" strictly with a *point in time*. For we must certainly ascribe *some* duration to the real present of consciousness [26].

We emphasize again that none of the foregoing statements represent actual explanations. They are not knowledge. They are only phrasings intended to draw our attention to what is peculiar about the fact of the unity of consciousness. The fact itself everyone experiences in himself. The finding that we now formulate is therefore to be thought of not as a *conclusion* inferred from the preceding considerations, but as a summary designation of that very same fact:

Wherever there is consciousness there is also unity of consciousness, and where there is unity of consciousness there is also memory. The total cessation of any capacity to recall would mean the cessation of consciousness itself, because the interconnectedness in which consciousness consists would have been dissolved.

Thus we see that the mere fact of consciousness by itself already provides a guarantee that the fundamental precondition of all thought — the dependable retention of an idea, the capability of memory — is to a certain degree fulfilled, since it is a precondition for consciousness itself. Despite the kaleidoscopic succession of ideas and the inexhaustible flow of ever new contents, consciousness, so long as it exists at all, possesses something that is unchangeable,

---

25 H. TAINE, Théorie de l'intelligence, 4th edition, Volume II, Appendix.

26 See too H. CORNELIUS, Einleitung in die Philosophie, 2nd edition, p. 231; F. SCHUMANN, Zeitschrift für Psychologie, Vol. 17, pp. 127 ff.; WILLIAM JAMES, Psychologie (translated into German by M. DÜRR), pp. 280 ff.

namely, its unity. This is why Kant was able to talk of a "pure original immutable consciousness" for which he introduced the name "transcendental apperception". It was also Kant who recognized, and even exaggerated, the unique significance of the unity of consciousness for the most basic questions about knowledge in all their profundity. In his involved way, he designated this fact as the "original synthetic unity of apperception", and the proposition that all intuitive manifolds fall under the conditions of this unity was for him the "supreme principle of all employment of the understanding" and served as the basis for the most important features of his theory of knowledge. Whether Kant was always right in the conclusions he drew with the aid of this principle we shall have occasion to discuss later. But the fact of the unity of consciousness — to which Kant assigned so important a place in his epistemology — will in my opinion have to occupy an even more dominant place at the very center of any metaphysics in the future[27].

The fact of consciousness itself thus guarantees to a certain degree (again in Kant's words) "that what we are thinking of is precisely the same as what we were thinking of a moment before". But only to a certain degree. That previous "moment" has only the duration of a "present", and if we cannot be guaranteed that ideas may be retained with assurance for appreciably longer time spans, then we seem to have helped very little. The continuity of consciousness can be maintained without its having to extend over such long stretches of time as are required to carry out a deduction. Consequently, extreme skepticism has apparently still not been deprived of every foothold. The following comments, however, do place its position very much in question.

First, it is possible for a person — through special preparations, frequent repetition, training, a certain adjustment of attention, or some other psychological means — to fill the momentary present with highly organized content and within this content to distinguish several ideas or somewhat complicated ideas. This is how it comes about that even relatively complex ideas, which serve to illustrate involved and difficult conceptual relationships, suddenly stand out in consciousness as clearly, say, as is needed to obtain a conclusion,

---

27 HANS CORNELIUS' book Transzendentale Systematik (Munich 1916) seeks to take the thought seriously, but misses its goal. It overshoots the mark in attempting to derive all possible knowledge, even the necessity of Euclidean geometry, from the unity of personal consciousness.

to carry out a deduction. Naturally there is no assurance that a particular analysis will be performed with full certainty by a particular person in this manner. But this is more than we can ask for. The real question is whether it is possible at all, whether it ever happens that deductions can be carried out with absolute certainty, whether any inference as such is ever safe from the threat of extreme doubt. That the correctness of one or another analysis is assured in the fashion described is something we experience as a fact. But there is no guarantee that we or someone else must experience that fact in the case of any particular analysis. We experience it in certain instances; indeed, we can even give empirically the approximate circumstances in which we are accustomed to experience it. And with this we might let the matter rest. For the unlimited power of skepticism is thereby breached.

But, second, we can still go a step further. If the unity of consciousness guarantees us that ideas are sufficiently constant throughout the duration of a present, then under certain circumstances (such as those we characterize psychologically as states of extreme concentration) it can erect on this foundation a certainty extending over longer intervals of time. This it is able to do (we can describe the process only metaphorically) by carrying over from moment to moment the consciousness of this constancy, integrating the successive present-differentials, as it were, so that at the end of a brief analysis we experience directly how its conclusion is joined, without any break, to its beginning.

Of course, careful introspection informs us that only conscious processes of extremely short duration are under consideration here. When a deduction is a bit more complicated, we immediately take refuge in repetition and verification so as to be certain that we are correct.

And then another thing is true here also. Although we have certainty free of doubt — indeed *prior* to any doubt — wherever the facts of consciousness described above are experienced, there is no guarantee that we *must* experience these facts under any given set of circumstances in connection with any particular problem. Such a guarantee is not contained in the fact of the unity of consciousness. The consciousness of an animal, of an idiot, fails when confronted with the simplest analyses, ones which a normal adult executes with confident ease; and the average man is denied insights grasped clearly by a Newton or a Gauss.

Here obviously we have come upon certain roots of intellectual endowment. We shall surely not err if we perceive differences in the intelligence of different consciousnesses as consisting, among other things, in a varying capacity to grasp their own contents as a more or less compact unity. The active mind of a clear-sighted thinker brings together complicated contents of consciousness into a stable unity. But everything escapes the mental view of one who is untalented; his ideas flicker unsteadily back and forth, and we say that he lacks the capacity for concentrated attention. His consciousness may possess unity just as does that of the cleverest person. Yet it is not a solidified unity; it resembles a collection of tatters that hang together by the thinnest of threads. And if man has an advantage over other animals because he possesses the faculty of "thought", this advantage would certainly seem to inhere in the fact that in the case of an animal the data of consciousness are more loosely associated. The less highly-organized an animal is, the more it lives, presumably, from moment to moment; its experiences follow consecutively, but they are not bound together as intimately as in the case of man. For the latter, the manifold of the most varied data of consciousness coalesces into a unity that becomes ever more comprehensive the more the individual possesses a true "personality" — a unity, indeed, that embraces virtually the entire span of his existence.

It is a great temptation to develop such thoughts further and to let them carry us into the domain of metaphysics. As it is, attempts have already appeared here and there to use the fact of the unity of consciousness as a bridge to the metaphysical[28]. But at this point we must turn back to the questions that first directed our attention to this fact about consciousness.

In general then we possess the capability of holding on to our ideas, throughout a minimal period of time, as firmly as is required to carry out analytic inference with full confidence. The unity of our consciousness guarantees that. But there is another fundamental condition that must be fulfilled — a condition that is indeed the prerequisite for that capability. We must be equipped with the ability

---

28 For example, H. Driesch (Philosophie des Organischen, II, pp. 380 ff.) regards "the unity of subjective experience in general and memory in particular" as one of the "three windows" through which we gaze into the absolute.

to determine whether ideas are the same or different. Otherwise, how could we know whether our ideas change or remain the same, how could we keep different idea separate? Without this ability, inference would be impossible.

This prerequisite is so fundamental that, while it was always assumed, it was never made explicit until Locke appeared on the scene. He correctly perceived its significance when he remarked that without it there could be no knowledge, no inference, no definite thoughts at all[29].

Now what is the situation with respect to this precondition? Does consciousness with its unity give us some assurance perhaps that the precondition is invariably met? No inferences of any sort are necessary to answer this question; we need only pay attention to certain facts that are always given together with consciousness.

Locke said that the prime capacity of the mind is to *perceive* its ideas, and in so far as it does so, to know of each one what it is and thereby also to perceive the differences by virtue of which one idea is not another[30]. But this mode of expression is most unfortunate and misleading; being still in use, it still leads to the gravest of errors. For it sets mind over against ideas as if mind were a receptacle into which ideas go to be accepted, "perceived" and compared with one another. It might then happen that different ideas, coming into consciousness, would be regarded as the same, or, conversely, that the same ideas would be held to be different. In order for correct thinking to be possible at all, it would thus be necessary to ascribe a special faculty to consciousness, the capacity not to be deceived in this process. The question would then arise whether this capacity is always present and to what extent we might rely on it.

But this of course is not the case. Consciousness is not related to ideas as the stomach is related to the food that it takes in and digests. Indeed, it is ideas that constitute consciousness. They need not first be perceived by some special act; their very existence as data of consciousness is identical with their being perceived. For them, *esse* is the same as *percipi*. Hence there is no need to postulate a specific capacity to perceive the contents of consciousness, and therefore no need for a special guarantee against being deceived in con-

---

29 Essay Concerning the Human Understanding, Book 4, Chapter 1, § 4.

30 *Loc. cit.*

9*

nection with such perception. There is nothing in my consciousness of which I am not aware; the two expressions say the same thing in different words. The data of consciousness are not *perceived* as different; they *are* different (see below, § 20).

But it will be said that I might be aware of different ideas and still not be aware of their difference. These two situations of course are not the same. Yet it is precisely the awareness of difference that is required, obviously, for all thinking and inference. Thus again doubts may arise as to whether the most necessary condition for thinking is ever fulfilled in our mind with any certainty.

But these doubts too shatter against the fact of the unity of consciousness. This unity shows us that although a difference of experiences and an experience of difference are not one and the same, yet within the mind they are so closely related that one cannot exist without the other.

For suppose two different contents of consciousness existed at the same time — say, an odor and a sound, or a green color and a red color in the visual field. Suppose also that the capacity to establish the difference was lacking, that is, the difference was not experienced as a fact and the experiencing individual lacked any datum that he or she could designate by the judgment "These phenomena are different" or "These phenomena are the same". The two experiences would then exist side by side without any relation or comparison. Each would exist only for itself, as if the other were not there at all. The two would, so to speak, know nothing of each other; no one would be able to say whether they were the same or different. In short, it would be just as if they belonged to *different* consciousnesses. Nothing would join them together; they would no longer form a unity, and we would have no basis and no right to declare that they were contents of the same consciousness. If differ*ing* contents belong to *one* consciousness, then by the same token they are differ*entiated*. We may also put it this way: differentiation takes place by virtue of the fact that different things are brought into relation with one another. And the unity of consciousness is a kind of being-related-to-one-another. Thus if different things are joined in the unity of the same consciousness, this means that they are differentiated. A similar conclusion holds with regard to equating things that are the same. Here again it is simply a matter of pointing to certain facts experienced in the very fact of the unity of consciousness.

Words intended to express this pointing-out must always appear imperfect and unsatisfactory.

As one can see, the set of facts involved here is quite similar to the one discussed earlier. At that time, we considered the unity of consciousness in so far as it comprises the succession of contents; here we have had in view the juxtaposition or coexistence of contents that is contained within that unity.

But the two facts appear together. We distinguish not merely ideas that are simultaneous but also those that follow one another directly, that take over from one another. This is the basis for the consciousness of *change*. It is a fact that our mind constantly experiences change or, what is the same thing, happenings, for a happening is a change. In experiencing a happening, we are directly aware of the difference between the state that follows and the state that precedes it. Here again it is not necessary to assume that the mind has a special capacity to perceive change, a capacity that might some day, perhaps, be lost and without which the mind could still exist. On the contrary, what we have once more is a property that belongs inseparably to the being of consciousness itself. After our earlier remarks, we need not dwell further on how this fact is derived from the unity of consciousness.

We stress, but only for the purposes of confirmation and elaboration, that precisely at this point one can go further — and some have gone further. That is, not only is every change, *when* one takes place in our mind, experienced *eo ipso* as a special fact of consciousness; it may also be said, perhaps, that change itself is a condition *sine qua non* of consciousness. For not only does no alteration take place in the mind without our being conscious of it; conversely, there would be no consciousness if no alteration were to take place. It would seem to be impossible for a sensation or a feeling to be constantly present without change during our entire existence. Hobbes long ago affirmed that a sensation extended without limit would cease to be sensed at all and thus would not exist in consciousness. *"Sentire semper idem et no sentire ad idem recidunt."* For example, we do not sense the bad air of a closed room until we step out into the open, although the possibility exists of comparing our sensations with the memory images of pleasanter odors. This possibility of contrast would be absent altogether if we assume that a certain content is continuously present in our consciousness. We could not imagine its nonexistence; hence we would not be able to compare its presence with the idea of its absence and differentiate accordingly. It would remain unnoticed; it would not be a content of consciousness. Thus every datum of consciousness seems to be something relative: it has existence only in relation to other data. This particular observation is of the greatest importance for any eventual metaphysics; its significance was first pointed out by Alexander Bain, who labeled it the "law of relativity". John Stuart Mill likewise recognized this law as certainly correct[31]. The observation may also be formulated as follows: nothing that persists unvaryingly is ever a content of consciousness. A consciousness in which nothing happened would be a consciousness without experience, and thus no consciousness. Consciousness presupposes change, a transition from one thing to another; consciousness (mind, soul) is a *process*.

Modern psychology is in full agreement with these views, and has fully adopted the "actuality theory" of mind. Here Wundt, in particular, performed a very great service by emphasizing again and again that mental contents are not things or substances, but processes or happenings.

To sum up, our consideration of the fact of the unity of consciousness has resulted in eliminating the misgivings evoked by the fleeting character of ideas and images. We have learned that this evanescent quality does not prevent the mind from carrying out simple acts of analytic inference. We thereby kept extreme skepticism from entering into the ultimate psychological fundaments of all thought, where it might have wrought great damage. Let us repeat once more that what is involved in this skepticism are not doubts about the correctness of the logical rules of analysis, as laid down for example in the syllogistic. Such doubts would constitute merely a misunderstanding. Rather, what we are faced with is a mistrust directed at our mental capacities. Because all conscious processes are fleeting in character, the question is raised whether with their aid it is in principle possible to represent strict logical relationships without error. Thus the problem turns on the relationship between mental processes and logical structures.

Besides the fleeting quality and temporal instability of mental structures, it is also their haziness — the indistinct boundaries between one idea and another — that can give rise to doubt. Further

---

31 JOHN STUART MILL, Logic, Book I, Chapter V, § 5, note.

effort must be devoted to this matter, if we are not only to convince ourselves that the human being is capable of faultless analysis but also to understand how variegated mental processes become proper surrogates for logical structures, how that which is imperfect completely fulfills the function of the perfect.

§ 18. The Relationship of the Psychological to the Logical

To carry our inquiry further, we must take up again a problem that has impelled the thinking of a whole series of contemporary philosophers to enter upon strange paths. The insight that concepts and other logical structures are not mental realities has led these philosophers to ascribe a special kind of "being" to them, and like Plato to counterpose the realm of real being and the realm of ideal being as two quite different and separate spheres. In acts of thought, however, the two realms must somehow come into connection or communication with one another; and thus the problem consists precisely in giving an account of how this is possible. The metaphorical, Platonist solution, according to which ideas are simply "intuited" by our mind, no longer satisfies us today.

It is an old truth that ideas or images are not the same as concepts, that mental activities are not the same as logical relationships. But only recently was this truth elaborated with full clarity — in the course of a feud against "psychologism", which appeared to look upon all logical entities, such as concepts and judgments, as psychological structures. I say "appeared", since psychologism was perhaps guilty more of a loose mode of expression, of a tendency to push certain questions aside, than of a complete failure to understand the true state of affairs. For example, that the image in my consciousness when I think of an ellipse is not really this ellipse, is not itself elliptical, was hardly disputed by the exponents of psychologism. Since most of them defended the view that concepts are products of *abstraction,* they must surely have had some inkling of the fact that a concept is not a reality of consciousness but, as it were, an unreal fiction. It must be clear to everyone that concepts do not possess existence as actual ideas. For example, as psychologists very well know, it is impossible to imagine a line, a stroke without breadth. Often the reasoning in support of psychologism has gone more or less as follows: "Concepts and judgments are products or structures of thought, thought is a mental process, therefore logic is the theory of thought and whatever pertains to logic belongs to the domain of psychology." But this is a lapse in thinking occasioned by the ambiguity of the expression "thought-structure". The term sometimes refers to a concept, sometimes to the ideas designated by that concept; or, following Twardowski, sometimes to the *content* of the idea, sometimes to the *object* of the idea (where by content is understood the process of consciousness that constitutes the idea, and by the object that which is designated by the idea, whether something real or simply a concept) [32].

This psychologistic lapse, however, seems to me to be no more dangerous for the foundations of philosophy than the explicit and carefully thought out doctrine that logical structures make up a sphere of their own, a domain of ideas that "exists" independently of the real world. This doctrine is not false at all provided we take the words 'exist' and 'independent' in a proper sense. But there is scarcely a Platonizing philosopher — even among those who do not wish to apply the word 'exist' to concepts [33] — who has not been led by the doctrine to entertain views that make it quite impossible to understand the true relationship of the two realms. These views have the same consequence in this respect as the Platonic myth, which enthrones the Ideas as real beings in some *hyperouránios tópos,* eternally remote from our world and inaccessible to any of our senses. Plato himself could not solve the problem; we recall his fruitless attempts to get clear about the way in which real things "participate" in the Ideas. Nor have his modern followers been able to advance one step beyond him. How then are ideas related to concepts, or mental acts of judgment to the propositions of logic? The answer we invariably receive (almost with disgust, in view of the considerations set forth in § 12 above) is that the latter are "grasped" in the former. But this locution is meaningless; and it cannot be made more palatable by using some such term as 'ideation' to designate the "act of grasping" ideal structures by means of real mental acts.

---

32 K. TWARDOWSKI, Zur Lehre vom Inhalt und Gegenstand der Vorstellungen, Vienna 1894.

33 One of them, for example, is BERTRAND RUSSELL, who prefers to say of concepts that "they subsist or have being" rather than that "they exist" (The Problems of Philosophy, p. 156).

These forms of expression offer *no* solution. But it makes matters even worse if, instead of speaking of grasping, we speak of *experiencing;* for this amounts to a *false* solution of the problem. Experiences are realities. If we use the word 'experience' in its usual sense — the only sense in which we have used it here — then 'something is experienced' means the same as 'something is a content of consciousness'. Experiencing is not an act. It is not an activity of consciousness that is somehow directed to an object and that seeks to bring it to consciousness, to make it its own, just as we pick up a coin and make it our own by the act of grasping it with our hands. When I say "I experience this", I am only using a verbally different expression for the judgment "This is a datum of my consciousness". Thus experience cannot be distinguished from experiencing and from what is experienced; it is all one and the same. For instance, a sensation of blue is an absolutely simple existent; one cannot separate within it the sensing of the blue and the blue that is sensed. This is one of the fundamental facts of descriptive psychology, on which there is no need to dwell and which is acknowledged even by psychologists who proceed in a more speculative fashion[34]. In *this* sense, however, concepts are not *experienced;* they are not real things at all, and are never present as components of an experience. (Also see below, § 20.)

Idealists of the Platonist tendency also understand this point, fundamentally. They resort to the same expedient to which philosophers have not infrequently had recourse in similar cases: if a proposition that is close to their hearts is not correct when words are taken in their usual sense, they construct a new sense for these words. In this way, of course, it is always possible to maintain the old proposition; but now it means something different. In the present instance, what happens is the following. Since concepts must somehow enter into a relation with real consciousness, with real experience, one simply says: if concepts are not experiences in the sense indicated above, then there is another sense of the word 'experience' and in this sense concepts are experienced.

Thus Edmund Husserl writes: "But when we speak of grasping, experiencing, being aware of, in connection with this ideal being, we do so in an entirely different sense than in connection with an

---

34 See, for instance, P. NATORP, Allgemeine Psychologie, Volume I, Tübingen 1912, Chapter 3, § 3 and § 4.

empirical or individually separate being[35]." Just what sort of "experiencing" the experiencing of an ideal being is — it is certainly not experiencing in the only sense of the word with which we are acquainted — one cannot properly ask. It is an ultimate; it is simply — experienced. At most, says Husserl, one can designate it with new names, and this he is not loath to do: thus, we experience ideal being "in an act of ideation grounded in intuition"[36]. He points out that every content of consciousness, as Brentano had already asserted, bears an "intentional" character, that is, it is "directed to an object" (whether this really holds for *every* content of consciousness we need not inquire into at this point). In perceiving, *something* is perceived; in imagining, *something* is imagined; in judging, *something* is judged. We cannot love without our love being addressed to a loved object; we cannot think without an object being there of which we are thinking. The objects to which our acts of consciousness are directed are not in our sense of the word experienced: the object that is perceived, judged, loved, is not really present in consciousness. But the being-directed-toward-an-object, the "intention", is indeed directly experienced. And this is how it is with concepts too. When I think of a triangle, although the triangle itself is not in my consciousness, the intention toward it is.

This doctrine, as we know, contains an element that is factually correct. We noted above (§ 5) that what actually exist are not concepts but conceptual functions, and this was the same as saying that what we experience are not concepts but the intention toward concepts — or, as we may also put it, that concepts are intentional, not real, contents of consciousness. The trouble is that none of this contributes in the least to the solution of our problem; it merely gives it a new name. For now we must ask: Is not the intentional experience as a real mental entity just as widely and unbridgeably separated from the ideal structures as ideas or images, say, are separated from concepts? How do I know to what my acts are directed? Am I not once again engulfed here in psychology with no prospect of reaching the domain of concepts and logic, the only domain ruled by the clarity and rigor whose possibility was so much our concern?

---

35 Logische Untersuchungen, Volume I, p. 128.
36 *Ibid.*, p. 129.

The answer we receive is: "Not by any means!" If we go about the matter properly, we find ourselves neither in logic nor in psychology, but in a new science more fundamental than both: phenomenology [37].

The basic idea of this science depends on the distinction between empirical intuition, through which real existing things are given us (as in perception, for instance), and a pure "Wesensschau" ("intuiting of essences"), through which we "grasp" the essence of the intuited objects (thus also of concepts) quite independently of their actual or possible being.

Examined in the light of day, however, this is nothing more than a strict rendering of the all too familiar distinction between essence and existence, between *what* something is and *that* it is. We can make judgments about the essence or being-so of objects — hence also about pure concepts — and construct whole sciences out of such judgments without introducing any judgments about real existence, about facts. Who would dare deny it? But this does not bring our problem one whit closer to solution; in fact, it is not even touched. What is more, the very point we are questioning is always assumed to have been already disposed of. We ask: How in general can non-real objects — concepts or judgments — be "given" to us when all that we are acquainted with as given are the real contents of consciousness [38]? Logical structures are not real; they

---

37 At this point the first edition of the present book contained a critical discussion of the phenomenological method. This is now omitted for the reason given in the preface. I mention this lest it appear that Husserl's very sharp comments directed at me in the preface to the second edition of Volume Two of his Logische Untersuchungen have deterred me from presenting a satisfactorily clear characterization of the phenomenological method. Husserl accused me of having read his book too hastily, but in the very same sentence misquoted my own. Further, he complained that I had falsely assumed that "ideation" was not intended as a real mental act. This was a misunderstanding. It arose because it seemed to me that after carrying through the *"Einklammerung"* ("bracketing") or *"Ausschaltung"* of all that is real, as is required for the phenomenological *"Schau"* ("intuition"), what would remain would not be a real process of consciousness but only a mere abstraction. The clearing up of this misunderstanding leaves untouched the arguments against phenomenology set forth in the text.

38 One can also use the expression 'the given' in an entirely different sense. This is what PAUL L. LINKE, for example, does in his Die phäno-

are not given as parts or aspects of mental processes. They are invented by us. All of our statements about them, however, are real acts of judgment; all that we know of them *must* be somehow contained in real mental processes, otherwise we would not be aware of them, we would not be conscious of them. Either the guarantee for the correctness of our logical analyses must lie in real facts of consciousness, or we have no guarantee at all.

Our mental structures, however, correspond only imperfectly to the perfect concepts they are intended to represent. On the one side there is imprecision, on the other absolute accuracy. How can the one come to be known to us through the other? The idealist speaks here of "grasping" one by means of the other, and thus evades the problem. He thinks of the process of grasping as already having been determined by what is grasped. The latter is regarded as something at hand, to which real thought processes can direct themselves; logical relations appear as enduring norms, which serve

---

menale Sphäre und das reale Bewußtsein (Halle 1912). By the "given" he understands "intentional objects" — for instance, that which is given in perception as the thing perceived, in memory as the thing remembered. What he has in mind is the *object* of an idea or image, regardless of whether a real object or only an imaginary one corresponds to the something perceived or remembered. So understood (*op. cit.*, p. 5), "no given as such is *eo ipso* real"; it is not real "in the sense of a real component part of our consciousness". On the other hand, we designate as the *given* only the actualities of consciousness, that is, experiences or real occurrences. In doing this, we find ourselves in the best agreement with ordinary usage, which, however, is not an especially happy circumstance inasmuch as the word 'given' suggests a donor and a receiver and thus readily evokes undesirable associations. Still these can be fended off by a suitable warning to which we herewith give utterance. Linke, moreover, designates the realm of the "given" (in his sense) as the "phenomenal sphere" and contrasts it with the sphere of reality: "These are two completely separated domains; there is no essential connection between them." (*Op. cit.*, pp. 29 ff.) He does not solve the problem of their mutual relationship, with which we are concerned here; he says only that the phenomenal sphere is not suspended in midair, since, to the given, mental processes correspond as real correlates. That the former cannot exist without the latter, we already know *on the basis of experience* (§ 6). The word 'given' is used in this same sense by R. HERBERTZ (Prolegomena zu einer realistischen Logik, p. 174) who, in a highly original turn of phrase, adds that all "given", all intentional objects (hence even mathematical objects, centaurs, nymphs), are real.

to regulate these processes. In reality, however, the situation is just the reverse. It simply won't do to define representing processes by means of the ideal objects to which they are directed; realities can be defined only by realities. The conscious processes in which we carry out logical analyses must be understood wholly in terms of their immanent psychological regularities without regard to that which they signify. How these processes can *nonetheless* fulfill their meaning-function is precisely our problem.

Naturally many a philosopher encounters situations where he cannot evade our problem. In such circumstances, he resorts to an appeal to *self-evidence,* which tells us that what holds of concepts and judgments is exactly what we, in our mental acts of thought, say about them. If, in rejoinder, we call attention to the fact that once again everything is being built on the insecure basis of a sub-jective psychical datum which lacks conceptual sharpness and may deceive us, he attempts to save himself by distinguishing between real and ideal self-evidence[39]. It is only the latter that is really in-volved. But this ruins everything again: How do we *know* anything about an ideal self-evidence or about its possibility? Its existence must make itself known *realiter* in some way in our consciousness, through a feeling of self-evidence or some other phase of mental reality. And then all the earlier objections are revived, and every-thing remains as it was before: the problem pursues us no matter how often we seek to elude it by some twist or turn.

We prefer to face the problem directly and calmly, prepared to affirm from the outset that there is actually nothing "there" except the real processes of consciousness, that it is through these pro-cesses that concepts are first fashioned. And we ask: How is it pos-sible for real psychological relations to furnish precisely what purely logical relations provide unless the two *are* the same, unless they possess equal sharpness?

The answer can be clarified with the aid of an analogy some-times employed to illustrate the difference between a mental process and a logical structure, but which is also useful in revealing the true relationship between them. Imagine a thinking-machine (as Jevons conceived it) or, something more familiar and practical, a calculat-ing machine[40]. Like the human brain, a machine of this sort is a

---

39　Husserl, Logische Untersuchungen, Volume I, pp. 50, 51.

40　This example is used by Husserl, *op. cit.,* Volume I, §§ 50, 51.

physical apparatus whose operations are of course fully determined by physical laws, not by the laws of arithmetic. A lifeless mechanism has no awareness of those rules; the multiplication table is not a component part of the machine. Yet the rules of arithmetic achieve due expression through the machinery, and do so with absolute, not approximate, accuracy. If I ask the machine for the product of 13 times 14, it comes up with the answer 182 and not, say, 182.000001. An absolutely exact result is obtained — without recourse to magic — even though physical machinery cannot possibly produce complete exactness in *every* sense. And this not because the laws of nature that govern the operations of the machine hold only roughly or approximately, but because of what is in the fullest sense of the term the infinite interlacing of all that happens. It is for this reason that no one process is exactly like any other. For example, the movement of a small wheel belonging to our machine depends not only on the operation of the lever but also, if to an imperceptible extent, on the position of the moon. In the case of a machine (assuming that it does not break down altogether), the inexactness that attends all physical constructions is expressed not in a false result, not in the appearance of wrong figures, but simply in the fact that, for example, the figures are not perfectly aligned, that the interval between them varies, that some of the tiny black particles of which the characters are composed become detached, or the like. From a physical standpoint, the calculating process of the machine indeed lacks precision. This, however, does not affect the result. What matters is not the alignment of the digits or their physical aspect, but the fact that these digits and no others show up in our field of vision.

It may be said perhaps that this example has not been very helpful, that it fails to touch the relationship we seek to elucidate. That the data supplied by the machine, despite small differences, still *signify* the same result may be due to the operations of the intellect, which gives meaning to the numerical signs and treats as the same those signs that differ only slightly. It is the intellect that first, on the model of the intuited concepts, introduces exactness and is thus able to abstract from and disregard accidental variations in the individual appearances.

It is of course correct that interpretation takes place first in the mind of an understanding observer. But what is decisive for us is that the necessary and sufficient foundation for the interpretation is already present in the physical structure, that under the given circumstances the interpretation is completely determined and any other one is excluded. Once we get clear about the means we use to effect this determination in a manner that is proof against objection, our problem is solved.

The situation is this. The sequence of integers is by its nature (i. e., by its definition) discontinuous, or discrete. Two integers always differ from each other by one or by some whole multiple of one, and never by an infinitely small amount. However all natural processes, as perceived by us, are continuous. One state of a physical system (unless quantum theory forces us to revise our conception) cannot pass immediately into a finitely different state, but must go through infinitely many intervening states each of which differs from its neighbors by an arbitrarily small amount. It was this point that Leibniz expressed in his *"loi de continuité"*. Hence physical processes are directly suited to the measurement of continuous magnitudes. For example, the length of a time interval is given by the position of the hands of a clock — always, of course, only within a certain approximation, since it is impossible to determine the position of the hands with absolute precision. But a calculating machine does not measure a continuum; it counts off discrete units. To be sure, the movements of the wheels and levers through which combinations of numbers are transformed into one another — for instance, 181 into 182 — are continuous processes; but the initial and final states are discrete. Although each of them is subject to the small variations noted above and could be confused with its immediate neighbors, the two are so separated from one another that they can be unfailingly distinguished.

It is no exaggeration to speak here of infallibility. That we are able in general to determine differences is a simple matter of fact (see above). Hence there must also be a threshold above which it is quite impossible to be mistaken about differences. This lower limit would still exist even if there were no instances in which we could specify it; and there are instances in which we can state with certainty that we have passed beyond it. I cannot give the distance between my home and the university (several kilometers) with absolute accuracy, but I can state with full assurance that it is more than ten centimeters. The length of a pendulum rod (one meter, say) cannot be determined with absolute exactness; indeed, it does not make sense to ask for its absolutely precise length. Yet we can say with full certainty that it is not one hundred meters and it is not one millimeter. In practice, the situation with respect to the threshold of distinguishability is even more favorable; very small differences suffice to guarantee that the threshold has been exceeded. Consider how slightly certain letters, say *h* and *k*, or certain numerals, say 1 and 7, differ from one another. Nevertheless we hardly need fear confusing them; and if the danger did exist, there is nothing to prevent us from increasing the difference in form or color of these letters and numerals to *any desired amount* and thus going still further beyond the threshold.

Even the most complicated configurations, however, can always be transformed continuously into one another by means of intermediate forms. Hence it is always possible with the aid of the continuous to imitate, as it were, any and all discontinuities. This is just as certainly possible as it is true that there are countable things in nature. For countability presupposes discreteness; yet in nature, strictly speaking, everything is in all probability continuous. I cannot say definitely at any mathematical point: Here is the boundary of the earth, or there is the surface of the moon. Yet we can distinguish earth and moon from one another with the fullest conceptual rigor. Discreteness of physical structure can be obtained even within a very narrow compass, as is shown by the case of the calculating machine. Another example is the roulette wheel: the spinning ball must come to rest each time on some specific number and there can never be any doubt as to which number it is. Within each numbered space, of course, the ball may occupy any of an infinite set of closely neighboring positions; but it always ends up in one or another compartment defined by the partitions that separate it from its neighbors, and to this compartment just one particular integer is assigned.

Once we understand how continuous processes can perform the function of the discontinuous, our problem is stripped of its difficulty. For the only difference between concepts and ideas, between logical structures and mental processes, with which we are concerned is precisely that between the discrete and the continuous. Concepts are sharply defined in so far as they are discrete or separate from other concepts; reality is hazily defined because, being continuous, it does not admit of absolutely sharp boundaries.

The thesis that continuous structures can assume the function of discrete ones may seem somewhat paradoxical. But this is only because at first sight it appears to contradict the intuitions on which we usually base the application of probability calculations to observations of nature. This application rests partly on what in a sense is an unlimited use of the notion of continuity. The laws of the distribution of errors furnish the probability, relative to certain observations, that the length of a pendulum rod, say, lies between 99 and 100 centimeters. But suppose I ask how great is the probability of an error, in all observations, of such magnitude that the actual length is 50 meters. Applying the laws of errors quite mechanically, I obtain as the value of that probability an extremely small fraction, but still not zero. Yet it is absolutely impossible physically to have erred in measurement to that extent, just as it is impossible in reality for the distance from my house to the university to be no more than 10 centimeters. In the case of errors of such size, the presuppositions underlying the validity of probability calculations can no longer be regarded as fulfilled. In *this* very broad sense, continuity does not extend arbitrarily far. A correct understanding of this fact, however, is very much hindered because in principle it is impossible to specify a point up to which these presuppositions are fulfilled. Consequently, the application of probability considerations to nature easily gives rise to the notion that discreteness, and with it determinateness (for we take discreteness to signify an absolutely determinate differentiation of structures), does not in any strict sense exist for us at all. But, as we have seen, this is not correct. Discreteness in our sense is possible within continuity. To be sure, the boundaries of differentiation are never determined with total precision; but it does not follow from this that the differentiation itself can never be made with full exactness.

Thus the problem of the relationship between mental processes and logical relations appears as a special case of the problem of generating discrete or countable structures by means of continuous ones. To demonstrate that this latter is possible is at the same time to solve our problem. The importance of this possibility has already been pointed out by thoughtful mathematicians. For example, Henri Poincaré has said: "In *analysis situs* inexact experiments may nonetheless suffice as grounds for a rigorous theorem. Thus if one sees that space cannot have less than two dimensions, nor four or more than four, then one is certain that it has precisely three, for it can-

not have two and a half or three and a half[41]." This holds even for
the most ordinary examples. It is absolutely correct to say that
people have two ears or two legs; it is not simply inaccurate but
utterly nonsensical to say that a person has 2.002 ears. Circumstances exist in which exact truths can be established by means of inexact experiences; this principle contains the full solution to our
riddle.

We may compare our brain to a calculating machine or a Jevons
thinking machine. Continuous brain processes lead to certain terminal states, just as these machines yield certain numbers or letters.
Parallel with the continuous stream of consciousness, certain discrete
states appear which, although joined by gradual transitions, do not
merge inseparably with one another. Certainly these states are experienced as different, and nothing more is required in order for
an exact logic of thinking to be possible. What we may too easily
fail to notice is that the condition for founding all logic is met once
it becomes possible to set up discrete structures. It is on this alone
that the possibility of conceptualization depends; strict differentiation is the only essential. If we refer to what was said above
(Part I, § 7), we realize that so far as the logical relationships of
concepts are concerned the intuitive content they designate is quite
irrelevant; all that matters is merely that they denote something
distinguishable. Concepts are determined logically only by their
being demarcated, by their being differentiated from other concepts,
and not by the intuitive objects with which they are correlated.

As a matter of fact, the relations beween discrete countable
magnitudes, even though they are realities, possess the same sharpness and rigor as the relationships of concepts. It is only the former
that we encounter in our consciousness; relationships of concepts
are nowhere, and it is correct to say that they do not "exist" at all.
We talk as if they existed, but this is only to simplify discourse. An
"ideal" being is precisely one that is not actual.

Idealistic logicians always point to the fact that psychological
laws are vague, and they conclude from this that absolute rigor is
to be found only in the sphere of the ideal, not in that of mental
reality. But here they commit a *petitio principii*. For those who hold
a psychologistic view have to concede that mental processes *in gen-*

---

41 H. POINCARÉ, Der Wert der Wissenschaft, 2nd edition, 1910, p. 50.
(French original, La Valeur de la Science, 1927, p. 68.)

eral are blurred and continuous. Nevertheless they claim that fully exact mental processes do occur, which then are the bearers of the logical. Moreover, it is certainly incorrect to say that all mental law-like regularities are vague or indeterminate; if the principle of causality is generally valid, then the events taking place in nature and mind conform to laws that no more admit of exceptions than the rules of formal logic. It is not that the laws are inexact, but that our knowledge of them is imperfect. There is a vast difference here. But we have just seen that despite our inadequate knowledge of the laws that govern mental events in detail, we do have exact knowledge of certain regularities. For example, without being able to specify its shape with absolute precision, I can still say with total certainty that the ring on my finger has three dimensions and is an instance of what the mathematicians call a "simply connected" spatial structure.

Intuitive ideas, once they are distinguished from one another with absolute certainty, can perform fully the task of concepts. For as we have already explained in some detail (Part I, § 5), concepts were devised in the first place simply in order to make sharp differentiation possible. We have now shown that this differentiation of mental quantities is in fact guaranteed by the element of discreteness that enters into the continuity of intuitive processes. Thus the problem of realizing logical relations by means of mental processes is now satisfactorily resolved.

§ 19. On Self-Evidence

The foregoing considerations have clarified the problems of pure thought by answering the question: What are the special features of mental processes through which we obtain unmistakable insight into the truth of judgments that rest on the analysis of concepts? In our discussion, we have often had to overcome widely shared preconceptions that prevent us from understanding the true state of affairs. In retrospect and as a summary, we wish to place our results in still clearer view by seeking to eliminate once and for all those fundamental errors that have constantly cast shadows across these problems and have obscured the ideas about consciousness entertained by philosophers, both ancient and modern.

As we mentioned above (§ 16), most thinkers have settled the question of the certainty of analytical thought simply by referring to *self-evidence*. The correctness of the principle of non-contradiction, and hence of all analysis, which is indeed based on this principle, has been held to be plainly "self-evident". Thus self-evidence has been viewed as an inescapable ultimate: every truth must eventually either find support in it or collapse into nothing.

This appeal to self-evidence as a court of last resort and final refuge we have repeatedly rejected on the ground that it is wrong-headed and impracticable. But advocates of the theory of self-evidence maintain that we labor under a cruel self-delusion if we suppose that we can get along without the notion. For no matter what I say, do I not always in the very nature of the case assume that my assertions and proofs are *evidently* true? When I point to certain facts, do I not presuppose at least that it is *evident* that these actually are facts? And is not this reference to *self-evidence* the terminal point we necessarily come to whenever a question is raised as to the basis for our conviction?

All of these protestations have really been answered already in our discussion above of a fundamental error made by Descartes (§ 12). There we saw that the foundations of what we know are neither certain nor uncertain; they merely *are*. They are not something evident, nor need they be; they are independently, self-sufficiently there.

The theorist who champions self-evidence asserts triumphantly that we can speak of a fact only if it is *(self-)evident* that a fact is actually present. But he is easily routed with his own weapons. For the existence of self-evidence would itself be simply a fact. Would we not then be obliged, according to the theory of self-evidence, to ask: How do I know that self-evidence is present? Is this self-evident? And if it is, must I not still ask: What assures me that it is evident? A self-evidence of a third order? And so on, *ad infinitum*.

Now we do, of course, establish truth by means of various data of consciousness, and we may if we choose call these self-evidence. But it is impossible to sustain the doctrine that there is a peculiar, irreducible experience of self-evidence, the presence of which constitutes a sufficient criterion and an unmistakable mark of truth. This is proved by the empirical fact that the experience of self-evidence occurs also in the case of notoriously false judgments. Any false claim that is defended with honest fervor may serve as an example. Thus the systems of such great metaphysicians as Descartes and Spinoza consist in large measure of false judgments which their originators nevertheless held to be the most certain of all truths.

I am aware that defenders of the doctrine of self-evidence maintain that in these instances what was experienced was not genuine self-evidence; they would have us believe that what was involved instead was a certainty "without self-evidence" [42]. This claim, however, is tangled up in a hopeless contradiction. On the one hand, if genuine self-evidence is experienced as essentially different from spurious (a certainty without self-evidence), then the two will never be confused with one another; there will be no mistakes about self-evidence — with the result that we shall have denied the existence of the very set of facts the theory was devised to explain. On the other hand, if there is no immediate difference between the two experiences, then we can decide only indirectly, by means of subsequent investigation, whether what is present is certainty with self-evidence or certainty without it. And this is an admission that a genuine criterion of truth is not to be sought in the experience of self-evidence, that other criteria are decisive, and these would have to be inquired into in connection with that subsequent investigation. Such criteria cannot themselves be experiences of self-evidence; otherwise we would be caught up in a circle. But then the claim that self-evidence is the ultimate criterion would be destroyed. Thus each alternative leads to a contradiction with the presuppositions of the theory. The conceptual distinction between self-evident certainty and certainty without self-evidence turns out to be merely an artificial construction, put together to uphold the contention that every truth announces itself to us through a special, infallible experience of self-evidence.

No issue has produced a greater confusion of ideas about the nature of self-evidence than the question of the validity of "axioms". In philosophical literature axioms are often described as "immediately self-evident", as judgments that carry within themselves the guarantee of their own truth. But if we may speak at all of such judgments, surely we cannot count among them the so-called axioms. We might perhaps include elementary perceptual judgments such as "This is blue" or "This feeling is pleasurable". But when we reflect that we can convince ourselves of the truth of a judgment only if we have pictured to ourselves the full meaning of the concepts that

---

42 See, for example, A. HÖFLER, Grundlehren der Logik, 4th edition, 1907, p. 82.

occur in the judgment, then we shall find it difficult to ascribe "immediate" self-evidence to axioms. For the concepts dealt with in the axioms are precisely the most fundamental of all; they are located at the highest levels of abstraction. Consider, for instance, the principle of non-contradiction or the principle of causality. How very rich in relations are the concepts that are linked together in these principles, or, more accurately, are first determined by them! As a matter of fact, the essence of concepts consists in relations; and the more abstract the concepts or the more removed from intuition, the more complicated are the processes required to represent them. What a manifold of interlaced relationships must we keep in view when, for example, we think of the concept of cause! How audacious then is the claim that the principle of causality is "immediately self-evident"!

Some writers, as we mentioned earlier, have attempted to get around the many difficulties in the theory of self-evidence by moving self-evidence out of the sphere of the psychological or subjective. They have sought to endow it with objectivity by declaring that it is not a mere feeling, or subjective experience, through which the truth of a proposition makes itself known to the one who judges; rather, it is a property of the judgment (as an ideal structure itself), and it is grasped correctly or not, as the case may be, in real acts of thought. When it is not correctly grasped, the result is illusion or error.

Obviously such assertions take the theory farther and farther away from its starting-point, so that it can no longer fulfill its original task. What the theory now comes to signify, in plain language, is that in addition to its truth, a judgment possesses also a specific distinguishing mark of its truth. For many authors the two coincide: self-evidence then is no longer merely the criterion of truth but its essence. Others distinguish between them, but in so doing strip their version of self-evidence of any meaning or function. For what point is there in establishing self-evidence if we can verify the truth of a judgment directly by the presence of its essential features? Moreover, the skeptical objections against a specific feeling of self-evidence, which we urged just above, remain standing in principle; now, however, they are directed not at self-evidence as a property of the judgment itself, but at its relation to the subjective experiences that are supposed to make its presence known to us.

In all cases, however, the basic error is that truth and the criterion of truth are conceived as something inherent in a single judgment, without regard to other judgments or to the realities. Yet it is quite certain that truth is not an immanent property of judgments. (This was a most important point in our inquiry into the concept of truth (Part I, § 10), and would have to be acknowledged on any impartial reflection.) On the contrary, it consists solely in the *relations* of judgments to something outside of them: in the case of conceptual judgments, relations to other judgments; in the case of assertions about reality, relations to reality, specifically those that effectuate a unique correlation.

Thus the experiences through which a truth is established can never be connected solely to the "self-evident" judgment itself. They must be joined to a consideration of its relations to something else, of its place within a totality (see above, § 10). When we establish a truth, certain data of consciousness appear that may of course be called feelings of self-evidence. But we should be clear about their nature and not assess falsely their epistemological significance. What their true nature is will emerge more clearly a little later (see below § 22).

§ 20. So-Called Internal Perception

We have seen that the theory of self-evidence is full of discrepancies and contradictions. And we have ascertained the *proton pseudos* of all these confusions: that those who use the expressions 'self-evidence' *(Evidenz)* and 'is evident' *(einleuchten)* speak and reason as if consciousness stood there face to face with and inspecting truths and the facts of its own consciousness. (Thus Stumpf says: "We designate as immediately given that which is immediately evident as a fact [43].") And then of course they require a special criterion by which to determine whether the inspection has been correct. But this is precisely what self-evidence is supposed to provide. To be sure, they cannot conceal from themselves the circumstance that one's own thought processes are not facts foreign to consciousness, but form part of it. Nevertheless, they persist in think-

---

43 "Erscheinungen und psychische Funktionen", Abhandlungen der Königlichen Preußischen Akademie der Wissenschaften, 1906, p. 6.

ing of them as severed from the subject or the "I", only then to tie them intimately to it again by an act supposed to be quite similar to the one which we imagine as setting up a connection between consciousness and things outside of consciousness: the act of perception. Thus they arrive at the notion of an "internal perception", through which the "I" supposedly becomes aware of its own states just as it becomes aware of external things through external perception. Since external perception takes place through the intervention of the sense organs, the supporters of self-evidence carry the analogy still further and speak of an "internal sense". As we know, this idea played a not inessential role in Kantian philosophy. Yet the notion of an internal perception, together with that of an "appearance" (indeed closely connected to it, a matter we shall touch on in Part III) is one of the most hapless ever fashioned by philosophical and psychological thought. This conceptual malformation has been responsible for a great deal of useless cogitation and many pseudo-problems of a malignant character.

It is helpful to glance briefly at the field on which the battle of opinions has taken place. We shall be all the more delighted with a viewpoint that from the beginning places us outside these bewildering difficulties.

The most vigorous champion of self-evidence and internal perception was Franz Brentano. Internal perception, he held, is absolutely self-evident, whereas external perception, as we know, can be deceptive[44]. In the case of internal perception, what is perceived is directly inherent in the perception; in the case of external perception, the object is given only indirectly with the aid of the sense organs. Now it has been justly pointed out that deceptive external perceptions cannot properly be termed sensory illusions, since these illusions have their basis in false interpretations or evaluations of sense data. The sense data themselves are neither correct nor incorrect; it is *we* who err in interpreting them. Taking into account that interpretations also figure in the case of internal perceptions, many have concluded that in this respect as well no essential difference can be established between the two kinds of perception. Those who count interpretation as part of the act of perception therefore assert that internal perception is as deceptive as external, while those who separate perception itself from the associated acts of inter-

---

44 Psychologie, p. 184.

pretation and assimilation quite consistently defend the view that external perception as such is just as self-evident and infallible as internal perception.

It was considerations such as these that led Husserl to recognize the untenability of Brentano's conception. But he did not go so far as to reject the entire problem as wrongly formulated. Instead he sought to solve it by introducing an additional distinction, thus continuing to tread old paths. He found that "the essence of the epistemological distinction drawn between internal and external perception" lay in the contrast between "adequate" and "inadequate" perception[45]. "In the first case, the *content* experienced is at the same time the *object* of perception. The content signifies nothing other than its own self. In the second case, content and object diverge. The content represents something that does not lie, or does not lie entirely, in the content itself, but is wholly or partly similar to it." In the first case, however, I think it makes no sense to speak of perception at all. The content simply *is* there, and this disposes of the whole matter. The concept of an adequate perception seems to me at least as dangerous and unfortunate as that of an internal perception. It has meaning and place only in those philosophical systems (and in fact is found only in those) that proclaim the concept of intuitive knowledge and would place the stamp of knowledge on pure perception. But everything belonging to this range of ideas has already been discussed so thoroughly that nothing more need be said about it here (see Part I, § 12).

It is interesting to see how disturbed the defenders of internal perception become when skeptics try to put it on the same plane with external perception and how hard they struggle to regain the firm footing which the theory was originally designed to provide. They make especially strenuous efforts to rescue the self-evidence of internal perception, for otherwise the entire theory loses its justification. Hugo Bergmann, in particular, has devoted himself to this task[46]. In an ingenious defense, and directing his remarks against Cornelius and Uphues, he combats a rather special form of the view to which our study has led us, namely, that the question of the self-evidence of internal perception is a false one because

---

45 Logische Untersuchungen, II, p. 711.

46 Untersuchungen zum Problem der Evidenz der inneren Wahrnehmungen, Halle 1908.

there is no such perception. It is unnecessary here to undertake an explicit refutation of his arguments; the refutation follows directly from the proof given for our own viewpoint. Indeed, looked at from this viewpoint, Bergmann's arguments *for the self-evidence* of internal perception become transformed into arguments *against the existence* of internal perception[47]. The true kernel of his arguments is simply an insistence on the absolute factuality of the given. Thus from what appear to be objections we may derive instructive confirmation.

Experimental psychology defends itself most tenaciously against our thesis that it is impossible to distinguish between a content of consciousness and its being perceived. This it does by pointing to the familiar fact, experienced over and over again, that so-called self-observation is uncertain. Comte, as we know, consistently denied that such observation was possible; but this view has not been accepted. Thus Külpe has the following to say about our problem: "... even for immediately present experiences we cannot assert in an unrestricted way the unity of consciousness with its object. Such facts as the just noticeable sensation and the just noticeable difference between sensations, for example, point to the conclusion that there are sensations and differences of sensations that we do not notice, of which we have no awareness[48]." Ever since Leibniz embarked on this course in his doctrine of *"petites perceptions"*, considerations such as these have gained rather than lost in significance. They play a major role in relation to the problem of unconscious mental states, and have contributed to making a problem of what, rightly viewed, turns out to be a question of terminology.

An especially instructive account is given by Stumpf, who takes a position in support of unnoticed and imperceptible contents of consciousness[49]. He discusses the example of a musical chord which on one occasion is heard as a simple quality but on another, if we are more attentive, is separated more or less distinctly into its com-

---

47 The same thing is true of Brentano's account in his Psychologie. There he differentiates internal perception (our mere "being-given") from internal observation, and correctly declares that the latter does not exist. He is also quite consistent when he rejects the unconscious.

48 Die Philosophie der Gegenwart in Deutschland, 3rd edition, p. 112.

49 Erscheinungen und psychische Funktionen, p. 34.

ponents. Were these components perhaps absent on the first occasion? To Stumpf such an assumption seems impossible, and he accepts as cogent the conclusion that the individual tones (as mental qualities, of course) are actually present in the chord all along but are noticed (we become conscious of them) only under certain circumstances. Against the criticism that his view involves an impermissible "reification" of mental contents, he defends himself as follows: ". . . But even if all this actually were a mere assumption, why must it be disallowed? Lately, chemists too have been taxed with the fallacy of reification because, for instance, they lodge within carbonic acid the two substances they later obtain from it ... yet surely chemists cannot be charged with a perverted way of thinking[50]."

But the comparison between the psychologist and the chemist seems particularly inapt in just this sort of case. For carbonic acid is not something that is immediately given; it is a substrate assumed to exist somehow behind or outside of the given sensations, which is intended to make the given intelligible. Or, if you will, it is a concept that designates certain interconnections of the given. And the same is true of oxygen and carbon. All three concepts — oxygen, carbon, carbonic acid — can and must be so determined in thought, their characteristics must be so defined, that they can best fulfill (in accord with the rules of science) the task for which they were originally constructed. It is entirely different with the data of consciousness. A chord heard is not some transcendent thing as to whose components and properties we may make various assumptions depending on what the explanation requires. It is not a concept which we may define one way or another; it is indefinable. It is something that simply exists, entirely removed in its determinations from our will or our needs. I cannot "explain it away"; I can make no hypothesis about its composition. Only in the case of objects that are not directly given can I do this sort of thing. The given is simply the actual, and is prior to all our assumptions. We are permitted to make assumptions only about that with which we are not directly acquainted. It makes no sense to advance assumptions about the composition of something with which we are acquainted; there is no place for them. If, in hearing a chord, we experience at one time a single sound and at another several tones, then the experienced chord — the directly given structure — is

---

50 *Ibid.*, p. 20.

different in the two instances. The experiences that are there the first time are *different* from those present the second time.

This difference in total experience is a brute fact, which cannot be interpreted away or declared to be an illusion. True, we can explain it by saying that the sensations themselves are the same in both cases but that certain mental acts, missing in one instance, were present in the other and have merged with the sensations into an experience of a different kind. But this interpretation is not necessary; nor is it the only possible one. We might just as well have taken the sensations themselves to be different in the two cases. That the sound, as a physical process, is the same both times is of no particular significance. For the same stimulus produces in general quite different sensations depending on the state of the subject. Sensations, together with their physiological correlates, may well be different for a person in a state of close attention than they would be otherwise. The hypothesis that seeks to attribute the difference between the two cases to the addition of a special mental act seems to me to be altogether unacceptable, if with Stumpf one conceives of this act as a mere *noticing (Bemerken)*. Noticing is identical with awareness. It cannot be regarded as a separate function of consciousness; it is itself consciousness and can never serve to explain the difference between two states of consciousness [51].

The attempt to rediscover in different mental structures the same elements unchanged — at one time noticed, at another time not — is probably a remnant of atomistic modes of thought in psychology, which even those who expressly condemn them fall back into at times. All we can say is: the sound heard as a unit is something other than the chord as analyzed. The moment we assert that the former is composed of the same sensations as the latter, we have slipped back into psychological atomism, which actually does commit an "impermissible reification" by looking upon different structures of consciousness as if they were mosaics put together from unchanged elements.

This approach is, strictly speaking, never permissible. The stream of consciousness is a true Heraclitian flux; every state of consciousness is a unity and cannot really be analyzed like, say, a chemical

---

51 On this question, see the admirable exposition by KURT KOFFKA, Probleme der experimentellen Psychologie, Numbers 1 and 2, Die Naturwissenschaften, 1917.

compound whose individual components exist also independently of each other. This point has often been remarked on, but never as forcefully raised and pursued as by Cornelius, with whose views on the matters discussed in this section I find myself generally in whole-hearted agreement. We cannot lay too much stress on the truth he expresses in the following words: "Actually nothing can be analyzed in any given content of consciousness without something *new* taking the place of this content; as soon as our analysis yields us knowledge that was not already *eo ipso* present in the given content, that content has thereby been replaced by something different from it[52]."

Our view is further confirmed when we observe how Stumpf seeks to meet the objection based on the indivisibility of unitary mental structures, and thus to justify his distinction between sensations and their being noticed. He cites an analogy: "Color and extension also form between them a whole, within which they can be separated from one another only by abstraction. Were we then to conclude 'Extension therefore cannot occur without color', we should be drawing a wrong inference. Indeed, the sense of touch reveals to us that extension does occur without color, although not without any qualitative element whatsoever. And there is nothing to show that this extension is perhaps an extension in some other sense[53]."

But the fact is that the word 'extension' does mean something quite different when applied to the data of different senses. For instance, the extension of a color and that of a tactile impression surely are not identical psychological data. It is only because *empirically* there is an exact correspondence between the ordering of tactile impressions and the ordering of visual impressions that we may refer to both in terms of the same objective ordering, called extension. We shall return to these relationships later when we consider the problem of space. Meanwhile, Stumpf's discussion does not establish the possibility of distinguishing between a sensation and its being noticed. This is not to deny, of course, that mental functions stand as a special class of experiences; we fully recognize the fundamental importance of this finding (see above § 5). But we reject

---

52 HANS CORNELIUS, Einleitung in die Philosophie, 3rd edition, 1911, pp. 313 ff.

53 CARL STUMPF, Erscheinungen und psychische Funktionen, p. 13.

the view that among these functions there is one that consists in *noticing* the contents of consciousness. There is no such thing as internal perception.

If we distinguish a sensation from its being noticed, in such a way that the sensation can be there even without a consciousness being aware of it, then certain consequences inevitably follow. What we call sensations become transcendent objects that confront consciousness and perhaps act on it, in just the manner we think of external perception as being the effect on consciousness of things-in-themselves. A doctrine with such consequences must naturally be characterized as metaphysical. Anyone who adopts it speaks of sensations in the same sense in which one might speak of a thing-in-itself, which lies at the base of, say, the perception of a table. They are unconscious in the same sense in which physical things are unconscious. Thus we arrive at the notion of an "unconscious mental something". We have just shown that the road leading to this notion is impassable. But are there perhaps other paths that might take us to it?

Now it is possible to show that we can attach an acceptable meaning to this combination of words only by adopting a totally inappropriate terminology. Thus far we have used the words 'mental', 'conscious', and 'directly given' as synonyms, and we shall continue to do so in what follows. It would therefore be a contradiction for us to speak of an *un*conscious mental something. We could speak this way only if we were to surrender our terminology and cease to identify "conscious" and "mental". But then insuperable difficulties would arise once we attempted to delimit the concept of the mental. For we would seek in vain some trait that would uniquely characterize "mental". Other attempts to extend the concept of the mental to the unconscious likewise fail. We shall come back to this matter later when we have occasion to deal with the definition of the physical and with the pseudo-problems attending its relationship to the mental.

We return to "internal perception". It should not be forgotten that this has also been spoken of in a somewhat different sense, one that is not so easy to attack. The expression 'internal perception of experience' has sometimes been applied to the processes of apperception, which are linked with the given and through which, as we are wont to say, the experience itself is elaborated. Dürr, for instance, presents the matter roughly in this way. He begins by defining internal perception as "the immediate grasping of processes of consciousness", and to this, of course, we cannot consent[54]. He then expressly affirms that the internal perception of a given consists of processes that follow one another temporally. Such perception is "something that is aroused only by experience"[55].

If this is what is meant by "internal perception", then it is not the target of our polemic. Such a version does not necessarily run into difficulties, for there is no objection to the concept of apperception rightly understood. But it seems to me quite inappropriate to attach the name 'internal perception' to the process of apperception. In the first place, we already have a term for this purpose — 'apperception'. In the second place, the use of the expression 'perception' suggests the incorrect atomistic notion that a "perceived" experience is contained unchanged in the apperceptive experience, except that it is surrounded, perhaps, by multitudes of new images and is, as it were, contemplated by them. In reality, however, the apperception experience is something *new* with respect to the originally given (the perception experience); the latter cannot be extracted from the former by analysis and separated from what remains[56].

It seems to me, however, that Külpe gives a most unsatisfactory turn to the theory of apperception when he says: "To experience a mental process, to *perceive,* to be conscious of the process, and to apperceive it, are thus equivalent expressions[57]." Here the distinction between perceived and apperceived data of consciousness, which

---

54 Erkenntnistheorie, 1910, especially p. 33.

55 *Ibid.,* p. 34.

56 R. HERBERTZ explores a similar way of speaking meaningfully of internal perception. He says (Prolegomena zu einer realistischen Logik, p. 190): "The processes of consciousness — while we experience them and through our experiencing of them — are not directly given at all. We must first bring their existence reflexively to consciousness ... in special acts of mental grasping. They are first 'given' us as objects of self-perception." In these sentences the word 'given' is used in an altogether different sense from the one we have employed here; consequently, the sense in which Herbertz speaks of self-perception is not identical with the one we have had to reject. In this passage, as in DÜRR, internal perception can be understood as apperception, and so has nothing to do with our problem.

57 Die Philosophie der Gegenwart, 3rd edition, p. 113.

was the original point of the theory of apperception, is altogether suppressed; for a merely perceived content would not be a conscious one at all, the unconscious alone would be apperceived and thereby lifted into consciousness. Here we have in its entirety the viewpoint against which we have had to direct these interpolated remarks: mental elements exist outside of consciousness (for they are indeed unconscious) and it is only through a special process — experiencing, perceiving, apperceiving — that consciousness takes possession of them. This process is supposed even to occur in varying degrees, for Külpe distinguishes five different levels of consciousness and holds that their existence has been demontrated experimentally[58]. But it should be noted that this result can not be read off directly from the experiment; the finding can only be an interpretation of it. A series of different experiences are interpreted as one and the same content in different modes of consciousness. But obviously we can also say — and according to our account this is all we *may* say — that different *contents* were there. For experience and the content of the experience are one and the same thing. Psychological experimentation is impotent in the face of this kind of question, for the solution to it must already be presupposed in the interpretation of any experiment. Take as an example (a favorite of Külpe's) the case of an experimental subject who, having been shown a sketched figure, is able to give its form but not its color. Yet every visual perception must have some quality; it must be black, grey or of some color. It is tempting to infer that the subject indeed had a sensation of color, but not in consciousness. Such an inference, however, is invalid, if for no other reason than that the report of an experience always comes *after* the experience. If a color sensation was necessarily present during the experience but is no longer there at the time of the report and no recollection of it exists, then we have the phenomenon that we call *forgetting*. And from experiments of this sort no more can be concluded than that under the circumstances described the data of consciousness can be so fleeting that they leave no disposition to recall anything and are promptly forgotten.

The modes of thought we have been attacking are deeply rooted. The very forms of expression of our language rest on the false assumption that the trinity of subject, act and object constitutes part of every experience or consciousness, just as perception presupposes

---

58 Die Realisierung, 1912, Vol. I, pp. 56 ff.

the trinity of perceiver, perceiving and perceived. We have already warned that the expression "the given", which we have constantly used here, also suffers from the same defect. It is even less advisable, instead of the "given", to speak of the "had"[59]: this term, if anything, calls to mind still more definitely the contrast between subject and object. The *Cogito* of Descartes, as we remarked earlier, contains the trap of a distinction between a substantivist "I" and its activity, into which Descartes fell when he added: *ergo sum*. For as is easily seen, his *sum* means for him the existence of a substantial "I". Lichtenberg's very true observation that Descartes should have said "It thinks" instead of "I think", is not only an inspired remark but should really be made the supreme guiding principle of psychology. In that science, we always talk — and our language scarcely allows us any other choice — as if consciousness were a stage upon which the individual mental elements make their entry, after having waited somewhere in the wings. These are then linked or separated, or however we may put it, by the "I" (by virtue of its "spontaneity", as Kant added, thus making matters even worse). As metaphors, these phrases may be allowed to pass. However, they describe nothing but the ceaseless change of qualities called "the stream of consciousness"[60]. Each of its phases is a new one and contains none of the preceding ones *realiter* within itself, even though it may be designated as the reproduction or apperception of an earlier experience. The stream of consciousness is simply an existing process; the "I" is the unified interconnection of this process, not a person who inspects and guides it. And the explicit consciousness of self is to be regarded not as a factor always accompanying the course of this process of consciousness but as just *one* content among others, which appears under specific circumstances from time to time. It was one of Wundt's invaluable services that he persisted in stressing the true state of affairs. He constantly fought against "the false distinction between consciousness and the processes that are supposed to constitute its contents", and held to his position with vigorous consistency[61]. Many unclarities and inadequacies would have been avoided if his arguments had not been so cavalierly pushed aside.

---

59 As Hans Driesch, for instance, likes to do.

60 The expression is due to William James.

61 WUNDT, System der Philosophie, Volume II, 3rd edition, p. 138.

§ 21. Verification

We have denied the existence of a special experience of "self-evidence", which infallibly points out to us the truth of a true sentence. The question then arises naturally: Through which data of consciousness may truth then be recognized? What is the criterion that assures us of truth? This question we have not yet answered directly; but we posses all the data required to do so.

Since we know the nature of truth and are acquainted with its properties, we can also specify how the truth of judgments must make itself perceptible to us. Truth can be found only where the characteristic features of the concept of truth are immediately at hand, or where there are data that have as a necessary consequence the presence of these features. Now truth is defined by a single, extremely simple characteristic: the uniqueness of the correlation of judgments with facts. Hence any sign or indication that permits us to determine whether such a uniqueness is present will furnish a criterion of truth. But there is only one immediate feature that characterizes the existence of uniqueness, namely, that only a single fact can be found that, in accordance with the well-established rules of designation, is correlated with the judgment under consideration.

The sciences long ago developed special methods to check the uniqueness of the designation of facts by judgments; these are the procedure of *verification*. They play a powerful role in the empirical sciences, since these disciplines are based on advancing their judgments first as hypotheses and then determining whether a unique correlation has been obtained by the judgment. If it has, then the hypothesis is counted a true proposition.

Our concern in this section is limited to proposition about concepts, since only the questions treated in such propositions can be reckoned among the problems of thought. At this point, however, we should like to settle quickly the question of the verfication of judgments about reality, which does not require any assumptions about the nature of the real (to be taken up in the next section) and which it would be awkward to treat again later on.

A judgment has meaning only in connection with other judgments. In order for a proposition to have meaning, there must be given, in addition to the proposition itself, at least the definitions of the concepts occuring in it. In the case of judgments about reality the definitions, in the final analysis, always go back in one way or another to what is intuitively given, and in the natural sciences and the social sciences and history, mostly to what is perceived through the senses. Thus every assertion about reality can be connected by a chain of judgments to immediately given facts in such a manner that it can be tested by these data. That is, matters can be so arranged that the presence or absence of specific data supplies the criterion for the truth or falsity of the judgment. This takes place in the following fashion.

Assume that we are to verify some arbitrary assertion about reality J. From J we can derive a new judgment J_1 by adding another judgment J' so chosen that J and J' together serve as premises for a syllogism whose conclusion is J_1. The judgment J' may be either (1) an assertion about reality or (2) a definition or (3) a purely conceptual proposition whose truth we assume for the moment has already been absolutely established. Now from J_1 we can, with the help of a newly added judgment J'', derive a further judgment J_2, where for J'' there are the same three possibilities as for J'. From J_2 and a new judgment J''' we obtain J_3 and so forth until we finally reach a judgment J_n of the form roughly: "At such and such a time and at such and such a place under such and such circumstances such and such will be observed or experienced." We betake ourselves at the appointed time to the appointed place and arrange the appointed circumstances. We then describe (that is, designate) our observations or experiences by means of a perceptual judgment P in that — on the basis of acts of re-cognition — we bring what is observed or experienced under the proper concepts and name it with the appropriate words. If P is identical with J_n, this means that J_n is then verified, and so is the original judgment J.

That is to say, we find that although judgment and fact have been correlated with one another along two entirely different paths, the same judgment both times designates the same fact. The correlation is therefore unique, the judgment true. Since the last member of the chain of judgments led to a unique correlation, we take this as a sign that the other members, hence the starting-point and the endpoint J, also fulfill the truth condition, and we count the entire process as a verification of the judgment J.

Strictly, of course, this conclusion is proof against objection if and only if the truth of the added judgments J', J'', ... has already been established. In turn, this is the case initially only if J', J'' ... are definitions or conceptual propositions, since these guarantee uni-

11*

queness by their very origin. But if they are assertions about reality, whose truth is not immune to all doubt, then uniqueness — assuming that the verification process has in fact led us to uniqueness and thus to the truth J_n — still does not, strictly speaking, establish the truth of J. For a conclusion may happen to be true even though one or more of the premises from which it was inferred are false. But since a purely accidental verification is in general highly improbable, verification does not lose its value. It does not, of course, offer an absolutely rigorous proof of the truth of J; it only makes it probable. But in return for that, it signifies a verification for the whole sequence of auxiliary propositions J', J'', ... For it also makes the truth of these judgments more probable, and on the same grounds that hold for J, since in principle they stand in exactly the same relation to J_n as does J. Each of these auxiliary propositions, in ordinary life or in science, is generally verified also through numerous other chains of judgments. Thus the individual results mutually support one another, and the uniqueness of the correlation becomes ever more secure for each member of the whole system.

What we have said can be illustrated by any example chosen at random from the sciences. Suppose a historian wishes to determine whether it is true that a certain event took place in the way in which it has come down to us. Initially he will have available various statements from some work of history and then perhaps printed or written reports or documentary records of the happening. These will have stemmed from witnesses who obtained this information about the event in a more or less indirect way, often through a number of intermediaries. From the data, the investigator may now possibly be able to infer the conclusion that a notation about the event is to be found among the records of a certain person of whom the sources make mention or in the chronicles of a particular city. He will then offer tentatively the proposition (J_n): "In such and such an archive there is a document with such and such a statement about the event." If such a document is actually discovered in the archive, then the exact same judgment (now as P) can be made on the basis of the intuitive perception of this document: the same judgment corresponds on both occasions to the same set of facts, and all judgments of the entire chain thereby count as verified.

This sequence of judgments is actually unimaginably long; it cannot be expressed or written down in its entirety. It contains an enormous number of auxiliary propositions J', J'', ..., most of which are never explicitly mentioned, since their truth is not in doubt. They are constantly assumed by us in life and thought, and just as often confirmed. For example, there are the assumptions — among the more familiar ones — that not all of a group of witnesses were deceived by hallucinations; or that parchment and paper preserve written characters unaltered and that these characters do not in the course of time change into others with a different meaning; and the like. Propositions such as these enter into every process of verification without exception. And because they are confirmed in every case, we cherish an unshakable belief in their truth.

The theory of knowledge of pragmatism, which some time ago caused a not inconsiderable stir in philosophical circles, places this process of verification at the center of discusson and maintains that the very essence of truth is to be found in it. That this thesis is totally incorrect we know from what was said in Part I. But the pragmatists (Peirce, James, Dewey in America, F. C. S. Schiller in England and others) did perform a genuine service by pointing out (specifically for assertions about reality) that there *is* indeed no other way to *establish* truth except through verification. This is actually of great importance. We add, however, the likewise important finding that verification always ends up in establishing the identity of two judgments. The moment it turns out that in designating a perceived fact we arrive at the same judgment that we had already on logical grounds deduced for this fact, we become convinced of the truth of the tested proposition. There is no other way to arrive at that conviction, since uniqueness, by its very nature, always expresses itself eventually in the fashion we have described.

But what of purely conceptual or analytical propositions? All the various considerations treated here as "Problems of Thought" are concerned with judgments of this kind. We know that they are valid *a priori*; for they state only what is already contained by definition in the concepts and hence require no confirmation by experience to be acknowledged as true. Thus a verification of the sort described just above seems unnecessary for conceptual propositions; it is not needed to disclose their truth. We also know that the fleeting and continuous character of mental processes does not prevent us from making correct analytic judgments and inferences and from recognizing that they have been correctly made. We have not yet, however, pictured in detail the acts of consciousness through which this comes about. We must do so now, in order to fill the place left vacant when we rejected the theory of self-evidence.

As we saw, it is of the essence of analysis or deduction that the content of the inferred conclusion is already contained completely in the premisses, so that the conclusion only appears to state something new. Combinations of signs that seem different turn out to be equivalent as soon as we go back to the suppositions expressed in the premisses. Hence if the inference has been correctly drawn, the uniqueness of the correlation of the concepts with one another must be revealed in the fact that, when we carry out the substitutions permitted or required by virtue of the conceptual relations laid down in the premisses, we obtain a pure *identity*. This is also the logical foundation for the way we confirm the correctness of the analysis (that is, the truth of the inferred conclusion). The process is exhibited at its clearest in the most perspicuous methods of analysis we possess: those of mathematics. In order to establish the correctness of some relation, say the equation $e^{ix} = \cos x + i \sin x$, we replace the symbols on both sides with their meanings — in our example, the series that define the functions — and we immediately obtain an identity. The correctness of the result can be verified in the same way in any other case, and every other deductively inferred proposition can be tested similarly. Take the schoolbook example of the mortality of Caius. In accordance with the assumptions expressed in the premisses, we can transform the inferred conclusion into a pure identity. For if in the conclusion we substitute 'a man' for 'Caius' (in accordance with the minor premiss) and if for 'a man' we put 'a mortal' (in accordance with the major premiss), the conclusion goes over into the tautology "A mortal is a mortal." Uniqueness is attested to by this identity.

Thus here too, as in the case of propositions about reality, the exhibiting of an identity provides us with a criterion of truth. In consciousness, of course, this showing of an identity takes place by means of more or less intuitive processes through which the discontinuous conceptual relations are copied, as it were. (The development of our discussion in § 18 convinced us that this is quite possible.) In order to grasp the truth of any general proposition I must first "understand" it; I must be clear about the meanings of the words and picture to myself the sense of the proposition. We may express this by saying that we understand a general proposition when we promptly supply it with an intuitive example. Insight into its truth occurs in just the same way, culminating in an identity experience through which certain representations or acts are proved to be one and the same. The identical logical relationship can be represented in the most varied ways; I can make a particular geometrical theorem clear to myself by means of any of an infinite number of figures; I can illustrate the validity of a form of inference with the aid of the most diverse examples. But quite independently of the nature of the illustrative pictures or figures (and assuming naturally that the "pictures" do run parallel to the logical relations), there will occur at the end the experience of an identity. And it is doubtless this experience that is commonly referred to as a "feeling of self-evidence". Whatever judgments we may be considering, whenever a truth appears evident to us, whenever, as it were, we say to ourselves "That's right" or "That's how it is", there is always an experience of identity. On the other hand, what is false makes itself known through an experience of nonidentity. How could it be otherwise? Truth is the absolutely constant, the eternally unalterable, the unique; whereas the false and the ambiguous show themselves in discrepancies, differences and deviations.

Of course, the occurrence of this "feeling of self-evidence", as we now see in accord with what was said above, is not an infallible criterion of truth. For an identity of the decisive data of consciousness may actually be present without the judgment, into whose consideration they enter, necessarily being correct. This can occur if the correspondence between the concepts or judgments and their intuitive representations is faulty, that is, if the element of discreteness in the continuity of the processes of consciousness, which we recognized above (§ 18) as the necessary condition for all exact thinking, fails to appear. It may then happen that by reason of this failure the same datum of consciousness comes to represent different concepts, and thus an experience of identity appears at the wrong place. The "fallacy of four terms" is an example of such a case. The mistake can be detected by thinking through the analysis again. For in the original case accidental circumstances had influenced the flow of the processes of consciousness. It is improbable that this will occur a second time in the same manner, especially if the reexamination is conducted by another person. Thus the discrepancy will be exposed.

To be sure, there is no psychological formula for altogether avoiding discrepancies, and for having the feeling of self-evidence always turn up in the right place. There is no guarantee that the correctness of a particular deduction will become evident to a particular consciousness every time. That would be too much to ask. It depends on conditions that we cannot completely satisfy at will. As a foundation for incontestable knowledge it suffices that under certain circumstances these conditions actually *are* fulfilled. And that this is the case, is a fact beyond all doubt.

For empirical statements and conceptual truths equally, truth is determined by means of an identity experience that constitutes the end result of a process of verification. But it is of supreme importance not to lose sight of the fact that, although they agree in this respect, a vast difference separates these two classes of judgments, an abyss that no logic or epistemology can bridge.

Suppose we have to verify a statement about reality that has been obtained by certain inferences, say a judgment about the character of some historical personage or about the properties of some chemical compound. The verification is then something quite new vis-à-vis the thought processes that led to the making of the judgment. It is an action through which man expresses his view about the surrounding world, and from which he expects a certain result. Whether or not this result is obtained depends on reality and its laws. Can we ever know with certainty that a judgment about reality must hold good? It seems at first that we could actually do so if only we knew the laws governing reality. But suppose we have studied fully all the law-like regularities of nature. How do we know that nature in the future will obey the same laws and that then too our judgment will be verified? Experience teaches us nothing about this, since it reveals only what is, not what will be. But a proposition, of course, is true only if it is confirmed *always* and without exception. As remarked above, what we can infer, strictly speaking, from a limited number of verifications is not absolute truth but only probability; for even in the case of false judgments a test of uniqueness may by chance yield a seemingly favorable result in a given instance. No matter how many confirmations there are, we cannot logically infer that a judgment must turn out to be true for all time. In order to be absolutely certain that a proposition will always be confirmed, that it is unconditionally true or universally valid, we would have to be able to *command* reality to furnish us in every test a perception that accords with the expected one. In other words, in order to make *a priori* valid judgments about nature, our consciousness would have to prescribe laws for nature itself; nature would have to be seen, in a certain sense, as a product of our consciousness. Kant, we know, believed both that this was possible and that it was the case; the highest laws of nature were likewise the laws of the knowledge of nature. Thus he sought to preserve and guarantee for us an absolutely valid general knowledge of nature, and to answer in the affirmative the great question as to whether absolutely certain knowledge of the real world is at all possible. In Part 3, we shall have to address ourselves to this problem, which we have often seen already looming in the distance.

There is no such problem for conceptual propositions or analytic judgments. In their case, the process of verification is not something new with respect to the derivation process; it is not independent of it. On the contrary, it rests logically and psychologically on precisely the same data as the process of derivation and in no way goes beyond it into an alien reality. The analogy between the two kinds of judgments with regard to their truth does not reach the point (as some might at first suppose and in fact have supposed) where the laws of consciousness play a role similar to that played by the laws of nature for assertions about reality. That is, we might be tempted to reason as follows: if I see now that a deduction is correct, this does not yet mean that the truth of the conclusion is absolutely certain; it is only probable. For what guarantee is there that I shall have the same insight in the future? Is it not possible that the law-like patterns of my consciousness might change, so that something that now is false will in the future seem true, or vice versa?

This line of reasoning misconstrues the facts on which the analytic process is based. A consciousness that is capable of setting up certain definitions is also capable of always understanding in the same way the analytic propositions that follow from them. In principle, the two processes are the same; a judgment in no way goes beyond what has already been put into its concepts, conceived as part of them. The question of whether a judgment is true has meaning only for a consciousness that can put together and understand the definitions of the concepts that occur in the judgment. But for such a consciousness the question is therewith already answered. I may of course become insane, the pattern of my conscious processes may so change that I become incapable of grasping a truth, for example that of the multiplication tables. But then I am no longer in a position to understand correctly the sense of any individual numeral. I cannot conceive a meaningful proposition about numbers at all, and the question of the correctness of such a proposition becomes pointless for me; I cannot even raise it. If a consciousness can understand an analytic proposition at all, it has *eo ipse* the capacity for perceiving its truth; both activities occur through the same processes. This holds, moreover, regardless of what kind of law-like regularity is displayed by the thinking consciousness. The character of the regularity has no bearing on the result; it is, so to speak, eliminated. Suppose I were transformed into a different creature with other senses and an altogether different mind which, however, for a being of that sort possessed a suitably high intelligence. The processes of consciousness (and their laws) through which I think of, say, the proposition $2 \times 2 = 4$, would not in the least resemble my present processes. Yet along this entirely different path I would still be able to perceive the truth of the proposition. Otherwise I could not understand the proposition at all, which contradicts our original assumption.

This means that in the case of analytic judgments I am guaranteed their absolute truth. I can be certain that they must always turn out to be true. ('Always' has the meaning of 'as often as I think the judgments'; if I do not or cannot think them, the question becomes meaningless.) Hence Leibniz was quite right when he referred to conceptual truths as *vérités éternelles*.

As for statements about reality or *vérités de fait,* on the other hand, it is entirely possible that I may understand and think them and may also have found them to be confirmed in a series of instances, but that in the future they might not be verified, and thus not be true. For what is required by the verification process in their case is not something already given with the understanding of the judgment itself. On the contrary, I must go beyond that understanding; I must examine the reality of the world.

This disposes of analytic judgments or conceptual propositions. They are not a problem, nor do they give rise to any further problems.

The problem of synthetic judgments, however, which holds within itelf all of the problems of reality, still awaits us in all its magnitude.

Part Three

Problems of Reality

A. *The Positing of the Real*

§ 22. Formulating the Question

To know something — as the first part of our inquiry showed — is to designate facts by means of judgments in such a way as to obtain a unique correlation while using the smallest possible number of concepts.

Thus far we have not considered at all the realm of facts, of designated objects. We have been concerned only with signs and the rules for combining them. At the same time we have learned that rigorous inference always consists solely in the combining of signs; inference substitutes certain signs for others and thus carries out the process of analysis whose laws are developed by formal logic.

We have also discussed the relationship of signs, judgments and concepts to the mental processes by which they are represented in consciousness. But even then we did not leave the domain of the problems of thought.

Now we move beyond this domain: we pass from the form in which knowledge is presented to us to the content therein presented. We turn from the signs to the objects designated. In so doing, we confront an entirely different class of questions, which we shall call problems of reality.

Questions of this sort are concealed in each and every synthetic judgment. An analytic judgment depends for its validity only on the rules of designation which are fixed, once and for all, in the definitions. In a synthetic judgment, however, concepts are joined together that were not put into relation with each other by any definition. Thus when I utter the synthetic judgment "Gaul was conquered by the Romans", the validity of my judgment rests not on any preexisting connection of concepts — it is not possible to deduce from the properties of the concept *Gaul* that one day Gaul would be conquered by the Romans — but on a factual relation among real objects.

But how do we know the facts of reality? Are they perhaps given to us directly? Do we infer them? Or in what other way do we become acquainted with them?

These questions recur with each fact about which we make judgments, and they must be answered if we are to be able to know whether our judgments are true. For before we can speak of any unique designation of objects, the objects must first *be there*. All of our questions, however, culminate in one: What are these objects, these "things" or "facts" with which our signs are correlated in cognition? What is it that is designated? What is reality?

For a question so basic, everything depends on how the problem is formulated. We cannot be too careful. Before we look for a solution, we must be clear on whether the problem as formulated admits of a solution at all and what it might possibly look like. What kind of answer can I expect to the question: What is reality?

Whatever the answer may be, it must itself be a judgment. But a judgment, as we very well know by now, is a sign for a fact and nothing more. An object is subsumed under a concept; the latter is correlated with it. This correlation takes place precisely in the judgment, which thus designates the whole state of affairs. A judgment cannot supply anything more. No matter what we try to do, no matter how many judgments we invoke to explain and clarify the concepts that are used, knowing — which indeed consists in judging — gives us only signs, never what is designated. The latter remains forever beyond reach. And anyone who insists that cognition ought to bring reality *closer* to us *realiter*, raises a demand that is *nonsensical* rather than, say, too high. We saw some time ago (I, § 12) that in cognition we neither can *nor want to* have the known object present; we do not want to become one with it, to intuit it directly, but only to correlate and arrange signs. That knowledge provides just this and nothing else is not its *weakness* but its *essence*.

Thus we see that anyone who might try to interpet our question as meaning "What is the designated, independent of the designation", would be mired down in hopeless misunderstandings. He would have posed a meaningless problem, since every question has to be answered with a judgment and is thus a request for a designation. Hence a formulation of this kind would be as sensible as asking: How is a sound to be heard if no one hears it?

It follows that the real cannot ever be given to us through any sort of knowledge. It is there before all knowledge. It is that which is designated, which exists before any designating. And this proposition itself and all the judgments we might make about it can only designate the real, never give or determine or create it.

This is a simple insight and follows purely analytically from the concept of knowledge. However, it has often been overlooked, with the result that recent philosophy has been led into many wrong paths. We shall return to this matter.

Meanwhile, we repeat that *acquaintance* with the nature of reality is not obtained through *knowledge* of reality. The former, where it is possible at all, must precede the latter, because what is to be designated is prior to the designating. Thus we are directly acquainted with the whole realm of our own data of consciousness; it is simply there, before any questioning, before any cognition. Nothing in it can be altered by cognition, nothing taken from it, nothing added to it. These immediately given data are the only reality with which we are *acquainted;* but it would be altogether wrong to conclude that therefore they must be the only reality, or even the only *known,* knowable, designatable reality. Such a conclusion, nonetheless, has often been drawn. This topic too we shall take up again later[1].

We return to our question: Which objects are real? The question has to be clearly understood. The situation cannot be that from a multitude of given things, we are to seek out the "real" ones in order to separate them from the unreal ones. Indeed, unreal things are never given us, since they are not there at all. The actual state of affairs obviously is that in the course of investigation we are led

---

1 In his Ordnungslehre (2nd edition, p. 381), HANS DRIESCH attributes to me the view that "there is acquaintance with reality but no knowledge" and refers to the above passages. But as the reader is aware, one of the most important claims I make is that there is knowledge of reality.

to designate the given by means of combinations of concepts and to form new concepts that do not directly designate anything with which we are immediately *acquainted*. The question then arises as to whether these latter concepts are correlated with anything "real", that is, whether the predicate "real" also is tied in with the features of those concepts. The answer, as we shall see, must be based on the interconnections between the concepts and certain elements of the "given", in accordance with the same methods that are applicable in other cases where the problem is to determine whether an object has a certain property. For example, that ether has a boiling point of 39^0 we determine through much the same methodology as we determine that electrons are real and that phlogiston or the "central fire" of the Pythagoreans is unreal.

In any event, it turns out that the question of the reality of an object, like other meaningful questions, can in fact be answered by effecting certain correlations and designations and is therefore meaningful. If we desire to fix its meaning more precisely, everything would seem to depend on the definition of the reality concept. But is it possible to give such a definition? Is this not one of those concepts whose objects can be exhibited only in intuition, only in experience? This appears indeed to be the case. For how could we trace the real back to something else, i. e., to something unreal? To specify how being differs from non-being would seem a hopeless undertaking. We shall in fact find our suspicion confirmed that to demand an analysis of the concept of reality is to ask for something that cannot be achieved. This is not to deny that there is a distinguishing mark, that it is discoverable, that it belongs equally to and characterizes all reality, so that it can serve at all times as a criterion for the "reality" of an object. The enormous importance of such a criterion for practical purposes is obvious; life is concerned only with realities, not with fictions. In practical life, moreover, we are never at a loss for criteria and need no help from philosophy. It is for the latter, however, to determine whether these criteria also retain their value for scientific knowledge and remain rigorously valid. For its own purposes, philosophy is obliged to reduce these criteria to a common formula. If it succeeds, it will have found a key to the solution of the most fundamental problems of reality.

No philosophical problem perhaps has been treated with more passion or has greater significance for the character of a philosophical system than the question: How wide is the domain of reality, what is to count as *real?* (In this discussion, we always use the word 'real' *[wirklich]* and the word 'real' *[real]* as completely equivalent.) Here we come up against the great problem of *transcendence:* whether and to what extent there are realities outside of or beyond the merely given, whether objects exist that are not given and to which the sign 'real' *(wirklich)* may or must be correlated. These problems are solved at one fell swoop once we have found a criterion and know how to apply it. And I believe that agreement on this point is far easier to achieve than we are apt to suppose in view of the violent doctrinal controversy that rages over the problem of transcendence.

Accordingly, the coming sections must be concerned above all with seeking out a characteristic feature of all that is real and with developing the consequences that follow from the result of this search. With this in mind, we shall consider the question Külpe has expressed in the form: "How is a positing of the real possible[2]?" Thereafter we shall have to come to grips with a different group of problems of reality that can be arranged under Külpe's question: "How is the *determination* of the real possible[3]?" Here the task is to examine what concepts must be correlated, generally or in individual cases, with that which is recognized as real: whether the real is to be designated as physical or mental, as a unity or a multiplicity, as spatial or non-spatial, as ordered or chaotic, or by whatever other technical terms we may employ. The method of inquiry throughout will consist in our establishing most carefully the possible and actual senses of such terms and then attacking all problems with the weapons forged in the first part of our discussion.

§ 23. Naive and Philosophical Viewpoints on the Question of Reality

The concept of reality is not a scientific one. It is not the product of some piece of research like, for instance, the concept of energy or of the integral. It does not belong to some specific science; in fact, strange as this may sound, the scientists could not be less

---

2 Die Realisierung, 1912, Vol. I, p. 4.
3 *Ibid.,* p. 5.

interested in its determination or definition. It is true, of course, that theorists always receive the stimulus for their investigations from reality. But so far as the actual interest of science is concerned, which finds satisfaction in the game of reducing concepts to one another, it is of no consequence whether these concepts do or do not designate realities. In either event, the cognitive process can take its course with equal vigor. The mathematician displays no less zeal in his preoccupation with ideal structures than the historian or the economist, whose interest is centered on reality. But even the latter two construct ideal cases; and in the inquiry into their general principles they work with simplifying abstractions. In the final analysis, all science is theory and all theory has unreal abstractions as its subject-matter.

Only life has to do with the concrete fullness of reality. The concept of reality is plainly a practical one. Behavior or action is occupied unceasingly and exclusively with realities and itself brings realities into being. It has long been recognized that here alone are to be found the roots of the concept of reality. Dilthey, in particular, has strongly emphasized this fact[4]; and Frischeisen-Köhler has sought to draw further consequences from it[5]. These authors have put their fingers on a highly significant point, even though we may not accept as sound the theoretical use they make of it.

It is only *philosophy*, and not the individual disciplines, that takes the concept of reality as the object of scholarly interest. It does so precisely because it is concerned with clarifying the most general foundations, which in all other fields are either accepted without proof or ignored. However, for its first orientation regarding the concept — this follows from what was said above — philosophy cannot turn to any of the individual sciences, but must seek to draw enlightenment from life and action. It must ascertain what the ordinary, naive person means when he or she ascribes "reality" to an object, and then it must ponder whether, for its own scholarly purposes, it can mean precisely the same thing by the word or whether the meaning must be changed to assure precision of thought.

---

4 WILHELM DILTHEY, Beiträge zur Lösung der Frage vom Ursprung unseres Glaubens an die Realität der Außenwelt und seinem Recht, Sitzungsberichte der königlichen Akademie der Wissenschaften zu Berlin, 1890, p. 977.

5 In his work Wissenschaft und Wirklichkeit, 1912.

As far as the naive, untutored individual is concerned, it is undoubtedly the objects of sense perception that make up the content of the concept *real*. But this statement, we must be careful to note, is not intended to report an assertion of the ordinary person or to reproduce his own formulation of the answer to the question of reality. It represents a later scientific formulation of the naive person's natural view. Such a person does not at the outset possess the concept of perception; the latter is a product of special reflection and arises as a result of observing and comparing the diverse dependencies of experiences on the sense organs. Observation soon leads us to distinguish the perceptual image from the perceived object; but originally, from the naive standpoint, the two simply coincide. A person does not say "I have a perception of a table" and proceed thereafter to infer the presence of a table. On the contrary, he says "I see a table". Without drawing any inference at all, he takes the object to be the immediately given, and does not distinguish it from the representation or image of the object. For him they are one and the same. Wundt uses for this unity the expression "object of representation"[6].

At this stage, there is no occasion whatsoever to form the concept of the real. That concept first makes its entry in the case of certain special experiences, such as dreams, the so-called sensory illusions, the false assertions of another person that must be checked. Here is the source of the notion of the illusory or the unreal, and hence a reason for constructing the concept of reality. Prior to this, there was nothing from which this concept could be delimited. The formation of concepts, as we know, presupposes differentiation.

As soon as this delimiting becomes necessary, we utilize as the criterion of reality that which we call perception, regardless of whether we already possess the concept of perception. If a person does not believe some object or other is real, there is only one way to convince him of its existence: we must take him to the object or bring it to him so that he can see it, handle it, or hear it. Then he is no longer in doubt. Suppose someone dreams that he is traveling in distant lands. After he awakens, a companion who has been keeping watch beside him through the night can tell him that the wandering was just an illusion, for his own senses testify to the fact that the body of the person who thought he was wandering

---

6 System der Philosophie, 3rd edition, p. 79.

afar lay there peacefully all the time. A separation is thus engendered between representation and object. The images in the dream were real; the object of the images, the wandering, was unreal, it did not exist.

It soon develops, however, that there are also cases in which an object is declared to be real without its having been perceived by the senses. A primitive man, who finds his companion torn to pieces in the forest, is convinced that a beast of prey is responsible, even though no human eye has ever caught sight of the animal. It is thus a sufficient criterion of reality if, instead of perceiving the object itself, we perceive the effects it has produced. The concept of causality is tied up in this way with the concept of reality. How clearly the former emerges in consciousness is a question that for the time being we can pass over without discussion. Life constantly poses the task of finding the causes of given effects, and in all ordinary situations experience quickly and easily supplies answers of sufficient probability. Indeed, learning from experience *is* nothing more than establishing such linkages.

With this, the objectives of daily life are completely taken care of. The perception first of the object and second of its effects provides in all cases a sufficient criterion of reality. Since not the object as such but only its effects need be given, the object itself comes to be thought of as so completely divorced from the perceiver that the naive individual can unhesitatingly answer "yes" to the question whether objects can be real without anyone perceiving either them or their effects. It is then natural that things outside of perception are thought of as continuing to exist just as they are given in perception — that is, equipped with all of their so-called primary and secondary qualities, spatial and temporal extension, colors, odors, and the like. In fact, from the pre-scientific standpoint, to *think* things means nothing other than to imagine them intuitively; hence they have to be thought of as fitted out with the intuitive qualities.

This is how the natural view of the world arrives at the position usually called "naive realism".

It is worth noting that from this viewpoint real objects are conceived of entirely as "things-in-themselves". The naive realist will always maintain, if he is pressed to take a stand on this question, that the being of a stone or of a heavenly body presupposes no relations of dependency whatsoever to other things or to perception, that they exist "in themselves". Indeed, the concept of a thing-in-itself is a widespread popular conception and was not first created, as is sometimes supposed, by a particular philosophical system. Quite the contrary. Kant, and Locke before him, borrowed it from pre-scientific thought. Notice how Kant introduces this conception into his philosophy, without definition, without any special reference to it as a specific fundamental concept of his theory. There can be no doubt that he simply assumed — and correctly — that the notion was a familiar one.

Can philosophy retain unaltered the criteria of reality accepted by the naive view of the world?

The first supposition put forward by the naive view — that the directly given counts as real — must of course be adopted. For here without question is the source of the concept of reality as such. In fact, this is acknowledged by all thinkers, and is expressly pointed out by some, von Beneke, for example[7]. The proposition "The data of consciousness are real" is nothing but the most primitive, if also preliminary, definition of the real, of existence (see above, § 12). It is preliminary because one soon admits more than the given into the extension of the concept of reality. The philosophical definition, however, undertakes not to go beyond but to render more precise the naive view by pointing out that *all* immediate data have equal claims to reality, that things given in perception have no greater claims than "subjective" data, such as feelings or fantasy images. Of course, the naive view does not deny the reality of "subjective" data; but it often neglects and even ignores them in comparison with the reality of what is perceived through the senses, especially with that of the "corporeal".

Just how we should further designate immediately experienced reality, whether we must say "The tree itself is given me" or only "The perceptual image or 'appearance' of the thing 'tree' is given" — is a question quite immaterial for us at this point.

But the second step of naive thought — in which not only the given but also the causes of the given are accepted as real, even though they are not given but are only assumed on the basis of the notion of cause — is one that philosophy views with greater caution. For in the first place, we here encounter the idea of cause, and this must be clarified before it can be accepted as part of the determination of the concept of reality. In the second place, no matter

---

7 System der Metaphysik, 1840, pp. 76, 83, 90.

how this clarification turns out, it seems certain in advance that reducing the concept of reality to that of causality cannot satisfy us epistemologically. For the concept of causality is obviously more complicated than the concept of reality and presupposes it as primary, since in any event a causal relation is exclusively a relation between realities.

But even if philosophy wished to follow the natural outlook in taking this step, there would still not be full accord. For, as we have just seen, pre-scientific thought already affirms a reality-in-itself that is not experienced either as such or in its effects, and to which therefore the earlier criteria are not applicable. Hence these criteria are no longer regarded as essential for the real; they are abandoned, and for the moment no substitute is provided.

As good as the psychological grounding and explanation of the prescientific view may be, just that poor is its epistemological justification. The majority of philosophers have not remained with the naive view. Rather, they have sought new points of view from which they hoped to find better and more unified criteria. Departures from the naive outlook have been in two directions. Some authors have attempted to perfect and supplement the popular view so as to achieve scientifically serviceable criteria. Others have rejected the steps taken on its own by naive thought and returned to the latter's starting point in order to hold fast to it in all of its purity. This second effort characterizes the standpoint known as "idealistic positivism" or "philosophy of immanence" and, less appropriately, "conscientialism". Most philosophers have chosen the first path and have arrived at various systems commonly designated as "realistic". We shall take a brief look at some of the intellectual structures in this category and thereafter examine especially the criteria of reality of immanence philosophy.

Our thoughts often move almost automatically along the following quite plausible path. In ordinary practice, as we saw, the predicate 'real' is first ascribed to what is immediately experienced, later to that which is assumed to be the cause of what is experienced. The question then arises whether the two criteria may possibly be reducible to one another. Now it is clear that the second cannot be subsumed under the first; it signifies something new with respect to the first. But the converse is certainly conceivable: the first criterion could be reduced to the second, and in that event would not have to be introduced as something independent. This would be the case if every given were itself the cause of another given. Then indeed the definition of the real as the "cause of the given" would fit both the experienced real and the real that is not experienced. As a matter of fact, it is quite possible to claim that whatever is experienced is the cause or part of the cause of something else that is experienced. Every datum of consciousness influences the later mental processes in some way; we can say that in principle an experience never vanishes from consciousness "without a trace", without leaving behind some disposition or other.

For the moment, let us disregard whether this definition of the real accomplishes anything very much. Let us instead ask whether we can follow further the path taken by the movement of popular thought, which tends to ascribe reality also to those objects which, as far as anyone knows, produce no experiences at all since no one ever perceives them. An attempt of this sort has in fact been made.

Certain thinkers have used the concept of cause, of effecting, as a springboard for a further leap into the realm of the transcendent. They have held that whatever ordinary thought has discarded, we may also discard from our philosophical characterization, and we shall still retain enough. That is, if previously we said that we call real whatever is the cause of experiences, we can now give up the relation to experience and still maintain the position that everything real is a *cause*. Anything that does not make itself noticeable in some way, never manifests itself, is in fact not *there*, is not real; whether we experience the manifestation of a thing, however, is accidental. Thus we capture the essential as opposed to the accidental if we accept the formulation: the real is that which *has an effect (wirklich ist, was wirkt)*.

Even our language seems to exert pressure in behalf of this interpretation and to demonstrate that it has caught the sense of the popular view. In German, the word 'real' ('wirklich') is derived from the verb 'to have an effect' ('wirken'). In Aristotle the concept ènérgeia coincides with that of reality. And Leibniz, too, declared: *"quod non agit, non existit"*. The best known advocate of this conception no doubt is Schopenhauer. Of matter, he said: "its being is its acting on something; it is impossible even to think of its having any other being" [8]. In another passage, he wrote that matter

---

8 Die Welt als Wille und Vorstellung, Volume I, § 4.

is "causality itself, objectively conceived"[9]. The reality of things, he explained, is their materiality: reality is thus the "efficacy of things generally". Today we find the same definition in many thinkers; for example, Benno Erdmann states: "Those objects are real that we conclude are efficacious[10]."

Undoubtedly this equating of the real with the efficacious is *de facto* perfectly correct. Yet it does not conclusively fulfill our purpose. Even though the real never appears in the world without efficacy, yet it can be conceived of independently of efficacy; it can be separated from it conceptually. And it is precisely the naive view that effectuates this separation[11]. That something can be real without leaving behind the least effect (for example, the last thought of a dying person) is an idea not at all foreign to this view. If we acknowledge the universal connection between reality and causality, we might of course utilize efficacy as a criterion of being, provided we knew how to recognize the efficacy or effectiveness of an object. It is clear that the question cannot be answered this way; it can only be pushed back and into a more complicated domain, much more difficult in fact to comprehend. For efficacy, as we have already stressed, is the more specific concept; its criterion presupposes that of reality. The latter concept is more general, since it is certainly possible at least to think of a being without efficacy (for example, one that disappears without a trace). Defining the real simply as the efficacious puts us at a further intolerable disadvantage in that it totally dissolves every connection with the immediately given, from which the concept of the real originated and with which it must later seek a tie if it is to find any application at all.

Nevertheless, speculation has at times moved even further from the starting-point. It has made the idea of reality into something still more volatile by assuming that it is not absolutely necessary to look for its essence in *causal* relations. On the contrary, the definition can be generalized: being can be sufficiently characterized through the existence of relations in general. As we know, Lotze conceived of the real in this manner as an all-sided "standing-in-

---

9 *Ibid.*, Volume II, Book I, Chapter 4; see also Abhandlung über den Satz vom Grunde, near the end of § 21.

10 Logik, I, 2nd edition, p. 138.

11 This is pointed out specifically by E. BECHER in "Naturphilosophie", p. 62 (Kultur der Gegenwart, 1914).

relation". But to say that he *defined* being as a standing-in-relation is to do him an injustice. He in fact complained that the statements usually made about the real only specified traits of being but did not define being itself[12]. But he then confessed that "what being means in the sense of reality and in contrast to non-being" is indefinable and can only be experienced[13]. As a matter of fact, a many-sided relatedness is by no means uniquely characteristic of real being; for we know, and Lotze knew just as well, that we can assert mutual relations among concepts, even though being cannot be attributed to concepts. Indeed nothing else can be asserted of them. Their nature consists in their standing in certain relations to one another. Numbers are not real things; but no one denies that relations hold between them. An entire science, arithmetic, has as its sole task to investigate the infinite manifold of these relations. No, Lotze does not define real being by means of relations. He comes only to the conclusion (which at the same time he identifies — erroneously, as was indicated above — with the position of the naive world view) that the reality of being consists entirely in the reality of relations[14]. But how real relations differ from purely ideal ones, according to him, also cannot be defined; it must be assumed, experienced immediately. In the end, Lotze too is compelled to think of real relations *de facto* as in turn causal, so that in substance his standpoint is not essentially different from the one that simply designates the real as the efficacious. Actually he contributes much more toward solving the problem that confronts us by his excellent polemic against Herbart, who defined being as "absolute position", a formulation on whose meaninglessness we need waste no words.

Let us now look briefly at some attempts at defining the real that move in the opposite direction. These stay close to the source from which the concept of reality flows, that is, they seek to hold fast to the directly given, to immediate experience, and especially to perception.

The natural world outlook accepts as external reality not only what is given in perception but other things as well. These other things, however, are represented as if they were given in perception and would in fact appear in perception if certain conditions were

---

12 Metaphysik, § 1.
13 Metaphysik, § 5, § 8.
14 Metaphysik, especially § 10.

fulfilled. Expressed in other terms, things themselves are conceived of as conditions of possible perceptions. This simple thought was clothed in a philosophical formula by John Stuart Mill, as we know. He declared that real objects are "permanent possibilities of sensation". For example, he said in his *Logic:* "The existence, therefore, of a phenomenon is but another word for its being perceived, or for the inferred possibility of perceiving it[15]." Since he did not assume the existence of things-in-themselves behind the phenomena, this proposition served as a characterization of reality as a whole.

In general we can grant that things signify possibilities of sensation for us. Yet this leaves undecided whether they are something else in addition. But regardless of whether or not this theory uniquely designates the concept of reality, our question is not resolved. Reducing the real to the possible must always be counted a *hysteron-proteron.* Consider how necessary it is to clarify the concept of possibility in philosophy! It always proves necessary to explain it in reference to reality; the possible is something that under certain conditions becomes real or actual, whose "being" thus depends on the "reality" of certain circumstances. Hence we are in a circle if in turn we seek to define the real in terms of the possible. In order to make the doctrine of the possibilities of sensation fully usable in any fashion we should have to be able to specify completely all the conditions under which sensations really do occur. This we cannot do; indeed, here is where the problem actually lies. Thus we can easily see that Mill's formulation does not in the smallest degree bring us any nearer to our goal. Moreover, when Mill notes at another place in the *Logic* that "to exist is to excite, or be capable of exciting, any state of consciousness", he locates — not altogether consistently — the criterion for the reality of objects in their *effects,* since the expression 'to excite' means the same as 'to cause'. The difficulties that lie in the concept of possibility are, in this formulation, concealed in the word 'capable'. Mill's views wander off in an uncertain direction from the immediately given; hence we cannot describe them as pure positivism, for which the standpoint of immanence is characteristic.

The philosophical endeavors we are considering here have as their goal a scientific formulation of the reality concept derived

---

15 Book III, Chapter 24, § 1.

from ordinary life. But this goal had already been attained in the older, simpler formulation of Kant: "Whatever is bound up with the material conditions of experience (of sensation) is *real* or *actual*." The concept of possibility is explained by means of the notion of "formal conditions" [16]. Thus he traces possibility back only indirectly, so to speak, to relations with the intuitive, or the simply given, while reality or actuality is traced back directly (this is what the word 'material' means). The systematic superiority of this view over that of Mill is easily recognized. At the same time, there is still an unacceptable vagueness in the expression 'is bound up with' *(zusammenhängt)*, which, moreover, is not lessened by the explanation which Kant adds: "The postulate relating to knowing the *reality* of things requires not immediate *perception* (hence sensation of which we are conscious) of the object itself whose existence is to be known, but its connection *(Zusammenhang)* with actual perception, in accordance with the analogies of experience which set forth all real linkages in an experience in general [17]." Here the connection *(Zusammenhang)* is explained as being determinable in accordance with the "Analogies of Experience", that is, in accordance with the fundamental principles of the permanence of substance, of causality, and of interaction. Once again we find ourselves referred to complicated synthetic statements. These may be entirely correct and from them we may perhaps be able to obtain the criterion we are looking for. But they do not answer our question for the simple reason that they do not set forth this criterion explicitly. Thus they say nothing about how the existence of those relations spoken of in the "Analogies of Experience" may be recognized. The criterion is not immediately experienced. And if it is inferred, the question then arises: In what way and on the basis of what principles can such an inference take place? Indirectly, of course, Kant does provide an answer; it may be taken from his doctrine of the "Schematism". There is no occasion here, however, to go into this obscure and quite vulnerable theory. What parts of it we can apply and must accept will be clear from the next sections.

Some recent thinkers have also adopted the Kantian formulation. Thus Riehl, for example, says: "'to be real' and 'to belong to the

---

16 Kritik der reinen Vernunft, Kehrbach edition, p. 202 (Raymund Schmidt edition, 1956, p. 266).

17 *Ibid.,* pp. 206 ff. (p. 271).

system of perceptions' mean one and the same thing" [18]. The great advantage of these expressions is that they make a fundamental point of bringing to the fore the need to connect the definition of the real in some way to the immediately given, that is, to sensation. At the same time, the impossibility of a purely logical definition of reality is correctly brought out. For wherever the definition of the content of a concept requires that we have recourse to the directly given, this always means that in our interpretation we are looking beyond that insurmountable limit to definition (see above Part I, § 6) which divides the realm of concepts from the realm of reality.

We must now endeavor to supplement and refine these formulations by introducing a characteristic feature that in every case allows us to decide whether an object stands in that special relationship to sensations (or to other experiences) which guarantees its reality. If we succeed in giving a rigorous form to the reality concept of ordinary life, then it will be easy to recognize whether philosophy can rest content with that concept or whether it must either go beyond it or turn back from it to the starting-point — in other words, whether the various realistic views or the strictly idealist, immanentist view will triumph against a rigorous critique.

Some general remarks should be made about the method to be adopted.

The attempt to press forward from the knowledge provided by everyday life and science to a secure philosophical truth may take either of two roads. The first, essayed by Descartes, consists in discarding one after the other all judgments held to be true if they are open to the least possibility of doubt, holding on only to what is absolutely certain beyond all doubt, and then on this narrow basis (we know just *how* narrow it is) erecting a structure of philosophical verities with the help of completely unassailable steps in reasoning. In this manner a *minimum* boundary is marked off for the domain of knowledge.

But the only absolutely certain method of thought is deduction, and deduction is a purely analytic procedure which furnishes no insights that are new in principle. Hence the doubt-free residue, composed of incontrovertible truths, cannot fundamentally be increased, and the system apparently erected on it is a mere will-o'-the-wisp, which only reflects the same background under different

---

18 Beiträge zur Logik, 2nd edition, 1912, p. 25.

illuminations. Whoever wishes to go further must use the very methods rejected during his period of doubting. And he must retrace many of the steps through which he reached his sanctuary of impregnable certainty.

The second road to philosophical truth consists not in eliminating all those judgments stemming from daily life and the sciences that for some reason are *open to doubt*, but in discarding only those that for some reason can be held to be *false*. The difference is very great indeed: the first course eliminates whatever can be doubted, the second only what is untenable. The first excludes everything that is not indubitably correct, the second that which is unquestionably incorrect. The first is obliged to round out into a complete, finished system the meager core that remains; the second preserves the system in that from the great block of what is believed and held, it carves away all falsehood, bias and misjudgment. The second road sets a *maximum* boundary for the realm of truth, one to which it can at most extend. The area of our realm of knowledge will be enclosed between the minimum boundary of the first method and the maximum boundary of the second. But just *where* between the two of them it lies, can scarcely ever be exactly determined.

There is no question but that rationally the second road is to be preferred as the more direct, the more reliable. It starts out from the assumption of an inexhaustible world full of variegated natural processes and thinking individuals; it cleanses the scientific world view of contradictions. (The habiliments of the resulting world view are determined essentially by the manner in which the judgments of physics are consistently joined to those of psychology and accommodated within the same system.) Compared to this road, the seemingly more rigorous one of radical doubt is in truth inconsistent; for scarcely is the goal reached when all steps must be retraced, and this can be done only by following the same course that the second road took from the very beginning.

In regard to the question of reality, the method of doubt is left with the claim that reality attaches to the contents of one's own consciousness, and in particular only to those experienced in the present, since judgments about what was experienced just moments before are no longer absolutely certain. This method surely cannot infer the existence of an external world, of the contents of the consciousness of another person, of a "thou". On the other hand, the method of eliminating falsehoods removes, as unreal, from the every-day picture of the world only those components that, if held as real, would result in contradictions.

§ 24. The Temporality of the Real

From early times — in Plato's system the thought is already fore-shadowed, if not expressed — the shadowy realm of concepts and the world of reality have been counterposed to one another as *timeless* being and *temporal* being. This introduces a determination of such universal and profound significance that it is neither possible nor necessary to alter or improve it. No one disputes that whatever is real for us is in time, and that concepts are timeless. Here we may rely on the *consensus omnium* and go on to the next step without fear of contradiction. On this point, no explicit justification or demonstration is required, only elucidation and clarification.

The temporality of all that is real is indeed a feature that can fulfill completely the role of the desired criterion.

Everything that really exists is there for us at a certain point in time. Events or things — everything is at a certain point in time or during a certain time interval. This is true regardless of what else we may believe about the "essence" of time; it is true independently of how we determine a point in time or of whether we ascribe to time relative or absolute character, subjective or objective validity. For the ordinary person, as for the sciences, whatever is real is in time; therefore we can always recognize the real by this trait. And if a philosopher asserts the existence of non-temporal realities, as does Kant, say, with respect to the things-in-themselves, nothing is altered in his doctrine by the fact that for our cognition the real never reveals itself except under the form of time.

A large sector of reality also possesses another feature that is not shared by anything unreal: *spatial* ordering. All real things and processes of the *"external"* world (a spatial expression itself) are characterized by the fact that a quite specific *locus* must be assigned to them. But, as we know, this is not true of all realities; many data of consciousness, which possess the full reality of what is directly given, are absolutely non-spatial. The emotions of joy or sadness, anger or sympathy that I feel are not somewhere in space; they are not given at a particular place (especially, of course, not "in my

head"). It makes no sense to ascribe spatial predicates to them.
The circumstance that all of reality is temporally determined, but
only part of it is spatially determined, is the source of a whole
series of philosophical questions. It contributes, for example, to the
psycho-physical problem, of which we shall speak later. Meanwhile,
this circumstance teaches us that both temporality and spatiality
may be viewed as *sufficient* criteria of reality, but only temporality
is a *necessary* criterion of all that is real.

Mere concepts are never at a place, are nowhere at a specific
time. The number 7, the concept of contradiction, the concept of
causality — these are not to be found at any place in the world,
not to be encountered at any time, not even (as we have quite often
emphasized) in the mind of the person who thinks the concepts.
What exist in the mind are only the real mental processes that take
over the functions of the invented concepts. And this is true, of
course, not only of general concepts, but of individual ones as well.
A specific place and a specific time can be ascribed to the Battle
of Pharsalus; but the concept of the Battle of Pharsalus is no-where
and at-no-time.

The same thing holds also for certain unreal objects not custom-
arily designated as concepts, for instance things or processes regarded as real but that later turn out not to exist at all. Let us consider an example. I think of a journey that I am going to take next
year. The journey, at least now, is something unreal; and if we
assume that unfavorable circumstances prevent it altogether, then the
predicate of being real cannot possibly be assigned to it. In what way
then must the imaginary journey differ from a real one? Surely not by
any contentual features. For absolutely nothing can happen to me on
the real journey that I could not just as well have pictured to myself in thought. The smallest occurrence, the least incident that can
take place on a journey, I am able to imagine down to the tiniest
detail. Every content of a perceptual image can also be the content
of a memory or fantasy image. This insight — that the real cannot
be distinguished from the unreal through any feature of content —
was expressed by Kant in the frequently cited proposition: "A hundred real thalers contain not a whit more than a hundred imaginary
ones." But the honor of having been the first person to express this
truth belongs to HUME (A Treatise of Human Nature, Book I, Part II,
Section 6): "The idea of existence . . . when conjoined with the idea
of any object, makes no addition to it." Thus we cannot recognize

from any feature of a concept whether or not that concept designates something real; for this we need an entirely new predicate,
some special relation to something else.

When someone has to specify the difference between my thinking of a real journey and my thinking of an imaginary one, he will
perhaps point out that in the latter case my thoughts are quite
indefinite. I can imagine the journey in this way or that; it is a product of my fantasy. Nothing compels me to provide it in imagination
with fully determinate, exactly fixed details. On the other hand,
when I think of a real journey, the smallest circumstance must be
determined down to the most minute detail. For if I allow the least
divergence or arbitrary alteration, then I am no longer thinking of
how the real journey proceeded; I am substituting something imaginary.

This account has an element of truth in it, but it needs to be
filled out and refined. For it is necessary to locate the quite special
kind of determinacy that the real possesses as contrasted with the
imaginary. This determinacy consists in nothing other than the fixed
spatial and temporal ordering, which assigns to each item of the real
journey a quite definite place, to each occurrence in the real world
a unique relationship with all other occurrences and parts of the
world. Every element of reality has one and only one place in time,
which is fully and firmly determined as soon as a unit of measure
and a reference system for time are chosen. A fixed spatial determination, moreover, is characteristic of most realities. But since this
does not apply to all realities (for example, the feelings experienced
on the journey), it follows that unique temporal determination alone
is to be regarded as a necessary characteristic of reality.

Now it may be objected perhaps that an exhaustively complete
temporal determination can also be ascribed to a merely imaginary
journey. The circumstances might be such, for example, that the
future journey must of necessity take place at a quite precisely determined point in time, on such and such a day, at such and such
a minute or even second; and everything could be planned and
aranged so that all of the individual phases by force of circumstance
occur in a manner that is precisely predictable. Then in thinking
about the future events of the journey, I would be compelled to
represent the individual occurrences at quite definite points in time;
there would be no room for an arbitrary exercise of will on my
part. But would the journey thereby become real?

It is the examination of just such a case that confirms our findings. For suppose we grant that the natural interconnections have in fact made it absolutely necessary that the events of the journey should occur in a quite definite way and at points in time known precisely in advance. This would mean that the events must happen this way and cannot possibly either fail to happen or turn out differently, that the journey is thus not an imaginary one at all, but possesses *future reality*. If natural circumstances determine with necessity the time an event occurs, this is the same as saying that the event actually does occur. Neither in our example nor, strictly speaking, in any other case will the circumstances ever be so completely in view that any predicted future event in its entirety would have to be fitted into a fully determined position in time. It will still always be possible for unanticipated events to cut across the predicted course of things, so that we can never judge with certainty whether or not what was only imaginary to begin with will also become actual. And this is always expressed in the fact that my imagination is not absolutely compelled to assign a unique point in time to that which is imaginary; an element of uncertainty and arbitrariness always remains. The same is true of the existence of past realities. It can never be determined with perfect certainty that the imagined past was real in the manner in which it is imagined; however, the more exactly we can locate it in space and time, the more sure we are that we have come upon something real.

A dream will be recognized, after we awake, as something unreal (that is, not the event of dreaming but the events dreamed of), because there is no compulsion to place it at a given point in time. It has left no traces with the aid of which it can be connected uniquely in time to the experiences of the present.

We may now regard as established the proposition that whatever ordinary life and science acknowledge as real is characterized by its temporality, by its having a fixed place in the general temporal ordering of things and processes. KANT expressed this truth (in the chapter on "schematism" in the Critique of Pure Reason) when he said: "The schema of reality is existence in some determinate time."

From the foregoing account it follows that the characteristic trait we have found is not a contentual feature. On the contrary, it is an external one, so to speak, which interweaves each real thing with every other.

But does our result fulfill the other condition that we have recognized as indispensable for a criterion of reality? This condition requires that everything be linked with the immediately given, because the concept of reality is rooted in the given and must admit of being pursued back to its roots. Now at first glance, our criterion seems not to satisfy this requirement. For time determinations are not directly given; they are not matters of simple experience. Rather, they seem to presuppose a well-defined objective measure and an equally well-defined reference system — concepts that lie outside of the immediately given. But a connection with the given is achieved once we make clear to ourselves the one way in which a temporal determination can be effectuated and a point in time defined. A point in time is fixed by specifying the interval between it and another point in time. For example, I say that Kant was born 13 years after Hume. If I then ask when Hume was born, I can answer only by relating that event to another point in time. I reply, for instance, "1711 years after the birth of Christ". Of what use is this to me, however, if I do not know when this latter event took place? But no matter what point in time I take as a reference point, the time specification always remains hanging in the air, as it were, and requires for its answer a new "when". Time determinations lack support or meaning unless there is a point at which the question "When?" no longer needs an answer.

Now there is just such a point: it is the *present moment*. I cannot ask "When is the present moment?", for this "when" is immediately experienced. Time determinations have meaning and purpose only for those events that are not directly present to my consciousness. In the final analysis, the meaning of a "when" is to be found in the interval between the "when" itself and that point in time which for me is the present. The present cannot be further defined; it serves as a fixed point of reference for all determinations and is indeed the only one that exists. Through it the relativity of the *beginning* of time is resolved for me. (The psychological and physical relativity of *duration* is not involved here; it is left standing as taught by the individual sciences.) Thus we see that if the criterion for the reality of an object is located in its existence at a definite time, the connection of all that is real with the simply given is expressed with full force and clarity. To exist at a specific time means to stand in a specific relation to the given, to the experienced "now".

Thus orientation in time is undoubtedly the characteristic that is exhibited wherever we speak of real existence, wherever we ascribe to objects that "reality" which cannot be defined but the sense of which everyone presupposes as fully determined and as governing all action and inquiry. In particular cases, various characteristics may help us establish reality; but these features all have in common the fact that through them what is real is assigned a definite position in time (and usually a definite position in space). This is what all methods of *"Realisierung"* (the justification of assertions of reality) come to in the end.

In reaching this conclusion — in developing, on the basis of the thought and procedures of practice, the criterion by which we can mark off the range of what is to count as "real" — we have created a firm foundation for the philosophical treatment of the problem of reality, and one that should not be too quickly relinquished. Obviously the philosopher, whatever his objective may be, has no right to endow the word 'reality' in advance with a new sense, differing from that fashioned and used by pre-philosophical thought. It is from there that philosophy's problems are posed, and problems cannot be solved merely through new definitions. The philosophical doctrines with which our reality criterion is not in harmony usually give us to understand that they do not in fact desire to erect a new concept of reality; their point is only that our criterion does not correctly capture what the ordinary person truly means when he speaks of reality, and hence must be stated in some other way.

In my opinion, it can be demonstrated that these doctrines are wrong. They proceed in a thoroughly dogmatic manner, that is, they set up their own particular reality concept in advance in order to avoid certain problems that otherwise they could not master; and they try to take their stand behind this sense of the concept as if it were the only natural, obvious or even possible one.

These philosophical systems, which maintain that the concept of the temporally determined does not coincide with that of the real, fall by their nature into two groups: one declares that the concept is too narrow, the other that it is too broad. The first is then bound to see in philosophy the discoverer of a new domain of reality located beyond that of science and everyday life. The second is obliged to criticize the simple standpoint of the naive man and of the scientist on the ground that it accepts mere fancies as "real", hypostasizes mere concepts and attributes meaning to pure hypotheses (mere "aids to description"). Both things have occurred often enough, and both tendencies play a role in the philosophical thought of all periods.

One of the historic tasks of philosophy has been to refute the first of these tendencies. Today we may regard this as having in essence been fulfilled and completed, approximately since the time of Kant's struggle against the old metaphysics. A critical examination of the second tendency, however, is still of very great importance today, and especially today. Such an examination will be taken up in the pages that follow. We shall develop there the positive consequences of the insights we have obtained, and in the process these insights themselves will be further confirmed. Our position with respect to the other tendency, which assigns an excessively wide range to the concept of the real, will then appear of itself, without our having to direct any special inquiry toward it.

§ 25. Things-In-Themselves and the Notion of Immanence

We claim that everything is real that must be thought of as being at a specific time.

The informed person will appreciate at once the significance of this proposition. He will realize how very far it takes us beyond the world of the immediately given. Once it turns out that the rules of scientific inquiry compel us to assign a definite position in space and time to an object, the real existence of that object is also assured in a philosophical sense. The object is more than a mere auxiliary assumption or a working hypothesis. For example, if in accordance with rigorous rules of scientific research the where and when of atoms can be given uniquely and definitely*, then they exist regardless of whether or not they ever directly reach perception — and also regardless of what else we may be able to say about their "nature", that is, regardless of the additional concepts under which we can subsume them.

Our criterion does not initially presuppose anything at all with respect to space and time (except that they somehow establish the

---

* Schlick would have revised this formulation in the light of the indeterminacy relations of quantum mechanics, of which he was fully aware two or three years after he wrote this sentence. [Translator's note.]

possibility of determining position in space and time in the sense discussed). It is clear, however, that space and time cannot be declared real in the sense of our criterion itself; for time is not at a certain time, space is not at a certain place. Here too contact with ordinary and scientific thought is preserved in the best possible way; for no one regards pure time or mere space as something real in the same sense as the pen in my hand or the joy in my heart.

Now objects whose reality is asserted without their being directly *given* are called (in our meaning of the term) *things-in-themselves*. At any rate this is the meaning we wish to assign to the term from now on. It seems to me that this definition brings out most clearly the problem that attaches to the concept. In what follows, the reader should at no time forget that the expression 'thing-in-itself' is to be understood in the stipulated sense alone.

The term can indeed be taken in many other senses. For instance, we may, with MACH (Analyse der Empfindungen, p. 5), believe that it must mean something that is left over when we think of a thing with all of its properties removed. This we are not concerned with. When we plead for the existence of things in themselves, we are saying merely that we may speak of real objects without thereby meaning that they are, in our sense, "given" as objects to a subject. Thus we are not postulating a hidden, unknown "bearer" of properties, an "absolute" in some metaphysical sense. For the moment, we do not care to make any judgments as to what is the case with things in themselves in these respects. Consequently, the bases on which the concept of a thing in itself recently has often been held *a priori* to be in disrepute are also not relevant to the concept as formulated here. Naturally, the word 'thing' is not intended to suggest that whatever exists in itself must be conceived of as somehow thing-like, or substantial. On the contrary, a "thing in itself" can just as well have the character of a process or a happening. We do not want to prejudge anything, and for this reason the word 'thing' at this point is in fact misleading. But since no neutral expression is available we shall continue to use the word, content with having specifically warned against any misunderstanding.

If the concept is defined in this manner, then, by the remarks just made, is surely follows from our criterion that things in themselves exist, since clearly many objects that must be thought of as temporally determined are not among the immediately given. (Were

13*

we to draw the conclusion that temporality, in Kant's sense, must be a property of things in themselves, we would be entirely wrong; but more of this later.) In recent times, as everyone knows, transcendent things — they can be so designated since they are located outside the realm of the given — have been the target of assaults launched from all sides, and especially by many positivists and Neo-Kantians. Any defense of things-in-themselves is looked upon almost as something old-fashioned, to be treated only with an indulgent smile. But this will not prevent us from going right ahead to investigate the question thoroughly.

Philosophers who reject things-in-themselves we shall call advocates of the *notion of immanence,* provided they demand more or less strictly that we remain in the sphere of that which is given or encountered and rule out transcendence. The individual schools of this tendency differ widely from one another, although more in terminology than in substance. A few of them have themselves designated their ideas as immanence philosophy (Schuppe, Schubert-Soldern and others). In so far as the view is stressed that all immediate data have the character of *consciousness,* we may (with Külpe) speak of "conscientialism". But this would not be accepted at all by many opponents of things-in-themselves, Avenarius for example. In his philosophy, neither the concept nor the word 'consciousness' actually occurs, and he would reject as entirely inappropriate the designating of everything that is given as "content of consciousness". At the same time, the Neo-Kantians of the Marburg school (Cohen, Natorp and many others) will have nothing to do with the "given". They insist on remaining in the sphere of "transcendental logic", which they would identify with the domain of real being and from which the fictitious things in themselves are excluded. But we do not need to discuss their position at this point (see below § 39).

Some thinkers interpret the immanence standpoint — and maintain that this is the only way to construe it — as holding that the idea of an object that is not the content of some consciousness is self-contradictory, and hence that a thing-in-itself is impossible. Only a few words are needed to dispose of this interpretation. It is summed up in the widely quoted words of Schuppe: "A thought that is directed to a thing makes this thing something thought; consequently, the thought of a thing that is not thought is an unthinkable thought[19]." The same argument, as we know, is found earlier in Berkeley and a number of other thinkers.

In the literature of modern epistemology it has been shown conclusively more than once that this inference rests on an equivocation — on a two-fold meaning of the word 'thinking' — and is therefore invalid. The expression 'a thing that is thought' (*'gedachtes Ding'*) may mean (1) an object created by thought, that is, an idea or representation within my consciousness; but (2) it may also mean an object only *intended* or *meant* in thought, that is, designated by means of some idea or representation of my consciousness and with which a thought in my consciousness is correlated. When we speak of a thing-in-itself, then of course it is "thought (of)" in the second sense; but by no means does it follow that it is also *thought* in the first sense. Schuppe's inference, however, conflates the two senses[20]. This pseudo-argument is especially easy for us to resolve on the basis of what has gone before. We have made it quite clear that thinking, in the sense relevant to knowledge, signifies nothing but the *designating* of objects. But that an object is not produced by our giving it a designation, indeed is independent of it and can exist without our correlating some sign or representation with it, is all contained in the very concept of designating. The above fallacy would never have been committed if the two meanings of the word 'thought' had been kept apart by the assignment to them of different terms.

Thus the concept of thing-in-itself is not *a priori* self-contradictory. But there are other reasons that operate against the assumption of a transcendent being and cause philosophers to confine the concept of reality to the realm of the given (or of "what is encountered", or of "contents of consciousness", or whatever it may be called).

These reasons must now be examined. They are to be sought — as in the case of any serious scientific assumption — in the fact that the opposite view is believed to lead to contradictions or at least to represent a completely superfluous, unnecessary hypothesis. Here the claim is that the positing of realities beyond the given either

---

19 WILHELM SCHUPPE, Erkenntnistheoretische Logik, p. 69.

20 See, for instance, the excellent discussion by W. FREYTAG, Der Realismus und das Transzendenzproblem, Part VII, 1902; also G. STÖRRING, Erkenntnistheorie, 2nd edition, 1920, p. 73.

leads on closer scrutiny to unsolvable problems, or else contributes nothing to the solution of the problems that do exist.

The first part of the claim is of course the more radical, and it should therefore be inspected first. Is it true that unsolvable problems (i. e., allegedly unavoidable contradictions to the postulates and rules of the sciences) arise if we regard as *real* not only the immediately given but everything for which these very rules and postulates yield specific spatial and temporal information? Is it true that these contradictions can be avoided only if we limit the concept of the real by reducing it to its first source, the immediately experienced?

There is no doubt that a withdrawal into the immanence standpoint obviates and makes unnecessary a whole series of philosophical struggles. Surely every serious thinker has at times felt the temptation to rid himself of tormenting problems by adopting the immanentist viewpoint. Just as Herbart believed that every able beginner in philosophy ought to be a skeptic, one might perhaps add that every conscientious scholar ought to work his way through the stage of immanence philosophy. It is a standpoint that makes it possible to forestall problems, to prevent intellectual conflicts from arising in the first place; this seems a better method than to treat them afterwards when they are fully developed. Moreover, this prophylactic procedure seems always applicable. For one thing is clear: whatever of the world is originally given, whatever is there prior to any intellectual evaluation, must be free of contradiction. Facts do not contradict one another; our thought must assume responsibility for all conflicts, which must have been brought about through one misstep or another. *Correct* thoughts about existing facts can never lead to contradictions; everything that is simply at hand is positive or affirmative, and contradiction becomes possible only through an act of denial (see above § 10). Thus we reach our positivist desideratum: in general, stay with the bare factual, carefully avoiding anything contributed by thought, and be satisfied with the mere description by means of judgments of what is at hand, without adding any hypotheses.

It is obvious, however, that a meticulously rigorous execution of this program would unfortunately mean a total renunciation of knowledge. Knowing presupposes some kind of thinking, and for this concepts are needed. These can be obtained only through systematizing the factual material, and this at once creates the possibility of errors and contradictions. Scientific description, which is explanation, consists in relating facts to and interpreting them through one another, with the help of acts of re-cognition [21].

Thus the extreme standpoint, if carried through with rigor, cancels itself out. But we may still hope to enjoy its advantages if we allow a minimum contribution on the part of thought. The immanentist claim, however, is precisely that the assumption of things-in-themselves does *not* form part of this minimum. For this reason the immanence view would desert the spatio-temporal criterion and go back to the very first, original standpoint, already abandoned even by the world outlook of the naive person. Only the most elementary presuppositions would be admitted — presuppositions of such simplicity that they are in fact common to all starting points and are never held in doubt. For example, AVENARIUS mentions as one such presupposition the "basic empiriocritical postulate of the fundamental sameness of human beings" (Der menschliche Weltbegriff, § 14). Likewise, we find in Mach simple arguments by analogy according to which, for instance, we are permitted to ascribe to our fellow man feelings and ideas similar to our own even though they are never given to us. These assumptions — to which surely there can be no objection — one can accept and be confident that they do not give rise to the dreaded problems from which one has taken flight.

What then are these problems?

Actually the problems basically are only one, not several, or at any rate the others converge in one and are solved simultaneously with it. It is the problem which, since Descartes, has remained at the center of all modern metaphysics: the question of the relation between the mental and the physical. When we trace back the various lines of thought, we see clearly that it is just this problem before which philosophers have taken refuge in the fortress of immanence lest, by remaining in the metaphysical positions of Cartesian dualism, the occasionalism of Geulincx, or Leibniz's Monadology and preestablished harmony, they expose themselves to the assaults of criticism. Even if one of the most prominent representatives of the view had not explicitly stated this to be the

---

21 That every judgment as such transcends the given is shown very well by W. FREYTAG, *op. cit.*, pp. 123 ff.

case[22], we could readily see that all forms of the immanence idea arise from a desire to escape the psycho-physical problem.

Now it is true, and generally conceded, that when we return to the most immediate standpoint — one which precedes philosophical reflection — the problem of the relationship between mind and body in fact disappears. No doubt it is through conceptual elaboration that this distinction is first introduced into the current of experiences, which initially constitutes the world for us. It is only necessary that the intellectual abstraction which effects the separation of mental and physical and assigns each its limits be cleansed of its errors and that its true meaning be established. There is no other way to overcome the problem. Kant, too, solves it by showing that the entire difficulty is "self-made" and springs from a "surreptitious" dualism[23]. It is remarkable that two thinkers of such different tendencies as Kant and Avenarius (as we shall show in more detail below, § 33) arrive in principle at the same solution — or rather dissolution — of the problem. It is a good sign that the truth has been found and an inhibiting difficulty finally deprived of its terrors.

Had Kant's philosophy been correct, it would have proved that the conquest of the psycho-physical problem is compatible with the assumption of things-in-themselves, since both are contained in his system. At the same time, the most important motivation for the immanence standpoint would have disappeared. Its defenders could no longer tell us: "Look, you must come over to our side if you want a completely clear view of the relationship between mind and body." But simply appealing to Kant is obviously not a sufficient argument, since he himself has so often been reproached because the thing-in-itself is the source, allegedly, of unsolvable contradictions in his system. Thus it is necessary to examine specifically and explicitly whether the immanence notion is justified in claiming that every transcendence beyond what is given introduces unresolvable contradictions into the explanation of the world.

We dispute this claim and must therefore show that the assumption of transcendent entities (that is, the existence of entities that are not immediately given) does not lead to any incompatibilities. The proof is best carried out indirectly, by showing that it is pre-

---

22 MACH, Analyse der Empfindungen, 5th edition, p. 24, note.
23 Kritik der reinen Vernunft, Kehrbach edition, pp. 326, 329.

cisely the immanentist system which suffers from difficulties grounded in the impossibility of reconciling the denial of things-in-themselves with the soundness of empirical research methods and their best established principles.

The view we are discussing is found in its purest form in Avenarius and Mach. We shall therefore present and critically review the essentials of the immanence standpoint with reference to these authors. In expounding the basic principles we shall follow Mach's account, which has the advantage of being more intuitive; for the exact logical analysis of the decisive points, however, we must look to the formulations of Avenarius which in their meticulous precision far surpass those of Mach.

The doctrine propounded by immanence philosophy is the following. If we strip away all unwarranted and superfluous additions made by thought, then we recognize that the world is an interconnected system of colors, sounds, smells, tastes, pressures, and the like. These "elements" (as Mach and Avenarius call them; Ziehen speaks of "*gignomena*" or "becomings") are always given in various combinations with one another; they can never be entirely detached from these combinations, and it makes no sense to ask what they are like "in themselves", apart from all relationships to other elements. These combinations are constantly changing; but there do appear among them relatively constant relationships which stand in contrast with the more variable ones, are comprehended in special representations or ideas, and receive their own names. For example, what we call *bodies* are relatively stably linked complexes of colors, pressures and the like. "What also shows itself as relatively constant is the complex of moods, memories and feelings bound to a specific material object (the body) and designated as 'I' (Analyse der Empfindungen, p. 2); "it is not that bodies produce sensations but that complexes of elements (complexes of sensations) form bodies." Just as elements can be assembled into my "I", so they can be assembled into other "I's"; "the relationship leads quite instinctively to the picture of a viscous mass that hangs together more firmly at a number of places (the I)" (*op. cit.*, p. 14). It is the task of science then to describe the mutual dependence of the elements in the simplest possible way. When I investigate the mutual dependence of elements that belong to the complexes called "bodies", I am doing physics; but when I study the dependence of any element on those that belong to the (never sharply bounded, of course) complex "I", then

I am doing psychology. "What differs in the two domains is not the subject-matter but the direction of our investigation" (p. 36). The elements *are* at the place where we perceive or experience them as spatially located, and not in the brain from which they are then first projected out into space.

Here we have in outline a grand world view of astonishing simplicity. It seems to be necessarily free from contradiction, since everything has been purged from it that does not belong to the realm of the merely given, a realm standing above all doubt. It appears to satisfy perfectly all the requirements of science once we understand "... that only the determination of *functional relations* is of any value to us, that it is only the *mutual dependencies of experiences* that we wish to know" (p. 28). This last assertion, of course, does contain a correct element, since all truths — and science is concerned with truth alone — are revealed to us only in specific experiences of verification (see above Part II, § 21).

In this view of the world there is no place for things-in-themselves and immanence philosophy is happy to get rid of what it regards as a superfluous and valueless product of our fantasy. Moreover, it may be said — these are the words in which Viktor Stern, an incisive critic of Mach, gives the latter's philosophy its due — "Nothing of value is lacking in this view of the world, neither other minds, nor the 'world' (that is, an infinite manifold of elements), nor order and law-like regularity in this world, nor the reality of this world, nor its development ...[24]"

The starting-point for the construction of such a world view is so well chosen that the immanence philosopher remains just as far from the dangers of dualism and materialism as from subjective idealism, which is always in danger of losing its tie with the external world altogether and slipping into the abyss of solipsism. To be able to examine this view critically one must become thoroughly familiar with it, and anyone who attacks it without this preparation will generally miss the target[25]. A sympathetic understanding of a philosophical system, however, consists in picturing to oneself

---

24 VIKTOR STERN, Die logischen Mängel der Machschen Antimetaphysik und die realistische Ergänzung seines Positivismus, Vierteljahrschrift für wissenschaftliche Philosophie 38 (1914), p. 391.

25 See Stern's very sound refutation, in the work cited above, of certain inadequate arguments directed against Mach.

just exactly what sense is assumed within that system by each question or assertion of everyday life and science. If we make the notion of immanence our own in this way, we shall soon notice that certain difficulties arise in interpreting all propositions in which we speak of bodies or processes whose elements are never given or, indeed, where the elements of an object are given to several individuals at once.

We shall now consider the first case.

§ 26. Critique of the Notion of Immanence

a) Unperceived Objects

There is no question but that in everyday judgments as in scientific ones we constantly talk of objects *not given* to any consciousness. I speak of the manuscripts now in my desk even though they are not being perceived at this moment by me or by anyone else; I cannot perceive them through the desk. True, the elements, of which (according to Mach) they are complexes, have often been given to me, and I can bring them to "givenness" at any time. All I need do is open the drawer and turn my gaze in a certain direction or let my hands carry out certain movements of touching. The situation is similar with all objects of everyday life. The man in the street is interested only in things that are, have been, or can be perceived by him or his fellow man. But science goes beyond this to things that, in virtue of its own principles, cannot be given to man. It makes judgments about the interior of the sun, about electrons, about magnetic field strengths (for which we do not possess any sense organs) and so forth. What meaning is there in these statements?

There are *only two possibilities:* objects that are not given either are or are not to be designated as *real*.

Anyone who accepts the *second* possibility thereby declares that the concepts of those objects are merely auxiliary ones without immediate meaning. We shall soon discuss this position. But before that we want to take a good look at the *first* possibility, which in fact is usually preferred although it does violate most clearly the fundamental principle of all ideas of immanence. But the immanence philosopher seeks to retain as much of the natural world view as possible; indeed, according to Avenarius, it is precisely the immanence philosopher who preserves and expounds this view in its utmost purity. And for just this reason he must permit himself a certain kind of transcendence. In fact, we have ascertained that all world outlooks can join in admitting without objection certain very obvious arguments by analogy even though these may involve transcendence. Indeed, in assuming a real past, we already transcend the merely given with every judgment we make; and if the immanence philosopher can conceive of his basic principle in so generalized a form that to posit certain *not*-given objects as real requires only this innocent transcendence and no more extensive kind, then he is likely to indulge himself without feeling guilty of any offense against his fundamental tendency.

1. Unperceived Things as Real

According to the view we are about to discusss, real objects exist even without being directly perceived in any way. Vaihinger, who calls this point of view "critical positivism", says, for example: "... we also call real those complexes of perception that do not enter into perception even once but are continually capable of being perceived[26]."

Since real objects are nothing but complexes of elements, it follows that elements that are not "given" must possess reality too. Here an enormous difficulty appears. "One and the same" body, depending on the circumstances under which we perceive it, is composed of quite different complexes of elements; we have seen that only a *relative* constancy can be ascribed to a body. Thus when I take the sheets out of my desk and look at them, the elements whose conjunction constitutes these sheets will be quite different depending on how and from what point of view I look at them. The elements will be different when I look at the sheets directly and when I look at them from the side, when I look at them under artificial illumination and when I look at them in daylight. Every little shadow, every movement alters the elements appreciably. One and the same body is never given a second time as *precisely* the same complex of elements. Which of these infinitely many complexes of elements actually exists when no one is perceiving the paper? The answer to this question is of decisive importance. But many immanence philosophers leave this point in obscurity, while others ex-

---

26 Die Philosophie des Als-Ob, 2nd edition, p. 89.

press themselves in a contradictory manner. We must therefore formulate the possibilities at hand with the greatest care.

For brevity's sake, let us designate the various complexes of elements (Russell calls these complexes "aspects") that, under various perceptual conditions, constitute an object, say, a sheet of paper, as C_1, C_2, C_3, ... They are of course infinite in number. The object itself, the sheet of paper, we designate by O. Now the hypothesis of the thing-in-itself asserts that O is something other than the C's and exists independently of them. On the other hand, immanence philosophy claims that there is no object O distinct from the C's, that O is identical with the C's. So long as I perceive the object, so long as a particular complex C_i of visual or tactile sensations is thus given me, I can simply set $O = C_i$ (where the equality sign is intended to express full identity and i always takes a different value for any change in the conditions of perception, so that basically O is always different).

But now the question that the immanence philosopher must answer is: Which C or which C's constitute the object O when it is *not* perceived, when no C at all is being *experienced* by me? Logically, only two answers are possible: either a quite specific C_i continues to exist in the intervals between perceptions (and is thus real without its being perceived by anyone at all) and this is the O; or, there are *several* C's — in the limiting case *all* possible ones — that remain real even when they are not given to anyone, in which case O is identical with the set of all real C's and is only a name for this totality.

The first of these possibilities need not of course be taken too seriously, and in fact has never been advocated. Obviously it would be arbitrary to the point of absurdity to single out one of the infinitely many C's, assert its continued existence outside of perception, and identify it with the real body. For instance, we would have to think of the sheet of paper as being observed in some quite definite state of illumination, in a particular position, at a particular distance, and select the corresponding visual perceptions as the true, actual paper. There would be no grounds whatsoever for such a choice, for nature does not in the least distinguish any one such complex of sensations C from the others. Further, it would be impossible to give any satisfactory accounting of the relationship between the complex that was singled out and the remaining C's which were given during the time the paper was being perceived.

The immanence philosophers themselves, as we said earlier, have seen how impractical this road is. So the only possibility that remains is the second, that the unperceived thing O is to be identified with the aggregate of the C's. Now it is clear that only the aggregate of all C's can be considered; for if we wished to pick out from the aggregate a particular group, the choice could only be absolutely groundless and arbitrary. Also, we should have to understand by all C's all *possible* complexes of elements or aspects, and not merely those that had in fact been given to some individual or other. For with each future perception of O infinitely many new complexes are experienced, and all of these must be allocated to the *same* object O. The identity of the perceived object with the unperceived one is, by this conception, automatically assured.

This describes the one possible view on the basis of which immanence philosophy can assert the reality of unperceived bodies. The world is an endless fabric of elements joined into certain complexes. What we call bodies are infinite, continuous sets of such complexes, which are all real in the same way and of which only a small, although infinite, part is experienced, that is, given to some "I" as "perceptions".

The only philosopher who has clearly developed this point of view and has acknowledged it to be a necessary consequence of the notion of immanence is BERTRAND RUSSELL (Our Knowledge of the External World as a Field for Scientific Method in Philosophy, Lecture IV). By correctly drawing on "physical laws" as the selection principle, Russell (p. 110) defines just what it is that determines what *belongs* to the content of a thing. "Things are those series of aspects which obey the laws of physics." The given aspects he calls "actual" and those not given "ideal". He does not assert the reality of aspects that are not given. Rather he says (p. 112): ". . . it is unnecessary . . . to assign any reality to ideal elements; it is enough to accept them as logical constructions." But he also does not deny them reality: "It is open to us to believe that the ideal elements exist; and there can be no reason for *dis*believing this . . ." The question of the reality of aspects not experienced by anyone is of secondary interest to Russell. He is more concerned with the question as to the *content* of the concept of physical thing. But since he declares that it is perfectly admissible to assume the reality of C's not experienced, we may regard him as a representative of the view under examination. The accounts given by all other immanence philosophers are self-contradictory, and — in order to conceal contradictions — unclear. They have not pressed ahead to Russell's bold position.

But his position is vulnerable. Two objections, it seems to me, must be raised, each of which is sufficient to make this immanence view untenable.

First, this conception gives no accounting of the fundamental differences that must be assumed to exist between experienced and unexperienced aspects. By assumption, both are equally real. What then distinguishes perceived aspects from unperceived ones? In Russell it would seem that only the being-perceived might do so. But it is scarcely necessary to show that a concept like this, which presupposes a subject, an object, and an activity mediating between them, has no place in the system. How does a complex of elements that "is given in a consciousness" differ from one for which this is not the case? To this question we receive no answer. And any possible answer would introduce as the basis for the distinction a new factor, and thus sacrifice the basic principle of the immanence standpoint. For the object would then consist of something quite *different* from the complexes of elements with which we are acquainted.

Second, it seems to me that Russell's conception of the world cannot be upheld from the viewpoint of the principle of economy. We are hardly in compliance with Ockham's "razor" — the old principle that *"entia non sunt multiplicanda praeter necessitatem"* — if we accept as real not only the actually experienced aspects of an object, but also the infinite sets of all possible aspects. Bear in mind that these possible C's include not only all the perceptions that would be given to any known creature, from bees to men, but also such perceptions as would be experienced by a merely *conceivable* being having sense organs with which we are completely unacquainted, even perhaps a dwarf as small as an atom. What an infinite swarm of aspects is posited here as real — an incalculable series, and one not even completely specifiable! Is this world view really simpler, more economical, provided with fewer dispensable posits than the plain world view of the cautious realists who, apart from the C's that are experienced, assume only the things-in-themselves that mediate between the C's? No one can accept such a conclusion unless he believes that the positing of real "things-in-themselves" comprises a much more extensive claim than the positing of real unexperienced complexes of perception, that a clear and essential difference exists between the two kinds of assumptions, that a sharp boundary line can be drawn between permissible and impermissible transcendence.

There are two factors (clearly present also in Russell) that engender such a belief. The first is the opinion that the concept of the thing-in-itself somehow contains the notion of *substance* in the metaphysical sense, the old category of the permanent "thing" with its "changing properties". To its opponents our O, as a thing-in-itself, appears as an eternally self-identical "essence" vis-à-vis the changing "appearances" C. Russell, for instance, develops his view quite openly in a struggle against the assumption of "permanent" or "indestructible" things. This assumption, he contends, is an illicit addition supplied by thought, for in truth only the ever-changing non-substantial aspects are given us. He is right — but the concept of a thing-in-itself need not contain any of these unwarranted, forbidden notions and, as we have defined it above, does not in fact contain them. As far as we are concerned, "to exist in itself" means no more than "not to be experienced by us"; and in this sense the unperceived "aspects" of Russell, in so far as they are held to be real, already have a being-in-themselves. No other kind of transcendence is present. The thing-in-itself need not be some unvarying, permanent metaphysical substance, and yet does not, for that reason, have to be a set of complexes of sensations. Rather (see the later sections of this book) we shall be able to regard it as a complex of processes and states and to see quite readily that we arrive at a much simpler, more compact picture of the world, one more in agreement with the spirit of the sciences, than if we interpret a thing as the set of all aspects.

The processes that constitute a thing must, of course, be thought of as not inconsiderably different from the complexes of sensations. And this is the point that is resisted by the second factor on which the view under criticism is based. This factor is the aversion to assuming the existence of realities with which we are *not acquainted (unbekannter Realitäten)*. We are aware of — in the sense of being immediately acquainted with — what red is, or sweet, or an aspect. And it seems more satisfactory to introduce hypothetically into our view of the world only those elements with which we could in principle be acquainted.

But the requirement that we admit as real only elements with which *it is possible to be acquainted* is in the first place totally unjustified. It is nothing but a vestige of the preconception that being acquainted with *(Kennen)* belongs to knowing *(Erkennen)*, and is indeed its more important part. In the second place, the view under discussion does not itself comply with that requirement. For an "unperceived aspect" simply cannot be the same as a "perceived aspect"; otherwise the distinction would be without meaning. And the two kinds of complexes must be different in a still deeper sense. Of all the aspects that, for example, form this room when no one is in it, none can be identical with an aspect experienced by someone who enters the room; for this latter aspect, as Russell too recognizes (p. 88), is "conditioned by the sense-organs, nerves and brain of the newly arrived man ..."; and all that can reasonably be assumed is "that *some* aspect of the universe existed from that point of view, though no one was perceiving it". We see that the hypothetically added complexes are ones with which in any case we are "not acquainted". Thus the struggle of immanence philosophy against the realistic assumption of things-in-themselves is a vain one, since this philosophy itself cannot get along without a fully equivalent assumption.

This actually concludes the critique of the particular form of the immanence notion that we have been discussing. Yet in order to disentangle problems that have been confused by much philosophizing, it is also useful to direct a critical glance at other fruitless attempts to achieve an unobjectionable formulation of the immanentist standpoint. In connection with these efforts we shall encounter some instructive contradictions and weaknesses of an entirely different kind.

In Joseph Petzoldt we read: "All the difficulties we experience in thinking of element-combinations of the optical and tactile qualities as existing independently of their being perceived stem therefore solely from the fact that we find it extremely difficult to free ourselves from the idea of absolute being, and do not immerse ourselves sufficiently in the notion of relative existence[27]." He then tries to prove (*op. cit.*, p. 188) that his view does not become involved in contradictions: "There is no contradiction (apart from the qualities that may be attributed to them) in the mere continued existence of things after they are perceived; they occupy their particular space and do not in the least disturb my present perceptions. Thus

---

27 Das Weltproblem, 3rd edition, p. 184.

a contradiction could lie only in the qualities with which I think of things as continuing to exist; and the contradiction would of course assert itself were I to think of all similar continued existence as absolute. But if I think of things exactly as already being different when perceived by different kinds of individuals and different in their continued existence for each individual — different for the color blind person, different for the deaf, different for the totally blind, different for some intelligence organized in a manner altogether divergent from human intelligence — then where could there be even one contradiction, or anything unthinkable?"

Petzoldt confirms (op. cit., p. 193) that existence (Dasein) "does not consist merely in being perceived". Of the early days of the earth, which no human eye saw, he declares: " ... the idea of that remote period is entirely dependent on us. But this does not at all mean that the time in question is a mere idea of ours. On the contrary, in its existence it is fully independent of us." Thus if existence is not identical with being perceived nor with being represented or imagined, the *esse* and *percipi* part company. This means that an object O exists even when the element complexes $C_1, C_2, C_3, \ldots$ are not experienced by anyone. The question then is: What is O? Petzoldt's answer is not that O is the aggregate of all possible C's nor that it is identical with any particular C. His answer is that it is identical with every single C, but with a different one for each individual! Expressed schematically then, for the first individual $O = C_1$, for the second $O = C_2$, and so forth, where it is to be noted that the equations are intended to express absolute identities. For Petzoldt, it is the concept of "relative existence" that makes these claims possible. But this concept is plainly self-contradictory, that is, it is a meaningless combination of words. For since C_1 and C_2 are by assumption different, then by the principle of identity one and the same O cannot be identical with both C_1 and C_2[28].

---

28 In the third edition of his Das Weltproblem (pp. 188 ff., footnote), PETZOLDT answered my objections to his viewpoint, unfortunately without going into the rigorous formulation of my argument as given above. I reproduce the essentials of his exposition here so that the reader can decide for himself whether Petzoldt has succeeded in avoiding the contraction: " ... Schlick holds the view that there is a contradiction here: I have shown only that different individuals may *think* one and the same thing differently [i. e., represent it intuitively differently — Schlick], but what I was required to show was that, for different beings,

It is clear that logically just two alternatives are possible here: either we allow the existence of only the experienced $C_1, C_2, \ldots$ and do not recognize an identical O (in which event we arrive at a new view soon to be examined), or we see O as only another name for the aggregate of *all* C's, as in the case of Russell's solution, which is nowhere clearly formulated by Petzoldt. He comes close to it incidentally when he declares (p. 211) that talk of "the same thing" is only a logical construction. But it is precisely in that passage, which is occupied with the interpretation of Einsteinian relativity, that the shortcomings of Petzoldt's philosophical relativism reveal themselves. However, we cannot go into this matter at this point. I have called attention elsewhere to the fact that the epistemological standpoint here described leads its advocates to assertions that violate the fundamental principles of all theory construction in physical science and fly in the face of empirical facts[29]. The case is inter-

---

the same thing could *be* something opposite — 'red and not-red, hard and not-hard, and this *independently* of its being perceived'. But this is precisely what I have shown; Schlick here simply ignores the words 'for different beings' even though he writes them down; and he ignores them because what he really demands of me is obviously an entirely different proof from the one he himself actually enunciated: the proof that one and the same *absolute* thing or *thing-in-itself* must be able to possess these opposite qualities at the same time — failing which I cannot maintain my claim that existence does not consist merely in being perceived. According to his view, the claim that things exist independently is not compatible with the doctrine that, for the perceiver, things *consist* only in perceived qualities. My account explicitly demonstrates the compatibility of these two points." Then several sentences follow, manifestly in complete contradiction to the passages just cited: "The independent existence of the unperceived poses no problem whatsoever. All that can be said about a thing considered as independent and thought of as detached from its relation to the central nervous system is that it exists, that it exists independently of its being perceived. Any problem as to *how* the thing is constituted is in principle unsolvable and furthermore even illogically formulated." But did the author not declare just a moment ago that things exist *with* their known qualities independently of their being perceived, even though with different qualities for different beings?

29 See my lecture The Theory of Relativity in Philosophy, at the one hundredth anniversary of the Gesellschaft Deutscher Naturforscher und Ärzte, Leipzig 1922; by the "very clear-headed and esteemed herald of relativistic positivism" cited on p. 65 I meant Petzoldt.

esting because it shows that, for an understanding and a correct application of a purely physical theory, one's epistemological orientation is by no means a matter of indifference, and that even for philosophical viewpoints there is a kind of confirmation of refutation through the facts of experience.

We conclude from our discussion that the immanence notion in the form evaluated thus far seems untenable. The claim that a non-given real object is simply an element complex continuing to exist as it was given to us when we perceived the object must be modified.

If I change the lighting and the position, and thus alter the relation of a body to myself and to the environment, or if not I myself but a colorblind person looks at the body, then new elements appear and a new complex is formed. Yet I still speak of the *same* body. Thus under different conditions the object is formed from other elements. Hence if the question "Which elements form the body?" is to have a meaning I must specify the totality of these conditions. If these conditions are disregarded, then the immanence philosopher must reject the qestion as wrongly formulated, since it impermissibly detaches the elements from the relations in which they are always encountered. They appear only in association with elements of an "I"-complex; a body is "given" only if certain relations hold between its elements and those that form my sense organs. The question "Which elements form a real object while it is not being perceived?" would be identical with the self-contradictory question "What does a thing look like when no one is looking at it?" A body that is not given cannot be built up out of the elements "blue", "cold", "hard", and the like. But what then is the constant something that justifies me in embracing under the concept of a single body the series of changing combinations of elements?

Manifestly it is the *law-like regularity* of their interrelationship. This law-like regularity, this aggregate of relations, thus constitutes the true nature of the body — a conclusion to which the doctrine we are discussing must come. Applied to our example, if I assert the existence of the sheets of paper in my desk, I thereby claim not that certain elements "in themselves" are present, but that under certain quite definite conditions certain elements will appear at certain places. *If* I then open the drawer, *if* I move my head to such and such a position, *if* the illumination is of such and such a nature, *then* the element "white" will appear at such and such a place and also the element "grey" (where the paper is more in shadow); if I reach out my hand, then certain other elements will appear (tactile sensations), and so forth.

Thus the claim that an unperceived thing exists means not that certain elements are actually there at the moment, but that they *would* appear were certain conditions fulfilled. But here we have exactly the same idea that constitutes Mill's theory of permanent possibilities of sensation; thus the viewpoint we are examining, if developed with consistency, leads inevitably to Mill. It is therefore open to the same objections.

We can not get around these objections by avoiding the word 'possibility' and speaking instead of "functional relations". MACH says at one place (*Analyse der Empfindungen*, p. 296): "But then I must say that for me the world is *not* a mere sum of sensations. Rather, I speak expressly of *functional relations* of *elements*. But this does not merely make Mill's 'possibilities' superfluous; it replaces them with something much sounder — the mathematical *concept of function*."

Logically, the mathematical concept of function is certainly sound enough. But especially from the viewpoint of the question of reality, it is something quite shadowy; for it is not anything real, but a concept. We must be very clear about this: if we say that a body consists in certain dependencies, in certain functional relations among the elements, then if we proceed to talk of the body as something real, we are elevating mere concepts — functional relations — to the realm of reality and hypostasizing them. Such a procedure is surely inadmissible.

Anyone who explains an unperceived thing as a mere law-like connection between things perceived seems to me to be arguing like a blind philosopher who defends the claim that a color, of which he hears other speak, is in truth nothing but a law-like connection of experiences of sound and touch. And no protestations by persons with normal vision can dissuade him; for no matter what others may tell him, color for him remains a sequence of sounds, and so he can persist in his belief.

Let us keep clearly in mind the significance of the mathematical concept of function and its application to reality. If I turn a piece of paper this way or that, or crumple it up, the elements of the complex "piece of paper" (as well as those of my hand that is holding it) change in a quite definite way. An alteration in the one goes together with alterations in the others; in darkness the optical elements disappear altogether and only the tactile elements remain. We can think of this dependency as being stated in a law with the aid of mathematical functions (of course, on theoretical grounds — which we shall go into later — we can never actually state the law). This law would then be a conceptual creation, an abstraction. Only the elements and their changes are *real*. This holds for any law, any general relation of dependency. Newton's Law of Gravitation cannot be designated as something that is real, but only as something that is "valid" (as Lotze put it). It is not *at* any place or *at* any time; what is real is solely the *behavior* of bodies, which we only describe through the Newtonian formulas.

We should also note something else: as long as the paper is perceived, we might indeed be able to say that its nature consists in the interconnection of the elements white, smooth, rectangular, and so forth. For, so long as the elements themselves are there, their interconnection is something real. But during the intervals between perceptions, when no eye beholds the paper and no hand touches it, we surely cannot say this, since the elements no longer exist. Certainly no one would dream of defining something real as a relation between unreal magnitudes. Under these circumstances, all that remains is to conceive of the body (the paper) as a functional relation between the elements actually given at the moment — for instance, my hands, which will in fact cause the paper to appear if they perform certain manipulations. One might seek to give legitimacy to a conception of this sort by pointing out that in one way or another all elements are connected to all others. But to seek the essence of reality as a whole in functional relations would be neither economical nor compatible with the natural, naive concept of reality.

No, this will not do at all. The abstract logical conditional proposition that certain elements appear *if* certain conditions are fulfilled (perhaps they will never be fulfilled) cannot possibly be understood as the entire content of the assertion that a body exists. For that would be to identify the validity of abstract propositions with the being of real things, something not at all in the spirit of immanence philosophy and contradictory to its basic idea. We would then have a new metaphysics that, like all the old rejected systems, makes concepts into realities.

Anyone who says that a thing of the external world *is* a law-like interconnection of elements that also exists when the elements themselves are not given[30], and believes that he has thereby imparted to things the same sort of reality possessed by a sense datum, for example — such a person has reified a law. The concept he has formed is identical with the concept of *force,* as it once dominated an outmoded phase in the development of the natural sciences. For him, the lawfulness of the interconnection has actually become a power that simply *produces* certain elements as soon as certain conditions are present. "The law recognized as an objective power, we call force", wrote Helmholtz (in notes to his essay on the conservation of energy). What is conceived in the concept of permanent possibilities of sensation or in the "objectively existing law" is precisely what used to be conceived under the concept of force — even if one is loath to call it that. The viewpoint we have been describing thus goes over into *dynamism;* for both, the world of external things is a world of forces. They designate it with different words, but that does not matter. In substance there is no difference between the two positions. In any case, the standpoint of immanence is thus abandoned. And this is what was to be proved.

The mistake consists precisely in the fact that what was attempted was a *definition* of the reality of a body. All such efforts are bound to lead to absurdities. They end up in Mill's explanation of the real in terms of the possible (see above § 23). The concept of the real cannot be reduced to unreal concepts; it must be taken from experience. Concepts and realities are incomparably different; that is the way they are. They cannot be transformed into one another. Only the recognition of this distinction makes logical thinking possible and any blurring of it leads to the great errors of the classical metaphysical systems. One of the characteristic features of immanentist positivism, however, is that it conflates real and purely conceptual relationships. MACH says (Analyse der Empfindungen, p. 296): "For the natural scientist, the gap between intuitive representation and conceptual thought is neither very great nor unbridgeable." No doubt this sentence can be understood in a sense in which it is completely correct (see above Part II, near the end of § 18); but it is false in any sense in which it may dispose us to construct reality out of the mathematical concept of function.

---

30 H. CORNELIUS, Einleitung in die Philosophie, 2nd printing, p. 271.

2. Unperceived Things as Unreal

The road we have travelled with Mach and Petzoldt thus far is now blocked; we must turn back. Let us survey that road once again.

The question of the "reality" of unperceived bodies had to be answered in the negative, if by "body" we understood nothing but the complex of elements given us when we perceive the body. For that reason, we tried with Mach and Cornelius to find the essence of a real body not in the complex of elements as such, but in the abstract law stating their interconnection. This undertaking too we recognized as logically inadmissible, and contrary to the sense of the whole problem.

Nothing remains then but to retreat to the second of the two possibilities mentioned above (see § 26, near the beginning). The positivist is now obliged to take seriously and preserve his point of departure: to designate only the actually given as real. What is "real" about a body is only what is immediately *given* of it at the moment; everything else is mere concept, a pure symbol of thought. No other position is compatible with the chosen point of departure; only in this way can one be faithful to the immanence standpoint in all its purity. The emphasis had been all along on the dependency of the elements on the complex constituting the "I". Accordingly, the elements must be left standing exactly as experience reveals them. But experience teaches us that, for instance, the optical elements of a body disappear when I close my eyes. Of course, on the basis of the statements of my fellow men who still see the body, I claim that it continues to exist; but when they too close their eyes or turn away or leave, then those elements are not experienced by anyone. They are no longer there for any subject and according to this view do not exist at all. The body is no more; for the elements, along with their alterations, that formed the body are no longer present. If I nevertheless continue to speak of it as something existing, I am only using it as a conceptual symbol for the prediction that the elements will reappear once I bring certain conditions into being.

The declaration that reality is to be denied to anything unperceived, regardless of whether or not it is "perceivable", also eliminates an inconsistency that often distresses us in the writings of Mach and others. On the one hand, reality is attributed to certain bodies because they possess perceivability, even though the factual situation is such that we never can perceive them (for example, the other side of the moon or substances deep in the interior of the earth*). On the other hand, the concepts of atom, electron and the like, created by physics and chemistry, are declared to be mere auxiliary aids to thought and not designations of real magnitudes, since they are not perceivable. But it is in fact impossible to establish a difference in principle between the two cases. For "perceivable" is a relative concept. When we ascribe this predicate to an object, we mean that under one or another set of conditions the object can be brought to "givenness". But for these conditions the possibilities are absolutely unlimited, and this deprives the concept of any definiteness. The conditions include a certain spatio-temporal relation to the perceiving sense organs, together with a certain composition of these organs. But what composition? One person perceives through his senses what another is unable to bring to givenness with his; a dog, with its more delicate organ of smell, lives in a world far richer in olfactory qualities than the world inhabited by man. It would be quite arbitrary, especially from the positivist standpoint, to make human beings the measure of perceivability. Beings might indeed exist, like Maxwell's demon, for whom — by virtue of a constitution that of course would bear not the slightest resemblance to ours — an atom would represent a directly given complex of elements. In short, just as reality cannot be defined in terms of possibility, neither can it be defined in terms of the possibility of perception. It is altogether impossible in this manner to determine a boundary that encloses the realm of the real and separates it from the unreal. To be consistent, positivism must declare as real only what is perceived, not what is perceivable. In the positivist view, all that is not given stands on the same plane; it is not real. The interior of the earth and the other side of the moon are mere conceptual aids, in the very same sense as atoms or electrons. Here no fundamental separation is possible.

We too, from the standpoint we find ourselves compelled to take, cannot make any distinction between these two kinds of objects of thought. But we do not assert that they are unreal; on the contrary, we declare that they are fully real and thus at the same time we deny any difference in reality between objects perceived

---

* This was written in 1925. [Translator's note.]

and objects inferred by rigorous methods. We attribute reality to both kinds equally.

The objects designated by means of natural scientific concepts (bodies, atoms, electrical fields, and the like) are not identical with complexes of elements. But they are just as real, and they remain so even if no elements are given at all. The properties and relations of these objects are never given directly; they are inferred. And this is true in the same sense, and to the same degree, of all objects of that sort, of the physicist's electron as well as of the bread on our table. On the basis of our experiences in viewing and touching the bread, we assume the existence of a relatively persistent object with which we correlate the concept "bread"; and on the basis of the experiences we have in connection with certain experimental investigations, such as those of Perrin or Svedberg, we assume the existence of objects that we designate by means of the concept "atom".

There is not the slightest difference between the two cases. And the claim, often heard, that the existence of molecules cannot be regarded as proved until such time as we can *see* them is wholly unwarranted. Seeing an object proves to me that it exists only in so far as I can infer this from the given visual sensations; and to make this inference I need a series of premises about the constitution of the sense organs, about the nature of the processes through which these sensations are aroused, and much more. If I do not experience the object "directly" but only observe its "effects", then the chain of inference will be lengthened by an additional member. But in principle nothing is changed in the least; the weight of the proof remains the same. The inference *may* become less certain through the addition of a new link; but this need not and will not be the case if the new premises are of the highest certainty that can be attained on an empirical base. To perceive an object is in the end to experience the effects that issue from it. Whether the effects are nearer or more distant cannot be the ground for any fundamental difference. Hence it is just as much a perception of a helium atom, for example, if I "directly see" it or if I follow its path (as C. T. R. Wilson did) in supercooled water vapor or (with Regener) observe the scintillations it produces when it strikes against a Sidot screen[31].

---

31 Using essentially the same argument, B. Bavink very nicely demonstrates the untenability of the distinction rejected by us. See his Allgemeine Ergebnisse und Probleme der Naturwissenschaft, 3rd edition, pp. 25 ff.

But we have digressed here to deal with our own standpoint, which will be developed more exactly later. We now return to the critique of the strict positivistic doctrine of immanence according to which all objects, in so far as they are meant as something other than mere complexes of elements, are not realities but pure auxiliary concepts — bread no less than molecules.

This doctrine, which strictly identifies reality with givenness, has been formulated by outstanding philosophers and has often been the object of critical discussion. It is no wonder that the arguments pro and con take typical paths, so that there is scarcely any prospect of adding new arguments of such character that they need only be uttered to gain immediate universal acceptance. *Esse = percipi* is the formula that typifies this point of view. The philosopher who adopts it does not of course want to designate as real only what he himself finds as given (otherwise he would be a solipsist, and none of the great philosophical systems has seriously defended solipsism); he wants to say only that nothing is real if it is not given to some subject. Or, as Avenarius expressed it, whatever exists is encountered as a term of a "principal coordination", a name he gave to the "intimate connection and inseparability of the I-experience and the environment-experience in every experience that is realized" (Der menschliche Weltbegriff, § 148). What we ordinarily call subject, is for him the "central term" of the principal coordination; the object he calls its "counter term". But he places particular weight on one point: the situation is not that the central member meets the counter member, but that both are something encountered, both "belong in the same sense to every experience". This view may also be described by the well known Schopenhauerian formula: no object without a subject. A thing-in-itself would be an object that is *not* a member of a principal coordination — an object that lacks a subject *cui obiectum est* (see E. LAAS, Idealismus und Positivismus, I, p. 183) — and such a thing does not exist.

We need only point out briefly the consequences that follow when we erase from the world of reality all that is not given. These consequences have often been developed in recent times, and I regard it as established that they are indeed irreconcilably contradictory to the principles of scientific inquiry.

Among these principles is in the first instance that of causality. This principle demands an unbroken interconnection of all that is

real so that real processes proceed according to strict empirical laws*.
But if we confine ourselves to *directly given* magnitudes, it is not
possible on the basis of experience to set up such laws governing
the continuous succession of these magnitudes. In order to fill out
the interconnections, on which all science rests, the causal sequences
must be supplemented with magnitudes that are not directly given.
For example, suppose unexpectedly I hear a clock strike. The clock
is in a distant room, and so placed that at the preceding instant it was
not given — acoustically, optically, or otherwise — to me or to any
other subject. It would be impossible to find a sufficient cause for
the sudden presence of the sounds in the whole range of what in
that preceding instant belonged to any principal coordination. Causal connections exist only between realities, not between concepts.
To confuse the two is to mistake the relationship between cause and
effect for that between ground and consequence. Nothing remains
then but either to acknowledge the existence of a transcendent reality or else to deny a universal law-like causal tie[32]. The immanence
philosopher is understandably reluctant to take the second alternative. And thereby he contradicts himself, since he also does not
want to accept the first.

The immanence philosopher is in the habit of answering these
objections by saying that his world is every bit as law-conforming
as that of the realists, since the so-called causal interconnection of
events amounts in the long run simply to a functional relation of
elements. All that can be established is the existence of elements,
and interpolating "things-in-themselves" as intermediaries does not
do the least bit of good. But to put the question this way is only

---

* Schlick wrote this before the development of quantum mechanics.
[Translator's note.]

32 See too FREYTAG, Der Realismus und Transzendenzproblem, p. 11;
STÖRRING, Einführung in die Erkenntnistheorie, pp. 144, 148; the essay
by V. Stern, cited above at the end of § 25; even Petzoldt, who on
just this account wants the "elements", as we saw, to exist independently
of *percipi*. PETZOLDT says (Weltproblem, 1st edition, p. 145): "Perception
shows that the play of light out there in the leaves and tree trunks depends on the sun and the clouds. If I step back from the window, I no
longer perceive sun and clouds, but the play of light continues. How
then can I reconcile the demand that this process display a law-like
regularity with the discontinuity in the very existence — not just the
being-perceived — of the clouds and the sun?"

to sidetrack the real difficulty, not to solve it. The problem is already unintentionally obscured by the fact that Mach, for example, always prefers to talk about functional dependency instead of causal dependency. For the expression "functional relation" seems just as well suited to interconnections of the purely conceptual as to those of real things, so that it appears not to matter whether the supplementary entities belong to the one realm or the other. But the question at issue turns entirely on relations among real things, which from antiquity has meant *causal* relations — regardless of what else one may have thought about the concepts of cause and effect. No problems can be solved by extending the term 'function' to relations of that sort.

But the heart of the matter is this: we are helped very little by the assurance that everything depends on everything in a unique manner and that the principle of causality is therefore preserved in any case. One could imagine a world of arbitrary chaotic events and assert the same thing of it. The claim that there is a causal tie has empirical meaning and a testable sense only in so far as one can specify the individual rules or laws in accordance with which the processes of the world run their course. All rigorous rules of that kind (that is, all natural laws) with which we are acquainted in fact express dependencies between magnitudes that are not directly given. Indeed, the fact of the matter is that in no case are we able to specify the mutual relations of the elements with perfect accuracy; for the quantities that appear in the precise formulas of the natural scientist never designate the immediately given or any changes in it; they always designate supplementary objects that are connected to the given in a rather complicated manner. And this is in the highest measure true precisely of the *most fundamental* laws of the physicist. Consider, for example, the equations of electrodynamics or of gravitation; the quantities that appear in them are related to perception only in an extremely roundabout and indirect manner. The reason for this lies in the truth, which we shall demonstrate later, that the "elements" in principle do not admit of quantitative determination.

But these significant facts are usually passed over hurriedly. "That it is easier",says MACH (Analyse der Empfindungen, 5th ed., p. 4), "for the scientist to pursue not the direct relations of these elements but the relations of relations, need not disturb us here." The fact is that it very much disturbs anyone who desires to work out a coherent, logically rounded picture of what goes on in the world. Such a person will find unsatisfactory the notion that the truly simple relations expressed in natural laws are to hold not between realities, between sensations, but only between mere concepts, such as electrons, frequencies, and the like — pure symbols of thought, which can stand only in logical, not in causal, relations with one another.

The viewpoint described here is not compatible with the causal principle. On this view, it is impossible to conceive of natural laws as laws that deal with changes in what is real; thus these laws are robbed of their original sense. This is not a totally devastating blow. For a supporter of the view could still say: very well, then we must surrender the notion that all reality can be unambiguosly incorporated, according to definite laws, into an unbroken causal system. (From his standpoint, there can be no question from the outset of looking upon the causal principle as an *a priori* one and the incorporation of everything into a causal system as an absolute necessity.) One can see, however, just how much is at stake here, so much in fact that none of the immanence philosophers is actually prepared to take this step, which from his standpoint is clearly unavoidable. It would be a blind and utterly unprofitable dogmatism indeed that, merely to maintain the proposition *esse* = *percipi*, would throw overboard the most basic presupposition of all inquiry for no other reason than the fear of things-in-themselves. Once this fear proves to be groundless, the whole position is deprived of any support.

As we have remarked, the concept of the thing-in-itself is held to be either self-contradictory or superfluous. That it is not superfluous we already know, since we saw that it had to be constructed in order to guarantee the unambiguous character of causal relations in nature. How groundless is the charge of contradiction was demonstrated earlier when we discussed the argument offered by Berkeley and Schuppe (§25). The same argument in other versions is also found in other thinkers. In fact, no basically different argument is ever adduced, and it is in the nature of the case that there is no other possible way to prove that everything must be an object for a subject. The supposed proof rests on a common equivocation and fallacy of four terms. Nonetheless we find that even Avenarius, brilliant as he is, makes certain statement that can scarcely be understood in any other way than as a repetition of the old argument, except that here the mistake is most cleverly concealed, that is, ab-

sorbed into tacit presuppositions. He says (Der menschliche Weltbegriff, p. 131) that we are not entitled to ask "whether the environment-constituent *in and for itself* (in the special sense of the theory
of knowledge) could be or might be thought of as characterized by
other sense qualities or by none at all — *at least in so far as we
are to understand by the expression 'environment-constituent ('object', 'thing') in and for itself' the counter term taken in abstraction
from the central term or from every central term.* Such a question is
unjustified since as soon as I think of an environment-constituent,
the constituent *is* already the counter term for which *I* am the central
term; but I cannot abstract from myself. To think of an 'environment-constituent (an 'object', a 'thing') in and for itself' is therefore
to try to think of something that can neither be thought of nor inferred; and to wish to determine positively, or *even only negatively,*
the character of an 'environment-constituent (an 'object', a 'thing')
in and for itself' is to seek to determine something that is unthinkable by means of things that are thinkable."

   This formulation has been regarded as superior to the usual one
(of Schuppe) because Avenarius' argument, in contrast to the other,
is directed not against the notion of a "thing that is not thought"
but against the thought of an *unthinkable* thing. What Avenarius
here condemns as a self-contradictory transcendence is "thinking of
something that, in so far as it is not something thought, is also
not something thinkable, that is, something for which there are no
thinkable conditions under which it would become something
thought" (F. RAAB, Die Philosophie von Richard Avenarius, 1912,
p. 157, note 330).

   This may be correct. But it holds only if by thinking is meant "intuitively representing". It is a fact that a thing-in-itself, that is, an
object that is not a term of a principal coordination, is as such not
intuitively representable; but that is all that Avenarius has proved.
He has not refuted the thinkability of a thing-in-itself, if by thinking is meant unique designation by means of symbols. For Avenarius,
an environment constituent, by definition, always signifies something
encountered or that can be encountered, or, in our terminology,
something *given,* that is, intuitively represented or representable; and
this, by its very nature, is always a term of a principal coordination,
never an "object-in-itself". That was why he carefully added: "at
least in so far as we are to understand, by the expression 'environment constituent in and for itself', the counter term *taken in abstrac-*

tion from every central term". But one arrives at the concept of a thing-in-itself not merely by thinking the central term *away,* but rather by thinking of something not given as *being added* to what is given. Thus the argument of this ingenious thinker proves only what was bound to be clear beforehand: that Avenarius' environment constituents are not things-in-themselves.

MACH too, as we have already noted, believes that one obtains the concept of a thing-in-itself by thinking *away* all the features of the *thing (Analyse der Empfindungen,* p. 5): "The obscure picture of something constant or permanent, which itself does not actually change when one or another constituent is omitted, seems to be a something *for itself.* Since we can remove each of its constituents *by itself* and the picture will still *represent* the totality and be recognized, we suppose that we could take *all* of these constituents away and something would still remain. Thus there arises in a very natural way the philosophical notion, at first impressive but later seen to be monstrous, of an unknowable *thing-in-itself* different from its 'appearance'."

We see again and again that the positivist directs his critique against a specially constructed concept of the thing-in-itself and then supposes that he has refuted the general idea of such a thing. The critique, within its limits, is quite valuable, but it does not possess the far-reaching significance attributed to it. And we, who have defined the concept in our own fashion (see above, beginning of § 25), are left entirely untouched.

b) Objects Perceived by Several Individuals

Thus far our inquiry into the immanence notion has in the main disclosed the contradictions to which this notion leads when we have to determine objects whose element are *not* given to any perceiving subject. The immanence philosopher, however, also becomes entangled in difficulties when he tries to get clear about what it means when *different* individuals make pronouncements as to one and the same real object. We shall now consider these difficulties.

The problem is simply this: suppose two different subjects state that they perceive the same environment constituent, say the lamp hanging from the ceiling. What meaning do the two assertions have from the immanentist standpoint? Defenders of this standpoint believe that this is simply a case of two principal coordinations with a common counter term. They lay special weight on this point in the clear knowledge that here we touch on one of the most momentous questions of philosophy, and they boast that they have answered it in the simplest possible way. In other words, what we have is not a thing-in-itself, which in some mysterious manner "produces" in different minds various processes called "sensations". On the contrary, one and the same object is directly given at the same time to several subjects. The elements are not in the brain, the head; they are not projected from there out into the room. They are simply out there where we experience them. They, and the places they occupy, can simultaneously belong just as well to the experience of the one subject as to that of the other. Thus MACH says (*op. cit.*, p. 294) that from his viewpoint, there is "*no* essential difference between my sensations and those of another person. The *same elements* are connected at many junction points, the I's." (It seems to me that at another place — p. 22 — he contradicts what he has just said: "When we speak of the sensations of another person, these of course have nothing to do with my optical space or with physical space generally; they are thought of additionally, and I think of them as *causally* (better, functionally) tied to the observed or imagined human brain.") And Avenarius says of the philosophical outlook that he has struggled to reach: "The natural view, which lies at the base of all empirical sciences, that the *very same* constituent of *my* environment can also be a constituent of the environment of another person, would appear, as such, to be tenable" (Der menschliche Weltbegriff, § 161).

Were this view really tenable, then the world picture suggested here would in fact possess a seductive simplicity and a marvelous compactness. The interrelation of the I's to one another and to the external world would seemingly have been brought under the clearest formulas with all difficulties disposed of. But unfortunately altogether insuperable difficulties do arise as soon as we seek to carry out the program in detail. Both physics and psychology teach us that it is impermissible to assume that two persons who simultaneously look at the lamp hanging there have exactly the same, much less identical, experiences. Since the two individuals cannot be at the same place at the same time, they must see the lamp from slightly different angles; and the distance from the eyes of the two individuals will not be exactly equal. Thus there is no doubt that the complex of elements each designates as "the lamp" will *differ*. Of course it might be said that, according to the world picture of the immanence doctrine, it is not necessary that precisely the same complexes of elements belong as counter terms to different central terms. It would suffice if after all only one or another element within the complex were identically the same in both principal coordinations; the remaining elements in the two complexes, while being organized in accordance with similar law-like regularities, could be more or less different. Thus a bridge would be built between the experiences of different individuals; both could be freely counted as inhabitants of the same world, and in addition, the advantages of the immanentist world outlook would be preserved.

In the first place, however, even this modest demand unfortunately can never be rigorously fulfilled. No form, no color is ever seen as *exactly* the same by two observers. The keenness of vision, the sensitivity of the eyes to color, and the brightness of the illumination will never be *absolutely* the same for both. How two observers perceive the lamp depends, as Avenarius himself constantly emphasized, on the constitution of *their* bodies, particularly the nervous system; and as similar as the bodies may be, we are never allowed to assume that two natural structures are absolutely alike. We must therefore say that in a complex designated as one and the same object by different individuals, there will never be elements that are absolutely the same for both with respect to quality, intensity, and the like.

In the second place, even if the elements were exactly alike, it still would not help. For they are still not *identical,* not "the same". Anyone doubting this need only think of what happens when one of the two observers closes his eyes. As far as he is concerned, the lamp has vanished. But for the other person it is still there; yet the identical object cannot be there and not be there at the same time.

Contrary to Mach and Avenarius, we have just determined that one and the same element cannot belong to more than one I, to more than one principal coordination. No matter how similar the experiences of different I's may be (which of course in principle is impossible to determine), it doesn't do us any good. As long as absolute identity is not present, the experiences are not the same. Consequently, an element that belongs to the experiential world of person A is something different from an element that belongs to the world of a second person B.

Well and good, the immanence philosopher might say, why make such a fuss about it? We shall simply have to give up this idea.

Even though different individuals never experience the same environment constituents, there still exists a regular relation between them, a mutual dependency, and this is all we want or need. If we were acquainted down to the last detail with the constitution of the two observers, then in principle we could also specify which elements were given them under the particular circumstances. Thus all questions that could possibly be raised could be answered; all meaningful goals could be reached along this road.

At first glance it certainly seems not to matter whether different individuals experience identically the same elements, or only like or similar ones. Closer examination, however, shows that through this latter alternative the entire view of the world is fundamentally changed. Just look at what the immanence philosopher must maintain if he adopts this position! No element, no environment constituent occurs in more than one principal coordination where the central terms are different subjects; the reality that is given to one individual is never given to another. In other words, every being has a world unto itself, into which absolutely nothing is projected from the worlds of other beings; each is separated from all the others by an unbridgeable chasm. True, there is a correlation between these worlds, in that the events of any one run parallel to those of the others and thus would be in harmony should one compare them (which in any event is impossible, since no being in one world can enter into the world of another); but a real world *common* to all individuals is out of the question.

The world picture that results is familiar to us from the history of philosophy: in its logical content it is completely identical with Leibniz' doctrine of the monads and preestablished harmony. On this view, every self with its total environment is in fact a monad. The Leibnizian proposition "monads have no windows" holds, since the monads have nothing in common and there is no exchange of realities. Even though the terminology and the detailed metaphysical determinations with which Leibniz decks out his monads may not be transferable to this picture of the world, the core remains the same[33]. There are as many worlds as there are terms; and the recip-

---

33 The understanding that a consistent doctrine of immanence leads to a monadology was expressed earlier by VICTOR KRAFT in his noteworthy book, Weltbegriff und Erkenntnisbegriff, 1912, p. 165. Bertrand Russell strongly emphasizes the kinship of his own theory with the Leibnizian picture of the world and consciously follows him.

rocal correspondence of the worlds of different individuals, which results in congruous and compatible statements, is simply nothing but a preestablished harmony of the purest form.

Of course a proof that the standpoint here described coincides with the theory of monads is not to be equated directly with a proof of the untenability of that standpoint. Perhaps a metaphysical system like the theory of monads cannot be refuted at all. Still we do see *that* we are led precisely to a metaphysical system, and we see what we must think of the claim made by immanence philosophy that it represents the only natural, metaphysics-free world view. This is proof enough for us; and no one would be more aware of its weight than the spokesmen for immanentist positivism, if they were to let themselves be convinced that it is correct. This is evident from the way Petzoldt, for instance, speaks about the notion of pre-established harmony in Spinoza and Leibniz. He says (Weltproblem, 1st edition, p. 94): "But this is nothing other than an explicit affirmation of a continuously occurring miracle, and thus a declaration of the abandonment and impotence of science."

How may one hope to escape the consequences to which we have been led? The supporters of Mach and Avenarius could at best return to an idea already discussed above by saying that the worlds of the different subjects are not hopelessly apart. When several subjects consider the "same" object, there is still something identical in their perceptions. But it is not to be sought in any individual element or complex of elements. What is identical is the *law-like regularity* of their mutual interconnections.

No doubt these regularities are the same for different individuals — not the regularities between the elements themselves, however, but the relations between the relations of elements. For these are the laws of nature. And if I believe at all in the existence of other minds, I shall also have to assume that they find the same lawfulness in nature that I do. But even this doesn't help; we are still left with a preestablished harmony. The claim that all subjects observe the same law-like regularities in nature is in fact only another expression for the reciprocal correspondence of the world pictures of the monads, for their mutual harmony, and nothing more. Only if it were something more, only if the common lawfulness were a real structure instead of a mere abstraction, could it play the role of a middle term between the individual worlds and be regarded as a real connection between them. But if anyone chose to declare that these pure connecting points, these relations of relations, are real as such, he would thereby dissolve the real into mere concepts and adopt a position that we have long since recognized to be untenable.

Thus the philosophy of immanence is deprived of its last refuge. Inevitably its universe breaks down into as many worlds as there are central terms present; and there exists among these worlds a multiple parallelism signifying no more than a mysterious correspondence, not a real bond. In order to present the world as a unified real system of causal relations, which it undoubtedly is, we must assume real connecting links by virtue of which a real connection replaces a logical correspondence. And this requires only a very obvious and very natural step: that we do *not* conceive the connecting points of relations of relations of elements (that is, the concepts without which we cannot describe the law-like changes of perceptions) as the mere auxiliary concepts demanded by the immanence notion; instead, we must see them as signs for realities, just as much signs for realities as are the concepts that designate something directly given. And we are acquainted with a criterion for determining with *which* concepts real objects, in contrast to mere fictions, are correlated: it is those concepts that, in the course of being derived from the given in accordance with empirical rules, have a *temporal* sign affixed to them. Thus we turn from the doctrines of immanence philosophy, which seeks to equate the real with the given, back to the criterion of reality that we had obtained above from the range of ideas found in everyday life and in science. With both of these, we adhere to the one natural standpoint — a standpoint that can be abandoned only if one believes that contradictions have been discovered in the concept of a thing-in-itself, that is, in the concept of something that is not given, that does not belong to any principal coordination. Once it is recognized that things-in-themselves in this sense are not impossible, it is easy to be convinced that they are not superfluous. And when their existence is acknowledged, the strict positivist standpoint is surrendered.

The transcendence thereby consummated is in principle not *more* of a transcendence than that which positivism itself admits when, for example, it reckons the *past* too in the realm of the real, even though it is not given and can never again be brought to givenness. Positivism admits the past because it has no ground for denying it and because the past is needed in order to make the present intelligible. Well, these are the very same grounds on which we acknowledge

realities that transcend consciousness: we have no ground for denying them and we need them in order to make the world of consciousness intelligible. The immanence philosopher is not content to declare the entire past a mere auxiliary concept, which he could very
well do; he recognizes its reality. Similarly, we claim full reality for
all temporally localized objects, and we have no grounds whatever
for declaring them pure auxiliary concepts that do not designate
anything real.

The soundness of our result is indirectly confirmed exactly where
consistent positivists seek to bring into congruence the environment-
constituents of different central terms. The poorly concealed concept
of the thing-in-itself peers out of their accounts at every turn.

We find such a hidden acknowledgement in AVENARIUS. Thus we
read (Weltbegriff, p. 162): "But if in general we allow the assumption that in these two principal coordinations the counterterm R is
one in respect of number, that is no reason to allow the more far-
reaching assumption that the counterterm R is the *same* in respect
of its *constitution* ... To the same extent that special conditions
are to be assumed in addition to the common ones, it is also to be
assumed that the make-up of the one R in one of the principal coordinations is determined differently than in the 'other' principal
coordination." This differentiation between the *one* real R and its
qualities, which may be different in different relations, is nothing
but an affirmation of the thing-in-itself, and in fact not in its most
advantageous or least objectionable form. Here we may simply
repeat our earlier line of argument (§ 26). At that time we designated by $C_1, C_2, \ldots$ different perceptions or complexes of elements
that are given to an individual at various times. Now we may use
these same symbols to designate the different perceptions that several individuals have "at the same time" of the "same thing" O.
The conclusions about the relationship of the one O to the many
C's and about the entry into the scene of the idea of the thing-in-
itself remain exactly the same.

An object is not a thing-in-itself, but an object for a subject or
a counterterm for a central term, only if it is nothing but the complex
of qualities it exhibits in the principal coordination in question. If the
qualities in another principal coordination are different, then what is
present in that coordination is not the same object. If we speak from
the standpoint of there being different central terms and yet one
and the same object, then we are talking precisely of a thing that

possesses qualities that belong to it independently of the central term, hence "for itself". Avenarius does this and thus acknowledges the existence of a thing-in-itself in the sense in which we too must sanction and require it. If he did not do so, then, as is evident from the passages cited, the connection between the worlds of the individual subjects would be ruptured. In order to safeguard this connection, and to prevent it from being destroyed even within the experiential world of the single subject, it is necessary to acknowledge realities that are not given. Without them, the sense of empirical laws of nature cannot be preserved. And it is not correct to say, as MACH does (*op. cit.,* p. 28) that "this relation to unknown, not given primitive variables (things-in-themselves) is purely fictitious and worthless."

It is this "unknown" *("unbekannt"),* which Mach emphasizes here, that has made things-in-themselves an abomination for so many philosophers. They will not countenance in their world picture any quantities with which we are not acquainted, which neither are given nor can be given. That is why they try to hold on so firmly to the dogma of the identity of the real and the given.

They behave in this manner because they have not yet entirely freed themselves from the old concept of knowledge — a concept that positivism otherwise has helped so much to overcome. At this one point they still conflate knowing *(Erkennen)* with being acquainted with *(Kennen),* that is, with pure experiencing, mere being given. They still look here for an answer to the question of what the real actually "is", an answer that can be supplied us only by direct acquaintance, by experience. What the "elements", in the case of Mach and Avenarius, "are" we know by direct acquaintance; colors, sounds, smells are simply given. It is not a judgment or a definition but experience alone that gives us information about their "nature". But this does not mean that the elements and their nature are *known* (see above I, § 12). At times we find a correct insight into this state of affairs expressed quite clearly even among spokesmen for positivism. Thus VAIHINGER (Die Philosophie des Als-Ob, 2nd printing, p. 94) says: "Being is only *knowable (wißbar)* in the form of unalterable successions and coexistences; it is not understandable, since to understand is to reduce something to something else, which cannot be done in the case of being." In this way, of course, we can never become acquainted with things-in-themselves; they are not knowable *(wißbar),* since by definition they are never *given*. But if we find this unsatisfying, it is only because we have lost sight of our goal. For do we want to *become acquainted* with the world? Do we not rather want to *know* it? It is the latter alone that is the task of philosophy and of science.

That a part of the world is given to us directly, while another and larger part is not so given, must be accepted as a contingent fact, so to speak. We have no interest in it as persons knowing; we do have an interest as persons *living* in the world. It is no service to the knowing person in particular if, in connection with the question of what an object *is*, we refer him to pure experiencing. For him the question only means: "Through which general concepts can the object be designated?" He can answer this question all the sooner in the case of things-in-themselves, since in general he is led to them by just these concepts. The individual sciences furnish us with concepts precisely of real objects that are not given, and that we have therefore designated as existing "in themselves". Through these concepts, then, we truly *know* what things-in-themselves are, and the wrongful accusation against them regarding their unknowability *(Unerkennbarkeit)* is in truth only a complaint about their being such that we cannot be acquainted with them *(Unkennbarkeit)*, that we cannot experience them, that they are not intuitively given — in short it is a reversion to the mystical concept of knowledge. The intuiting of things is not cognition nor a precondition of cognition. The objects of cognition must be *thinkable* without contradiction, that is, they must admit of being designated uniquely by means of concepts; but they need not be intuitively representable.

That such representability is still often demanded by positivistically oriented thinkers is an odd sort of bias. The circumstance that psychologically every thought is bound up with intuitive processes of consciousness, and cannot take place without them, easily leads to a conflating of conceptual thinking and intuitive representation in the epistemological sense. In Petzoldt's book, which we have cited a number of times, this pervasive confusion of thinking and representing, of mere designating on the one hand and intuitive depicting on the other, is revealed with particular distinctness. The prime source of his mistakes in reasoning is that he takes thinking to be pictorial representation and not conceptual correlation. His basic error is expressed in its most striking form in a sentence on p. 201 of his Weltproblem: "To represent the world, or (!) to think it, means precisely to represent or to think it with qualities, whereas the question about the world in itself specifically disregards all sense qualities." It is true that somehow we must represent the mutual relationships of concepts intuitively if we are to be able to grasp them; this, however, we can do in as many different ways as we please, and epistemologically it does not matter how we do this. The successful scientist for the most part has a strong inclination toward the intuitive; his mind is crowded with a multitude of very clear images as illustrations of the conceptual relations that he has worked out. It is natural that he finds these images the essential factor in knowledge and that he regards the intuitively representable as the sole object of knowledge. But in fact the sensible representations are more or less accidental and subsidiary, as far as the problems of epistemology are concerned. They are essential only for the psychological viewpoint.

The non-representability of realities that are not given is thus no objection to their existence or to their knowability.

B. *Knowledge of the Real*

§ 27. Essence and "Appearance"

From the foregoing considerations we have gained the insight that the area of the real is not to be identified with the area of the "given". It most certainly extends much farther. Our critique of attempts to establish this identification did not have simply a negative character. Every argument directed against such efforts was at the same time a proof of the existence of realities that are not given, that transcend consciousness.

We emphasize once more that with this we have answered the question raised earlier, whether there is any reason for philosophy to abandon or modify the criterion of reality that can be extracted from the procedures of everyday life and science, namely, the criterion of temporality. It has turned out that there is no such reason, that only dogmatic presuppositions have made it seem desirable to many philosophers to narrow the real down to the given. These presuppositions have proved to be without foundation. The criterion of temporality has again come into its own, and thus our first problem of reality — the question of the *positing of reality* — may be counted as in principle solved. Of course, the application of the general principle to the individual case remains a subject for special research. The latter with its empirical means must find out whether the criterion of reality is actually fulfilled in the particular situation, that is, whether the data at hand not only make possible but require a temporal ordering of the objects under study (in the case of natural science objects, a spatio-temporal ordering). Once the decision has been made in this way, philosophy must simply accept it; the question is settled for philosophy too.

We come now to the second problem of reality, which embraces the most fundamental questions of philosophy: the *determination of the nature* of the real, the *knowledge* of the real.

Here again it is necessary first to clear the field for positive cultivation by rooting out certain dogmas, which would draw a boundary between the real that is given and the real that is not given in such a way as to make it impossible to attain clarity about their mutual relationship.

The concept of reality stems ultimately from experience, since the real that is given is the only one with which we are *directly acquainted*. Yet even at the time it is formed, the validity of the concept of reality is already extended to a being beyond experience. And philosophy — as usually happens in the case of such developments — immediately proclaims that the conceptual sphere that is farthest from the source is the most excellent and most important. In our case, this means that the real beyond consciousness is declared to be a higher order of reality, a more genuine being, in comparison with which the world of consciousness is only a shadow and a fleeting reflection.

It was Plato, as we know, who pushed this strange view to its extreme and developed it most brilliantly. For him, the supersensible world of ideas is the highest in every sense, including the rank ordering of *value,* which he himself — or rather along with the Megarians — was the first to conflate with the logical rank ordering of conceptual generality. He thereby brought confusion into questions of a world outlook for more than 2000 years, by giving all "idealism" a more respectable aspect. On the very same terrain, however, there was also erected the conception of materialism, which in its admiration for the solid reality of physical objects simply forgets that there also exists a real world of consciousness, or believes that it may be treated as a *quantité négligeable.* While no epistemologically oriented philosophy has gone quite that far, one finds a tendency to downgrade experiential reality in favor of the transcendent even in those systems that consciously take as their point of departure the primordial reality of the immediately given and strive to give it its full due.

This applies especially to Kant. This characteristic tendency breaks through quite forcefully in his practical philosophy. But even in his theory of knowledge, the being of that which is not given — the things-in-themselves — is counterposed in striking fashion to the being of that which is given. The latter, as is well known, he calls *appearance*. Thus there is introduced into philosophy the distinction between things and appearances, which, ever since Kant, has played a similarly large role with both the opponents and the supporters of his doctrine.

For Kant, things-in-themselves are unknowable. And to the question: "What then do we know?", he answers: "*Only* appearances!" In so far as unknowability here means what we would call "not being open to direct acquaintance" *(Unkennbarkeit)*, Kant of course is right. But he takes it to mean this and more. He wants to deny the knowability of things-in-themselves *in our sense* also when he says that they do not admit of being designated by our general concepts, of being brought under the "categories" of our understanding. We shall have to return later to these ideas of Kant and to the grounds he offers for them. What interests us here at the moment is that his positive determination of the nature of transcendent things is exhausted in the supposition that they are simply there. Their existence, however, was defended by Kant — though some of his interpreters might deny this — with all the clarity that one might wish. (This would be true even if the only passage in Kant's writings that testifed to it was the second remark to § 13 of the *Prolegomena*.) He thereby adopted the viewpoint generally designated today as "phenomenalism"*: a transcendent reality is acknowledged to exist, but its knowability is denied.

According to the doctrine of phenomenalism, we have awareness and knowledge not of the *nature* or *essence* of things-in-themselves, but only of their appearances. For the phenomena are precisely appearances of things. In Kant's view, of course, appearances are

---

* The term 'phenomenalism' here is of course used in a sense quite different from that found in Anglo-American philosophy. [Translator's note.]

real; time and again he emphasizes that appearance is not to be confused with *illusion* or *pretense.* Moreover, the sensible world of bodies has the same full reality and objectivity with which it confronts everyone in daily life and natural science. But Kant distinguishes the empirical character of its reality from the being of things-in-themselves. In fact, according to Kant, reality is a category, and as such may be predicated only of appearances, not of transcendent things. (Kant also accepts as valid an existence that is not a category, as can be seen in his remark on the Paralogisms of Pure Reason in the second edition of the Kritik der reinen Vernunft, Kehrbach edition, pp. 696 ff.) Thus inevitably the reality of things-in-themselves is evaluated as something more genuine and fundamental; the world of natural things is "only" appearance. The concept of a phenomenon presupposes something that appears, and consequently is not a phenomenon, but — one can scarcely express it in any other way — is *more* than appearance. Thus the thought constantly arises that things-in-themselves possess a "higher" reality.

Since for Kant all data of consciousness have the character of phenomena, each datum points to or suggests a being of which it is an appearance. Thus we are required to assume the existence of realities that are not given even when we are not led to this assumption on other grounds, such as the rules of empirical research. Our own feelings and other subjective experiences are conceived of as appearances of a being with which we are not acquainted. This is the Kantian theory of an inner sense — a theory lacking any kind of factual support and resulting solely from the separation of essence or nature and appearance.

It is precisely by means of this theory of an inner sense that we can best establish the soundness of the claim we now want to make: that the thing-appearance pair is in general a very poor piece of concept formation and that the concept of appearance should be banished from philosophy. For what does it mean to say that mental realities are not experienced as they really are, that we become acquainted only with their appearances? The very reality of consciousness from which we derive our whole concept of being is thereby pronounced a second grade being, since it is said to be merely the appearance of something else and not something that is sufficient unto itself, not pure being. This is the same as removing the concept of being from the soil in which it has grown. Earlier we found it necessary to oppose all efforts to constitute a special reality for the mental and to distinguish it from the merely given, or experienced (see above, Part II, § 20). The arguments adduced there against inner perception and an inner sense also prove that a duality of essence and appearance within mental reality is impossible.

But we must likewise reject the view that designates certain data of consciousness, especially "perceptions of physical bodies", as appearances of transcendent things. For even if this conception does not dispose us to ascribe a higher, more genuine existence to the things-in-themselves than to their appearances in consciousness, it still misleads us into counterposing two kinds of reality, whose reciprocal relationship then gives rise to problems as unsolvable as they are unnecessary. Specifically, what sort of relationship are we supposed to be characterizing if we say that a certain content of consciousness, a perceptual image, for example, is an *appearance* of a thing? Does this mean it is a part of the thing — a part that extends or flows into consciousness? This is out of the quesion, of course; for if any such part did reach into consciousness (as ancient theories of perception assumed), then the thing simply would not be transcendent. Or is the appearance supposed to be an adumbration, an imitation, a picture of the appearing object? Needless to say, no one wants to defend such a view any more, least of all a phenomenalist. Expressions of this sort can be regarded only as figures of speech.

The relationship we are discussing can be made clear only by means of images taken from the empirical world. Just as the contrast between illusion and reality finds meaningful application in that world, so too does the contrast between essence and appearance. For example, we can count the geometrically defined figure of a physical body as belonging to its essence or nature, the different perspectival views as part of its appearance. Is the relation between thing and phenomenon of the same kind perhaps? Manifestly not, for according to Kant, the entire body itself is only appearance. But the existence of phenomena must somehow be conditioned by the existence of things. Indeed, KANT (Prolegomena, § 13, Remark 2) defines appearances as "the representations that they (the things) bring about by affecting our senses". Appearances then are said to be the effects that things-in-themselves produce on consciousness. It is at this point that the Kantian theory has long been subject to sharp criticism because the concept of cause, which in this view has

validity only for appearances, here is applied to the things-in-themselves. If the criticism is correct, then the relationship of things to
phenomena becomes something unique and inexplicable, which
must simply be accepted and cannot further be clarified. Be that
as it may, Kant in any event assumes — as does every form of
phenomenalism — that there is some sort of correspondence or
correlation between things and phenomena. And for this the causal
relation is still the best image in the realm of empirical reality. In
fact, we often speak in everyday life of an effect as if it were an
appearance of a cause: fever is an appearance of illness, the rise in
the thermometer an appearance of warmth, lightning an appearance
of an electrical storm, and so forth. But just as the concept of cause
is ambiguous (since ultimately every process depends on innumerable conditions), so too the notion of appearance thus conceived
lacks any fixed reference. Is a perceptual image, for example, the
direct appearance of the perceived body? Can I not also conceive
it rather as an appearance of the nerve processes when the sense
organs are stimulated, or even as an appearance of the brain processes that we assume as running parallel to my perceptual image?

We see how indeterminate the concept of appearance is and to
what difficulties it leads when we try to reach it using experience
as a starting-point. The fact is that we can obtain the concept only
if we already presuppose a difference in reality between the world
of consciousness and the transcendent world. Indeed, it is nothing
other than the expression of the severing of these two worlds.

Many philosophers state in even clearer terms that they actually
do detect here a difference in reality. Thus, Külpe uses the term
'actual' *('wirklich')* only for the immediately given, and the word
'real' *('real')* to refer exclusively to the world that transcends consciousness. Yet according to him, there is a "close relation" between
actual *(= wirklich)* objects and real *(= real)* ones (Die Realisierung,
1912, pp. 13, 14). Of course these distinctions are to begin with
purely terminological in nature, and as such outside the question
of truth and falsity. We are free to designate just the immediately
given as actual *(= wirklich)* and to differentiate transcendent being
from it as real *(= real)*. But we must demand that terminological
stipulations be suitable, and this they are only if they are properly
adapted to the factual foundation. In the present case, it seems to
me, this requirement is not satisfied. The fact that there are real
things, some of which are given and some not given, may indeed

justify us in distinguishing two classes of real things, but not in assuming two different kinds or levels of reality. Also, Külpe's terminology allows the positing of an unconscious mental reality to seem more natural than is in fact justified, for it permits us, for example, to speak of sensations that are real (= *real*) but at the same time are not also actual (= *wirklich*).

From a purely formal viewpoint, we would likewise be permitted, with Kant, to designate as appearance any real thing that is given and to assign all that is not given to a realm of things-in-themselves. But this manner of designating suffers from the same mistake in that it implies different levels or grades of reality. For the word 'appearance' always suggests something lying outside that appearance and without which the appearance would not be there. On the other hand, a thing-in-itself can very well be present without appearing. It is therefore something that exists in its own right, something independent, in contrast to the appearance. There is a one-sided dependency between thing and appearances that robs appearances of that independence which is an inseparable part of the concept of the truly real.

Now there is no set of facts that either forces or justifies such a counterposing of two irreducible realities, of which one rests entirely on itself and the other is dependent on the first. On the contrary, we obtain a much simpler and hence more satisfactory picture of the world if we ascribe the same reality to all objects without distinction, so that they are all in the same sense self-dependent but also in the same sense dependent on each other. This means that the happenings in my consciousness not only are conditioned by the transcendent world but in turn also exert an influence on it. And the interrelations of the two realms are of exactly the same kind as those that hold between processes within one of the two realms. At any rate, there is no reason to assume other kinds of dependencies; consequently, we retain the view that they are in principle the same, so long as the facts do not compel us to give up this simple assumption.

Thus we seek to make do with the hypothesis — or, if you will, to follow out the postulate — that the mutual dependency of elements that are simply given is governed in principle by the same law-like regularity that governs not only processes in the transcendent world but also the relations between that world and the contents of my consciousness. It is no more possible to designate one or another happening within my consciousness as an appearance outside of my consciousness than it is for me to conceive of one or another content of my consciousness as an "appearance" of some other content of that same consciousness. The main point is to carry out with the utmost consistency the view that *all* parts of reality, no matter what connections they may have, are simply correlated with one another; none of them represents the "essence" of the world more than any other. The correspondence between extramental objects and the data of consciousness is a mere correlation, no different in principle from the correlations that we are able to effect among the data of consciousness themselves. On this conception the assumption of extra-mental objects does not signify an "unnecessary duplication" (PETZOLDT, Weltproblem, p. 190). In the sequel, a number of additional reasons will be given for concluding that this view of ours is not impracticable.

In any case, one of the positive results of our examination of immanentist notions is this: from them we may learn to recognize the immediate data of consciousness as self-dependent being, as full-fledged reality. In agreement with these notions, we reject the Kantian concept of appearance. Our perceptions, ideas and feelings are not something secondary, not mere appearances; they are independently real in the same sense as any transcendent "things". There is only *one* reality; it is always *essence,* and does not admit of being broken down into essence and appearance. There are, to be sure, different kinds of real objects, indeed infinitely many; but there is only one kind of reality, and it is to be ascribed to all objects equally.

It is only with this formulation that we remain faithful to the original sense of the concept of reality. Its source was the immediately given, which is absolutely real; and our whole formulation of the problem in the preceding sections was aimed at determining whether we must in addition attribute this *same* reality to still other objects. Whoever describes the reality of these other objects as being of a different or novel kind strips the problem of any sense and invents a concept of reality that lacks any foundation in actual experience and with which our own concept has nothing in common.

Phenomenalism owes its name to the concept of "appearance" and claims that we know only appearances, not the essence or nature of things[34]. It is a totally untenable doctrine, and a rigorous proof can be had that its viewpoint is self-contradictory.

We have repeatedly emphasized that things-in-themselves must of course be regarded as unknowable if we believe, with Kant, that in order to know a thing it is necessary to intuit it directly. And we have shown on each such occasion that this is something we cannot accept. For cognition cannot be thus defined; fundamentally it has nothing to do with intuition. This position is further confirmed by a closer scrutiny of phenomenalism. As is soon evident, it is impossible to maintain that we cannot say anything more about things-in-themselves than that they exist. Transcendent objects are supposed to be the grounds or bases for phenomena; hence to every difference in the phenomena there must also correspond a difference in the objects[35]. For if this were not the case, then the character of the appearance would ultimately depend on the subject alone. And we would arrive at a purely idealistic view of the world, such as that developed by Fichte, who thought this was the only way in which the Kantian system could be given a consistent elaboration. According to Fichte's doctrine, the self creatively produces appearances from itself, and does so without needing any assistance from transcendent objects.

Such are the consequences to which we are undoubtedly led unless we reject the phenomenalistic presupposition and assume that, on the basis of relations among appearances, something positive can be said about the mutual relations of transcendent things. And statements of this sort constitute *knowledge* of the things; such statements contain much more than the mere affirmation that the transcendent things exist. For instance, in order for me to perceive the window on my left and the door on my right there must be some underlying basis in the things of which the door and the window are appearances. That is, if the basis lay solely in the subject, then

---

34 The word 'phenomenalism' is not always used in the same sense. For example, HANS KLEINPETER (in his work Der Phänomenalismus) uses the term to designate philosophical currents that we have just criticized in §§ 25 and 26.

35 This is acknowledged likewise by many modern criticists; for example, see R. HÖNIGSWALD, Beiträge zur Erkenntnistheorie und Methodenlehre (1906), pp. 115 ff. PETZOLDT (Weltproblem, p. 190) seems, in his criticism of the above passages, to have overlooked the fact that there I was describing not my own viewpoint but that of phenomenalism.

both objects would necessarily be entirely subjective. For otherwise, the ground for localizing the door to the right of the window, and not vice versa, would lie only in something objective, transcendent; and by the above presupposition, it cannot lie there. The assumption that transcendent objects exist would then lack all sense and purpose; we would be right in the middle of subjective idealism and an end would be put to phenomenalism.

Thus even if space, for example, were only an individual determination of form of appearances, and not of things-in-themselves, it would still not follow that therefore *nothing* in the world of things-in-themselves corresponds to the spatial ordering of the world of the senses. There would still be some kind of ordering, only not a spatial one. Kant was quite clear about this — a point that at times is still overlooked. RIEHL is entirely right when he says (Der philosophische Kritizismus, I, 2nd printing, 1908, p. 476): "It follows from Kant's theory, even if Kant himself did not expressly say so, that there must be a reason for every particular empirical determination of space and time in the object that appears." And Kant himself declared (in a passage cited by Riehl): "I fully grant that space and time have both subjective and objective grounds." It is of course difficult to see how Kant could expect to reconcile this insight with his doctrine that the categories of multiplicity and relation are not applicable to things-in-themselves.

In short, it must be assumed that something or other in the things-in-themselves corresponds to or is uniquely correlated with each individual determination of the "appearances". And this is quite sufficient for us not only to know the world-in-itself but to know it to the same extent and in the same degree that we know the world of the senses. Cognition requires nothing more than the possibility of unique correlation. Indeed, we must also declare — and we have said this before — that in general *every* cognition of things of the senses is at the same time a cognition of transcendent reality; our concepts are signs for the one as well as for the other.

If by the "essence" of things we understand something that is knowable at all, then surely the empirical sciences supply us with knowledge of the essence or nature of objects. In physics, for instance, Maxwell's equations disclose to us the "essence" of electricity, Einstein's equations the essence of gravitation. With their help, we are able in principle to answer all questions that can be raised with regard to these objects of nature. If this is granted, then, by virtue of what was said above, we likewise possess a knowledge of the things-in-themselves. And the only one who cannot admit this is a person who insists on understanding by the essence of something real nothing except what is directly given, an immediately experienced quality; but this latter (we need only refer once more to our account in Part I, § 12) is not knowable, it is something with which we can only be acquainted.

There is still another quarter from which we can see how impossible the phenomenalistic position is. Since the characteristic feature of everything real consists in the fact that it must be represented as temporally ordered, the phenomenalist claim amounts to this: there are things of which we know that they exist at a specific time, but of which *beyond* that we know nothing. But the very nature of cognition absolutely excludes the possibility of a knowledge limited in just this way. For the empirical rules that lead to the incorporation of an event or thing in the temporal order already presuppose, for their application, that we have a multifarious acquaintance with the relations of that event or thing to others. In the last analysis, fixing an object in time always takes place, as we explained (see § 24, near the end), by relating it to the present moment; and the data required for that purpose are all bases for knowledge of the object. Thus temporal determination is impossible without additional knowledge of the object. The bases for a temporal orientation are always bases also for incorporating the object into other sets of relationships, and thus bases for knowledge. A mere temporal sequence is empty and without foundation. For us to be able to ascribe a determinateness to an object, there must be indications of some sort that the temporal sign is to be coordinated with precisely this object; but the aspects supplied by these indications can be asserted as properties or relations of the object. For example, how could we assert that there must once have been an Ice Age if we were not able at the same time to make a multitude of positive statements about its nature? Unless we could do so, we would have no idea at all of what is meant by an Ice Age! We can assert the existence of an object only if we know what kind of object it is, only if we are at least acquainted in one way or another with its nature. If we know nothing about *what* sort of thing it is, about its essence, we can say nothing about the fact *that* it is, about its existence. The two cannot be separated. The same holds for the things-in-themselves that presumably "underlie" the "phenomena" of the Ice Age.

Only through the necessary determination that they do indeed correspond uniquely with the phenomena are the things-in-themselves, thanks to the wealth of relations of the phenomena, woven together into a network of correlations — and it is by virtue of this that they are also *known*.

Let us summarize. There is only *one* reality. And whatever lies within its domain is in principle equally accessible, in its being as well as in its essence, to our cognition. Only a small part of this reality is ever given to us. The remainder is not given. But the separation thus effectuated between the subjective and the objective is accidental in character. It is not fundamental, as the separation between essence and appearance is supposed to be — a separation that we have recognized as not feasible[36].

§ 28. The Subjectivity of Time

Since temporality is the criterion of reality, and since reality must be ascribed to the transcendent world, it would seem to follow that the things of the transcendent world are temporal in the same sense as the immediately given world of consciousness. This would also appear to follow with respect to spatiality, since in the case of natural objects spatial and temporal determinations go hand in hand. Thus the conclusion seems inescapable that the realm of transcendent objects is extended in time and generally in space as well, that consequently the doctrine of the subjectivity of space and time — given such wide recognition since Kant — is incompatible with our results. For on this doctrine both space and time are merely forms of our intuition and do not apply to the things-in-themselves.

But this conclusion would be premature. Our findings do not provide premisses adequate to sustain it.

In order to see how our results relate to the Kantian theory of space and time — what, if anything, they imply as to its correctness or incorrectness — we must first be very clear about the meaning of that theory. And this requires that we hold quite firmly to the sharp distinction we sought to elaborate when we drew a fixed, impassable

---

36 On the matters discussed in this section, see my paper Erscheinung und Wesen, Kantstudien, 1918.

boundary line between the intuitive on the one hand and the conceptual on the other.

We must completely dissociate the subjective experience of temporal succession from the objective determination of time. The former is something directly given or intuitive, the latter is a purely conceptual ordering. The indefinable, indescribable experience of succession and duration, this qualitative and ever-varying aspect, furnishes no objective determination of intervals in the sequence of events. This experience constitutes the subject matter for psychological studies of "time awareness" and can provide us with a means for estimating time but never for measuring it. Rather, as we know, the way we measure time is to select certain simple periodic processes (passage of a star through the meridian, the coinciding of an hour hand with a particular position on the clock-face, and the like), use them as fixed reference points in the continuous course of our experience, and designate them by means of numerals. Thus we correlate events with a one-dimensional manifold, a purely conceptual structure, in which, after choosing an initial point and a reference system, we assign to each event a numerically defined position (date, hour, second, and so forth). This continuous sequence can and must be extended beyond the given reality and applied in like manner to the reality that is not given. This, indeed, was the reason why such an ordering was able in the first place to serve as a criterion of reality. To every interval between two numbers of that one-dimensional manifold there corresponds in the realm of consciousness a difference in the qualitative aspect of the consciousness of time (perhaps an indescribable experience of "right away", "soon", "a long time ago" and the like). But with reference to transcendent reality, no such aspect of course is experienced, since this reality is not given.

In the case of time (and likewise in that of space), Kant did not clearly distinguish between intuitive experience and a conceptual ordering. The two were hopelessly conflated and confused. But anyone who desires to sort them out correctly must ask: What is this temporality that the theory of the subjectivity of time denies to the transcendent world? Is this the content of the experience of duration, of earlier or later, an experience not otherwise describable? Or, is it merely an ordering in the form of a one-dimensional continuum, by which we designate the time sequence for purposes of exact description (chronology, mathematical physics)? It may well be that the subjectivity of time should be affirmed in the one case and denied in the other. If we are to come to a decision, we must have a clear picture of the various possibilities.

Let it be established at the outset that, as regards our criterion of reality, time naturally is to be understood not in the sense of intuitive being but only as a conceptual ordering. An object is real if the empirical correlations necessitate its being given a quite definite place in the one-dimensional continuum that we associate with succession as experienced. Thus the reality criterion is obviously compatible with the subjectivity of time as experienced.

The one-dimensional continuum is a type of ordering that need not serve only to designate the temporal ordering of reality. It may also be applied in innumerable other ways to order intuitively given data: the scale of musical pitch, of intensities of a sensation, perhaps even the scale of feelings of pleasure. We can designate any of these by the number sequence just as well as we designate intuitive "time". Of course, as compared with these other examples of one-dimensional orderings in the realm of the given, succession in time is something quite unique and plays a quite specific universal role in the law-like interdependency of all experiences. There is no doubt that temporality is a uniform property connected with *all* experiences.

For this reason it is altogether misleading to talk, as MACH does (Analyse der Empfindungen, XII), of a *time sensation*. For one can speak of a sensation only in relation to a particular sense organ. Hume is quite right when he says (Treatise of Human Nature, Book I, Part II, Section III): "Five notes played on a flute give us the impression and idea of time, though time be not a sixth impression which presents itself to the hearing or any other of the senses. Nor is it a sixth impression which the mind by reflection finds in itself." However, Mach's discussion seems to me to be substantially correct in so far as it makes clear that temporality is part of our immediately intuited experience; the only objection is that throughout he inappropriately calls this experience sensing. When I hear a tone, the perception does not consist of the tone plus the sensation of duration. Duration is bound up with the perception of the tone just as inseparably as the pitch or intensity of the tone.

And duration is a property not only of sensations but, as we have said, of all experience. There is no sense organ that senses time; the entire self experiences it. This will be no surprise to us if we recall the peculiar role that temporality plays in relation to the unity of consciousness, which we have to regard as the most essential feature of the individual self (see above, Part II, § 17). The system of recollection, which constitutes the unity of consciousness, is a temporal one; the peculiar tie that within consciousness joins past and future by means of the present seems to underly both temporality and the unity of consciousness in equal measure. Whether we shall ever be able to say anything more detailed about these interconnections must be left undetermined.

If we now ask whether "time" in the second sense — as conceptual ordering, as something objective — holds also for extra-mental reality or has only a subjective sense, there can be no doubt as to the answer. For a temporal ordering unquestionably relates to transcendent things just as much as to the contents of consciousness. What makes this possible is its character as a purely conceptual sign. That things-in-themselves can also be ordered in accordance with the one-dimensional schema of the number sequence is not especially significant. On the contrary, it is perfectly obvious. This is not what constitutes the objective validity of the temporal sequence. Rather, this validity is based on the fact that a certain way of carrying out this ordering is distinguished from all others, that we are led to it directly by those principles with the aid of which we have constructed the whole conceptual system that we use to designate the facts of the world. We shall talk about these principles briefly in the following sections; a detailed treatment must, because of the specialized character of the concepts involved, be left to the philosophy of nature.

Time, as a mere schema of ordering, thus certainly has trans-subjective meaning. But this does not settle anything regarding the question as to whether the intuitive experience of temporal duration and temporal succession is merely subjective. The concepts by means of which we order empirical data temporally can certainly be applied to the transcendent world as well. But this is not to say that in their transcendent application they must also have the intuitive content that in their immanent use constitutes the temporality of the conscious processes, which can only be experienced, not described. We can also say quite properly of objects beyond consciousness that they "succeed one another". Yet this is not to attribute to them the specifically intuitive aspect which, for example, distinguishes the ordering of points in time from the ordering of space points on a line. The former do indeed follow "one after the other", but in a very different sense, which also can only be experienced but not conceptually demarcated. Do duration and succession exist in the realm of things-in-themselves in just the same way as they are experienced in our consciousness? Or is the transcendent correlate of temporal succession only a non-intuitive ordering that can be *known* exhaustively with the aid of our concepts, but cannot be identified with and must not be confused with the ordering of experience with which we are directly *acquainted?*

The question has to be formulated with great care. For it would be meaningless if its answer presupposed acquaintance with the transcendent order, something with which we on principle can never be *acquainted.*

But precisely for this reason we are able to say that the thesis of the *objectivity* of intuitive time, as taught by some philosophers, is not provable under any circumstances (see, for example, LOTZE in his Metaphysik and STÖRRING in his Erkenntnistheorie, 1920, pp. 185 ff.). Beyond that, however, the following may be asserted in behalf of the mere subjectivity of intuitive time.

Processes to which "objectively" equal durations are ascribed may still be connected to different experiences of temporality. An hour creeps by slowly or rushes past, depending on whether it is filled with boring or interesting content. Theoretically there is no limit to the variations in speed that a consciousness, by reason of its differing intuitions of time, may subjectively ascribe to the course of events. The natural scientist, K. E. VON BAER (Welche Auffassung der lebenden Natur ist die richtige?, 1862), has painted in an especially vivid manner the diversity of world pictures presented to a being depending on whether he undergoes a vast number of experiences in what for us would be a short time, or contrariwise, is subjected to an existence poor in experiences during what we would consider a "long" interval of time. His remarks have often been cited by philosophers, for example, Liebmann, Heymanns, and Störring. Were our whole life compressed into a half hour, without subjectively seeming shorter, then plants would seem to us as unchanging as mountains do now. The course of a year would appear comparable to our most remote geological epochs, and anyone who experienced the setting of the sun could learn only from the history books of a long forgotton past that it had ever risen.

Thus if the self-same time can be experienced in so many different ways, which of them is to count as transcendently real? Our intuition of time, or perhaps that of a bird, whose pulse beat is so much faster than that of a human being, or of the short-lived mayfly, or of a creature "for whom a thousand years are but a day"? None of these ranks above any other, and it becomes quite impossible to ascribe to an intuitive experience of time anything other than a subjective significance. The objective course of events can be neither fast nor slow; here these relative concepts lose all meaning. By the same token the course of events cannot be temporal in the intuitive sense. The transcendent ordering in which it has a place is not intuitively representable.

What is true with respect to experienced time is that, at any given instant, one moment in it can be distinguished from all the others: the "now"-moment of the present. We are accustomed to calling only the presently experienced moment real; the past is no longer real, the future is not yet real. We must agree that giving this sort of preferred treatment to one point in time above all the others makes no sense for the transcendent world. In such a world, past and future reality can lay claim to the predicate *real* in the same sense as the present does. Or, more exactly, the difference among these times is not absolute, is not objectively *there*. We are compelled to accept such an assumption by considerations drawn from the theory of relativity. These teach us that the concept of simultaneity is relative. That is, the determination as to whether two events occurring at different places are simultaneous turns out quite differently depending on the state of motion of the observer. Hence when we join all "present", and therefore simultaneous, events of the world into an all-inclusive "present time", this union depends on the physical system with respect to which this assembling was undertaken. It is impossible to fix a total state of the world as "presently real" in an unambiguous manner; there is no basis in the extra-mental world for singling out a present moment in contrast to the past and to the future. This has meaning only for the world of immediate experience. On this point, then, the claim that time is subjective is correct.

Were it necessary, further evidence for the subjectivity of time as experienced could also be obtained from the theory of relativity. This is the fact that, from a purely formal viewpoint, time measurements play quite the same role in the description of the world as do space measurements. We may then infer by analogy that, with respect to the question of reality, space and time are on the same footing. The subjectivity of intuitive-spatial data, which will be apparent in the next section, may thus also be taken as support for the arguments relating to intuitive-temporal data.

There is still another line of reasoning that is well suited to making clear the subjectivity of the temporal in the sense already explained. It is developed most ingeniously in P. MONGRÉ's Das Chaos in kosmischer Auslese (Leipzig 1898) and FRANZ SELETY's Die wirklichen Tatsachen der reinen Erfahrung, eine Kritik der Zeit, Zeitschrift für Philosophie und philosophische Kritik (Volume 152, 1913).

Let us imagine that the stream of contents of our consciousness has been broken up into successive segments and these segments have been interchanged with one another in a random manner so that the sequence of our experiences is all mixed up. And let us then ask what difference this rearrangement would make as far as our experience is concerned. The answer would have to be: None at all! We would not be able to notice any change and we would believe that our experiences had retained their previous sequence. For suppose we singled out some momentary state of consciousness. How would we know that certain experiences had preceded it and that certain others will follow it? We could know this only from the fact that every state of consciousness contains certain components that we call "recollections of past events" and certain others that we call "anticipations of coming events". Thus once a particular state of consciousness is present, we would also be compelled to believe that we had experienced the past preserved in that state as "memory" and had before us the future held in that state as "expectation", independently of what experiences "really" had preceded or would follow. And since the same holds good for any arbitrary state of consciousness, it is clear that we would never notice such an imagined reordering. But an alteration in the stream of experience that is not experienced is only a fiction, only a change of designation, not a real change. All of this is true, of course, only if we are allowed to think of the stream of consciousness as broken up into strictly separated segments. But if this is permissible, the consideration just outlined establishes that a true, intuitive succession is not even experienced in consciousness itself, that time is not an intuitively given ordering. Rather, what we find are only qualitative differences between contents of consciousness ("memory" components, and the like). It is these that supply the foundations for the purely logical process of ordering the given one-dimensionally, just as certain qualitative properties of sounds provide the foundation for a one-dimensional ordering with respect to "musical pitch". This being the case, it follows on the one hand that there can be no talk of an *objective* existence of intuitive time, and on the other that the nature and possibility of the correlation between the one-dimensional conceptual continuum and the objective world is made clearer and more plausible, since its purely logical character is already revealed in connection with the ordering of the given.

We sum up: time as an intuitive quality must be counted as purely subjective. But the time order as a one-dimensional continuum has, in its correlation with the world of things-in-themselves, objective meaning in the same sense as any other instance of designating by means of concepts.

§ 29. The Subjectivity of Space

Much of what we have said about time holds *mutatis mutandis* for space. Here too it is necessary to distinguish between the spatial as intuitively representable extension and the spatial as a system for ordering natural objects, achieved with the aid of pure concepts. This system can be realized in a manner quite analogous to the arrangements of objects in the time sequence, the only difference being that what is now involved is not a one-dimensional continuum but a three-dimensional one. As we noted above (Part I, § 67), one of the most significant accomplishments, epistemologically, of modern mathematics was to establish the fundamental difference between geometry as a system of pure judgments and concepts in which all that matters are mutual logical relations, and geometry as the system of intuitive spatial structures and their relationships, with which these concepts and judgments are correlated. The first system corresponds with the second in every respect, of course. But it is fully independent of the latter in that it *need* not in any way be conceived of as a description of the laws that govern the intuitive geometrical structures. As we saw, this was proved by the fact that the very same geometrical propositions can be given an intuitive content in the most diverse ways. Hence it follows quite rigorously that none of these contents belongs *essentially* to those propositions in such fashion that they can mean only that content and no other. For us of course this result was quite natural, since we have recognized concepts from the beginning as mere *signs* for objects; thus the meaning that belongs to a sign does not inhere in it as something essential, but is imparted to it only by the act of designating.

Now it follows, exactly as in the case of time, that when we incorporate an object into this three-dimensional reference system, we are not thereby committed to ascribing to the object a spatial character in the intuitive sense. Whether this must be done is a question that remains completely open. It might be that spatiality, as Kant intended, is to be attributed only to our sensible representations, which form part of given reality, and is not a property of transcendent or not-given reality.

Nevertheless the ordering of reality, both given and not-given, may be expressed (although — unlike what holds in the case of time — with exceptions) by means of the same three-fold system of numbers, and to that extent it is one and the same ordering. But it may, to begin with, be called spatial only where it enters into experienced reality. We have no right to ascribe to things-in-themselves an existence in space if by such existence is meant something intuitive; the transcendent world is not known to us intuitively.

Perhaps the cogency of these considerations will become more apparent if we try to clarify them in a negative fashion. Suppose we do not want to make the distinction drawn here between intuitive relations and conceptual orderings, but hold to the belief that the former are always given along with the latter and constitute their essential content. We would then have to conclude that the transcendent world is indeed in space. For unless we wished to seek refuge in subjective idealism, we would have to attribute, as we saw a while back, some kind of ordering to the transcendent world. And if this ordering, which manifestly must be in exact agreement conceptually with the spatial ordering, can fulfill this requirement only if it itself has the characteristic of spatiality, then the things-in-themselves would also have to be ordered in space.

One philosopher who does not make this distinction, and who thus does not effect a separation in regard to space between a type of conceptual ordering and that which is intuitively representable, is Eduard von Hartmann. Consequently he arrives at the conclusion that space is transcendently real. That is, having gained the insight (as we did) that the transcendent ordering of things must be related to the same conceptual system as the spatial ordering of the objects of experience, he takes this to be "a logically cogent proof of the spatiality of the transcendent system of relations" (Das Grundproblem der Erkenntnistheorie, p. 110). HARTMANN says that what are involved here are "quantitative, three-dimensional, continuous reference systems that are permutable in their basic measures" (*ibid.*, p. 109), and he believes that one and only one object can fit this definition, namely, the space of our intuition. But we know from what has been said before that this is altogether wrong. We found, for example, that the aggregate of all number triples is a manifold that falls under this particular concept and yet does not itself possess the characteristic of spatiality. For what compels us to conceive of a number, say, as an intuitively representable interval between co-ordinates? Additional objections can be presented in detail from the standpoint of the mathematician; but what has already been stated is sufficient refutation.

On the basis of the position we reached in Part I, we can add the general and decisive comment that it is absolutely impossible in principle to define space purely conceptually (that is, through implicit definitions, see § 7). We could no more make clear by means of concepts what space is to a creature who possessed no sensible-spatial experience, than we could give a person born blind an idea of yellow or red through mere definitions. We can of course so define concepts of manifolds that intuitive space falls under them. But since its intuitive character cannot be affected by the definition, we can always conceive of any number of other objects that differ only in that their intuitive character has been replaced by another one, and that also fall under the concepts. In other words, we can never infer the intuitive character of an object from the fact that it falls under a certain formal definition. Thus even if the transcendent order of things belongs to the same type of manifold as the spatial order of our perceptual representations, it does not follow that we must attribute to it also spatiality in the intuitive sense.

For it might be that these spatial determinations signify nothing beyond incorporation into the conceptual system described above. It might be that they are not intended to assert that intuitive extension — a feature characteristic of the perceptual representation of a body, for example — is a property of transcendent objects in quite the same way, differing only numerically. This latter, in fact, must be accepted as being the case only so long as we have not yet learned to draw the distinction between intuitive extension and the conceptual system; for then we could understand by a spatial determination only the attribution of spatial and temporal qualities as we are acquainted with them through sense perception. As we know, Boyle and Locke marked off such qualities as "primary" in contrast to the sense qualities as "secondary", because they were thought to belong to the real objects outside of consciousness itself.

The issue is between Locke and Kant. Let us ask: Does the specifically spatial character of space, that is, the intuitive content by which the three-dimensional continuum first becomes a space, belong to transcendent objects too? In other words, are such objects located in the perceptual space of our intuition? Do intuitive-spatial relationships also exist independently of their being intuited?

The answer to this question is easier to find and establish than one might suppose at first glance. The ordering of things-in-themselves is not only numerically distinct from the intuitive-spatial ordering of our sensations, it is essentially different; transcendent objects cannot be localized in the space of intuition. For the objective ordering of things is *unique,* whereas there are many perceptual spaces, and none of them in itself has properties that stamp it as the sole bearer of that ordering.

We can easily understand this fact and its significance if we look briefly at the psychological peculiarities of the representation or idea of space.

Spatial intuition is a matter of sense perception. Regardless of whether one leans more toward nativistic views or more toward empiricist views on the question of the origin of the idea of space, regardless of whether one holds that the spatial ordering of sensations is something that is connected to them beforehand or is something that accompanies them only because of a process of association, it is still certain that spatiality is a specific, intuitive kind of ordering of sensations. But we have various classes of sensations, since we possess sense organs of several different kinds. And within each of these there is a more or less distinct spatial order. This ordering, however, is specific for each sensory domain and in its intuitive nature bears no resemblance to the orderings of the other domains. For example, there is a visual space, a tactile space, a space of sensations of movement. They exhibit no common intuitive features. When I intuit visually the shape of my pencil, the experience I have cannot even be compared with the experiences I have when I touch the "same" shape. There is no quality common to both that might be separated out from them as the genuinely spatial quality.

This conclusion is confirmed by the experiences of persons born blind who have then been operated on. For such persons, the spatial qualities of the visual sense are something totally new in relation to those of the sense of touch or of movement. They find in the former nothing of that with which the latter had already acquainted them. Patients who are able to orient themselves in tactile and kinesthetic space do not have the slightest knowledge of how to orient themselves optically in visual space. We may then rigorously infer the conclusion formulated by RIEHL as follows (Der philosophische Kritizismus, II, p. 139): "... that the various basic components in the construction of space — motion, figure, magnitude, direction — are different for the two senses, that consequently there is no other tie between the representations derived from these two senses than that which *experience* produces."

It is a fact that the connection between the different sensory domains comes about only because certain spatial data, say of the visual sense, under certain circumstances always correspond in experience to certain data of the other senses. For example, when I *see* the table lamp at a certain distance in front of me, after certain sensations of movement in my arm (I reach out my hand), there occur certain *tactile* sensations in my fingers (I touch the lamp); when I perceive visually a pencil-shaped body, I can always bring into being, by suitable measures, the same sensations of touch that I experience in touching a pencil. In this way, the spatial experiences of the different sensory domains are uniquely correlated with one another, and this is why all of them can be brought under a single system of ordering, which by this very fact also becomes the type of ordering for transcendent things.

There are still those, of course, who defend the view enunciated by Locke that the sense of sight and the sense of touch have as a common constituent, so to speak, the same space sense. We found Stumpf maintaining that the very same spatial extension can be experienced in several sensory domains (see above § 20); and MACH too supports this view (Analyse der Empfindungen, p. 111, note 2).

Both writers cite the case of Saunderson as confirmation. "If Locke were wrong", declares Mach, "how was the blind man Saunderson able to write a geometry intelligible to those who can see!" But this ignores the difference that exists between the intuitive meaning of the word 'extension' and the purely conceptual sense. The latter is defined by a system of relations, and it is geometry that has the task of laying down that system. Thus geometry, and hence Saunderson's textbook, has nothing to do with the intuitively given, which in the case of sensations is called 'extension'. The theorems of geometry, as we explained above (§ 7), are completely independent of extension. Sensations are related to one and the same space only because experience creates associations between them through which they are brought into one and the same ordering. Even Mach says quite correctly (just before the cited passage): "All systems of space sensations, no matter how different they may be, are connected by one common associative bond, the movements they serve to direct."

If now we ask again whether the intuitive spatial qualities belong to transcendent objects, this question, by virtue of what we have just discussed, is seen to be very much like the problem of whether or not sense qualities can be asserted of things-in-themselves. When many different qualities have equal claim to being ascribed to a thing, this is an indication that none of them belongs to it. Similarly here. We have many different experiences of qualities of spatiality, and we do not know which ones we should carry over into the objective ordering. All of them have an equal right, and this suggests that actually none of them can be chosen, since there is no basis for distinguishing one of them above the others. Different perceptions correspond to the same "space" not only within different sensory domains but also within one and the same domain. For example, a given bodily form presents a quite different visual aspect depending on position and distance; such a body also supplies the sense of touch with essentially different data depending on the portion of the skin it touches. Locke found his principal argument for the transcendent reality of space in the fact that the different senses provide us with the same assertions about the spatial properties of things. Now we see that this is not true at all of intuitive spatiality; on the contrary, in this respect the assertions in question have no similarity with one another. This being so, the Lockean argument collapses as far as our problem is concerned.

Nevertheless, there are other ways in which one might perhaps attempt to uphold the transcendent reality of space in the intuitive sense.

In the first place, one might wish to dispute the thesis that each sense has to be allocated its own special space. One might argue that it is simply not correct that there exists a visual space, a tactile space, and so forth, that what we designate as space is always a fusion product of data from different sensory domains on the one hand and of various data from the same sensory domain on the other. On this basis, "the" representation of space would be precisely this intuitive fusion product and, as such, *one;* its qualitative properties would then be what must be asserted of the things-in-themselves. And they *could* be asserted, since here the conflict of different qualities would disappear and each would come into its own.

But this notion leads to psychological impossibilities. There is no such thing as a mental fusion product of disparate sensory domains. There is no idea or representation that is neither optical, nor kinesthetic, nor tactile, and yet has in itself something from all of these. Spatial visual representations are closely associated with the corresponding tactile and kinesthetic representations (together they form what Herbart and Wundt called "Komplikationen"). But they do not fuse with one another into a unity, any more than the representation of a word, say, consists of fused representations of the sound, the typeface, the movements of speaking and writing. Each of these is an independent representation of a word, linked to the others only through firm associations. Also it is not necessary to have an associative concurrence of representations from all the disparate domains in order to form an intuition of space. Otherwise a blind person, for example, could have no intuition of space, since he would be totally without the necessary optical elements. The fact is, however, that the tactile-kinesthetic representations he possesses do supply him with a space intuition that is complete for its kind, just as the optical elements by themselves provide an intuition of space that in a quite different way is also complete. Thus there is no unified, unique mental structure that alone represents all spaces. The spatial is given us intuitively in several ways that differ *toto genere* from one another; it is different for different sense organs and for varying attendant circumstances. It is precisely this fact that speaks for the subjectivity of the spatial.

In the scond place, it might be possible to explain the spatial-intuitive as objectively real by picking some sense and transferring its data over to the transcendent world, at the same time granting the subjectivity of the other senses. We may not, of course, do this without reasons, and these, as we have said, are lacking. But even if there were some basis for preferring one sense over the others, within the province of that sense the various qualities of the space intuition would come into such conflict, display such relativity to and dependence on circumstances, that it would be impossible to conceive of any one of them as part of an objective definition of things.

To convince ourselves of this, let us consider the structure of visual space, beginning with the visual space of a single eye rotating around its center, but otherwise at rest. Are all the properties with which we conceptually endow the objective ordering of things given us intuitively in this space? In other words, is our optical space likewise the physical space? Everyone knows that this is certainly not the case. We at times designate two lengths as objectively equal even though intuitively they are completely different — that is, when one of them is at a greater distance from us than the other. In optical space, as we know, all straight lines, suitably extended, return to their starting-point (for example, the line of the horizon), and all straight lines viewed in perspective intersect at a point in the visual field. When I turn my gaze toward the ceiling of a room, each angle of the ceiling appears greater than a right angle; hence the sum of the angles of the rectangle is greater than four right angles. Similarly, when I look at a drawing of an arbitrary plane triangle, I find that because of perspectival distortion the sum of its angles is always greater than two right angles, and the larger the triangle the greater is the discrepancy. In short, the optical space we have described is *not* the Euclidean space in which we usually order physical objects. It is a "spherical" space, for which Riemannian geometry holds true, not the ordinary Euclidean geometry. Even though optical space is a spherical one, our empirical data with respect to it are compatible with the assumption that physical objects possess Euclidean metrical properties. And we account for this by the fact that we can correlate spherical space point for point with Euclidean space so that the same conceptual system of ordering may be taken as a basis for the description of both. Actually the structure of visual space is even more complicated. For we see with two eyes, which moreover we move around freely along with the head and the body. The result is a very great variability of intuitive spatial magnitudes. Thus physical-objective space is not at all identical with visual space; it may be thought of as a conceptual construction that can be erected on the basis of visual space, provided we sacrifice the intuitive character.

Now it might be supposed that objective space is identical with the *space of touch*. But even the most superficial examination of the latter's special features shows that this cannot be so. Tactile space is an amorphous, even more indefinite structure than visual space; its law-like regularity is unimaginably more complicated. Since the sense of touch is spread over the entire skin, it can represent one and the same physical-spatial datum (say, the distance between the two points of a divider compass) by an almost endless array of qualitatively different impressions, depending on where the sensations occur. For example, as far as the sense of touch is concerned, two lines may intersect that objectively are everywhere at a fixed distance apart (two compass points moved along the skin with a constant interval between them will at many places yield two impressions, but at others only one). Thus we see that the continuum of tactile sensations is something entirely different from physical space, although it can of course be uniquely correlated with it. Tactile qualities are not properties of objects. Even three-dimensionality, which we attribute to the ordering of objects, would seem scarcely to be derivable from the data of tactile space.

As for the other sense data, only sensations of *movement* (that is, sensations of muscles and joints) may be regarded as essentially involved in the formation of the intuition of space. We need to devote a few words to them here, since Heymanns (in connection with some remarks of Riehl) has advanced the hypothesis that it is to this class of sensations that we must look for the sole source of the representation of space, and that these sensations furnish us with just that Euclidean physical space within which natural science orders all objects [37].

But it is not possible to uphold the premises from which Heymanns seeks to deduce an identity between the physical Euclidean space and the space of kinesthetic sensations. In the first place, cer-

---

[37] G. HEYMANNS, Die Gesetze und Elemente des wissenschaftlichen Denkens, 2nd printing (1905), § 56.

tain presuppositions about the structure of sensations of movement that he accepts cannot be confirmed by psychological observation. He takes no account of the undoubted differences that exist among the data belonging to this sensory domain, data that are quite different for each muscle and joint. And he introduces the assumption, for which no direct verification is given, that there are but three pairs of qualitatively different kinesthetic sensations (feelings of direction, as Riehl called them), corresponding to the paired concepts before-behind, left-right, above-below. It is clear that this hypothesis is offered to explain the three-dimensionality of space, but it lacks any objective basis.

In the second place, the way in which "feelings of direction" are treated in the Riehl-Heymanns hypothesis is open to the most serious objections. HEYMANNS says (loc. cit., p. 206): "We call the data that cannot be further described, and according to which a person born blind distinguishes between different directions, the quality, and the other data that he takes into account in measuring his way, the quantity of the feeling of movement." Now one may of course introduce such terminology. But in doing so, one must understand clearly that what is here designated as quantity is experienced as quality; this is evident from the sentence quoted. Kinesthetic sensations, like all mental magnitudes, may not be treated directly as quantities in the mathematical sense, that is, as extensive magnitudes which are divisible and can thus be combined into a new sensation in such a way that the components are preserved in it unchanged. (See, for example, my discussion in § 5 of the paper, Die Grenze der naturwissenschaftlichen und philosophischen Begriffsbildung, Vierteljahrsschrift für wissenschaftliche Philosophie, Volume 34, 1910). In order that such sensations may be susceptible of quantitative description, a system of numbers must be correlated to the system of qualitatively different elements. And the way this is done is quite arbitrary, just as the temperature scale that we correlate with sensations of heat can be selected as we choose. Now Heymanns selects a system of numbers in such a way that the numbers used to measure the hypothetical feelings of movement behave exactly as if they were ordinary Cartesian coordinates. It seems that Heymanns entirely overlooks the fact that any number of other correlations would do equal justice to the facts. He offers a proof that the axioms of geometry are valid in his system. But this is not at all surprising; for the measurement relationships were chosen so that precisely this would be the case. The calculations involved in his proof simply unfold what is contained in the presuppositions he added. They have nothing to do with kinesthetic sensations, and they teach us nothing about the structure of the spatial intuition that rests on them.

We thus arrive at the conclusion that kinesthetic space is no more identical with physical-objective space than is tactile or visual space. It is an intuitive continuum whose structure can provide us with the occasion for the conceptual construction of an objective ordering of things; the data of kinesthetic sensations correspond uniquely of course to this ordering, but this gives them no advantage over those of the other two senses we have discussed.

I thought I should add this observation on the Heymann hypothesis because in this way we can once again bring out clearly the difference between a purely conceptual ordering and an intuitive structure correlated with it. Conclusions inferred only from the former should not be confused with statements about the latter.

Whatever else might be said about the epistemological relations of kinesthetic sensations to the concept of space has been presented in an incomparable fashion by HENRI POINCARÉ (La relativité de l'espace, in: Science et méthode, Book II, Chapter 1).

We may summarize our results by saying — and now it will no longer sound paradoxical — that physical space, and hence the spatial properties of physical objects, is *not at all* representable intuitively. That is, the spatial properties of the contents of representations are not identical with those of physical objects. Perceptions, no matter to what sense they may belong, can only provide the ground on which the conceptual edifice of physical space is erected.

It is extremely important for us to be clear that physical space is at the same time metaphysical space. It represents the ordering schema of the things-in-themselves; there is neither the possibility of nor a basis for distinguishing between the ordering of extramental objects, which physics explores, and the ordering of the things-in-themselves, of which epistemology speaks. The two orderings are absolutely identical. The physicist, as will be shown later, cannot define the object of his science in any other way than the philosopher defines his thing-in-itself.

Let us suppose, for example, that a physical die is presented to perception in various ways: visually by our beholding it from a certain viewpoint, kinesthetically by placing our hand or some other part of the body along its sides, tactilely by bringing it into contact with our skin at one or another spot. This can all take place in any number of different ways and the result is indefinitely many intuitive data. With respect to these data, the objective configuration of the die is a schema, so to speak, that brings them all under one formula. This schema no longer contains anything of the intuitive data, for these depend collectively and individually on the relative position of the die with respect to the peripheral sense organs. All of these dependencies — for which allowances can be made through the rules for perspective in the case of optical impressions and in the case of kinesthetic and tactile ones through rules that admittedly are very hard to formulate — are completely removed from the schema. The subjectivity of space intuitions is eliminated, and all that remains is the objective ordering, which no longer contains any intuitive element and consequently should no longer be designated as spatial. (We note that the elimination of subjective elements from the ordering schema does not at the same time bar all relativity; it is not true that whatever is "objective" must also be "absolute". The objective may still contain relativities that rest on the mutual relationship of physical bodies, for instance, the relationship of a measurement apparatus to the bodies and processes measured. The problems that arise here belong not to general epistemology but to the philosophy of natural science. It is in this latter discipline that the problem of space can be studied in its totality; our concern has been only with the limited question of whether or not the world of things-in-themselves is spatial. On these matters, see HERMANN VON HELMHOLTZ, Schriften zur Erkenntnistheorie, edited and introduced by Paul Hertz and Moritz Schlick, Berlin, and my book, Raum und Zeit in der gegenwärtigen Physik, 4th edition, 1922*.)

Intuitive spatiality or extension is denied of things-in-themselves. But we may and must affirm that they can be arranged into a multidimensional manifold, through which we represent spatial relationships mathematically. This result may also be expressed by saying, with STÖRRING (Einführung in die Erkenntnistheorie, p. 223):

---

* English translation, by H. L. BROSE, Space and Time in Contemporary Physics (Oxford University Press, 1920). [Translator's note.]

". . . space is to be rated . . . as transcendently real in so far as it can be defined in terms of mathematical analysis." One may, if one wishes, attach the term 'spatial' *('räumlich')* to the transcendent ordering as well, or distinguish "the spatial" *("das Räumliche")* as the intuitive from "space" *("Raum")* as a conceptual construction. Whoever regards space as definable will have to adopt this latter position (this is what WUNDT seems to do in Logik, I, pp. 493 ff., although his definition certainly cannot satisfy the mathematicians). But anyone who does so must be clear that in using the word 'space' he is also designating, for example, the set of all number triples. As a matter purely of terminology, of course, this sort of thing is admissible; but it seems to me that the original sense of the word has here been shunted aside in a very inopportune way. Only a lack of clarity about this whole situation could have given rise to the fruitless dispute as to whether space is really intuition or concept. It is best that we continue to designate only the ordering of the sensible-intuitive as 'spatial' and as 'space'. Where on occasion we must use these words to name the ordering of transcendent things, we shall for greater accuracy always add a characterizing adjective; thus we shall speak of a *transcendent* or an *objective* space. Similarly Becher, with whom I am in substantial agreement, calls the relations in the transcendent world "spatial in a metaphorical sense". Another serviceable expression would be 'intelligible space', used earlier by many metaphysicians, including Leibniz, Herbart and Lotze.

The intuitive character, and hence the undefinability, of what was originally understood by space has been made especially clear by ZIEHEN (Erkenntnistheorie, pp. 63 ff.), who incidentally uses the expression "locality" for spatiality. As we know, Kant attempted to prove, by a special demonstration (in the "metaphysical exposition of this concept"), that space is not a concept but a pure intuition. But for us his arguments are devoid of meaning, because they rest on presuppositions that are foreign to us. Our concept of the intuitive does not coincide at all with what Kant calls pure intuition.

Nor can we make use of the grounds that Kant adduces for the subjectivity of space, even though we are persuaded that the thesis he desires to prove by means of them is true. These grounds fall into two groups. First, from the *a priori* character of our geometrical knowledge Kant infers that space must be a subjective form of the intuition. This was the only way he could explain the possibility of valid apodictic statements about the properties of space, which, he believed, form the content of geometrical propositions. We shall soon see that we cannot share the Kantian view of the nature of geometrical truths, so that as far as we are concerned the demonstration fails. Second, Kant finds grounds for the subjectivity of space (and time) in the so-called antinomies of pure reason. He believes that in considering the universe reason necessarily entangles itself in contradictions that arise because we wrongly regard space and time as determinations of the things-in-themselves. But these contradictions — except for the "psychological paralogisms" — are by no means as unavoidable as Kant supposed. And even if they were inevitable, we would still have to argue against the assertion (as LOTZE did in his Metaphysik, §§ 105, 106) that the way out chosen by Kant actually overcomes the difficulties. The correct element in Kant's thought will be discussed later (see below, III, § 33).

Thus there is nothing we can do with all these famous arguments of the Kantian philosophy, much as we would like to have their weight on our side. Nor, of course, do we need them; the preceding developments, which rest on psychological insights are in my opinion fully decisive in themselves.

§ 30. The Subjectivity of the Sense Qualities

In order to find out which properties may and which may not be ascribed to things-in-themselves, we must refer back to those considerations that led us to assume that things-in-themselves do exist. For, according to what was said in § 27, the grounds for this assumption already contain the grounds for any determination or definition of such things.

Our critique of the notion of immanence has shown us that we must assume the existence of transcendent things as real intermediaries among experiences, which themselves lack an unbroken continuity. This is true of experiences that belong to the same individual consciousness and especially of those that are distributed among different individuals. It is the transcendent realities that constitute the (identical) objects to which man refers by word and concept in his social intercourse with his fellowmen. We long ago convinced ourselves that the role played by these identical objects cannot be taken over by complexes of elements, that is, combinations of sense qualities, since these are *never* the same for different individuals (see § 26 *b*). This fact, established by psychology and physics, made it absolutely impossible to regard the sense qualities (red, warm, loud and the like) as properties of things-in-themselves. Or, in our terminology, the (psychological) concepts by which we designate sense qualities cannot also be used to designate transcendent objects. "Naive realism" unthinkingly does just this, and attributes these qualities to objects-in-themselves. This leads to contradictions, for naive realism is obliged to make mutually incompatible determinations of one and the same object. For example, it must assert that the same body is red and not red, cold and not cold. Thus naive realism is recognized to be untenable and must make way for the view that sense qualities are "subjective".

Sensible qualities are elements of consciousness, not elements of a transcendent, non-given reality. They belong to the subject, not to objects.

This insight, as we know, has its origin in antiquity. It is present quite clearly in Democritus. But it was then lost to philosophy for a long period during which the naive realism of Aristotle prevailed, and was only revived in the modern era (Galileo, Boyle, Locke). Not until quite recently was it again subjected to significant attack, especially through the ideas that we described and argued against in §§ 25 and 26. These ideas in fact represent a renewal of naive realism, as their advocates not infrequently like to emphasize. But we have analyzed this doctrine sufficiently. Other philosophers, Herrmann Schwarz and Henri Bergson among them, have opposed the subjectivity of sense qualities along different lines[38]; this doctrine, however, seems to be so fully assured by the positive grounds adduced for it that it is not necessary here to go into the arguments of these writers. (A lively critique of their arguments may be found in JULIUS SCHULTZ, Die drei Welten der Erkenntnistheorie, 1907, pp. 41—51; a historical treatment of the question by FRISCHEISEN-KÖHLER appears in the Vierteljahresschrift für wissenschaftliche Philosophie, Volume 30, pp. 271 ff.)

---

38 HERRMANN SCHWARZ, Das Wahrnehmungsproblem, 1892, and Die Umwälzung der Wahrnehmungshypothesen, 1895; HENRI BERGSON, Matière et mémoire, 1896.

It must be emphasized that the doctrine that denies *sense* qualities to transcendent objects does not thereby assert that these objects can possess *no* qualities at all. Something of this sort has often
been supposed by those who, misunderstanding certain fundamental results of the natural sciences, believe that these results lead to
a purely quantitative, quality-less view of the world. But there is no
basis at all for this position. We shall return to the question in more
detail later.

That sense qualities are subjective is beyond doubt. The same
considerations that establish the existence of things-in-themselves
also teach us that such concepts as *red, warm* and *sweet,* which
designate elements of consciousness, cannot be ascribed to things-in-
themselves. They cannot be used to designate objects unambiguously
and without contradiction.

We are in exactly the same position with regard to the question
of the transcendent existence of sense qualities as we are with respect to the question of the transcendent reality of intuitive space.

In both cases, the same arguments forbid us to assume that the
intuitively given not only exists in consciousness but is repeated in
exactly the same way in the realm of the things-in-themselves. We
have established that things-in-themselves do exist, and that they
can be designated by concepts; but we have also determined that
such concepts do not include those of sense qualities. The latter
are unsuitable for the unambiguous designation that all knowledge
requires; they depend on the state of the perceiving subject, and in
the absence of such a state are utterly devoid of meaning. A transcendent thing cannot be "yellow" or "warm"; nor can it be spatial,
and for the same reasons. For intuitive spatiality likewise exhibits
wide-ranging dependencies, as well as the greatest of differences
among various sense organs and individuals. Indeed, the intuitively
spatial aspect of the perceptual representation of an object can vary
more and in a more pronounced fashion than its sensible qualities.
Intuitive spatiality undergoes modification even in the case of tiny
changes in position that have no perceptible effect on the qualities.
The apparent shape of a body varies much more readily with the
external circumstances of perception than does, say, its color.

It is worth remarking that although spatiality exhibits even less
constancy than do the sense qualities, the subjectivity of sense qualities attracted attention much earlier than the subjectivity of spatiality.
But this is not difficult to explain. Precisely because of the boundless

flux of spatial data, we had to accustom ourselves, even in child-hood and prior to the formation of any scientific ideas, to working with the objective ordering schema instead of with the intuitive data. In the case of sensible qualities, on the other hand, this was neither necessary nor possible as far as the needs of everyday life were concerned. What the psychology textbooks generally refer to as the genesis of the *intuition* of space is actually the development of the capacity to form a conceptual ordering and apply it correctly. As must be the case with any concept, every detail of the ordering schema is of course represented by means of an intuitive image. Since from the inception of spatial experience, intuitive spatiality and the conceptual ordering have thus always stood in place of one another, the two are not distinguished. Thus there is ascribed to the spatial a fixed, objective character that by rights belongs only to the ordering schema.

But once this important and necessary distinction is drawn with appropriate rigor, we cannot help but find highly absurd the notion that the qualitative aspect of spatiality, which attaches for example to visual or kinesthetic sensations, also exists in the objects in themselves when no one perceives them. The content of the image of "extension" is different for each sense organ and for each situation. Like sense qualities, it can be regarded as a property only of subjective representations, not of objective things.

Let us consider exactly what it means to ascribe transcendent reality to a content of consiousness, whether it be a sense quality or spatiality. It can only mean that something exists in the world of things-in-themselves that in every respect is like something in the world of consciousness. Thus we would have one object with two or more exemplifications, one located in consciousness and the other in the transcendent world.

But there are only two possibilities under which this assumption is meaningful.

The *first* is that there is nothing contradictory or miraculous in supposing that consciousness and a content of consciousness may be readily separated. It would then be the most natural thing in the world for an object to be a content of consciousness at one time, and at another to exist apart from consciousness and thus outside of it. If this notion must be rejected, then a *second* possibility would still remain: that an object, wherever it appears, is always the content of a consciousness.

We take the second possibility to be realized, obviously, wherever on empirical grounds we must in any event presuppose the presence of a consciousness. If a companion and I look up at a cloudless sky, I naturally assume that the content "blue" is present in his consciousness too — if not in absolutely the same way as in mine, then at least in a very similar manner. In a concert hall, each sound sensation is duplicated just as many times as there are listeners in the hall. We need not spend any more time on this point, although for obvious reasons the existence of similar sensations in different consciousnesses does not admit of a rigorous proof. Indeed, even in the case of animal consciousness, we do not hesitate to assume the existence of contents that are similar to ours, or at least comparable to them. This then is not the issue. The question is: Can any datum that is found within my consciousness also occur outside of it, *without being* the content of some other individual consciousness?

This question, as we know, has been answered in the affirmative by many philosophers, especially by partisans of "objective idealism". The fundamental contention of all idealism is: "All being is conscious being" *("jedes Sein ist Bewußtsein")*. Thus idealism is obliged to reject out of hand the first of the two possibilities cited above and characterize all reality as the content of consciousness, whether or not it belongs to an individual consciousness, whether or not it is like the contents of an individual consciousness. In this way, the transubjective external world becomes for the idealist the content of a "supra-individual" or "metempirical" consciousness, a "consciousness in general", a "world-mind", or whatever else it might be called. And for the idealist, the possibility exists initially that qualities, such as "warm" or "blue" or "extended", also exist outside of consciousness. Thus the question as to whether sense qualities and space possess transcendent reality makes perfectly good sense to him. From his standpoint, however, he must of course answer the question in the negative, since the arguments we have adduced here for the subjectivity of sense qualities and space retain their full force. Hence for the idealist too, although transcendent qualities are by their nature the contents of an all-embracing consciousness, they must still differ essentially from our sense experiences.

But we of course have no reason to adopt the idealistic viewpoint. On the contrary, we may presuppose a consciousness in the transcendent world only where we are compelled on empirical grounds to do so, that is, only where observation reveals living organisms, possibly equipped with a nervous system (see below, § 35). The idealist is moved to construct his metempirical consciousness not by any special observations but only by virtue of his fundamental thesis that being and consciousness are identical. But this thesis has been refuted by the considerations set forth in § 26. Hence the idealistic view here described is no longer an issue for us.

With this, we eliminate one possibility of giving meaning to the question of the transsubjective reality of conscious qualities. We must now examine the other, listed as the first above. When it is asserted that qualities as given are objectively real, can this mean that such qualities — for example, blue or cold — exist outside of *any* consciousness, hence absolutely in themselves, and yet are identical with a blue or a cold that is the content of a consciousness?

Actually we already answered this question when we made clear (Part II, § 20) that distinguishing consciousness from its contents is meaningless. The word 'consciousness' in the sense discussed here is only a general name for the immediately given. It does not denote some character that, so to speak, is added to the given from the outside and that it might lack. Hence whatever does lack this character is not identical in nature with the given or the conscious; it is something else. If we take consciousness away from a mental content, then that content itself is no longer there. When consciousness disappears, its contents disappear. We cannot imagine a green that is not a seen or conscious green. We cannot imagine an experience that ceases to be experienced and yet continues to *be*. Were we to say that this sort of thing might be the case even if we were unable to imagine it, we would be forgetting what the question means. For what is at issue here is precisely the existence of objects supposed to exist exactly *as* we imagine them. Once we say that these objects exist outside of consciousness in an unimaginable form, we have already answered the question in the negative. We may advance the theory — this has indeed been done — that images are formed and disappear as a result of the fact that something or other "rises above the threshold of consciousness" or sinks beneath it, a something that also can exist outside of consciousness (as something unconscious). But these magnitudes that rise above and fall below this threshold would still be essentially different when outside of consciousness; as objects of which we were not conscious, they would no longer be intuitive images but unknown hypothetical structures. And the threshold theory, far from explaining and so disposing of this essential difference, would simply have presented it in its own way — and this by means of metaphors that have no genuine explanatory value.

Thus every attempt to bring to mind this possibility runs into the contradiction of the imagined unimaginable, the intuited unintuitable. The question as to whether any conscious quality may also exist in essentially the same manner outside of consciousness thereby receives a negative answer. Alternatives that presuppose the existence of such a quality are thus seen to be without meaning. Everything intuitive — sense qualities, spatiality, and anything else of the sort — is *eo ipso* subjective. To ask about its objectivity is to accept a meaningless formulation of the question. That which is beyond consciousness cannot be repeated within it unchanged. The concept of an "adequate knowledge", as it arises in the minds of some philosophers, would among other things require just such a repetition, a "wandering over" of transcendent objects into consciousness.

The reader will have noted that the considerations advanced here bear a certain similarity to the idealistic argument against transcendence that we had to reject in § 25. As a matter of fact, these considerations may be viewed as the useful kernel contained in that argument. The latter would scarcely have fascinated so many clearminded thinkers had there not been some evident truth concealed within it. The idealist's attempt to prove that a being outside of consciousness is *totally* impossible was naturally bound to fail. But what he did succeed in proving was the impossibility of the extramental existence of objects that are imaginable or representable. We recall (§ 26 b, near the end) that the error on which the idealist argument foundered was the conflation of imagining and thinking, and hence of the unimaginable and the unthinkable or impossible. This mistake is corrected if we carefully distinguish imagining (= depicting intuitively) from thinking (= designating by means of concepts). Once we do this, the ideas of Berkeley and his followers no longer appear entirely meaningless, even though they do not contain the truths ascribed to them by their authors. Rather, these ideas express a different truth: that transcendent things are not imaginable, that nothing in their nature is quite like the content of an image or representation, that consequently all data of consciousness are subjective. No such datum can be simply a copy of a transcendent quantity. Transcendent magnitudes, as we said above, are open to knowledge *(erkennbar)*, but not to direct acquaintance *(kennbar)*.

It is instructive to examine one of the familiar formulations of the idealist argument from this point of view. Take, for example, the demonstration offered by JULIUS BERGMANN (System des objektiven Idealismus, p. 91): "All contents of perception are inseparable from their being perceived; being perceived is so much a part of the nature of whatever is perceived, and hence of every perceivable determination, that nothing of it remains when it ceases to be perceived. But all the determinations that we include in the concept of a body are perceivable. Hence it is of the nature of the world of bodies to be an object for a perceiving subject." What is correct in these words can be extracted with the aid of a few simple comments. Bergmann proves nothing against the existence of transcendent things, since such things need never be thought of as perceivable, that is, as intuitively representable. Thus the minor premiss does not hold true of them. But the images of "bodies" (the sensible qualities together with extension), through which we represent things intuitively, do in fact belong to the subject by their very nature, as set forth in the major premiss. Whatever is imaginable can, as such, only be the content of a consciousness; it is subjective.

I should like to close this discussion with a brief terminological observation. Authors frequently speak of the *ideality* of time and space, meaning by this what we have here called subjectivity. This use of the term goes back to Kant. Many writers follow his example and refer in general to the reality of whatever belongs only to consciousness as *ideal* being. We have deliberately avoided this mode of expression. For the word 'ideal' has long been used as the opposite of 'real'; indeed, these writers have explicitly contrasted transcendent being as the real with the ideal being of the contents of consciousness (see, for example, BENNO ERDMANN, Logik, 2nd edition, p. 138). As a consequence, two different kinds of reality have been introduced terminologically. We have already discussed our reasons for not accepting this mode of designation (§ 27). Putting matters this way conveys the impression that a lower order of reality is to be attributed to ideal being, to the given contents of consciousness, than to transcendent reality. Even if this notion is far from the minds of those who employ such terminology, misunderstandings may still arise. The ordering of transcendent things is not a bit more real than the ordering of the contents of consciousness that we call space and time. That is why we refrain from designating these latter as *ideal*.

§ 31. Quantitative and Qualitative Knowledge

The ordering in space and time of the contents of consciousness is likewise the means by which we learn to determine the transcendent ordering of the things that lie beyond consciousness. This transcendent ordering is the most important step toward a knowledge of these things. We must give an exact account of how this step is accomplished.

The main points that enter into consideration here have already been set forth in Part I, § 9. We saw that establishing an identity — this is what all knowledge consists in — means, as far as external things are concerned, locating things at the same point in time and space. Everything in the external world (as we said toward the end of § 9) is at a particular place at a particular time; and to find one thing in another is ultimately to assign to both of them the same place at the same time. We must now make this definition more precise by specifying that when we use the expressions 'space' and 'time', we mean the transcendent ordering of things. In the earlier section, we were not yet in a position to call attention to the distinction between the transcendent and the intuitive meaning of these words. But we did indicate briefly that the determination of the position of objective things refers not to visual or tactile or any other intuitive space; rather it refers to a correlate that is to be thought of in terms of concepts.

The important thing now is to get clear about how we proceed from the intuitive spatio-temporal ordering to the construction of the transcendent ordering. This always happens in accordance with the same method, which we may call the *method of coincidences*. It is of the greatest significance epistemologically.

If I look at my pencil from different sides, no one of the complexes of elements that I experience is itself the pencil (see § 25, above). The pencil is an object different from all these complexes; it is definitely a "thing-in-itself" in our sense. As far as I am concerned, all of these complexes, which depend on lighting, distance and the like, merely represent the object, that is, they are correlated with it. The details of their relation to it can be determined by physics and physiology only after the properties of the object are ascertained more closely, that is, only when we succeed in the manner explained above (end of § 9) in designating it uniquely by means of general concepts. Here, as we have pointed out, the most important role is played by those concepts of ordering that assign the object its place in the transcendent schema.

If, while I am looking at the pencil, I touch its point with my finger, a singularity occurs simultaneously in my visual space and in my tactile space: a tactile sensation suddenly appears in my finger, and the visual perceptions of the finger and of the pencil suddenly have a spatial datum in common — the point of contact. These two experiences, which are entirely disparate, are now correlated with one and the same "point" of transcendent space, namely, the point of contact of the two things "finger" and "pencil". The two experiences belong to different sensory domains and are in no way similar to one another. But what they do have in common is that they are singularities or discontinuities in what is otherwise a continuous field of perceptions surrounding them. It is through this feature that they are picked out from the field. This is how they can be related to one another and correlated with the same objective point in space.

A clear example of the process through which the transcendent ordering is recognized can be found in the reports, often cited in philosophical literature, regarding persons born blind who have been operated upon [39]. According to these reports, one such person learned to distinguish visually between a round piece of paper and a rectangular one by virtue of the fact that the latter exhibited singularities or discontinuities (namely, the four corners) whereas the former did not. Up till then the person had been acquainted with circles and rectangles only from tactile experience; in the case of circles, the experiences were continuous, but they contained four singularities in the case of rectangles. It was this common feature that made it possible to relate the new experiences correctly to the

---

39 DUFAUR, Archives des sciences physiques et naturelles, Volume 58, p. 232.

familiar tactile perceptions and hence to interpret the new experiences properly.

It is not only the sensations of different sensory domains but also the sensations of different individuals as well that serve in this manner to determine the schema of transcendent ordering. If I wish to direct the attention of a large audience to a point in a figure on the blackboard, I put the tip of my finger on that point. And although everyone present has a more or less different visual perception, what is common to all of them is that the finger tip and the point of the board coincide. Due to my action, these two objects, previously located at different places, now occupy the same location. Here we see the uniqueness of correlation without which there would be no transcendent ordering of objective space. Two perceptual objects that touch one another in visual or tactile space (have a "locational" sign in common) must correspond to transcendent things that share a "point" in the objective ordering schema. Otherwise, a single place in a perceptual space would be correlated with two places in transcendent space, and this would contradict uniqueness of designation.

The whole process of ordering things rests on effecting coincidences of this sort. Two objects are made to coincide with one another (as a rule, optically), and this produces singularities inasmuch as the locations of these two otherwise separated elements are brought together. Thus in the transcendent space-time schema, there is defined a system of distinct positions or discrete places that can be enlarged at will and extended in thought into a continuous manifold that permits the complete incorporation of all spatial objects.

Obviously not every experience of coincidence in a sensory domain can be interpreted as a coincidence in the objective sense. When the moon comes between us and a star, it seems that the star is right at the edge of the moon; but we know very well that the star is not really at the same place as the moon, but is an enormous distance farther away. Two compass points may coincide as far as the sense of touch is concerned even though in reality they are separated. In short, objective coincidences are never experienced directly; they are inferred or constructed from just such experiences. The rules in accordance with which this takes place are treated in more detail in the philosophy of science. These rules, while interesting structurally, are quite simple. They do not lead to any basic difficulties.

Determinations of space and time are always effected by means of *measurement,* and all measurements, from the most primitive to the most advanced, rest on the observation of spatio-temporal coincidences such as those described above. The process is most easily followed in the case of exact scientific determinations. In the final analysis, every precise measurement consists always and exclusively in comparing two bodies with one another, that is, in laying a measuring rod alongside the object to be measured so that certain marks on the rod (lines on a scale) are made to coincide with specific points on the object. All measuring instruments, no matter how constructed, apply the procedure. The tailor's yardstick, laid end over end along the cloth, is an illustration of the principle; and so is the physicist's thermometer in which the top of the mercury column reaches a particular mark on the scale. In the case of most instruments, what we observe is an *indicator* coinciding with a certain position or number. A familiar example is a *clock.* We call attention parenthetically to a fact most important for the theory of space and time, namely, that time itself is measured in no other way than by the observation of *spatial* coincidences.

(We note, but do not pursue further, a circumstance that is of the greatest importance for the philosophy of science. A comparison of two bodies becomes truly a *measurement* only if we presuppose that it makes sense to speak of the *interval* between two points on a body — say, the length of a rod — as a magnitude that can be attributed to the body independently of its position and situation. For only in this way does it become possible to compare different distances by applying a measuring rod, to set the parts of a scale equal to one another and to specify how many times a certain distance (the unit of measurement) is contained in another distance. If the measuring rod were to change in an unknown manner when transported from place to place, then no meaning could be attached to speaking of the same intervals at different places.)

Since precise measurement always amounts to establishing coincidences, only *distances* are directly measurable, and not all of these. For it is often impossible in practice to get close enough with a measuring rod to the distance that is to be measured; for example, the distance from the earth to the moon can be determined only indirectly. But with the aid of mathematical relations, we can infer it from directly measured magnitudes. The theory of geometrical knowledge shows that we can do so by purely *analytic* means (we do not have time here for a proof of this). Apart from the presuppositions indicated above, which are required for any measurement, no basically new assumptions are necessary. Thus the indirect measurement of spatial magnitudes presents no new problems. In principle — and hence from the standpoint of epistemology — it is all the same whether I establish the length of the earth's meridian directly by applying a surveyor's chain or determine it only indirectly through triangulation.

Not only in the exact sciences, but beyond them as well, every spatio-temporal ordering can in principle be reduced to the same foundation. For in ordinary life, whenever we specify a position we do so by means of data that rest on approximate coincidences and in turn make such coincidences possible. And the same thing is true of all time measurements, whether in the life of an individual or in history. If we are satisfied with approximate specifications in terms of years, months, days and the like, we must understand that these are all concepts that in the last analysis are determined only by the course of the heavenly bodies and how they coincide with certain positions (meridians, vernal equinox, and so forth).

What is accomplished by incorporating things into the transcendent order?

An enormous advance in knowledge. To know is to find one thing again in another. In the variegated, multiform relationships among the experiences of various individuals (and of *one* individual under differing circumstances), what is found through this method is a common ordering; one objective world is discovered amidst the abundance and confusion of subjective data. The identically same objects of this world are found again in the most varied relations to elements of the world of consciousness. For the concepts that are applied to transcendent objects are defined by means of relations to or correlations with the given. It is the *same* pencil that is in contact with my right hand, is at a certain distance from my left hand, at certain distances from my two eyes, and so forth.

We saw earlier (Part I, § 9) that in every judgment there is a statement of identity, since that which is cognized is held to be identical with that as which it is cognized. And we learned that a really complete identification, without which there is no knowledge, is possible in the case of real objects chiefly where one (or both) of the two objects that have been ascertained to be one is defined as a term of a *relation*. This is the case with regard to the ordering of the objective world. An object determined by that ordering stands in various spatio-temporal relations to all the other objects in the world and appears in all of these relations as one and the same; it is found again in each of them as one of their terms. Thus incorporation into the transcendent ordering schema becomes a finding again of identical objects in the most varied relations. And it would be a colossal advance in knowledge even if those relations were entirely different qualitatively and in no wise reducible to one another.

In reality, however, these objective relations are of exactly the same kind qualitatively. Their differences are all discovered to be purely quantitative and therefore reducible to one another.

We should now like to clarify what this fact means and what enormous significance it has for our knowledge.

Each relation of the kind in question is determined by specifying a number of magnitudes — the location of a point, for example, by giving three coordinates of space and one of time. In virtue of the methods for measuring described above, this is accomplished ultimately by specifying the length of certain distances. But the length of a distance is the *number* of units it contains. Distances are *extensive* magnitudes. They are divisible; they are built up out of equal parts. One and the same unit of length is found again in all lengths; the only variation is in the number of units. Thus lengths are reduced to one another *quantitatively* and there is no more perfect kind of knowledge. The finding again of one object in another occurs in its most perfect form where the latter is nothing more than the sum of replicas of the former. Indeed, part of the concept of a sum is that the summands enter into it completely and unchanged, that the summand remains identically the same both within the sum and outside of it. Every number can be thought of as a sum of ones. Accordingly, every number, as applied to reality, already expresses knowledge, namely, the knowledge that in the quantity measured the unit will be found again as many times as is called for by the number. The essence of quantitative knowledge thus consists in the fact that it dissolves the known object into a sum of units that — unaltered and exactly alike — can be found again in the object, and counted.

In this manner, first all spatial magnitudes (distances, angles, volumes), and then time intervals (thanks to the concept of velocity), come under the sway of numbers. Relations of the objective spatio-temporal ordering are reduced to a mere counting of units, and thus to each other. This is not true, of course, of the intuitive space-time relationships. So far as intuition is concerned, the various relations of position and time are in general entirely different qualitatively; for example, a horizontal and a vertical segment, or one laid to the right and another to the left, as a rule are not at all of the same quality intuitively. On the other hand, number concepts, and hence quantitative knowledge, refer throughout to the *transcendent* ordering. It is of the greatest importance to take note that the *objective* world is the subject-matter of quantitative knowledge. What numbers in natural science directly designate are not relations between immediately given elements, but relations between transcendent magnitudes, whose objective "position" is defined through correlation with experiences of coincidence. With the aid of this method, each of these "positions" or "points" of the objective ordering system (each "world-point", to use the language of modern physics) can be fixed by assigning four numbers, and the system in its totality can be conceived of as the set of all number quadruples. These four numbers themselves need not signify distances; but their values must ultimately be determined by the measurement of distances.

The method of coincidences breaks distances down into units, and the counting of the units then constitutes what we call measuring. This is the way *number,* and hence the concept of quantity, gains entry into knowledge. If we are thus able to gain mastery over the world of things by means of a system of numbers, we owe it entirely to our *spatial* experiences; for it is in these that the experience of coincidences takes place.

We saw before (Part II, § 18) that in the ceaseless flux of the processes of consciousness, exact thought is achieved only by discovering the discrete in the continuous. We now observe that the same thing is true, strictly speaking, for all exact knowledge, since the principle of coincidences, too, rests on picking the discrete or discontinuous out of the continuous course of perception.

Thus for the spatial ordering of things, knowledge is obtained in principle in the most perfect way, that is, quantitatively. But the question then arises: Exactly *what* is in this spatio-temporal ordering? In other words, by what additional concepts can the objects incorporated in the ordering scheme be designated?

To begin with, how do we accomplish such a designation? There is only one possible way: we must exploit the *relations* through which these objects are defined for us. For they are not objects of *direct acquaintance;* they are not given. As explained above (Part III, *A*), we come to posit them as realities only through establishing certain relations, certain correlations with the given.

The pencil not only has a definite place in optical or in tactile intuitive space, but in the former it has a particular color as well. Can we think of this color itself as something that must be located in the transcendent ordering schema at the "position" occupied by the objective thing "pencil"? We have already seen that this is not possible. As sense qualities, colors are subjective; they belong in the intuitive space of vision, not in the objective space of things. Thus the objectively existing pencil cannot be subsumed under the concept "yellow". We do, however, need some concept or other in order to be able to carry out a unique designation. At first, the only thing that seems possible is to assume that some quality with which we are not directly acquainted is at the place occupied by the surface of the pencil. This quality I designate as a "property" of the pencil, a property with which I correlate the yellow of the content of my consciousness, just as I make a certain transcendent location correspond to the visually intuitive place of the yellow. I must then correlate this *same* quality with the colors that all other individuals experience in their "perceptions of the pencil". Whether their color experiences are the same as mine is irrelevant and forever undecidable. What matters is only that the correlations be effected uniquely; and this is always possible if we take into account the fact that each perceiving individual stands in a different relation to the pencil. The differences in the statements of the individuals can then be explained by the differences in their relations to the pencil. These relations, of course, are conditioned by the locations of the individuals and the character of their nervous systems.

We can now consider the following as generally established. Suppose I hold up a second pencil next to the first one — a pencil of exactly the same make, which therefore has the same color for me. All other observers will likewise make the judgment: "The color of both pencils is identical." Moreover, any individual who has once designated this color as 'yellow' will always use the same designation for it under the same circumstances; in total darkness, all observers will state that the pencil is not given them through any color experience at all, and so on. In addition to agreements, which extend even further than in the case of judgments of intuitive spatial relationships (see § 30), there are also discrepancies, for example under such circumstances as colorblindness, looking through tinted glass, or the like. But in any case, the unknown quality or "property" is defined by means of its relation to the corresponding color experiences: it is the one identical quality that stands in differing relations to those different mental elements.

At this cognitive level, a separate quality in the transcendent object would have to correspond to each of the infinitely many nuances of color that I am able to perceive in the intuitive objects of the visual sense (assuming the same circumstances of perception). Each such quality would be a something-in-itself; each would stand unknown alongside of all the others and would not be reducible to them.

Clearly science would have to make every effort to move beyond this highly unsatisfactory stage. Indeed, we know that today it has succeeded brilliantly in doing so. Physics replaces the unknown qualities with wave states and correlates different frequencies of objective waves to the different subjective colors. Now these frequencies are no longer mutually irreducible. As temporal quantities, they admit of being known quantitatively. They can be measured by counting units; hence, in view of what was said above, they are completely knowable through one another. The determination of frequencies (or of wave lengths) takes place of course with the help of the method of coincidences, as when we measure the intervals between interference bands, determine the position of a spectral line on a scale, or the like.

But we must not suppose that science, in consequence of these results, has eliminated all qualities. This is certainly not the case. For the light waves that correspond to colors are, as we know, electromagnetic in nature, that is, they consist in periodic variations in those qualities that physics designates as electrical and magnetic field strengths. They themselves, however, retain their qualitative character even though they are at the same time extensive, hence divisible, magnitudes, to be thought of as the sums of units and thus subject to the concept of number.

Let us illustrate this advance in knowledge from a qualitative to a quantitative level by means of an example that is more instructive since it is connected more closely to the progress and state of our inquiry.

When an object touches my skin, I have a thermal sensation the quality of which depends on where the contact takes place and what kind of body was previously in contact with that part of my skin. The same body of water may seem cool or warm depending on whether the hand dipped into it was previously in contact with warmer water or colder water. The different thermal sensations I have in touching a body under various conditions are correlated by the physicist with *one* identical quality: this he calls "temperature". Under circumstances that otherwise are the same, an intense sensation is based on a different temperature than a mild sensation, and the difference between the two temperatures is first conceived of qualitatively. The physicist, however, utilizes a certain device to make the temperature subject to mathematical treatment. He correlates numbers with the various temperaures, and in so doing makes use of the approximate correspondence between the quality of the thermal sensation and the volume of a certain body (the mercury in a thermometer tube, for example). Now this volume is an extensive magnitude and can be measured by the method of coincidences; but at this stage of knowledge this is *not yet* true of the temperature itself. Temperatures are not broken down into additive parts; they cannot be reduced to one another. It makes no sense to say that a temperature of 20 is equal to twice a temperature of 10. The numbers 10 and 20 are correlated with certain temperatures only by virtue of an arbitrary stipulation, that is, by assuming one or another thermometric substance together with a scale. The insight employed here is simply that temperatures may be ordered in a one-dimensional series. We could also, in accordance with some arbitrary agreement, correlate numbers with the pure colors of the spectrum or with tonal pitch, without knowing anything about the wave character of the physical structures that correspond to them. An ordering of this kind would of course not provide any knowledge of the nature of what was being correlated with numbers. At this stage, which is known as pure thermodynamics, measuring temperature would be something fundamentally different from measuring say, the length of light waves; for it would not be bound up with knowledge of the magnitude being measured.

Not so the next higher stage, that of the so-called mechanical theory of heat. This theory identifies heat with the mean kinetic energy of molecules in motion — certainly an extensive magnitude. By definition, this magnitude is constructed out of spatial and temporal quantities (namely, velocities) in such a manner that it can always be conceived of as composed additively of parts. Temperature differences now are no longer qualitative for the physicist. Temperature as a special quality is altogether eliminated from the physical world outlook. It is completely reduced to the mechanical concepts of mass, space, and time; it has thus become measurable in a strict sense and its nature has become completely *known*.

The examination of these relationships clearly yields the following conclusion: qualities are fully known — that is, completely and uniquely designated by means of combinations of concepts already at hand — only when we succeed in reducing them quantitatively to one another. And they are thereby totally eliminated, in their character as specific qualities, from our picture of the world.

The possibility of quantitative determination is thus not only a welcome supplement to knowledge, needed to give it a more precise form. It is the indispensable condition for any complete knowledge at all. Only the quantitative — thus ultimately the additive — reduction of magnitudes to one another permits the one to be found again fully and unchanged in the other, that is, as parts in a whole, as summands in a sum.

This process of eliminating qualities is at the heart of all advances in knowledge in the explanatory sciences. The most ancient philosophical assumptions about the qualities of objective being are directly derived in a natural way from sense data. For example, the sensations provided by the sense organs in the skin (and the muscles) are clearly the basis for describing reality as comprised of the "four elements": water is that which is moist, fire that which is warm, earth that which is heavy and hard, air that which is light and yielding. In textbooks it is still customary to divide physics into mechanics, acoustics, optics, heat. This division rests entirely on the differences between the sensory domains: mechanics corresponds to the tactile and muscle senses, acoustics to the ear, optics to the eye and heat to the sense of temperature. In physical theory, of course, these separations have long since been abandoned. With the passage of time, there has been a gradual elimination first of the sensible qualities and then of the objective qualities that replaced them, until finally all that remains is a very small number of qualities that cannot be reduced any further (for instance, electrical and magnetic field strengths, as mentioned above). From them, physics constructs the entire objective world, and all the magnitudes that occur in its picture of the world are represented as spatial or temporal combinations of these fundamental qualities. The latter may be conveniently designated as "intensities".

At times it is said that in the quantitative description of reality qualities are simply ignored or discarded or neglected, and that the quantitative world picture is necessarily the poorer in that it provides only a partial account. But this view is entirely wrong. Scientific research does not simply leave qualities out of consideration. On the contrary, it insists on uncovering the quantitative differences that correspond to the qualitative ones. That such quantitative differences can always be found is indeed a remarkable empirical fact. For example, wherever I experience different sounds, I can also measure different frequencies. Qualitative differences are not simply there *outside of* and in addition to quantitative differences; the latter run fully parallel with the former. It is this fact that makes the quantitative picture of the world *complete* in itself. The addition of qualities would not enrich or supplement the picture; it would only be another kind of description.

Obviously science in its account of the world cannot get along without qualities. It cannot regard nature as a play of pure quantities. To speak of quality-less atoms and the like does not make sense; for quantity is an abstraction that presupposes the presence of something of which it is the quantity. Nothing can be without being some way; being and being a quality are the same. (This point has been stressed especially by E. BECHER; thus he says in his Philosophische Voraussetzungen der exakten Naturwissenschaften, p. 87: "All that is, is quality . . .") Even the objective spatio-temporal manifold must be understood as something qualitative, and this without prejudice to its extensive character. For this manifold must be somehow distinguishable from other four-dimensional manifolds that, quantitatively, are exactly the same.

Moreover, once the mutual dependency of individual magnitudes is finally discovered, there is a certain arbitrariness in designating any particular intensities as the fundamental ones — the ones to which all the others will be reduced. Due to the pervasive mutual relations, I can always express the qualities hitherto accepted as fundamental in terms of some of the remaining qualities and thus select the latter as the ones to which all other qualities are to be reduced. To cite an example: in the construction of Newtonian mechanics I need not, as is customary, take mass, time and distance as the fundamental concepts. I can just as well use volume, velocity and energy as the base to which to reduce all the other magnitudes occurring in mechanics. Which possibility I select is merely a matter of practical convenience.

It would therefore be a dubious metaphysical interpretation of the scientific world view to say that in the external world no qualities exist except the "intensities" whose quantitative variations constitute the building blocks of the universe of physics. For the physical world picture is a system of concepts and must not be confused with the world itself. We can designate the realities of the world uniquely by means of complex concepts formed by putting together a small number of elementary components. But these realities themselves can also always be conceived of as "simple". This is most easily grasped if we bear in mind the above mentioned element of arbitrariness in the choice of the ultimate building blocks of the world picture. Thus the "universe in itself" must be described as a manifold of infinitely many different qualities which are so interwoven and interdependent that they can be designated by the quantitative conceptual systems of the natural sciences. These systems serve to reproduce the law-like regularity of the coming to be and the ceasing to be of the qualities. (The words 'coming to be' and 'ceasing to be' are of course to be taken in a metaphorical sense, for it is not changes in intuitive time that are involved here, but positions in the objective ordering.) Each of the qualities of the external world can be correlated with a concept formed by combining the concepts of other qualities. This is precisely how the law-like regularity of the totality of interconnections expresses itself; for this regularity alone makes such a correlation possible. To discover the regularity is to know the external world — to find the most general again in the individual and thereby to know the latter.

It is in this manner that the objects of the external world, the things-in-themselves, are determined as regular connections of qualities. (A study of the details of this cognitive process must be reserved for investigations in the philosophy of science, which I propose to report on elsewhere.) Thus an atom or an electron is to be conceived of as a union of qualities that are bound together by definite laws, and not as a substantial *thing*, which bears its qualities as properties and can thus be distinguished from them as their bearer. Hume's critique of *this* concept of substance is still entirely sound. If, like Machian positivism (see above, § 25 beginning, § 26 A2), we used the expression 'thing-in-itself' to designate substance in this sense, then the struggle against the thing-in-itself would be entirely justified and most necessary. The very idea of a kernel independent of its properties and merely the bearer of them is incorrect, since the kernel itself would then be something without properties. We need not concern ourselves any further with this idea. We do not encounter it at all in our analysis and the process of acquiring knowledge of nature can be made intelligible without it. It is thus proved to be dispensable. I have pointed out elsewhere (Naturphilosophie, Berlin 1925) that in specific cases natural science also finds itself compelled by empirical, experimental facts to abandon the old concept of substance. In the last analysis, all knowledge is a matter of relations and dependencies, not of things or substances.

A question about the true essence of one or another quality is answered by incorporating that quality into the quantitative conceptual system and thus reducing it to the fundamental intensities selected as a basis. And once completely found, this answer is definitive in character. Whoever supposes that the "real essence" of qualities is not sufficiently determined thereby and demands, say, that we gain direct acquaintance with them as with the conscious qualities of pleasure, pain, yellow and the like — such a person has once more fallen into the error of conflating experiencing and knowing, an error that we have so often recognized as a cause of confusion (see § 12, Part I). So far as the qualities of the universe are concerned, whatever can be provided at all by knowledge will be supplied in full by the natural sciences in the fashion already described. These qualities will be completely *known*. True, we shall never be *directly acquainted* with them. But our urge to know has no reason to seek such acquaintance; for it would be of no help.

Just the reverse is true of the qualities that make up the content of our consciousness. With them we are directly acquainted. But how do matters stand as regards *knowing* them? Compared with knowledge of the qualities of the external world, the situation evidently is rather bad. For psychology, whose subject matter includes the study of qualities with which we are subjectively acquainted, surely cannot measure up to the natural sciences with respect to the extent and cognitive worth of its findings. Clearly there is even a difference *in principle* between them. The fact is that introspective psychology can never go beyond the stage of qualitative knowledge. For such a psychology, the endless manifold of mental qualities is plainly irreducible; each is something new relative to every other and exhibits no extensive properties. Each sensation, for example, is by its very nature simple and indivisible. The relationship between a stronger and a weaker sensation of yellow is not such that the stronger consists simply in a weak sensation added to a second weak sensation. Rather, the stronger sensation is experienced as something that is qualitatively different from the weaker one and as equally simple and indivisible. No one can deny the truth of Kant's famous words that "mathematics is not applicable to the phenomena of the inner sense, and their laws".

All mental regularities discovered by the introspective method (for example, the laws of association, of attention, of acts of will) at most assert that the presence of certain data is the condition for the appearance of certain other data. Thus these regularities do give us causal knowledge, but the causally connected terms themselves do not thereby in any way become *known*, as is the case with quantitative causal knowledge. Rather, each term continues to retain its own individuality. It would take an infinite number of concepts to describe completely the manifold of experiences. For since the latter are irreducible, we would have to supply each of them with its own concept.

Is there no way then by which psychology too can reach the level of quantitative knowledge — the only level at which the goal of knowledge can be completely realized?

We have just gotten to know the procedure — that of quantitative concept formation — by which natural science gains mastery over qualities. The question we must ask is whether this procedure can be applied also to the subjective qualities of consciousness. By what was said above, in order for the procedure to be applicable, there must be spatial variations that are connected to the qualities in a fully determined, unique way. If this is the case, then the problem can be solved by the method of spatio-temporal coincidences and a *measurement* will be possible. But the procedure of coincidences consists essentially in physical observation and there is no such thing in the case of the introspective method. It follows at once that psychology can never reach the ideal of knowledge along the path of introspection. Accordingly, it must try to make use of physical observations for its purpose. But is this possible? Are there spatial variations that depend on the qualities of consciousness the same way, for example, that in optics the width of the interference bands depends on the color, and in electricity the deflection of the magnetic needle depends on the strength of the magnetic field?

Now we know that an exactly determined, unique correlation is in fact to be assumed between subjective qualities and the objectively inferred world. Extensive empirical data teach us that we can find, or at least must assume the existence of, "physical" processes uniquely connected to all experiences. There are no qualities of consciousness that cannot be affected by forces acting on the body. Indeed, we are even able to blot out consciousness altogether by a simple physical procedure, such as inhaling a gas. Our actions are linked to our volitional experiences, hallucinations to bodily exhaustion, fits of depression to digestive disturbances. In order to study interconnections of this kind, the theory of mind must abandon the method of pure introspection and become *physiological* psychology. This discipline alone can arrive at a theoretically complete knowledge of the mental. With the aid of such a psychology, we find it possible to correlate concepts with the given subjective qualities just as we are able to correlate them with the inferred objective qualities. The subjective qualities thus become just as knowable as the objective qualities.

It was shown long ago that the part of the objective world connected most directly to the subjective qualities of a self is that which is designated by the concept of the brain, in particular the cerebral cortex. Hence in the exact world picture of scientific knowledge, the numerically describable concepts that must be substituted for the subjective qualities are simply certain brain processes. It is to these that the analysis of the mutual dependencies inevitably leads. Even though we are immeasurably far from knowing exactly which individual processes are involved, at least the path is indicated: cerebral processes must be substituted for subjective qualities. This is the only hope we have of fully knowing the subjective qualities.

A knowledge of qualities, whether they are objective or subjective, is always obtained in the same way: the qualities are replaced

by the sign system of natural science concepts and thus are eliminated from the *world picture* of exact science. This is not to say,
of course, that they are eliminated from the world. On the contrary, they alone are real, and the scientific world picture is only
an edifice made up of conceptual signs.

In sum, a definitive knowledge of qualities is possible only
through the quantitative method. The life of consciousness is thus
completely knowable to the extent that we succeed in transforming
introspective psychology into a physiological, natural scientific
psychology — ultimately into a physics of brain processes.

It might be supposed that mental magnitudes could also be
measured and thus quantitatively mastered in a less direct way without an exact investigation into the nervous processes. For instance,
Fechner's psychophysics seems able at least to handle sensations
numerically by measuring stimulus strengths, a procedure that does
not require us to look into the nature of the central nervous processes.

But even if we grant that Fechner's psychophysical method can be
freed from all of its imperfections and applied to something other
than sensations (which to all intents and purposes seems impossible), we still would not be able to acquire knowledge of the mental in the fullest sense. True, a correlation of numbers with mental
magnitudes would have been obtained in accordance with some
arbitrary scale. But these magnitudes would not have been reduced
to something else and would remain quite unconnected with one
another. Hence we could not speak of knowing the nature or essence
of something. The situation would be exactly the same as in the
example from physics considered above. The nature of "temperature" remained unknown so long as "temperature" itself could be
measured only by correlating numbers on the basis of an arbitrary
scale. But the mechanical theory of heat, which introduced the mean
kinetic energy of molecules in place of temperature, at the same
time supplied a natural principle for quantitative treatment that
excluded any element of the arbitrary. Only when quantitative
relations do not merely reflect an arbitrary stipulation but, as it
were, follow from and are perceived from the nature of the things,
do they represent a knowledge of the *essence* [40]. Just as temperature

---

40 On the difference between measurement in the true scientific sense
and measurement in the sense of a mere correlation of numbers accord-

is here reduced to mechanical determinations, so the data of consciousness, if they are really to be known, must in general be reduced by means of natural principles to physical determinations. In the case of temperature (that is, the objective quality of heat), this is possible only through hypotheses about the molecular structure of matter; similarly, knowledge of subjective mental qualities requires physiological hypotheses that go deeply into the nature of brain processes. Unfortunately, the present state of research does not yet allow us to formulate such hypotheses with the specificity needed to attain this ultimate goal of psychology.

§ 32. The Physical and the Mental

These reflections lead directly to a problem that, since about the time of Descartes, has been at the center of all metaphysics: the relationship of mental to physical, of mind to body. In my opinion, this problem is one of those that owe their existence to a mistaken formulation of the issue. As a matter of fact, from the vantage point we now have gained, we see unfolded before us a world picture without those dark recesses in which the special difficulties, so feared under the label of the psychophysical problem, might find a hiding place. Viewed from this standpoint, the problem is solved even before it can be raised. This we shall now demonstrate. However, in order to set our minds completely at rest about the question, we must also uncover the source of the error that allowed the question of mind and body to become such a tormenting problem.

We defined the concept of the mental some time back (see, for example, § 20). As we said then, it designates the "directly given", which is identical with "content of consciousness". And surely we need not elucidate the meaning of these expressions any further. But until now there has been neither necessity nor occasion for a definition of the physical. This must now be supplied. Actually,

---

ing to some artificial principle, see J. VON KRIES, Über die Messung intensiver Größen und das sogenannte psychophysische Gesetz, Vierteljahrsschrift für wissenschaftliche Philosophie 6 (1882), p. 257; also my paper, Die Grenze der naturwissenschaftlichen und philosophischen Begriffsbildung, § 5, *ibid.*, 34 (1910), p. 132. (At the time I wrote this paper, I was not aware of von Kries's work.)

as will soon be evident, nothing more is needed to reach full clarity about the alleged problem than to bring distinctly to mind those characteristics that make up the concept of the bodily.

The universe presents itself to us as an infinite manifold of qualities. Those qualities that belong to the context of consciousness we have designated as subjective; they are the given, that with which we are directly acquainted. Contrasted to them are the objective qualities; these are not given and are not open to direct acquaintance. The former are of course what we call *mental,* and we have used this name for them. Should we now designate the second group, the objective qualities, as the physical? It would certainly seem quite plausible. But we can do this only if the concept thus defined refers precisely to that which we wish to capture with the ordinary language expression 'physical'. On closer inspection, however, this is not the case.

True, we usually understand by 'physical' anything — be it a thing, process or property — that is not counted as a part of the inner world of a conscious being, that is, anything that does not belong to the context of one's own self or to that of another consciousness. Our objective qualities would seem to fall under this concept of the physical, at any rate if we leave aside the doctrines of those thinkers who believe we must make room for an "unconscious mental". But in ordinary life, as in the sciences, everyone includes in the concept of the physical still other features, and it is just these that are taken to be essential. However, they are not made sufficiently clear, are located in entirely the wrong place, and must be held responsible for the origin of the "psycho-physical" problem. These are the features of *spatiality.*

The bodily and the extended have been thought of not only as belonging inseparably together, but, often enough, as absolutely identical. (See Descartes, for example.) Spatial extension has always been part of the definition of physical body. That is why Kant used the sentence 'All bodies are extended' as an instance of an analytic judgment. Spatiality is *the* essential feature of all that is physical in the ordinary sense. This customary sense ignores the difference to which we had to attach the greatest weight — the difference, namely, between the spatial as intuitive datum and "space" as the ordering schema of the objective world (see above, § 29). The latter, for want of a better expression, we called 'transcendent space' (§ 29, near end). At the same time, we emphasized that in employing this expression we introduced a metaphorical sense for the word 'space', which must be very carefully distinguished from the original use according to which 'space' always refers to something *intuitive*. But this intuitive spatiality, as our preceding discussions have shown, cannot be attributed to the extramental, to the objective qualities.

Now we know that representable or imaginable *extension* is a property of precisely the *subjective* qualities. Spatiality in this sense is thus possessed not by objective being but, on the contrary, by mental or subjective being. The popular concept of the bodily therefore joins together features that, *realiter,* are incompatible: a body is supposed to be a thing-in-itself (that is, something that is not a content of consciousness), yet at the same time it is burdened with the intuitive, perceivable property of extension. Since the two characterizations are not compatible, the ordinary concept of the physical (bodily, material) must give rise to contradictions. It is just these contradictions that make up the psychophysical problem.

All great philosophical problems, indeed, rest on troubling, tormenting contradictions. They exhibit themselves externally in certain conceptual antitheses. And it is precisely the reconciling of these antitheses that signifies the solution of the philosophical problem. Some examples of paired conceptual opposites are freedom-necessity, egoism-altruism, essence-appearance (see § 27). Another is our own pair of concepts: physical-mental, body-mind, matter-spirit, or whatever other designation we may choose.

We have come to see that the traditional concept of the physical is defective or ill-formed. Ought we then, as it seems we must, reject the use of the term altogether and say that there aren't any physical bodies at all? This, of course, would not be right. Somewhere there must be a domain in which the term has legitimate application. Otherwise the expression could never have acquired the outstanding methodological and practical significance that it in fact enjoys. There must be some way of specifying and delimiting the subject-matter of "physics". We have now determined at least negatively that we would fall short of this aim were we to accept the term 'physical' simply as the designation for all *non-mental* qualities. We also have the means, as a result of our earlier discussion, to solve the problem positively.

It seems to me that there is only *one* way to establish the genuine sense of the word 'physical'. To ask for the true meaning of the word can only be to ask for the meaning that the word actually has, specifically in the science whose peculiar subject-matter is the physical, namely, physics. No solution of the problem can be satisfactory if it constructs a special concept of the physical and sets it up *ad hoc* in such a way that a conflict with the mental does not arise. The concept of the physical must be drawn from the particular science that found it in rough form in pre-scientific thinking, sharpened it, and gave it clarity[41].

As a preliminary, however, it is important to show that if we hold to the viewpoint to which the investigations in the preceding chapters have led us, we no longer have a mind-body problem, we no longer need fear a contradictory opposition of body and spirit.

The world is a variegated structure of connected qualities. Some of them are given to my (or to some other person's) consciousness and these qualities I call subjective or mental; others are not given directly to any consciousness and these I designate as objective or extra-mental. At this point, the concept of the physical does not appear at all. Earlier we were obliged most emphatically to reject the mistaken idea that a different kind or a different degree of reality must be ascribed to these two groups of qualities, that one group is to be characterized as merely an "appearance" of the other. On the contrary, they are all to be regarded as, so to speak, of equal value; one group belongs as much to the pervasive connectedness of the universe as the other. We cannot say that the roles they play in the world differ fundamentally. In the universe, generally speaking, everything depends on everything else, each happening is a function of all other happenings, no matter whether the qualities involved are subjective or objective. Whether I now see red or experience joy will depend as much on my previous experiences (thus on mental qualities) as on the presence of certain extra-mental qualities, which I am able to know through the methods described in the preceding sections. Conversely, extra-mental qualities will depend on changes in mental qualities. The former, for example, are certainly functions of my "volitional" experiences, since objective events are undoubtedly influenced by my actions. When I experience the sensations of firing a revolver and hear the report, obviously something

---

41 For this reason, it seems to me that ROBERT REININGER's Das psychophysische Problem (Vienna 1916), in which a special philosophical concept of the physical is created, does not solve the real problem.

happens at the same time in the extra-mental world. Beyond question, there is a thoroughgoing dependency or "interaction" among the various qualities of the universe, thus between, say, those that belong to my consciousness and the extra-mental ones designated by the physical concept of "body outside of my body".

Now all of this is quite natural, and fits easily and freely into the picture we have gained of the world. No problems are created. There is no reason for us to accept any other assumption, to ask whether what exists, perhaps, is not a universal pervasive interconnectedness of the real, but a "preestablished harmony" between consciousness and the "external world". Such a question can be raised only if we proceed from an entirely incorrect starting-point.

It might seem that in respect to the mind-body problem we must side with those thinkers who champion psychophysical interaction. But this is not so. What is obvious to begin with is only that we must assume an interaction between conscious experience and extra-mental processes, between an "inner world" and an "external world". But we cannot decide whether to designate this interaction as psycho-"physical" until we have come to an agreement about the concept of the physical. Thus far, at any rate, we have found no reason to call the extramental *as such* "physical". And we must also remember that those who raise the mind-body problem, and attempt to solve it, understand by "physical" something *other* than our extra-mental qualities. They base themselves on the ordinary notion of an intuitive, spatially extended body. But this concept is self-contradictory, as we have just shown. We must now see how we can express *without* contradiction what is really intended in the traditional concept of the physical. We shall then likewise have determined the particular meaning we must associate with the word 'physical' in the future.

To this end, we need only look back to the considerations developed in the preceding sections. There we saw how natural science succeeded in constructing its purely quantitative picture of the world. The elimination of secondary qualities in this picture gave rise to the concept of physical matter as a quality-less but extended stuff — a concept that dominated the philosophy of nature from the time of Democritus to that of Descartes, and on beyond Kant.

This world picture has been fundamentally transformed and refined by the modern development of physics. What stands in the center of physics today is no longer the concept of extended "substance" but the more general one of spatio-temporal process. At each stage in this development, however, we are able to read off the concept of the physical with equal clarity and certainty: reality is called "physical" *in so far as it is designated by means of the spatio-temporal quantitative conceptual system of natural science.* We saw earlier that the world picture of natural science is no more than a system of signs that we correlate with the qualities and complexes of qualities whose interconnected totality forms the universe. Moreover, the expression 'world picture' is itself not the best one to use; it would be preferable to say 'world concept'. For in philosophy the word 'picture' is better confined to the intuitively representable, whereas the physical representation of the world, although conceptual, is entirely non-intuitive. Thus the space of physics, as we have seen, is not in any way (intuitively) representable; it is a wholly abstract structure, a mere scheme of ordering. Of course the components of the physical concept of the world, like all concepts, are represented in our thought processes by means of intuitive images. And obviously when we illustrate objective spatial relationships, we utilize in the first instance those images that belong to an intuitive space, that of the visual sense, for example. (Visual space is by no means the only possibility, just as the objective ordering of time may be represented in thought not only by intuitive time experiences but also — as in the case of graphs — by visual spatial images.)

Thinking that has not yet been epistemologically clarified is apt to conflate the concept not only with the real object it designates, but also with the intuitive representations or images that serve as proxies for the concept in our consciousness. When we think of the scientific concept of a particular body, we do so by means of representations, such as visual images, that bear the intuitive feature of extension. On the other hand, the rigorous *concept* of body contains nothing of this; it includes only certain numbers, which specify the "measurements" or "configuration" of the body. Moreover, as explained in detail above, this does not signify the objective presence of intuitive, spatial properties in the actual object; such properties belong only to perceptions and images, not to anything extramental. What it does signify is the non-intuitive, non-representable ordering in which the objective qualities of the world are situated.

Accordingly, we must distinguish three domains the confusing and conflating of which have actually been responsible for the psychophysical problem. These domains are: 1) reality itself (the complexes of qualities, the things-in-themselves); 2) the quantitative concepts of the natural sciences correlated with reality and forming in their totality the world concept of physics; and 3) the intuitive images by means of which the magnitudes cited in 2) are represented in our consciousness. Here 3) is of course a part of 1), that is, a subdivision of the part of reality we designate as consciousness.

In which of these three realms should we seek the physical? The answer is easily found and, in my opinion, stands out quite clearly. No one will deny that when we speak of the physical, we always have in mind something *actual*. Hence the word 'physical' is undoubtedly bound up with objects of the *first* domain. But the tie is not direct or unconditional. Rather, 'physical' is bound up only with those real objects to which concepts of the *second* domain are or can be correlated. This is all that we can say in advance. And for the present the question remains entirely open as to whether *all* the objects of the first domain can be designated by means of the conceptual system of the natural sciences, or whether such a designation may be possible only for a *portion* of reality. It is thus an open question whether or not the *whole* world can be conceived of as something physical. The third domain and the mental generally (which is a subdivision of the first domain) are not involved at all in the conceptual determination of the physical. In particular, there is not the slightest reason to ascribe some special role to the mental in regard to whether it can be designated by the concepts of natural science. Hence there is no reason to suppose that the boundary of the physical (the reality that can be described by means of spatio-temporal concepts), if there is such a boundary, coincides with the boundary between experienced and non-experienced reality, that is, between mental and extramental qualities.

But the simplest hypothesis, and one which is made plausible by empirical results that will be presented shortly, is that such a boundary does not exist. Rather, spatio-temporal concepts may be used to describe *any arbitrary* reality, without exception, including the reality of consciousness. The fact that we describe the latter also by means of what are called "psychological" concepts does not give rise to any philosophical difficulty, does not create any antithesis between the physical and the mental.

Hence 'physical' signifies not a special kind of reality but a special way of designating the real, namely, by forming the natural science concepts required for a knowledge of reality. The term 'physical' should not be misunderstood as denoting a property that belongs to one part of the real but not to another. On the contrary, it denotes a species of conceptual construction; like the terms 'geographical' or 'mathematical', it designates not some peculiarities of real things but only a way of representing them by means of concepts. Physics is the system of exact concepts that our knowledge correlates to all reality. I say to *all* reality, since according to our hypothesis the *entire world* is in principle open to designation by that conceptual system. Nature is all; all that is real is natural. Mind, the life of consciousness, is not the opposite of nature, but a sector of the totality of the natural.

That with this conception we have hit the mark becomes even clearer when we examine critically other attempts to find a definition of the physical that is immune to objection.

Modern thinkers who occupy themselves with this question for the most part strive to reduce the difference between body and mind to a difference in the mode of consideration. Two philosophers as different in orientation as Mach and Wundt agree that physics and psychology deal ultimately with the very same objects; they merely treat them differently. Thus, says Mach, if we direct attention to the dependency of a particular "element" on those elements that form our body, then that element is a mental object, a sensation; on the other hand, if we study that same element in its dependency on other "elements", then we are doing physics and it is a physical object. "It is not the *subject-matter* but the *direction of inquiry* that is different in the two domains" (Analyse der Empfindungen, 5th edition, p. 14). But in the last section and in earlier ones (§§ 25, 26), we established that this account does not give a correct picture of the essence of physical research. The immediately given elements never enter of themselves into the theories of physics; they are always eliminated and only what is substituted for them is called 'physical'. But these substitutes are the concepts of quantities, which stand in place of the given qualities. These latter, in themselves and however looked at, remain *mental*. The yellow of a sunflower, the pleasant sound of a certain bell are mental magnitudes; "yellow" and "sound" are psychological concepts. Physical law-like regularities deal not with them, but with frequencies, amplitudes and the like, and these are never built up out of subjective qualities.

Wundt characterized the standpoint of natural science as that of mediate experience and the standpoint of psychology as that of immediate experience. And he emphasizes that "the expressions 'external experience' and 'internal experience' refer not to different objects but to different viewpoints we adopt in conceptualizing and treating scientifically what is in itself unitary experience" (Grundrisse der Psychologie, 7th edition, p. 3). But the concept of mediate experience too is not suitable for defining the physical. The concept of the physical, says Wundt, comes into being "by means of abstraction from the subjective factor contained in every real experience"; the natural sciences consider "the *objects* of experience in the character they assume when thought of as independent of the subject". On this view, the physical coincides with the objective, a conclusion which we have already had to reject as inapt and which on closer view becomes meaningful only if we presuppose that what is different is not merely the viewpoint but also the *objects*.

It then seemed more hopeful, in connection with the definition of the physical, to lay weight on a reality that (in contrast to the mental) is not directly experienced. We succeeded in setting up a definition of the physical only with the intervention of the mental, and it is in this sense that the expressions 'mediate' and 'immediate' are to be understood. But one must bear in mind that mental qualities also can be objects of mediate experience, to wit, those that belong to the consciousness of another person. For as we know, we establish their existence only through arguments by analogy. Plainly, the proper view, however, was that the *physical* was that reality which *in principle* is accessible *only* to mediate experience. This indeed was the objective that MÜNSTERBERG sought with his definition that 'mental' signifies that which can be experienced only by a single subject, 'physical' that which can be experienced in common by several subjects" (Prinzipien der Psychologie, Vol. I, 1900, p. 72). He is supported by A. MESSER (Einführung in die Erkenntnistheorie, 1901, p. 121). But this definition would count as satisfactory only if the expression 'can be experienced' had the same meaning in both instances, only if there were some sort of experience through which both domains were given to us. But this is not so; for a mental quality is directly or immediately given and always to the one subject who experiences it. On the other hand, in the case of an extra-mental object, to say that it can be known through experience is *not* the same as saying it can be experienced. Its relation to us is an indirect one, and it can stand in such a relation to many subjects at the same time. But this is equally true of the mental life of another person: any number of subjects can have indirect experience of it. This, of course, is an entirely different sort of experience. But this difference is precisely the main point, and so long as it is not captured by the definition, we fail to mark off the bodily from the mental. Hence the Münsterberg formulation does not advance us a single step.

ERNST MACH also sought a definition (Erkenntnis und Irrtum, 3rd edition, p. 6): "the totality of that which is immediately present for *everyone* may be called the physical, and that which is immediately given to just *one* person the mental". But on this definition, there is absolutely nothing that corresponds to the physical: for as we learned earlier (26B, above), the identically same element can never be given to different individuals.

Furthermore, nothing is gained by distinguishing between two kinds of experience, "internal" and "external". On the contrary, it is highly misleading, for exactly the same reasons cited above (Part II, § 20) in criticizing the notion of an "inner perception". If in addition, as too often happens, sense perception is reckoned as part of "external" perception, the sense qualities themselves are drawn into the domain of the physical, something we have already recognized as being inadmissible.

Suppose we corrected these various attempts at definition by replacing the two kinds of perception or experience (invoked to mark off the physical from the mental) with the unobjectionable dichotomy between given and not given reality. We would still not succeed in obtaining a serviceable concept of the physical. For, the reasons that prevented us from simply designating as physical the not given real qualities would still exist. These transcendent qualities, as we have shown, lack all the properties that are essential to the natural science concept of the physical as well as to the popular concept.

As we have remarked several times, there is an extensive body of quite definite experience that speaks for the applicability of physical concepts in designating immediately experienced reality, and hence mental reality. In preceding sections, we satisfied ourselves that the only possibility of acquiring a *complete* knowledge of the mental lay precisely in applying the quantitative concepts of the natural sciences to the designation of mental qualities and their interconnections. And the empirical data clearly indicate in what way this must occur: the complex of concepts of certain "brain processes" must be correlated with the world of consciousness. We know that our conscious processes run their course undisturbed only if certain parts of our brain remain intact. Destruction of the occipital lobe eliminates the ability to see, destruction of the temporal lobe does away with the capacity to verbalize, and so forth. These findings, as far as they go, establish only that there is an inner relation between the physical object "brain" and the experienced reality "content of consciousness". If we now wish to conceive of this relation only as one of mutual dependency and thus as causal (in the manner of a dualistic theory of mind-body interaction), the consciousness or the self would be a particular object different from the "brain processes" and could not, in principle, be designated by means of physical concepts. For on this assumption, the concepts of brain processes would be regarded as designating something else. And since concepts of processes outside the head are certainly not involved, no physical concept whatsoever could be correlated with the content of consciousness. Moreover, it would then be impossible to make even our brain processes intelligible physically, that is, to explain them on the basis of physical causes. For their causes would in part have to be sought in mental processes which cannot be represented by means of physical concepts; physical causality would have gaps, and this would have a totally upsetting effect on the concept of natural law and on the formulation of laws of nature.

But all these complications in the world picture are quite unnecessary. They can easily be avoided if in place of the dualistic assumption we introduce the much simpler hypothesis that the concepts of the natural sciences are suited for designating every reality including that which is immediately experienced. The resulting relation between immediately experienced reality and the physical brain processes is then no longer one of causal dependency but of simple *identity*. What we have is one and the same reality, not "viewed from two different sides" or "manifesting itself in two different forms", but designated by two different conceptual systems, the psychological and the physical.

In speaking here about the brain and brain processes, we must keep very clearly in mind a three-fold distinction: the expressions 'brain' and 'brain process' may refer 1) to the reality, that which exists in itself, and this is nothing other than the experienced brain processes themselves; or 2) to the physical concepts that designate this reality (the concepts of ganglion cells, nervous excitation, and the like); or 3) to the intuitive ideas or perceptions that serve as representatives for us of these concepts, and thus to the perceptions we have when we look at a person's brain after his skull has been opened or observe a ganglion cell through a microscope. The worst mistake that can be made in viewing the psychophysical problem — a mistake that, strangely enough, is made time and again — is, without noticing it, to substitute for the brain processes themselves, which are to be regarded as identical with the mental processes, the perceptions or images of the brain processes. These perceptions are experienced reality; they are themselves mental processes. But they belong to another person, the one who is looking at the brain of the first individual. They are of course in no way identical with the experiences of this first individual; they do not run "parallel" to them. Instead, they stand to them in a relation of causal dependency; for what I perceive of the brain of a person will, speaking theoretically, depend on what is going on in his consciousness.

Just which particular brain processes are to be correlated with specific experiences we are unable to say at the present stage of our knowledge. The study of brain functions is still in its infancy. But we must assert the possibility of a universal correlation, and this postulate must be satisfied if the mental is to be *known* at all, that is, designated by means of concepts that can be reduced to one another. We cannot regard *all* cerebral processes as signs of consciousness; so far as we know, in the case of a sleeping or unconscious brain mental life is lacking. But we do not even know *how* the physical processes to which mental data correspond (subjective qualities standing in the context of a consciousness) differ from those physical processes that are signs for objective qualities (qualities that belong to no consciousness). We shall have more to say about this in the next sections.

Thus we are led on purely epistemological grounds to the viewpoint of psychophysical parallelism. We should be quite clear, however, about its character. It is not a metaphysical parallelism; it does not denote a parallelism of two kinds of being (as in Geulincx) nor a single substance with two attributes (as in the case of Spinoza) nor two forms of appearance of one and the same "essence" (as in Kant). Rather, it is an epistemological parallelism between a psychological conceptual system on the one hand and a physical conceptual system on the other. The "physical world" *is* just the world that is designated by means of the system of quantitative concepts of the natural sciences.

§ 33. More on the Psychophysical Problem

In order to put our minds completely at ease concerning the mind-body problem, we must see clearly how the flawed concept of the physical is responsible for the contradictions in this great problem. The consideration of this matter is also quite instructive with respect to the history of philosophy.

We have already recognized the basic error that gave rise to the mind-body problem with all of its pitfalls. The mistake lay in considering the physical as something real that possesses intuitive spatial extension. It was only in comparatively recent times that the source of the evil was uncovered. Before then, it was thought that the cause of the difficulties had been sufficiently identified when one pointed to the fundamental *difference in kind* between the mental and the physical. That things so different as body and mind could act on one another seemed totally incomprehensible. Thus there were two domains of reality, and no one knew how to build a bridge between them, although no one was willing to assume that they exist as two absolutely separated worlds having nothing to do with each other.

But even if the physical and the mental were in fact two different domains of the real, no difference in kind, however great, could constitute a serious obstacle to the existence of a causal relation between them. For we know of no law stating that things must be of the same kind in order to act on one another. On the contrary, experience everywhere shows that the most disparate things stand in a relation of dependency to one another and thus interact with one another. And even if experience did not show this, there is surely nothing in the concept of interaction to confine its applicability to things of the same kind. Indeed, why shouldn't it be possible for an effect to differ to any extent whatever from the cause? No, there must be something in addition to the mere fact of difference. Other very special reasons must be adduced by anyone who wishes to deny the possibility of interaction.

At this point we begin to see that the *spatial* factor is somehow to blame for the genesis of the problem. But at first the real interconnection was not properly grasped. After Descartes had characterized the difference between physical and mental in terms of the opposition between thought and extension, KANT had the following to say (Kritik der reinen Vernunft, 2nd edition, edited by Kehrbach, p. 699): "As we know, the difficulty ... lies in the assumption that the objects of the inner sense (the soul) differ in kind from the objects of the outer senses, since the inner sense has only time as a formal condition, but the outer senses have space as well." Here Kant has not yet uncovered the real root of the problem (which, however, does not prevent him from setting out along the correct path to its solution) — Why cannot the spatial and the non-spatial act upon one another? Actually no reason is given. Indeed, modern thinkers (such as Stumpf, Külpe, Becher, Driesch, among others) have often insisted that no known law excludes such interaction and hence it should be regarded as entirely possible. Thus further studies would be needed to reveal the source of the psychophysical contradictions, which in fact lies concealed in the *spatial* relationship between the mental and physical realms.

The error in these formulations is immediately obvious to us. It was a mistake to designate the mental simply as non-spatial. We have long known that, on the contrary, our representations of space are derived wholly from the spatial determinations of *sensations*, that extension in the intuitive sense is an attribute only of mental quantities or magnitudes and *not* of physical things. As long as this fact remains hidden, and we draw no distinction between intuitive spatiality and the objective ordering of things, we immediately fall into contradictions. For then the physical and the mental fight each other, as it were, for possession of space; they put forward conflicting claims that could not possibly be fulfilled at the same time.

For the physical world, as our imagination pictures it, not only is spatial, it comprises *all* that is spatial. It singly occupies the whole of space and tolerates nothing else beside it. The qualities of sensations have no place in this world picture; the "secondary qualities", as we have seen, are necessarily and correctly eliminated from it. They do not appear in the laws that govern dependencies in the

physical world. Everything that happens in that world is determined solely by physical magnitudes.

This principle, thanks to which the physical world claims the
whole of space for itself, is usually called the "principle that causality in nature is closed". This principle is not laid down by the
natural sciences out of arrogance or lust for power. On the contrary,
its validity rests on the fact that the natural sciences must banish
the sense qualities from their completed conceptualization and that
consequently it becomes impossible to grant any place in the natural
science world picture to magnitudes belonging to the realm of the
immediately given.

A natural scientist might be content for a time with this state
of affairs. But a psychologist or a philosopher must raise the question: What then are the sense qualities, if they do not belong to
the objective world, if they are not properties of objective things?
The answer we are given is: They are states of consciousness. We
may let this answer pass. But as soon as we go further and ask
where these states of consciousness are, we are at once confronted
with the great contradictions that constitute the psychophysical
problem.

The easiest thing, it seems, would be to dodge the question
altogether by rejecting it as wrongly formulated: the mind is non-
spatial, there is no need to assign a location to consciousness. And
just this, no doubt, was the basis for advancing the theory that the
mental is non-spatial. Unfortunately, however, this solution is not
practicable, as we know. Certainly a great deal that is mental is not
localized; grief, anger, joy are not any*where*. But this is not true
at least as regards sensations. In so far as they are there, they are
mostly at a definite place and with a definite extension. But what
location do sensible qualities have — for example, the whiteness
of this piece of paper that I see before me? Natural science tells
us explicitly that the whiteness is not at the location of the physical object "paper". All that science finds there are physical things
(matter, electrons, or whatever else we may call them) in certain
physical states. Earlier (§ 30) we showed clearly that the attempt
to locate the whiteness in the physical object leads to contradictions. The only other place that might still be considered is
the brain. But the sense qualities are not there either. If someone
were able to investigate my brain while I was looking at the white
paper, he would never find the whiteness of the paper there; for

nothing can be found in the physical object "brain" except physical brain processes.

Thus the sense qualities cannot be at the one or the other location in physical space. The positions to which they must lay claim are already occupied by physical things, which precludes the presence of the qualities. And this not because different qualities cannot occupy the same place at the same time — that would be a completely dogmatic assumption — but because the notion that a mental quality can be at the location of a physical thing is ruled out for reasons we cited earlier. The physicist's world is complete in itself; the world of the psychologist cannot be fitted into it. Both of them struggle for the possession of space. One says: "White is at this place." The other says: "White is not at that place." It is these contradictory localizations and nothing else that constitute the real psychophysical problem.

Contradictions are indeed present. But only an unclear formulation could induce anyone to suppose that the problem lies in the difficulty of imagining "how a brain process becomes a sensation" or "how the spatial can act on the non-spatial" or how the qualities of sensations "are projected out of the mind into space". These matters may have been regarded as inexplicable, that is, not further reducible, things to be simply accepted. The mind-body problem, however, was always something larger and weightier, something that was felt to involve incompatibilities, and only thus could it have gained the central position it now occupies in modern metaphysical systems.

Of course, for us these particular contradictions do not exist. For we know that what is to be understood by 'place' will vary depending on whether we apply the word to the mental, which is immediately given, or to the objective world. In the first case, it denotes an intuitive datum; in the second, a position in a non-intuitive ordering. In this situation, no conflicts can arise, as far as we are concerned. But only if we learn to make this distinction can they be avoided. Yet it is all too easy for philosophical reflection, without noticing it, to slip into a position from which this important difference appears to have been transcended. The contradictions of localization then become insurmountable and the psychophysical problem unsolvable.

In trying to localize the mental, we get off at once to a false start if, with natural science, we focus on the spatial conditions under which sensations come about. Then we see a bridge of physical processes erected between the material object of perception and the sense organ, and between the latter and the cerebral cortex. Mechanical vibrations from a plucked string enter my ear, and from there an impulse is sent along the nerves to the hearing center of the brain. The result is that we are led to regard the excitation of the brain as the immediate condition for the experience "sensation", and this in turn misleads us into lodging the experience in the brain and thus in the spatial interior of the human body. And if we also — perhaps not explicitly — locate the sense qualities themselves in the cerebral cortex, we then, without being very clear about the details, usually go on to suppose that the mental dwells somewhere within the head of our fellow men, that consciousness is situated *in* the body.

In doing this, we commit the grave error against which Avenarius warned most emphatically and which he termed *introjection*. Once this error is committed, the road is closed to the solution of the psychophysical problem. The sensible qualities are located at the wrong place, and the contradictions described above can never be overcome.

Avenarius gave the clearest characterization of this fundamental error, and fought it most energetically. According to him, introjection is eliminated if we in our own deliberations return to the starting-point of reflection. A mental quality is something that is immediately given, simply experienced; hence reflection cannot be a prerequisite for determining just where the mental quality is situated. The whiteness of the paper before me has never been in my head. Every attempt to locate it anywhere except out there at the spot where I see it is bound to fail. It *is* there, it is to be found there; this is a directly experienced fact, and facts of consciousness cannot be explained away. To assert that whiteness was really first experienced in my brain and then "projected outside" is even more nonsensical than to assert that a toothache is actually felt as a headache and then projected into the tooth.

Clearly, as far as Avenarius is concerned, the sensible qualities win the struggle for the possession of space. For him, as for Mach, it is the familiar "elements" that in their variegated multiplicity fill up space and agglomerate into bodies and "I-complexes" (see § 25). Obviously, it does not make any sense at all to look for a place for consiousness among the elements, since they themselves all belong to consciousness (although Avenarius avoids this term whenever possible). The outcome had to be just this because the sensible qualities have the prior, directly given and indisputable claim to space. On the other hand, physical objects, atoms, and the like are not things of the same immediacy. We arrive at them only through inferences or intellectual constructions, which admit of the possibility of being so modified that their claims do not come into conflict with the absolutely undeniable claims of the "elements". To be sure, the Mach-Avenarius philosophy did not examine the claims of the physical objects with the same acuteness and energy it displayed in establishing the compelling character of the claims of the elements. Hence, as we showed above (§ 25), this philosophy was unable to clear up the situation. Avenarius was able to avoid confusing intuitive space with the objective ordering of things because he denied the existence of the latter altogether. But before him, a great thinker — Kant — had already understood how to avoid the error of introjection without being obliged to strike out along such a radical path.

On closer examination we see that Kant determines the relationship of consciousness to space in exactly the same way as does Avenarius. Like the latter, Kant sides with the mental qualities in the battle over space. He does so through his doctrine (with which we agree) of the subjectivity or "ideality" of space. According to this doctrine, space — here, as we know, this means intuitive spatiality — is not something that exists beyond consciousness; it is something connected with our intuitive representations. Spatially determined objects are not things-in-themselves, but representations of my consciousness, or, as Kant unfortunately calls them, "appearances". Thus from Kant's standpoint too, it is nonsense to seek a spatial position for the mind. The mental is not located in a man's head; rather, a head is itself only a representation in consciousness. Introjection is thus overcome *de facto*. Kant rejects as untenable the distinction, characteristic of introjection, between a perceived intuitive body outside the mind and the perceptual image within the mind. For him, as for Avenarius, the two are one and the same.

In view of the zeal with which differences of philosophical systems are commonly emphasized, it seems very important to me to stress their agreement wherever it may be found, especially when it concerns two viewpoints of such outstanding historical significance as the criticist philosophy and the positivism of Mach and Avenarius.

The orientation and terminology of the two systems are of course so different that they must first be divested of their outer garb before we can discern their complete internal accord on the points under discussion.

According to Kant, the objects of the intuitive world are "appearances", representations, contents of consciousness. Avenarius would have totally rejected these designations. Like us, he does not use the concept of "appearance", and therefore has no need to introduce the concept of the ideality of space. He expressly rejects, as a starting point, the "idealistic" view that whatever is given belongs from the outset to a subject and is thus perceived as subjective (see, for example, Der menschliche Weltbegriff, 2nd edition, p. IX). He avoids introjection through a cautious description of the given. Kant, on the other hand, eliminates introjection by subsequently correcting a world view already influenced by scientific thinking, and therefore arrives at somewhat different formulations. Basically, however, the two thinkers surely do not mean anything different when one speaks of environment-components, the other of appearances, as being images in consciousness. The role they accord these things in their overall picture of the world is of course different in the two cases; but the meaning is the same, so that what we have here is only a difference in terminology. When we designate the whiteness of the paper as mental or as a content of consciousness because we have experienced it, Avenarius could have no objection. At most he would say that the terminology is inappropriate because of the ideas so readily associated with it. Properly used, however, the terminology is not unsuitable at all, and has history on its side. Hence we also have used the terms 'immediately given', 'mental' and 'content of consciousness' as fully equivalent here.

Thus we may say: Kant brings space into consciousness. Avenarius extends consciousness over space.

These are merely different ways of expressing exactly the same thought — that the sphere of sensuous consciousness coincides with intuitive space. The relationship of the spatial to consciousness is, in both of these philosophers, identically the same.

Avenarius looked at the world through entirely different eyes than did Kant, and was probably not aware that in this instance he had traveled part way along the same road with him. That the two thinkers, despite the difference in their natural tendency, moved along the same path could hardly be explained unless it was the path to truth. And this is indeed the case. The only way to determine the relationship between space and consciousness is by gaining the insight that introjection is untenable; for in this context introjection is identical with the doctrine of the subjectivity of space or, to be more exact, intuitive spaces.

The positivists like to stress the contrast between their views and those of Kant, and habitually do not notice the significant agreement. It is therefore all the more worth emphasizing that in Petzoldt we find a correct insight into the identity between Kant's theory of space and the empirio-critical barring of introjection. Among other things, Petzoldt says of Kant: "He, however, makes a clean sweep of that barbarous *quid pro quo* that permits psychological sensations to enter the brain along with physiological stimuli — sensations which must then, of course, be shifted outside again [42]."

The elimination, or rather the avoiding, of introjection is a necessary condition for the solution of the psychophysical problem. But, as our critique of Avenarius' world picture has already indicated, it is not a *sufficient* condition for reaching a generally satisfactory view. Also the further elaboration of the Kantian system shows that new contradictions may arise in the mind-body problem even after we have come to know that consciousness cannot be localized in space, but that on the contrary space is located in consciousness.

To be sure, Kant himself thought that his view provided basically complete clarity. Thus in the first edition of the Kritik der reinen Vernunft (Kehrbach edition, p. 329, A 391), he says: "... all the difficulties regarding the connection of thinking nature with matter arise without exception from allowing the dualistic view to creep in, that matter as such is not appearance, i.e., a mere mental image ... but is the object itself, just as it exists outside of us and independently of all sensibility." For Kant there can be no talk of interaction between spatial objects and consciousness. We need only reflect that bodies "are not something outside of us, but merely representations within us; the situation therefore is not that the motion of matter produces representations in us, but that matter

42 Das Weltproblem vom positivistischen Standpunkt aus, 1st edition, 1906, p. 163.

itself is a mere representation" (*ibid.*, p. 326, A 387). Natural bodies, such as my own body, my nervous system and brain, all interact with one another; but then the causal chain is closed. These bodies do not act on my consciousness, for they are all only "appearances", that is, modifications of this consciousness itself. Thus the qualities of sensations are not produced in consciousness by the action of bodies and then projected out upon those bodies by consciousness. These qualities belong to the bodies from the outset; they are at precisely the places where they are perceived or experienced. Hence they belong to consciousness, since whatever is spatial belongs, as representation, to consciousness.

Thus far everything appears to be in good order. We seem to have avoided the awesome contradictions that beset the problem. The "secondary qualities" are situated in the intuitive space of the consciousness that perceived them. But the thing-in-itself, which according to Kant's theory corresponds to the perceived body, is non-spatial. Kant no doubt assumed that an objective ordering of the things-in-themselves corresponds exactly to the subjective spatio-temporal ordering of "appearances" (see § 27). Thus he distinguishes quite clearly between intuitive spatiality and the transcendent ordering. But he fails to mark off from one another the intuitive spaces of the various senses and instead constantly speaks of "the" space, which he then pronounces to be a form of the intuition. Yet when we move on from the spaces of the senses to the construction of the *one* space of physical bodies, the latter is no longer something intuitive. It is only a concept, which designates the transcendent ordering of the real. The Kantian notion of a *single* intuitive space is therefore an impossibility. And it was inevitable that the contradictions, which happily had been avoided up to that point, would again slip into the system through the gateway of this incorrect concept. On this basis, it is impossible to obtain a satisfactory definition of the physical. As the passages cited above indicate, he designates matter as appearance, and thus as mere representation, because it has spatial properties and spatiality is a property of intuitions or representations. But the truth of the matter is that physical objects — the objects dealt with by physics — are non-intuitive; they are divested of all secondary qualities and of spatiality. For these latter all vary with the observer, they change with the angle of vision, the position, the lighting. But a physical object is the identical object that is independent of all such variation and is that to which these different perceptions are related. It does not possess intuitive spatiality. It is not a representation, but a thing designated by a non-intuitive concept. Inasmuch as the realm of physical objects, according to Kant, must in turn find its place in intuitive space, the earlier conflicts reappear. The road to a definitive solution of the problem is blocked. For now the sense qualities again move into the space belonging to matter, to bodies. And, as we know, the claims of the physical and the mental are absolutely incompatible with one another. Thus in Kant too we still find that self-contradictory definition of the physical which is responsible for the mind-body problem. Physical bodies are quite certainly *not* realities in intuitive space.

From every direction then, we find ourselves led back to the result we have already reached: by 'physical' we must understand not a special kind of reality, but a particular *mode of designating* reality.

But if this way of designating is applicable to all that is real, then it is also applicable to the mental. Hence if there is any correlation at all, as is needed for knowledge, it must necessarily represent a parallelism. Under these circumstances, there is no sense whatsoever in speaking of a psychophysical interaction, although of course mental events do depend causally on events we call physical, and *vice versa*. But we are equally justified in calling mental events physical, and so the interaction is a physical one like any other; it would be unwarranted and misleading to give it a special name. On the other hand, the expression 'psychophysical parallelism' is entirely suitable for characterizing our view that one and the same reality — namely, that which is immediately experienced — can be designated both by psychological concepts and by physical ones.

All systems that have been refined through epistemological insights have therefore almost instinctively rejected the notion of interaction, even though at the time they lacked a correct understanding of why it is impossible. In the case of Spinoza and Leibniz, the parallelism is still metaphysical, as it is for Kant. In Kant, mental structures are only one variety of "appearances", namely, those of the "inner sense"; we must assume, consistently with his system, that one and the same thing-in-itself can "appear" both to the outer and to the inner sense, that is, both as physical and as mental.

It is instructive to consider Mach's position on the question of parallelism. He held that an "element" is to be counted either as

physical or as mental depending on the context in which it is studied. The law-governed dependency by virtue of which an element
belongs to a "body" is entirely different from that which is the
basis for an element belonging to a certain "self". Between these
two sets of dependencies a precise correspondence is supposed to
hold: to the law-governed succession of elements making up the
course of my experiences there is said to correspond a succession
of definite elements out of which my "brain" is put together for
some observer who could perceive this brain in all of its detail.
It is in this sense that MACH speaks of the principle of the "complete
parallelism of the mental and the physical" as being "almost self-
evident" (Analyse der Empfindungen, 5th edition, p. 51). But from
our vantage point, we recognize that this correlation is not paral-
lelistic in character, but causal (see above, end of § 32). For, the
perceptions that an observer has while investigating my brain processes are real mental magnitudes, just like my own inner life that
I experience during this investigation. Between these two series of
real processes there undoubtedly exists a dependency that we call
causal. The perceptions of the imaginary brain observer are conditioned by my own experiences. They are the *effects* of these experiences, just as much as the sensation of pain in the cheek of someone whose face has been slapped is an effect of the feelings of anger
in the mind of his assailant. In both cases, of course, the effects are
indirect; that is, they are mediated by intervening real magnitudes
(objective qualities).

In order to free our viewpoint of any remaining unclarities or
misunderstandings — experience shows how easily they creep in —
it is useful to go over once more the entire set of relationships under
discussion with the help of an illustrative example. Imagine an individual A who is looking at, say, a red flower and thus has the
experience "red" in his consciousness. At the same time, a second
individual B observes A's brain through an opening in A's skull.
Assume that B has at his disposal enough knowledge and sufficiently fine means of observation to be able to follow in the smallest and most exact detail those processes that occur in A's brain
when and only when A is looking at the red flower.

The various realities and concepts involved here are the following:

To begin with, there is a thing-in-itself called 'flower', with
which we can never be directly acquainted but which we can easily

come to know and then designate by means of concepts from the natural sciences — botanical concepts that describe the structure and form of the flower in objective space, and physical concepts in so far as we correlate with the thing "flower" the concept of a system of innumerable molecules, electrons, or the like.

A second reality is *A*'s experience, which we designate by means of the psychological concept "red" and which is real in itself in the same sense that the transcendent object "flower" is real. This second reality can be described therefore by physical concepts just as the flower was, and this is what happens with the aid of *B*'s observations. It turns out on the basis of *B*'s experiences that the very same entity that *A* labels 'red' can be designated by the physical concept "brain process of *A*".

As a third reality that enters the situation, we have *B*'s visual experiences, those colors and shapes that are present in *B*'s visual field while he is looking into *A*'s brain, say, with a microscope. To the various parts of this experienced reality *B* will attach such psychological names as 'gray', 'round', 'dark', and so forth. At the same time, however, he will know that he can, with equal justification, also apply to them certain physical conceptualizations, such as "processes in the complex of molecules constituting the thing I call 'my brain'".

The relationship here of these three realities and of the concepts correlated with them seems perfectly clear. And it might border on the incomprehensible that such a relationship could appear at all problematical and lend momentum to the "psychophysical question". The blame for this falls on certain odd confusions in consequence of which the reality designated by a concept is conflated with the concept itself and in turn the concept is conflated with its intuitive representatives, thus with other realities. First, the physical concept "process in *A*'s brain" is conflated with the reality itself that is designated by this concept, and we have two realities instead of one; that is, in addition to the experience of red in *A*'s consciousness we have the physical process in *A*'s brain. Then we conclude that the two must either "run parallel" or interact. But the fact of the matter is that only *one* reality is present, a reality that at one time is designated directly by the expression 'experience of red' and at another indirectly with the help of physical concepts.

But this is not all. We go on to confuse these same physical concepts with a quite different reality, namely, the real experience of B who is observing A's brain. When we say to ourselves "B actually does see A's brain", we treat the intuitive images in B's consciousness as though they themselves were the physical object "A's brain" and as though in these images the properties of the transcendent thing "A's brain" had been directly "grasped". But the truth is that the experiences of B, the images that are the content of his consciousness, are only the intuitive representatives that in his own consciousness stand in place of the abstract concept of the physical body "A's brain". These experiences become representatives (proxy representations) of this abstract concept because in their totality they actually were the occasion for the formation of the concept. There is no closer relationship between them. To us it makes no sense to designate B's visual experiences as "appearances" of the thing "A's brain". It would also be misleading to speak of A's experience as an "appearance" of the flower. Rather, the flower, the content of A's consciousness (called the "perception of the flower"), and the content of B's consciousness (called the "perception of A's brain") are all realities of the same rank. Between them there exists a relation of indirect causality, that is, a causality mediated by connecting links. For surely the processes in the object "flower" must be regarded as participating causes of A's experience of red, and this experience in turn is a cause of B's content of consciousness, since the observations that B makes of A's brain depend on the contents present to A's consciousness. If we designate all the realities that play a part in this entire process by physical concepts, we obtain an uninterrupted causal physical chain: effects (light rays) proceed from the flower, reach A's eyes and are conducted by nerves from his retina to his brain. From the brain further effects (light rays, again) extend out to B's eyes and from them quickly arrive at B's brain. In principle, this causal chain is fully accessible to our cognition; but there is *direct acquaintance* only with individual links of the chain, on the part of A with individual links in the middle of the chain, on the part of B with the terminal members. As to the links known by *acquaintance,* there is a parallelism in the mode of designation: they can be correlated with psychological as well as with physical concepts. But between the links themselves — between these real processes in the world — what exists is not a parallelism but a causal relationship.

We shall not seek to elucidate and confirm these ideas further by comparing them with the formulations of prominent thinkers.

It should be clear by now that our own path has led us to a basically simple view defensible in every respect. There is only one aspect that needs a somewhat strengthened defense and we shall treat it in the next section.

§ 34. Objections to Parallelism

As we know, the doctrine of parallelism in contemporary philosophy has been combatted on many fronts. Due to the influence of a number of important thinkers who embrace the doctrine of interaction, parallelism has been forced out of the dominant position it long occupied. Now we know that once we agree about the true character of the concept of the physical, all interaction is certainly ruled out. But we can of course seek to retain the notion of interaction if by 'physical' we wish to understand something *different*. This in fact is what is done by the supporters of the notion, often without expressing themselves clearly about the concept of the physical on which they base themselves. For this reason, if for no other, it is useful to examine their arguments; their presuppositions are thus more readily revealed. If we are then able to show that these assumptions are unproved, the attacks on parallelism will have been repulsed and the theory made the more secure.

In discussing the various arguments against parallelism, we are not concerned with those aimed at its metaphysical forms — at the doctrine that body and mind are two different "modes of appearance" of one and the same thing-in-itself, or the view that there are two quite independent realms of reality between which there nonetheless exists a preestablished harmony. Among the arguments put forward by advocates of interaction, however, are some to the effect that a thoroughgoing correlation of quantitative concepts with mental qualities is absolutely impossible. Such arguments would rule out precisely that which we have recognized as *necessary* for an exact knowledge of the processes of consciousness.

Against the reduction of psychology to brain physiology — this indeed is what the demand made by our parallelism comes to — it has been argued that no physiological theory can give a satisfactory account of even the simplest mental law-like regularities. (The keenest arguments along these lines have been advanced by E. BECHER, especially in his book Gehirn und Seele, 1911. Somewhat

similar misgivings have been expressed by VON KRIES in his Über
die materiellen Grundlagen der Bewußtseinserscheinungen, 1901. He,
however, does not regard these objections as insuperable, and has
worked in the direction of overcoming them.)

All physiological hypotheses start from sense perception as the
most important source of mental life in general. In perception, nerve
stimuli are conducted from a sense organ (say, the retina of the
eye) to a central organ (say, the visual area of the cerebral cortex).
After they fade away they leave behind certain traces, residues or
dispositions that are utilized to explain memory images and association. The various residues are bound to one another by "threads of
association"; and if one of the residues is stimulated, then under certain conditions the stimulus radiates out through the threads to
other residues, is communicated to them, and in response to this
latter physical process there is a revival in consciousness of the representations that correspond to these traces in the brain. For example,
when I look at a portrait of a friend, certain cells in my optic center
are activated. A connection is set up with other centers, such as the
acoustical, and residues are aroused there that correspond to the
tonal image of the name of that friend. His name rises to the surface
of my consciousness.

Yet even in the case of a process of such seeming simplicity, as
soon as we try to construct an exact picture of it that will fit the
empirical facts, we run up against enormous difficulties. Let us take
note of a few of them. For one thing, it is difficult to imagine even
the nature and location of the residues. When I look at a friend
from afar, the retinal image in my eye is small and from there
a certain part of my brain is stimulated. If I see him at closer range,
larger and other parts of my brain are activated. For nerve fibres
also lead from other points on the retina to other ganglion cells of
the visual apparatus. Thus the memory traces in the two cases will
be different. Any good friend, however, I have seen not only at two
different times but in thousands of different situations and at all
sorts of distances. There is not the tiniest area of my retina on which
his image has not already been projected. Hence the entire visual
domain has participated in forming the optical memory residue,
and each cell, moreover, in a thousand different ways corresponding
to the large number of perceptions in which it was active. Obviously
there can be no thought of localizing the memory trace at some
narrowly bounded place in the sensory domain (much less in a single

cell, as was still supposed some decades ago). And if we reflect —
to stay with optical memory images — that it is the same cells
again that participate in *all* other visual perceptions and consequently in the formation of all other visual residues, we see at once
that the physiological hypothesis roughly sketched above is totally
unsuited to convey knowledge of mental law-like regularities. It
assumes the existence of residues that are bound together by
"smoothed out" pathways and yet are spatially separated. However, it cannot make intelligible how such a separation might come
about. As our discussion has shown, residues are necessarily super-
imposed on one another. They must mingle with and dissolve into
one another, since they vie with each other for a place in the corresponding area of the brain.

The difficulties are further aggravated when we try to give an
account of how it is possible for the residues individually to be ex-
cited in a quite different order from the one in which they were
formed, and when we try to examine more closely the physiology
of perceiving and imagining. (An example is the role played by
what are called *Gestalt*-qualities.) And this is not to mention the
difficulties involved in giving an account of the higher mental functions, such as abstraction, logical thinking, and fantasy.

Thus as ordinarily formulated, physiological hypotheses are unable to provide an explanation for mental events. Some thinkers
have therefore concluded that at the point where it fails, the physiological theory must be replaced with a mentalistic theory. In other
words, we must revert to the assumption that the mental, the mind,
is a reality of a *special kind*. This reality resists description by the
spatio-quantitative concepts of natural science and has its own
peculiar law-like regularity, which we know from experience as
"psychological".

According to this conception, the contrast between physical and
mental designates a difference that is essentially *real*. The "physical"
is that reality whose nature can be described by quantitative concepts. The "mental" is that reality for which this is not the case.
Thus here the two concepts take on another sense. This new definition *could* coincide with the distinction we made earlier between
objective and subjective qualities (which may also be expressed as
the distinction between the extramental and the mental). But this
is not the case if one assumes, as most of these thinkers do, that
there is such a thing as *unconscious* mental being. For the property

of belonging to a consciousness is the characteristic, necessary feature of the reality that we designated above as subjective or mental. In our view, whatever is unconscious is as such extramental or objective, and cannot be called subjective or mental; but an unconscious mental being is quite compatible with the conception under discussion, it does not contradict the definition of the mental that forms part of the conception. Under the new definition of the concepts, the notion of an interaction between mind and body is not only meaningful, it must even be asserted as necessary. This is the position taken by the representatives of the conception, and in so doing they are thoroughly consistent. One may then speak without contradiction of a psycho-"physical" interaction; but notice that the word 'physical' here is used with a different meaning than in ordinary speech. For what it denotes is not the bodily, the intuitively extended, but a class of things-in-themselves, of transcendent qualities. In judging this doctrine, we must always keep in mind that in the modern theory of interaction the word 'physical' must be used in this quite distinct and different sense — if we are not to come to grief on the contradictions of the mind-body problem.

From what has gone before, it is already clear why a theory of interaction according to which two kinds of real being exist cannot but remain unsatisfactory. The two kinds of reality are supposed to differ in that only one of them can be subjected to the rule of quantity, of physics. But the applicability of physical concepts, we found, is a postulate that must be fulfilled if complete knowledge is to be possible at all. Thus this interaction doctrine excludes the possibility of reducing psychological laws to other laws of nature and thereby sets up in advance a certain limit beyond which knowledge cannot go.

A further drawback is that the doctrine does not yield any serviceable working hypotheses. For it is not based on a specific hypothesis about the nature of mind, from which the facts of mental life may then be unequivocally derived. On the contrary, it is content with the statement that what constitutes the special nature of the mental is precisely that its processes take place in just the way in which we are acquainted with them and not otherwise. We are obliged to ascribe to the mind all the necessary properties without being able to give an exact account of their interrelationship: the mind possesses the capability of having and processing perceptions, of retaining residues, and of connecting them and reviving them in representations; yet we lack any hypothesis by means of which this manifold might be unified. If we desired and were able to set up such an hypothesis, who would guarantee that we would not then encounter difficulties as great as, or even greater than, those that confronted us in the case of the physiological theory cited above?

The whole doctrine of interaction stands or falls with the proof that the qualities given in consciousness actually differ from the non-given, "physical" qualities in that there is no possible way of correlating them uniquely with a system of quantitative concepts. But has such a proof been presented? Has it been demonstrated that there is any being that does not fall under the definition of the physical upon which this doctrine is implicitly based? Or does the possibility remain that the *whole* of being, without exception, may be described with the aid of physical concepts?

It is my conviction that such a possibility does in fact exist. The objections we have considered do not establish in general and in principle the absurdity of every physiological theory of consciousness.

Of course, the mentalistic hypothesis must also recognize the part played by the brain in the occurrence of mental processes. For it is a fact of experience that certain mental disturbances are conditioned by particular disturbances in the brain. According to the theory of interaction, the mind must act on parts of the brain, and *vice versa*. And the points where these influences take effect must be located somewhere in these parts; exactly where, remains a matter for physiological theory. In any event, therefore, we do need a physiological theory; and it would be methodologically absurd if we did not seek to make do with it alone and instead declared that a mentalistic hypothesis is necessary, before it had been conclusively proved that a physiological hypothesis was impossible. But no such proof exists. For the objections discussed above show only the inadequacy of the attempts made thus far to formulate a physiological hypothesis; they cannot establish that a physiological — in the final analysis, physical — explanation is in principle impossible. There is no general principle on which to base such an impossibility proof. On the contrary, it seems entirely conceivable that we might, with the aid of a "physical" system, produce results that are fully analogous to the processes of consciousness considered above. We can imagine a gramophone or a moving picture machine so perfected by vastly complicated arrangements that it can reproduce received impressions in a fashion comparable to the performance of memory, and fall no more short than would conform to the difference between the plasticity of living matter as compared with the rigidity of the materials out of which we usually construct our physical apparatus.

It is obviously no ground for objection that we do not know of any structure in the brain externally resembling such an apparatus. For what is at issue here is the underlying principle — that of the transformation of temporal succession into spatial juxtaposition — which can operate in the one case as well as in the other. It was this fundamental principle that R. SEMON, in particular, recognized as the necessary basis for psychophysical theories and termed the principle of "chronogenic localization" (in his Die Mneme als erhaltendes Prinzip im Wechsel des organischen Geschehens and Die mnemischen Empfindungen). It seems methodologically unwise to attempt to construct any special hypothesis so long as we lack a positive foundation in the form of exact knowledge of the processes taking place in the ganglion cells of the central nervous system. What is of concern to our epistemological inquiry is not whether some particular theory is correct but whether a theory is *possible* at all.

We have all the more ground to assert the possibility of a physiological theory of mental processes since we can already give certain positive indications concerning the path leading to it. We pointed out above (§ 4) that what is really characteristic of a perception or a representation, what forms the content of a memory residue, is not some part or detail of the representation but primarily its "*Gestalt*-quality". For example, what is recalled ordinarily are not the single notes, but the melody which is composed of them and which is a specific property of the whole that consists of the individual notes. In order then to find a physiological theory of mental processes that will do justice to their special character, we would have to investigate whether the "physical" brain processes also possess *Gestalt*-peculiarities; and it is among these that the physiological correlates of the representations and other mental processes would have to be found. This is the path that WOLFGANG KOEHLER has taken (see his Die physischen Gestalten, 1921) and his conception promises to be fruitful in detailed applications as well. His view of the psychophysical problem, I am especially happy to say, seems not to deviate from the one presented here (see W. KOEHLER, Bemerkungen zum Leib-Seele-Problem, Deutsche Medizinische Wochen-schrift, 1924, Number 38).

The arguments against parallelism discussed thus far were reject-ed because they did not get down to basic principles. We must therefore pay all the more attention to two other arguments, which from the very outset involve matters of principle.

Both proceed by comparing the manifold of mental reality with that of the physical conceptual system and both find the two do-mains incommensurable.

The first objection stresses the *simplicity* of many experiences and contrasts this with the complicated character of the correlated physical processes. When I hear a simple tone, this is an absolutely unified sensation that cannot be further broken down. It is impos-sible to distinguish any parts in it or to exhibit any elementary ex-periences of which the sound might perhaps be a composite. It is an ultimate, indivisible *element* of mental life. On the other hand, its physiological correlate — in our terminology, the scientific con-cept correlated with it — is apparently extremely complex. The physical processes, and the substance in which they occur, are enormously complicated. From among the innumerable cells of which the brain is composed, a goodly number go into action when a sensation takes place. The living substance of each of them, as we know, contains many millions of molecules, each protein mole-cule hundreds of atoms, which in turn break down into still smaller particles, the electrons. All of these particles are undoubtedly *real*, that is, the concept of an atom or of an electron designates a com-plex of real qualities. And now the concept of a brain process, in which so many complexes of qualities take part, is supposed to designate a single quality, namely, this simple sound! Is this not a truly unsolvable contradiction? This objection is so basic that there seems to be no escape from it.

Nevertheless I believe that a way out can be found, and in a very natural manner. All we need do is keep in mind what we ac-tually know about the processes under discussion. and how much latitude there is for physiological hypotheses. We know very well that innumerable ganglion cells, each consisting of innumerable mole-cules, are active in any sensory process. But we do not know *which* process is to be associated with a simple sensation as its physical correlate. Certainly the correlate is not the total brain process, but only some part of it. Which part we cannot of course say, since we are not sufficiently cognizant of the process as a whole. Thus it may be a very small partial process, one that is extremely simple. The most we can conclude from the objection we are examining is that the process *must* indeed be a quite simple one. Only that sort of process, and not one extending over rather large parts of the brain, can be used as a sign for the simple quality of a sound sensation. We have had to assume that the complicated total process in the brain is necessary in order to bring forth that simple quality in precisely the right way and in the right relationship; but the quality itself can be as elementary and indivisible as one may wish.

It seems to me that the objection is thus stripped of all its force. But we can bring into play even heavier weapons, supplied in earlier sections, and refute the basic argument with one equally basic. We saw above (§ 31) that the essence of scientific knowledge lies in correlating a system of concepts with the aid of which the manifold qualities of the world can be reduced to one another. But we expressly pointed out that in principle the choice of the ultimate elements that serve as building blocks for the system of concepts is arbitrary, and that as a consequence the concepts "simple" and "composite" are fully relativized. A unique designation of the world is possible in terms of arbitrarily many different conceptual systems, and what appears in one system as an ultimate element will be described in another by an intricate combination of concepts. Now the number of simple mental qualities is infinite, whereas the number of simple concepts in our system of knowledge is quite small, for it is in the nature of knowledge that this number be kept to a minimum. Once the elementary concepts for certain qualities, or combinations of qualities, are assigned, then the remaining qualities must necessarily be designated by means of composite concepts. And none of this leads to any contradiction.

It has been argued that brain processes consist in rearrangements of atoms and electrons, and thus in the movements of constant or invariable magnitudes (E. BECHER, Zeitschrift für Philosophie und philosophische Kritik, Vol. 161, pp. 65 ff.). Hence, by the basic principle of parallelism, mental experiences also cannot be anything other than transitory processes in relatively enduring objects. For the processes in the brain particles are not separable *realiter* from the brain particles themselves. The *motion of an atom* and an *atom in motion* can be divorced from one another only in abstraction; they are not different things but a unity, just as a sound and the intensity of the sound are a unity. It is therefore impossible, or nonsensical, to assume that what corresponds to mental being is a motion but not that which moves; rather the "movement of the particles" must be explained as a conceptual sign for a unitary mental entity. If the inner life is the reality with which the concept of a brain event is correlated, then it is at the same time the reality that is designated by the concept of a brain substance. But this contradicts experience altogether. Consciousness cannot be the essential nature of brain particles, for the latter may persist where the former is lacking (as in sleep or death). The life of consciousness does not itself meet the above requirements at all: mental qualities are not experienced as transitory modifications of a constant mental being. A sensation does not present itself in consciousness as a changing state of something that endures; on the contrary, it appears and disappears in relative independence.

This argument, however, fails to touch our conception. It presupposes a concept of substance that we must regard as incorrectly formed and that accordingly has no place in our view. For what is brain substance? What is a material particle? The reality we designate by means of this concept is — as we established earlier (§ 31) — an interrelationship, a unity, of changing qualities and not a sum of constant qualities. If we keep this in mind, one thing becomes clear: we have no right whatsoever to conclude that if a process in an atom is to serve as a sign for something mental, the atom itself must also be mental. The process may indeed correspond to a certain mental quality without our having to claim that the numerous other qualities connected with it, and belonging with it to the same complexes, are also mental. Here we must be on guard against the narrow preconceptions that attach themselves to familiar pictures or images. What is required is only unambiguous correlation. For the rest, things that belong together in mental reality may in a physical sign system be separated; and *vice versa,* things that are united in the world of qualities may be quite far apart in the conceptual representation. The mental elements out of which the I-complex is built may belong to entirely disparate physical complexes. And the elements that are brought together into a complex by a physical sign need not stand in any relationship in consciousness to one another: if one of them is mental, the others need not on that account also be mental.

But there is no point in speculating further about the possibilities nor in depicting any particular hypotheses in greater detail. We still lack any empirical basis on which to judge them so long as we know no more about the processes involved than is possible in the present state of research. Nothing more need or can be shown here than that the objections considered have certainly failed to demonstrate the impossibility of a physiological theory of mental life and hence of parallelism. The objections seem to hold only if we forget that in the case of physical concepts we are concerned with signs and nothing but signs. If we carefully guard against any false comparison of the signs with the reality designated by them, the apparent difficulties disappear and the probative force of the counter arguments dissolves into nothing.

A very tempting and ingenious comparison of this sort was made by Driesch and was regarded by him as an absolutely conclusive disproof of parallelism [43]. Like the arguments just discussed, it sets the manifold of the mental world against that of physical concepts. While the arguments we disposed of above rested on the notion that the concepts of physics are too complicated to be correlated with simple mental experiences, Driesch conversely points to the kaleidoscopic abundance of mental events, which can never be exhausted by the scanty conceptual world of physical processes. As he sees it, natural science in general does not have at its disposal enough concepts to provide an unambiguous correlation for all mental magnitudes. In physics there are only a few basic elements from which the whole of nature is constructed. These, according to Driesch, consist of positive and negative electrons and "ether atoms". All substances are composed of such elements and in the final analysis all events are nothing but motions of these three fundamental kinds of things, that is, spatio-temporal rearrangements of them. On the mental side, however, we have not three or four, but infinitely many qualitatively different basic structures. And we cannot believe that this endless multiplicity could possibly be equalled by the endless multiplicity of the spatio-temporal combinations on the physical side. For the latter would provide sufficient conceptual material just to designate the experiences of intuitive succession and juxtaposition. The spatio-temporal ordering of our representations corresponds to the objective ordering of things, and hence cannot correspond in

---

43 HANS DRIESCH, Seele und Leib, Leipzig 1916.

addition to the qualitative makeup of the representations. Therefore we, with our physical concepts, are quite helpless in the face of the infinitely richer multiplicity of the mental world.

Nevertheless, this apparently unassailable argument is unsound. It relies on a comparison between two infinite sets, and anyone versed in the matter knows how easy it is for fallacies to arise here. No one familiar with set theory will be deceived by the proof presented above. We shall disregard the objections that can be made against the quasi-mechanical startingpoint of Driesch's reasoning. (Modern physics no longer accepts the view that whatever happens is to be conceived of as mere motion, as the motion of electrons and ether.) Instead, we shall assume that the factual conditions to which the new idea is supposed to apply are in principle actually present, and then ask whether the conclusions that this prominent philosopher of science felt obliged to draw really do follow.

The fact is that these conclusions do not follow. This becomes clear if in the first place we reflect that the multiplicity of our experiences of juxtaposition and succession, on closer examination, is much more narrowly bounded than, and falls short of, the multiplicity of the possible arrangements and movements of physical things. We are apt to exaggerate the power of our imagination and to forget that the space perception threshold sets narrow bounds to the multiplicity of experiences. As difficult as it is for us actually to *represent intuitively* 1000 objects, just that easy is it to form the *concept* not only of 1000 objects but of 1000^{1000}. Very small as well as very large space and time intervals cannot be represented intuitively, nor can very fast or very slow movements. Concept formation, however, can proceed as far along these lines as we desire. In this respect therefore it is richer than the immediate experience of the ordering of representations and thus may be well suited as a source of material for designating mental qualities. But we shall not pursue these thoughts any further, since there is a second counter-argument more fundamental in character and fully decisive in its own right.

In the second place, then, it is impossible to prove, as Driesch tries to do, that the two sets under comparison — mental qualities on the one hand and physical concepts on the other — cannot be correlated with each other or, as the mathematician would say, are not of the same power. Driesch rests his proof on a showing that the one set is properly included in the other. Specifically, he argues that the set consisting of the physical domain is included in that of the mental, since the whole of the former corresponds only to a proper part of the latter, namely, spatio-temporal experiences. But as every mathematician knows, this argument proves nothing at all in the case of infinite sets. If I mark off a small part of a line segment, the part is completely contained in the whole. Yet, as can be proved quite rigorously, it is possible to set up a correspondence between the points of the part and those of the whole line such that to each of the infinitely many points of the whole there corresponds just one point of the part, and *vice versa*.

Someone might reply that the set of physical structures is related to the set of mental magnitudes not as a smaller segment to a larger one, but as a structure of fewer dimensions to one of a greater number. But this would not help; for set theory also shows that this too offers no obstacle to a one-to-one correlation. One of the "paradoxes" of infinity, yet rigorously provable, is that a part of a surface, say a square, can be "mapped" onto a line sigment even though the line (we may think of it as having been drawn inside the square) contains only an infinitely small portion of the points of the square — since I can, of course, draw within the square infinitely many other lines that have no point in common with the given line. Each point of the segment can be correlated with a point on the surface notwithstanding the fact that these are structures of different dimensionality. The mutual correspondence can be carried out quite unambiguously. (Here, to be sure, the correspondence cannot at the same time be *continuous,* or rather, if the mapping is continuous, it cannot at the same time be unambiguous. But as we have already suggested in our remarks directed against the previous objection, correlation does not involve continuity. It is not necessary that continuous transitions of the correlated physical structures correspond to continuous transitions of mental qualities, or *vice versa.*) And so, like all the others, this final attempt to prove that parallelism is impossible also fails

§ 35. Monism, Dualism, Pluralism

The result we have arrived at is to be welcomed in the interest of a unified, truly satisfactory world view. For the dualistic world picture put forward by the supporters of interaction necessarily carries with it the renunciation of complete knowledge of the world.

On that view, the universe divides into two realms. Only one of these, the "physical", is open to exact, quantitative concept formation; the other, the world of the mental, can never be made subject to such conceptualization. The concepts of the various mental magnitudes must always stand side by side; they do not admit of being derived from one another, since, as we verified above, such derivation can be achieved only by the quantitative method of natural science.

All the reasons offered in support of this two-fold division, and for the special position of mental qualities, we have found to be untenable.

The system of quantitative concepts furnishes us with a remarkable and unique means of knowing the world, so far as the latter is not given to us in *direct acquaintance*. And there is no reason to suppose that this system must fail in regard to the given world of qualities known by acquaintance. On the contrary, we believe that it is possible to apply it universally so long as there is no rigorous proof that we err in so believing. In science, it has never proved to be sound policy to surrender a belief of this sort too soon. Nothing harms inquiry so much as the pronouncing of an *ignorabimus*, and we must be on our guard against uttering one prematurely.

Thus we are thoroughly convinced that all the qualities of the universe — all being whatsoever — are of one kind in so far as they can be made accessible to knowledge by means of quantitative concepts. In this sense we embrace a monism. There is only *one* kind of reality, that is, we need in principle only *one* system of concepts to know all the things of the universe. And there do not exist in addition classes of things that this system does not fit.

Such a monism seems to me to be as comprehensive and far-reaching as reason's need for unity might desire. At the same time, it is the only kind of monism that can be arrived at by epistemologically refined thinking. It has all the useful features that made nineteenth century materialism so successful with a public which, unburdened by epistemological scruples, found satisfaction in materialism's strong drive toward a unified, closed world picture. And recently a revived materialism, under the more general name of monism, was hailed by the same kind of public and for the same reasons. These views attracted favor because they put their trust in the unlimited applicability of the quantitative mode of thought used by physics to gain knowledge of its world. This was a legitimate feature, which can and must be fully preserved even in a world view that has been subjected to the most rigorous of critiques. To have expressed this trust by the proposition "All that exists is matter" was of course naive, inadequate and philosophically erroneous. And the error was compounded by the acceptance of a completely uncritical concept of matter, with the result that materialism was incapable of seeing, much less solving, the simplest philosophical problems. This materialism, moreover, presupposed a kind of mechanistic explanation of the world which in the meantime had been abandoned by natural science itself.

Nevertheless there was a healthy tendency here, and all that had to be done was for the critic to remove the unhealthy part and set materialism on the right track. It is one of the great services of the Neo-Kantian schools to have undertaken this particular task; I refer especially to FRIEDRICH ALBERT LANGE and his excellent History of Materialism. The so-called Marburg School of Neo-Kantians, under the leadership of Hermann Cohen and Paul Natorp, also held to a correct view on at least this point. Let me cite a passage from NATORP's Allgemeine Psychologie (1912) that shows his agreement with the matters discussed in the previous section. He writes (p. 12): "But what then becomes of psychology? ... As far as what are involved are causal laws for so-called mental events, psychology becomes simply a careful, methodical, scientific inquiry into sensory and brain physiology, an inquiry that is not confused by any metaphysical prejudice."

It is only in the precisely circumscribed sense mentioned earlier that our outlook may be termed monistic. As a metaphysical view, however, monism in any of its well-known forms cannot withstand criticism. In this respect the counterpart to materialism — known as spiritualism or psychomonism — is no better situated. Where materialism claims that all that exists is matter, psychomonism believes itself justified in asserting that everything is of a spiritual or mental nature.

That such a viewpoint is untenable must already be clear from the considerations set forth in the preceding section. In earlier parts of our inquiry it may have appeared that our findings could be made to harmonize with spiritualist or psychomonist ideas. We repeatedly called attention to the fact that we cannot assume any basic difference in kind among the qualities of the world; rather, the division between given and non-given qualities, between the subjective and the objective, is accidental or contingent in character. What then is more plausible than to say that since the qualities with which we are directly acquainted are mental, and since they do not differ fundamentally from the qualities with which we are not directly acquainted, therefore these latter are also mental! In that case, everything in the world would as such be mental in character. Now my own consciousness offers me the sole possibility of being directly acquainted with qualities as they are in themselves, and there I find them to be mental magnitudes. But then, it seems, I must conclude that if I could be acquainted in the same way with the other qualities, I would come to know them too as mental. Thus I may assume that as such they are likewise mental, the same in kind as my sensations and feelings, differing perhaps in shading and gradation but still endowed with the special character of mental being.

This argument from analogy is so thoroughly plausible that the metaphysics to which it leads has always had numerous adherents, and its defenders may be found even among the outstanding thinkers of our time. It is the same argument by which Schopenhauer, for example, sought to prove that the true essence of all that exists is *will;* he believed that in everything immediately given he could find an experience of will as the characteristic feature of the mental.

Yet the psychomonist world view suffers from enormous deficiencies. The argument for it outlined above is open to the gravest objections. These objections become evident as soon as we try to make quite clear what it *means* to assert that all that is real is mental in character.

We have used the word 'mental' to designate everything that is immediately given, that is, everything that is connected to a unified consciousness. Does the thesis of spiritualism or psychomonism understand the term in the same sense? Does it wish to assert that there are no qualities in the world that are not connected to any consciousness? Obviously the thesis neither desires to do so nor can it; for if it did, its standpoint would be identical with that of the immanentists. As we recall, the immanence doctrine rests on quite different foundations (see above, §§ 25 and 26). For it *denies* any transcendent being. Spiritualism, on the contrary, requires such a being and seeks to explain it. Moreover, we know that not everything real is a content of consciousness. In earlier sections we learned the reasons why we cannot maintain that all being designated by means of natural scientific concepts is mental. For example, the essential reality *(das Ansich)* of a person's *total* brain cannot possibly consist in his mental life; the latter can be based only on certain limited, partial processes in the brain. In point of fact, the arguments of Becher discussed by us above were expressly directed against the spiritualist form of the doctrine of parallelism.

The only way out of its difficulties for psychomonism is to assume *ad hoc* the existence of consciousnesses not otherwise required by the facts of experience. For instance, since the brain processes in an unconscious individual cannot betoken the presence of a consciousness in the individual, the question arises: to whose consciousness do the realities designated by these processes belong? Here, of course, a spiritualist metaphysics can appeal for help to the notion of a "supraindividual" consciousness and assert that the magnitudes in question belong to the consciousness of some higher being, such as God. It may also ascribe to each living cell or material particle a spirit or mind of its own and thus locate those magnitudes in various subindividual consciousnesses. But obviously this is to plunge into a boundless stream of hypotheses that cannot in any way be justified. A conscientious investigator may infer the presence of a consciousness only where there are quite definite characteristic indications, in particular those we count as the signs of *life*. And even these alone do not suffice, as is shown by the example just cited.

The entire psychomonist doctrine rests on an argument from analogy. But if we wish to employ such an argument, we must actually conform to the analogy: we may assert the existence of another consciousness only where we find conditions analogous to those which, by experience, are bound up with our own consciousness. If we observe that our own consciousness disappears altogether when the nervous system is disturbed or damaged in certain ways, then how can we justify the assumption that a mental life exists where no nervous system is present? How can we view a planet or a stone or an electron as a conscious being? We cannot assume the existence of even the most elementary sensation if no organ analogous to our sense organs is present. True, the poetic prowess of a Fechner has painted the similarity between the forms and processes of organic and inorganic nature in so seductive a fashion as almost to provide grounds for boldly inferring the existence of atomic and stellar minds. But on closer inspection, this semblance disappears and we see before us not actual analogies but metaphors and similes with which science cannot accomplish anything. Although they are enjoyable as poetry, they cannot help us obtain new knowledge.

The spiritualist belief in the mental character of all that is thus turns out to be untenable if "mental" is identified with "conscious". Here the alternative for the psychomonist is to abandon the identity. He may then announce that his thesis is not refuted by the finding that not all reality is a content of consciousness; for anything that is not conscious is unconscious, and does not thereby cease to be mental.

But anyone who adopts this standpoint runs into the greatest difficulty when called on to answer the question: What *sense* then do you attach here to the word 'mental'? What does it mean to say of a quality that it is mental in character although unconscious? A psychomonist who speaks of the unconscious mental in this context obviously has in mind that the reality so designated is in some way like the reality of consciousness. Now we ourselves have unceasingly urged such a thought in so far as we have warned, time after time, against assuming a fundamental difference between the world of consciousness and the transcendent world. But is it a proper formulation of this insight if we say that transcendent being also is mental? I do not think so. For this would presuppose assigning to extra-conscious realities a quite special property which they would have in common with mental magnitudes and which at the same time would be a characteristic feature of the mental magnitudes. This common trait would constitute the sense of the word 'mental', and if we could not specify the trait, the word would lack any definite sense. But it is in fact impossible to determine in any positive way a qualitative similarity or mutuality between given conscious being and non-given extra-conscious being, to separate out of the concept of consciousness a specific feature that belongs in the same manner to the extra-conscious. For if we abstract consciousness from a content of consciousness, then we abstract the entire content; and we have no feature left over, still less one that would serve to characterize mental being. If we apply the word 'mental' as the psychomonist does, then we know only that the term is supposed to designate some property that belongs to all reality without exception. But we are unable to specify this property more precisely. Thus the "real" and the "mental" become interchangeable concepts; we gain nothing and express no new knowledge when we substitute the latter for the former.

In general, the great danger in any metaphysical monism is that it readily becomes a word behind which a philosophical truth only seems to lurk. When I proclaim that all being is fundamentally one, my statement has a meaningful ring. When I declare that the world, multiform as it may appear, is basically only *one,* my utterance seems to be as profound as the ἕν καὶ πᾶν of the Eleatics. Yet such general pronouncements, taken in themselves, are completely meaningless; a concept loses all sense if I broaden its scope to designate absolutely everything[44].

I have already said that the magic charm of spiritualism is more poetic than scientific in character. For what leads to the formulation of such a doctrine is not actually knowledge but intuition (see above § 12). In the final analysis, the wish to be acquainted with *(kennen)* extra-conscious reality, as we are directly acquainted with the conscious world, is father to the idea that this reality is mental in nature. We suppose that if an extra-conscious quality could be made directly accessible to our experience, that is, be immediately given, then we would have roughly the same experience as if a sensation or a feeling had appeared in our consciousness. Thus the quality would be something mental. We have emphasized many times that this wish for direct acquaintance stems not from the will to *know* but the will to *behold,* to *experience.* Thus it has nothing to do with science and philosophy. Moreover, since it is self-contradictory, it is of course impossible of fulfillment. To wish to know how the extra-conscious is experienced in consciousness is the same as asking what a color looks like if no one sees it, or how a tone sounds if no one hears it. It makes no sense to call something 'mental' that does not belong to the mind of any conscious being.

Thus the materialist and the spiritualist forms of the metaphysical doctrine of monism are equally untenable. All the more significant, then, is the epistemological monism at which we have arrived and which is expressed in the principle: "Whatever is real is open to designation by quantitative concepts." *This* homogeneity, which is asserted of all being, is no empty word; it has a definite testable meaning and signifies genuine *knowledge.* But such homogeneity is of no consequence so far as experience is concerned. As regards the kind and value of an experience, it makes no difference through which concepts it can be designated for the purposes of

---

44 PETZOLDT, in his Weltproblem, several times makes similar use of the principle that a concept becomes idle and meaningless if its extension is broadened to excess.

knowledge. Hence this monism provides no occasion for the sort
of controversy over questions of value that has raged so hotly in
connection with materialism.

In one respect, of course, dualism might still seem to stand un-
refuted. Mental qualities have that special relationship which, as
the interconnection of consciousness, has so often occupied us. And
in this way they are distinguished from all other qualities that do
not enter into such a relational bond. Does this not represent a dualism as to the relationship holding among the mental on the one
hand and among the nonmental on the other, and does this not
basically amount to the same thing as a dualism of being? But certainly involvement in such an interconnection is part of the "essence"
of mental reality. Individual mental qualities surely cannot be separated from the interconnection without their ceasing to be; they
have no existence outside of it (see above, § 17).

Now this interconnection is indeed something quite special. Since
the physiological correlates of mental magnitudes are not yet in any
instance completely known, science thus far does not possess quantitative concepts by which to designate the interconnection of these
magnitudes in consciousness. But once these concepts are found,
the unity of consciousness will be recognized as being only one of
many interconnections and will be reduced to them. The problem
of consciousness will then be solved. Until then, however, we need
to bear in mind that the unity of consciousness is unique for us
only because it coincides with the self, so that the difference between
this particular interconnection and all others amounts to the antithesis between subject and object, beween the I and the not-I. We
are *directly acquainted* only with the interconnection of the I; and
again it is meaningless to ask whether an interconnection of extra-
conscious qualities would turn out to be of the same kind *in case*
we were directly acquainted with it. For if this were the situation
we could experience it directly; it would then be a consciousness
interconnection, and not one of extra-conscious qualities. This desire to be directly acquainted with extra-conscious qualities is once
again an expression of the metaphysical need for intuition; it has no
connection with knowledge, and to gratify it would be of no help.
To know is not to make the external world into an inner world.

The antithesis between consciousness and the external world
certainly can be neither blurred nor abolished. But to acknowledge
it is not to erect a dualism between the kind of interconnection that

exists among the conscious and the kind that exists among the extra-conscious. Rather, it is to distinguish and single out the interconnection of consciousness from the multitude of other interconnnections exhibited by the world in all its abundance. Thus at most one may, if one wishes, speak of a *pluralism.*

In this sense, however, every sensible and philosophically honest world view must be pluralistic. For the universe *is* variegated and manifold, a fabric woven of many qualities no two of which are exactly alike. A formal metaphysical monism, with its principle that all being is in truth *one,* does not give an adequate account; it must of necessity be supplemented with some sort of pluralistic principle. Some place must be left for the truth that there are infinitely many varieties of qualities; for the world is not cold and monotonous but multiform and constantly changing. And if so many people have turned away from the gray world picture of materialism, they did so because they missed in it the pluralistic element. Materialism seemed to rob the world of that endless qualitative multiplicity which constitutes its most indubitable reality.

Both pluralism and monism, each in its own way, contain a part of the truth. It is only dualism from which no good can be extracted. A bifurcation of the world into physical and mental, essence and appearance, a realm of nature and a realm of mind, or whatever form the antithesis may take, can not be defended, can not be justified on scientific grounds. The diversity of being is not two-fold, but infinite. This is the truth in pluralism. But there is also some truth in monism: in a different sense everything is unified and homogeneous. Variegated reality is governed everywhere by the *same* laws. Otherwise it would not admit of being designated by the same concepts: it would not be knowable. To know is to find the one in the other, the same in the different. To the extent that the world is knowable, to that extent is it unified. The unity of the world can be shown only by the fact that it is knowable. It has no other meaning.

C. The Validity of Knowledge of Reality

The question of the validity of knowledge is usually said to be the characteristic problem of the discipline to which this book is devoted. Why is it, then, that this question, which should have been placed at the very beginning of our inquiry, is first accorded due recognition in the title to the final section? Has everything that went before been merely a preliminary?

The fact is that the preceding developments already contain in essence the answer to the question of validity. To speak of "valid" knowledge is basically a pleonasm. Knowledge that is not valid is not knowledge but error. When we succeed in ascertaining the essence of and the approaches to knowledge, we also know what valid or true knowledge is and under what conditions it comes into being.

We have traced the processes by which knowledge of reality is obtained in science and, as we hope, we ourselves have thereby obtained knowledge. How certain is the ground over which we have traveled in so doing? Assuming that they follow their normal course, do these processes always lead to absolute truth? Or, can the most certain judgments about reality lay claim only to probability? And then how great is this probability? What are we to understand by this concept, which we have not yet dealt with explicitly and hence have not yet studied in its relationship to truth? Does our knowledge have an absolute validity, or is it valid only for humankind since it is the product of human intellectual activity?

The answers to these questions must already be contained in the investigations we have carried out. For, as we said above, every proposition about knowledge is at the same time a proposition about the validity of knowledge. To be valid is to be true; therefore we should be able, from what we have determined about truth, to derive whatever there is to say about validity. Thus if we go back and review these findings, it will be possible to reach the solutions obtainable from our vantage point by the easiest and shortest paths.

§ 36. Thinking and Being

We may regard the question of validity as settled for one class of judgments, namely, *analytic* judgments. They formed the real subject matter of the second part of our inquiry. Since an analytic judgment asserts of an object only what is contained in the definition of the object, it therefore correlates with the object a sign that by agreement is fixed as a sign for that object. It provides a unique correlation in conformity with the definition of uniqueness, and is thus absolutely *true*. The proposition "Analytic judgments are absolutely valid" is itself an analytic judgment. Such judgments have nothing whatever to do with *knowledge* of reality, and may therefore be completely separated from it. Their realm is that of thinking, not of being.

While analytic judgments contain no *knowledge* of reality, for that very reason they nevertheless hold for reality. This circumstance has given rise to a misunderstanding, a pseudo-problem, over which philosophy has often labored in vain. A wrong formulation was reached concerning the problem of the relationship between "thinking" and "being". To clear up this misunderstanding we must once again speak about analytic judgments, even though for us these judgments are no longer problematic, no longer pose any questions.

There is no doubt that analytic judgments can be *about* real things and are not intended merely to say something about concepts. The Kantian proposition that analytic judgments involve only concepts, whereas synthetic judgments involve the objects of concepts, is meant to say something correct; but in this formulation it can be misunderstood. If, with Kant, I include the trait of extension in the concept of a body (which, if we recall § 33, is a startingpoint not without its dangers), then of course the proposition "Bodies are extended" claims to be valid for all *real* bodies and is in fact applicable to them. It has more than just a *concept* as its subject matter, in contrast for example to a purely logical judgment, such as "The extension of a concept varies inversely with its intension." Thus we see that there are propositions about reality that possess absolute validity because they are analytic. This state of affairs has given rise to misgivings among skeptics and speculations among metaphysicians, none of which are justified.

The metaphysicians have wished to conclude that thinking and being are identical, or that being possesses a quite special rationality compelling it to behave according to the laws of thought. Real things, too, they say, obey the fundamental laws of identity and contradiction (as we know, the principle of analytic inference may be formulated in these two laws) and are thus subject to logic, to thought.

The skeptics, on the other hand, who desire to find a way around this line of argument, are for just this reason suspicious of the whole state of affairs. They incline to the conclusion that it is wrong to ascribe unconditional validity to analytic judgments. Thinking has no power over being, and reality need not obey the law of contradiction. The law of contradiction is simply a law of thought; the thinking of other creatures may obey quite different laws. The claim that analytic judgments have absolute validity for things outside of thought as well must therefore be in error. Even if it is *unthinkable* that one of the fundamental laws of logic might be given the lie by reality, this still does not place reality under any obligation. Reality need not conform to our thinking; unthinkability is by no means the same as objective impossibility. Just as there are non-Euclidean geometries, so there may be non-Aristotelian logics in which the law of contradiction has no validity. And creatures whose thinking follows any such logic would have the same right to deny the validity of analytic judgments as we, by virtue of our human reasoning power, now have to champion their validity.

A formulation corresponding to the viewpoint of the metaphysician may be found in HERBERT SPENCER's Principles of Psychology: "When we perceive that the negation of the belief is inconceivable, we have all the possible warrant for asserting the invariability of its existence ... we have no other guarantee for the reality of consciousness, of sensations, of personal existence." JOHN STUART MILL offers a skeptic's retort to this passage when he says that inconceivability is not a criterion of impossibility (Logic, Book II, Chapter VII, § 3).

Mill's objection is certainly motivated by a correct idea. He is doing battle here against Spencer as a representative of the *doctrine of self-evidence,* which we criticized above (§ 19). But it is precisely the conflating of the problem of self-evidence with that of the real validity of analytic judgments that has produced the entanglement. Neither the metaphysician nor the skeptic, neither Spencer nor Mill, is right in this matter; neither sees the correct way to pose this question. We may best unravel the knots if we consider an example. The proposition *"facta infecta fieri non possunt"* ("What is done cannot be undone") is indeed an analytic judgment and hence absolutely valid. It asserts of everything that is done that it is not not done, and this follows from the law of contradiction alone. Does it make sense for the skeptic to doubt that the law is correct or for the theologian to ask whether God, who is all powerful, can change the happened into the not-happened? It does *not* make sense. This way of posing the question treats the judgment *"facta infecta fieri non possunt"* incorrectly as knowledge, as something different from the judgment "facta sunt", and asks whether the first may be false when the second is true. But the truth of the matter is that both judgments say exactly the same thing; they are identical in sense and differ only in form. One can be transformed into the other through a mere analysis of the phrase 'is done'. When I pass from the second to the first I do not obtain some ontological truth, some new knowledge of reality; I only bring out the meaning that attaches to the phrase 'is done'. It is exactly as if I wanted to ask: Can a pain that I feel also be at the same time no pain? Can a blue that I see, also and at the same time, not be blue? In these instances, it is much easier to grasp the situation than in the case above, which is veiled by the complicated meaning of the concept "is done". Of course, I am also free to designate the blue as not-blue; but then either the word 'blue' has a different sense than it had before or the particle 'not' is used in a sense that departs from ordinary negation. Similarly, anyone who applies the terms 'done' (or 'happened') and 'undone' (or 'did not happen') to the same event only changes the sense of the words. (But it is an entirely different matter if a theologian asks whether God could make things go on in the world *as if* a past event had not taken place; this question is meaningful, and the answer to it would be a synthetic judgment.) A person can, if he so desires, call the judgments "*A* happened" and "*A* did not happen" both true; but then what he understands by truth is something other than uniqueness of designation.

The principles of identity, contradiction and excluded middle say nothing at all about the *behavior of reality*. They simply regulate how we *designate the real*. They are laws that refer to the correlation of concepts with reality and for this reason they necessarily hold of reality. As we pointed out above (§ 10), the principle of contradiction is merely a rule for the use of the words 'not', 'none' and the like in designating the real (and, of course, nonreal objects as well). In other words, it defines negation. Anything that contravenes the principle is termed *unthinkable,* and the unthinkable is then indeed absolutely *impossible*. But this does not constitute a violation of reality by thought; for impossibility in this case does not refer to any behavior of being. On the contrary, it concerns the designation of being by means of concepts and judgments and thus, if one wishes to put it that way, the relationship of thinking to being.

To say that what is impossible for thought might yet be possible for reality is, with Mill and Spencer, to confuse unthinkability and unimaginability, for in fact 'inconceivability' has both meanings. Imagining, the flow of intuitive mental images, is a real process; imaginability and reality do not coincide. But thinking is correlating concepts with real and other objects. Unthinkability signifies that it is impossible to carry out certain correlations, and thus depends on nothing but the established rules of correlation. While the laws of imagining are facts that we learn from experience, we arrive at the rules for correlating not through experience but through stipulation.

It is impossible to declare consciousness, sensations, or personal existence to be unreal (an impossibility that Spencer regarded as so significant). For it is only from these that we first derive our concept of real existence. This concept serves to designate them not on the basis of any knowledge, but by virtue of the meaning with which we have endowed the word 'real'. It is the old Cartesian error (see above, § 12) to conceive of such existential propositions as knowledge. In truth they are analytic judgments of the simplest form, that is, disguised definitions.

I think it is now clear why analytic judgments, and with them the principles of pure logic, must hold with incontestable certainty of real things. There is nothing remarkable about this and nothing philosophically significant. Any formulation that makes it seem problematic is to be rejected. For this reason I regard it as misleading to speak of a non-Aristotelian logic that would be related to our ordinary logic of analytic, deductive inference in the same way as non-Euclidean geometry is related to Euclidean geometry. Such a new logical system would differ from our Aristotelian system only in appearance, only in its verbal expression. I can of course imagine setting up a system of logical axioms in which, for example, the principles of contradiction and excluded middle have no place. In this new logic there would be judgments that were neither true nor false, and judgments that were both true and false at the same time. But a closer examination of its seemingly quite strange principles would reveal that the new logic yields and signifies only a shift in meaning of familiar logical terms. The words 'true', 'false', 'not', 'all', 'none' and the like would no longer have their old sense. But combinations of words could be found that would have the same meanings as those possessed by the old terms. Were we to reintroduce these latter, we would be back again with the old logic, and we would recognize the new logic as nothing more than the Aristotelian clothed in other dress. The reason is that logic, if we disregard its accidental garb of words, images and acts of thought, includes only what pertains to the unique designation of objects — or, if another expression is preferred, to the *determination* of objects. Since the various logical systems, much as they may seem to deviate from one another, still always have the same significance and cannot furnish anything other than determination and correlation, they are in truth identical with one another and differ only in their linguistic or psychological form.

EDGAR ZILSEL, a modern supporter of the notion of a non-Aristotelian logic, writes in his book Das Anwendungsproblem (1916, p. 150): "The rational is the unique form that stands above all logics and is common to them all; it is their inner consistency, the circumstance that all their propositions are *determined* in respect both to their foundation and to the way in which they are derived from the axioms; in short, the rational is determinateness, precision itself." Let me say that I am in full agreement with these statements; but, unlike their author, I believe that the rules of formal logic already set forth in pure form what is common to all logics, if one disregards the outer garment, and that these rules furnish nothing more than the rules of "determination" in general. That is why it seems to me impermissible to use the word 'logic' in the plural; for what distinguishes the different "logics" is not something logical, but merely something psychological or linguistic.

Thus the skeptical notion of a multiplicity of different logical systems cannot bar us from attributing to the logical (that is, to the rules of analysis) absolute validity for real things.

The entire second part of our inquiry was devoted to the proof that all deductive thinking is analytic in character and may claim unlimited validity. The reflective person has ever been astonished at the fact that our thinking, with its intricate and extended deductions, can so penetrate the workings of nature that bold, far-reaching inferences obtain exact and surprising confirmation by events. Consider, for example, the predictions of astronomy, which reach out over centuries and yet are fulfilled to within seconds. Here, if anywhere, we seem justified in speaking of a preestablished harmony between thinking and being or in concluding that our understanding dictates the laws of nature.

22*

But surprise at this state of affairs is warranted only in part. A distinction needs to be made here. When I say that deduction has absolute validity for real things, I include of course the proviso that the premisses of the deduction agree with reality. Then surely the conclusion, which is the result of analysis, also agrees completely with the behavior of things. How we come into possession of premisses that designate uniquely the facts of the world is indeed quite remarkable and raises questions to which we must address ourselves, for *a priori* it is doubtful whether we possess any valid propositions of this sort. But anyone who does *not* doubt the validity of the premisses ought not be surprised that the conclusion proves true, no matter how long and complicated the intervening deduction. The conclusion says nothing new, nothing that is not already contained in different terms in the premisses; it is only a formal restatement. For example, if we regard it as settled that the familiar laws of gravitation correctly describes the behavior of the heavenly bodies, then it should be obvious to us that correct calculations based on those laws will be confirmed by observations. For, the special cases, which are subject to observation, are contained analytically in the general laws. The general laws are only an abbreviating expression for the special cases.

This state of affairs has often been incorrectly understood. Philosophical wonder *(thauma)* has, as it were, been focused on the wrong point. The reason is that we are not able, from the conclusion of a deduction, to recognize the premisses that led to it. Deductions are formed by combining judgments, and judgments are signs for facts, for relations between objects. The peculiar feature of signs for relations is that when they are combined the result is always simpler than the totality of signs that have been put together. Thus the situation is different here than in the case of concepts, which are signs for objects or things. Here combinations produce structures that are much more complicated, and are never as simple as the combined elements in themselves. A large number of letters cannot give rise to a simple word, a large number of simultaneous sensations cannot result in a wholly simple perception. The combining of judgments, on the other hand, always leads to a simplification, since the common elements drop out. That is, judgments can be combined and used for the purposes of deduction only if they contain common middle terms, which are then eliminated through the process of inference. From a number of premisses a *single* conclusion can be drawn; complicated calculations can lead to *one* simple formula. This may be seen most clearly in the case of algebraic procedures, which are only abbreviating symbols for certain syllogistic processes (see above, § 14). The whole of mathematical analysis is basically nothing but a combining of judgments — a process in which certain common parts cancel out so that new simple results emerge that are all contained implicitly in the original premisses. But only implicitly. And for this reason the illusion may arise that a special bridge is required between premisses and results, a bridge that might perhaps be present in thought but absent in the external world — as if the deductively obtained result might perhaps not agree with the world of actual facts.

But suppose the individual judgments that were combined to yield a conclusion were as clearly recognizable in that conclusion as the letters in a written word or the individual notes in a melody. The situation would then be as little cause for astonishment as the fact that a melody may be represented by an ordered sequence of notes, each of which signifies a single sound of the melody. The whole problem as posed would appear to us about as sensible as the question of whether something in nature that extends three one-thousandths of a meter must be exactly three millimeters long. Through the work of thought we obtain *new* simple signs for new empirical relations. And if experience does exhibit these new relations, if, say, a solar eclipse does take place as predicted *provided* the facts and laws of nature are taken properly into account — there is nothing strange about this at all. It is just as obvious as the validity of any other analytic judgment.

The presupposition here throughout is that the premisses of the deduction are true. That this presupposition is so often fulfilled is indeed a just cause for wonder. How is it that we are able, by means of judgments, to designate real facts in a strictly unique manner? How do we know, for example, that the laws of celestial mechanics, on which we base our prediction of a solar eclipse, hold so universally that they describe the planetary paths of past centuries just as accurately as those of today? What, in short, is the situation regarding the validity of synthetic judgments, of judgments that not only hold for reality but also express some *knowledge* of reality? It is precisely because such judgments are synthetic that their validity is far from obvious.

§ 37. Knowing and Being

With Kant, we called *synthetic* those judgments that attribute to an object something not contained in the *concept* of that object. The relation between subject and predicate in a synthetic judgment is not given by a definition; it is established by knowledge. The question of the validity of such judgments can be resolved only on the basis of insight into the nature of the cognitive act. We must accordingly turn back to the results of the first part of our inquiry. Not only do we find there the elements required to solve our problem; we also find the problem itself, which had already made its appearance on several occasions. At the time we were obliged to postpone an answer, even though the question troubled us very much. We were disturbed because there seemed to be no road that could lead us to indubitable, exact knowledge of reality. Now it is time to examine systematically the various possible paths. Perhaps there is some way to the earnestly sought goal of absolutely valid truths about reality, but the approach may not have been visible from the course taken thus far by our inquiry.

Let us then proceed step by step along the boundary between knowing and being so as to determine whether there is some opening that leads to the desired rigor in judgments about reality. In particular, let us look carefully at those places where outstanding thinkers believed they might be able to find such an opening.

The *real* embraces our experiences and whatever is connected with them according to certain rules (we have searched out these rules above, III A). To know reality is to find again one real object in another. Such knowledge always reduces in the final analysis to a re-cognition or an identifying with one another of intuitive or nonintuitive contents of consciousness. Due to the fleeting character of experiences, this act of comparing and finding the same is always subject to an uncertainty that, although harmless and of no significance for the practical conduct of science and everyday affairs, is always present theoretically and stands in the way of absolute infallibility. We never know for sure whether we have not falsely correlated a concept with some real object. We never know whether the features of the object do not in fact deviate somewhat from those that constitute the concept selected. The only means we found for producing fully exact concepts, therefore, was to free them entirely from the real. This we did by means of implicit definitions, which define concepts exclusively by means of concepts and not by intuitive measures, not with reference to the real (see above, § 7).

Is it possible to pass with certainty from the realm of reality to that of rigorous concepts? Can we build a bridge between the two?

Now even if we found such a secure connecting link, we would have gained only a very modest advantage so far as knowledge of reality is concerned. For the course of our experience is a temporal one. Suppose at a given moment I perceive a real object and am certain that it falls under concept A and that it can also be designated by concept B. On the basis of my perception I can utter the judgment "A is B". But this judgment, as it stands, has validity only for the moment of observation; it is a proposition for that moment. I can do no more with it; it does not help me achieve those ends for which I make judgments about reality. Thus if I were to encounter object A again, how would I know that this time too it may be subsumed under concept B. In other words, how could I be certain that once I have found the proposition "A is B", I can henceforth assert it as a valid premiss in future inferences?

How do I know that the comet, whose return at a definite point in time I can predict, will submit without deviation or interruption to the same laws of motion that have governed its path according to all previous observations? Why are you confident that the cup of water you take from a spring during a long walk on a hot day will quench your thirst? Might it not poison you even if all the other properties characteristic of water remain unchanged? Is it absolutely out of the question that your dog, who day after day lies loyally at your feet and does not allow any stranger to come near you, might suddenly attack you and try to tear you to pieces?

These examples make it clear that at every moment of our lives we must assume countless judgments as true, if we are to be able to act, indeed, even to exist at all. Are these judgments really beyond all doubt?

The fact is that they are *not* absolutely certain. A synthetic judgment, which ascribes a particular property to some real thing and thus asserts a real interconnection of traits, never has the character of a universally valid truth. A detailed proof of this proposition is not necessary today, since it is no longer seriously disputed. No matter how discontinuous and non-linear the development of philosophy may be, we can nevertheless in our day consider extreme rationalism as definitively refuted. No philosophical system is able any more to pretend that it can, with apodictic certainty (that is, through mere reason), provide information about, say, the number of planets or the special properties of a chemical element. Philosophy can never revert to that confusion of thinking, knowing and being from which such a rationalism arises. There is only one form in which an apodictic knowledge of reality is still discussable, namely, the one discovered by Kant.

As we know, he sought to preserve a modest place for rationalistic ideas by advancing the considerations that follow:

If knowledge, as he correctly said, is to conform with reality, it cannot possibly be absolutely valid. Future experience can always give the lie to any statement that I make. For my knowledge can be governed only by experiences that I have actually had, not by remote or future ones of which I knew nothing at the time I made the statement. My truths can be universally valid, they can hold also for realities not yet experienced, only if reality is in some way governed by knowledge. If something like this were possible, it would indeed be the *one* way to rescue a strictly valid knowledge of reality (as we pointed out above, near the end of § 21). Hence we need only examine this particular pathway to arrive at a definitive answer to our question.

Kant not only sees this pathway as a possibility, he regards it as actually existing. The laws obeyed by the objects of experience are in his view at the same time the laws in accordance with which experience itself as a cognitive process takes place. And this explains why we can with certainty make judgments about reality that are necessarily confirmed by all future experience, and thus are synthetic *a priori*. For when something is given to me in experience, it is by that very fact subject to the laws of experience. In this context, 'experience' signifies knowledge grounded in perception. Kant had found this meaning of 'experience' already present in Hume, who also employed the word in a sense other than that of mere perceiving. This usage best accords with what we encounter in ordinary speech. We call someone "experienced" not simply because he has seen much, but because he also knows how to *evaluate* what he has perceived. The only difference is that Kant understands by knowledge nothing but exact, absolutely valid knowledge.

Kant develops his basic thought in a two-fold manner.

First, with the aid of this thought he attempts to overcome the vagueness and haziness of intuition, so dangerous to the rigor of knowledge. According to him, our sensuous intuition, fleeting as it may be, is subject to strict laws. This conformity to law, revealed when we abstract from all sensationlike elements in intuition, Kant calls *pure intuition*. When we leave out the content of sensation, what still remain are the *forms* of the intuition, namely, space and time. This is the theory of *a priori* forms of the intuition, used by Kant to explain the possibility of pure mathematics, the apodictic validity of mathematical judgments. For example, geometry is simply the science of the spatial form of the intuition. Its propositions hold with absolute rigor because we cannot of course have spatial perceptions and images in consciousness without the spatial form being imprinted upon them by the very makeup of our consciousness.

Second, Kant also wishes to utilize the same principle for those synthetic judgments that relate not only to the spatial and temporal forms but more generally to reality in space and time. Some of these judgments too possess absolute validity; the possibility of such judgments is explained by carrying over the basic idea from intuiting to thinking. Just as our intuition is tied to certain forms, so certain root concepts (the "categories") are said to be inalienably characeristic of our consciousness, and thinking in all of its operations is subject to these categories. The judgments in which these root concepts are displayed must necessarily be true of reality because our consciousness cannot think of or conceive reality except in terms of these categories. Reality is itself a category; the real for us is that which we must think under this category. Thus the real — that is, what we experience as real — conforms to our thinking. We can express certain propositions about reality *a priori* (these propositions Kant calls principles of "pure natural science") and their objective validity is made intelligible in the fashion indicated.

These notions developed here have, in connection with a remark of Kant himself, been likened to the feat of Copernicus. Just as Copernicus, against the apparent evidence of the senses, held that the earth revolves around the sun, so the Critical philosopher maintains, against the prevailing view, that objects are governed by knowledge and not the other way around. We must examine separately the two applications — forms of the intuition and categories of thought — that Kant makes of his basic idea, if we are to be able to pass judgment on his answer to the great question of knowledge. We shall do so in the sections that follow. But first we must clarify certain important aspects of his attempted solution.

It is clear that the Kantian solution, even if correct, would not signify a resounding triumph for rationalism. For the *a priori* knowledge that his theory allows us has no concrete, material meaning in any individual case either in scientific research or in our daily life. Propositions that express merely the forms in which (according to Kant) all of our experience must appear are quite general. For example, we might assert with apodictic certainty that each single real event has a cause. But in no case would we be in a position to decide *a priori* which cause belongs to which event; we would never be certain that we had found the right one. Or, we might know quite well that something constant (a "substance") must underlie all changes in nature; but this does not permit us to believe, say, that the scientific principles of the conservation of energy or of mass have been elevated to the rank of absolutely valid truths. It is quite possible for subsequent experience to prove that the principle of the conservation of energy (or of mass) is incorrect without Kantianism having been refuted. Kantianism would still maintain that in the long run observed variations are to be conceived of as modifications in something absolutely constant, and that science advances precisely by seeking out this enduring or constant something. Thus the application of the category of substance would not be prevented, only deferred. If mass or energy did not fulfill the condition of constancy, then a new substance would have to be found that satisfies this inescapable demand for permanence. And so forth.

According to this conception, the most general laws of nature are identical with the rules governing knowledge of nature. These supply only an empty framework within which the advance of the individual sciences takes place, and which is filled out by their advance. The framework takes no part in the advance itself. Thus *a priori* knowledge here plays a role quite different from the one it assumes in the rationalistic system of a Descartes or a Spinoza. Such knowledge provides only the most general forms to which the cognitive functions of consciousness are tied. It is understandable that, to devotees of the old metaphysics, the Kantian Criticism appears as one that "grinds everything to pieces".

Now synthetic *a priori* propositions are valid only for "appearances", only for the world of representations on which are imprinted the forms of intuition and thought. This is the one world with which we are acquainted, whereas the world of things-in-themselves is for us unknowable. We cannot know or specify anything about the latter world, except the boundary that marks it off from the world of appearances. Kant was obliged to undertake this partition of the world in order to rescue universally valid knowledge for at least one of the parts. As I believe I have shown above (§ 27), the notion of such a separation is to be blamed on a wrong concept of knowledge, and constitutes a very dangerous obstacle in the path of philosophy, one that must be removed by eliminating altogether the concept of appearance as incorrectly formed. When this is done, a key pillar of the Kantian system is removed, and we are then compelled to adopt an extremely skeptical and cautious attitude toward it. Examination of the doctrine of synthetic judgments *a priori* will confirm in detail that this attitude is correct and will describe more exactly the position we must take regarding the transcendental philosophy constructed by Kant.

We have often had occasion to remark that for Kant the existence of *a priori* valid knowledge of reality is a settled fact. In his opinion, the mere fact that there are sciences is proof beyond doubt that such knowledge exists. It has often been argued — I believe without justification — that Kant never really made this assumption. But the passages in which he expresses himself to this effect are so clear and so numerous, and the passages that admit of a contrary interpretation so isolated and ambiguous, that I cannot possibly agree with the modern Kantians on this point, even though many of the most acute students of Kant's philosophy have upheld such an interpretation. (Aloys Riehl, in particular, has been a most energetic advocate of this view.) It has been said that Kant refers to the factual existence of valid synthetic judgments *a priori* only as an example, and does not use it for any further inferences. But against this is the circumstance that Kant, in the numerous passages in which he rejects attempts at an empirical proof of the most basic principles, always does so on the ground that it would then be impossible to explain the indubitable fact that such principles are universally valid. Thus, as against LOCKE and HUME, he says (Kritik der reinen Vernunft, Kehrbach edition, p. 111): "But the empirical derivation, which both have hit upon, is not compatible with the reality of the scientific *a priori* knowledge that we possess, namely pure mathematics and general natural science, and this incompatibility thus refutes the derivation." But we can use a fact for purposes of refutation only if we have no doubt that it exists. Here, as in all similar demonstrations, Kant assumes that we are in possession of valid *a priori* judgments. It has been said by many that first he *proved* the validity of these judgments, for to assume the validity would have been to offer a circular argument, something of which we cannot believe him capable. But his concern was only to prove that such judgments are possible. He formulated the question as follows: Here we have synthetic knowledge that is *a priori* valid of empirical objects. How can I explain this? How must the knowing consciousness be constituted if this fact is to be intelligible? Thus Kant presupposes that science exists, and his goal is simply to infer from it the nature of the creator of science, namely, human understanding. (Kant often stated that for him it is a matter of *human* understanding only, that he makes no claim to have provided a basis for constituting an understanding in general. On this point, see the Kehrbach edition, pp. 61, 66, 663 ff. This must be emphasized in opposition to the view of many Kantians.) He rests the "transcendental deduction", which is intended to explain the objective validity of these judgments, on the concept of *experience*. But he so defines the concept of empirical knowledge as to include, implicitly, synthetic judgments *a priori*. In assuming that we do possess experience, he assumes that such judgments are valid.

There is no need here to trace the interrelationships of the Kantian ideas any further. Besides, the dark corners of his system have already been looked into often enough. It was necessary to go this far in order to clarify the presupposition on which he bases his attempt to subject nature to the governance of universally valid thinking. We may now concentrate on examining this presupposition. If it does not stand up, then we shall know that the Kantian endeavor has miscarried. And the majestic display of acuity in the *Transcendental Aesthetic* and the *Transcendental Analytic* will have failed to secure for *a priori* knowledge a last small space — a site which, although very modest in comparison with the claims made by the old metaphysics, would still be a quite respectable resting place.

§ 38. Is There a Pure Intuition?

When they assert that there are synthetic judgments *a priori*, Kant and his followers point in the first instance to mathematics. Our inquiries in the earlier sections, however, have already yielded considerable clarity about mathematical judgments. There is no doubt that mathematics contains strictly valid truth and that mathematical judgments are to that extent *a priori*. But the absolute exactness of mathematics, as we showed in § 7, may be regarded as guaranteed only in so far as it is a science of mere concepts. We saw in the case of geometry, for example, that it is possible to abstract from all intuitive content of mathematical concepts by defining them through implicit definitions. And modern mathematics not only has acknowledged that it is possible to introduce and determine concepts in this fashion; it has found itself *compelled* to follow this path because in no other way could it ensure the rigor of its propositions. Geometrical concepts must thus be considered without regard to the intuitive content with which they may be filled and are usually thought of as being filled.

Mathematics, viewed in this way, consists of purely conceptual propositions. It yields no knowledge of reality, and hence it need not concern us here. Its truths all follow syllogistically from a system of axioms, and this axiom system has the significance only of a definition of the basic concepts. Consequently, the axiom system consists of nothing but *analytic* truths, which merely develop the relations between the basic concepts fixed by the definitions. In this sense, geometrical judgments are of course *a priori,* but they are not at all synthetic.

And here we come to the question raised earlier but postponed till now: Do mathematical propositions possess a meaning that goes beyond the range of the purely conceptual? Do they retain their apodictic validity when we impute an intuitive content to mathematical concepts? If so, then the sense of such expressions as 'straight line', 'plane', and the like, would no longer be thought of as being determined merely by implicit definitions; they would be taken to signify the spatial structures we are accustomed to designate by these expressions. The question thus becomes: Is geometry as the science of space also an *a priori* science?

Were the answer yes, we would have to accept as universally valid the notion that spatial structures sustain just those relations with each other that are laid down in the implicit definitions of the basic gemetrical concepts. But then they would no longer be definitions but synthetic propositions, because the sense of the words would have changed. The axioms would now deal with intuitive magnitudes, not concepts.

The individual theorems of geometry would of course follow purely analytically from the axioms as before. And the fact that they held true of spatial structures would offer no further problem. Whoever found this fact puzzling could lay the blame only on a wrong formulation of the question, something we warned against in § 36. Kant's view was that the derivation of geometrical theorems from the axioms takes place with the aid of intuition and cannot be obtained without it. This view must be corrected. A major finding of modern geometry, so we learned in § 7, is that in no case do proofs require intuition; they can be conducted by purely logical deduction.

But while all of these corrections are methodologically extremely important, they leave the main point untouched. So long as the axioms are synthetic judgments *a priori,* any theorem, even though derived analytically from the axioms, must be regarded as synthetic. For the theorem says the same thing as the axioms: the content of the axioms includes analytically that of the theorem; the theorem presupposes that the objects of which it treats have precisely the properties laid down by the axioms.

Now according to Kant the statements of geometry as a science of space do possess apodictic validity and are therefore *a priori.* They are also judgments about reality, since space, although not itself a real thing of course, is held to be the *form* in which sensuous reality is always given to us. It is the form of our intuition, and through the science of geometry we recognize the law-like regularity of this form as *pure* intuition. This regularity must naturally be a quite definite one, which can be expressed by means of a quite definite geometrical system, such as that of Euclid. For only if the regularity is fixed once and for all as the law-like form of the sensuous consciousness can it prescribe *a priori* the form or shape of the world of experience.

Over many centuries Euclidean geometry was thought to be *the* geometry of space. The idea never occurred to anyone that the properties of space might be described by axioms other than the Euclidean, which were held to be absolutely valid. All of this seemed to speak for the correctness of the Kantian conception and at the same time for the Euclidean character of the pure intuition whose existence he assumed. This in fact is also the opinion of the present-day Kantians. They admit of course that geometries other than the Euclidean are conceivable; but they believe that only Euclidean geometry can be represented intuitively and therefore that physical objects must necessarily appear to us in Euclidean space. Yet even if someone were to assert that the law to which our intuition conforms is non-Euclidean, he could still retain intact the rest of the Kantian position. So far as I know, however, no one has ever advanced such an assertion. But the opinion has been offered (V. HENRY, Das erkenntnistheoretische Raumproblem, Berlin 1915) that while some specific geometry must of necessity be the sole one valid for the space of intuition, we shall never be able to decide which one it is; science can only supply us with an ever closer approximation and can never establish the validity of the axioms with apodictic certainty. According to this view, the synthetic *a priori* judgments of geometry must always bear for us a problematic character. What is unsatisfactory about this view is obvious. It claims that we are in possession of synthetic judgments *a priori,* yet at the same time denies that we can ever specify them. Geometry would thus lose its value as far as knowledge of space is concerned.

What also seems to speak in favor of the Kantians is the indubitable fact that sense experience can never compel us to base the description of nature on a particular geometry. Experience can never prove that a certain geometry is the only one valid in empirical space. The reason is not only because, due to the indistinctness of perception, small deviations from Euclidean geometry are always possible, but because the empirical facts can be brought fully into accord with *any* geometry we wish, if only we express the laws of nature in an appropriate formulation. It was HENRI POINCARÉ in particular who drew attention to the peculiar way in which geometry is independent of experience (especially in La Science et l'hypothèse and Science et méthode). I have discussed this matter in detail elsewhere (Raum und Zeit in der gegenwärtigen Physik, 4th edition, Berlin 1922) and therefore need not repeat the arguments here. If experience as such cannot decide unambiguously which geometry must be taken as valid for our space, this seems to favor the Kantian view that the character of space is determined independently of experience by the form of our intuition.

Empirical, sensuous intuition cannot establish for us the validity of axioms. True, we believe we can see immediately that, given a straight line and a point not lying on it, only one straight line can be drawn through that point parallel to the given line. But suppose a third straight line is drawn that forms with the second an angle of a millionth of a degree. Empirical intuition can never tell us with certainty whether the new line will ever actually intersect the first line, for the simple reason that an angle that small is not intuitively representable. Yet from Euclid's time until today, most people have thought that they could immediately grasp the correctness of the Euclidean parallel postulate. This, it seems, could only become intelligible if our consciousness in fact had at its disposal a "pure" intuition that far exceeds the certainty of the sensuous intuition of space and could thus have the significance that Kant ascribes to it.

To refute the Kantian theory, it is not enough to point out that today a great many mathematicians — if we may continue with the same example — do not by any means find the parallel postulate completely obvious. Invoking subjective convictions has no meaning for this sort of question. It would be merely an appeal to faith, and would involve us in all the inadequacies of the theory of self-evidence (see § 19).

The existence of a "pure" intuition alongside of or rather within empirical intuition can be more easily called into question along a different route. It so happens that certain supposed insights have been shown by mathematical analysis to be *false*. Naturally this is fatal for the theory. A necessary form of the intuition cannot deceive: the whole point indeed is to explain its correctness, its validity. Instances may be found, it seems to me, in the examples that follow.

Anyone who relies on intuition must surely judge that a tangent can always be drawn to a perfectly continuous curve. But this is an error. There are curves (Weierstrass was the first to write an equation for one) that are fully continuous and yet do not possess a tangent at any point (since their equation is nowhere differentiable). Here, then, intuition leaves us in the lurch.

This sort of example already suffices, in my view, to establish that the doctrine of a pure intuition is untenable in special cases. But we need not spend time or place weight on them. We must still reject the Kantian notion on more general and quite fundamental grounds, which we have already fully developed in the earlier chapters.

The basic point is that the validity of geometrical propositions cannot be grounded in a pure intuition for the simple reason that the space of geometry is not intuitive at all.

There is not just one intuitive space, but as many as there are spatial senses. Thus there is an optical space (actually two of them, since man is a two-eyed creature), a haptic space, a space of kinesthetic sensations. All of these differ fundamentally from one another. The space of the geometer, however, is but a *single* one, and it is not identical with any of these other spaces. It has quite different properties from them (see above, § 29). It is a conceptual construction and grows out of the spatial data of the individual senses with the aid of the method of coincidences described earlier. This method correlates uniquely the individual elements of the subjective spaces with one another, and this in turn leads to the formation of the concept of "point" in objective space.

Objective space (as well as the space of everyday life) is something *added* in thought to the intuitive-spatial data of perception. And it is just as easy to add non-Euclidean relationships as Euclidean ones. For what is involved here is only the adding of *concepts,* through which the intuitive data are interpreted while their makeup of course is left entirely unaltered.

Kant continually speaks of "the" space, declares it to be intuitive, and contrasts it only with the unknown ordering of the things-in-themselves. We, on the other hand, are directly acquainted with several intuitive spaces and these we contrast with the ordering of physical bodies, an ordering that is precisely the space of geometry. Its non-intuitive character cannot be doubted (see § 29 above, near the end). In the intuitive spaces the Euclidean axioms are *not* valid. For example, we saw earlier that visual space is a Riemannian space, and the spaces of tactile and kinesthetic sensations certainly may not be counted *a priori* as Euclidean (see § 29). With this we have answered the question, posed at the beginning of this section, as to whether geometry retains its validity when we attribute an intuitive sense to its concepts. The answer is in the *negative.* That certain geometrical axioms should be peculiar to our space-intuition is out of the question. For we possess no intuition of geometrical space.

Geometrical space is a conceptual structure that we set up in such a way that with its aid we can express the laws of nature in the simplest possible form. This alone is decisive for the choice of geometrical axioms. But notice that the setting up and selection of axioms in this manner does not wait until a science of physics has been developed. The experiences of everyday life are already richly permeated with a knowledge of law-like regularities in nature; even the very concept of a body could not have come into being without certain geometrical concepts. The point of view we have suggested guides mankind unconsciously, as it were; and it has taken a most ingenious series of investigations (like those of Poincaré) for us to be able to recognize *that* this point of view does guide us.

Euclidean geometry has served as the geometry of everyday life, and until a short time ago it seemed to provide the proper foundation for all the purposes of natural science. The new physics, however, in one of its boldest and most beautiful moves, has concluded from the Einsteinian Theory of Gravitation that we cannot make do with the Euclidean metrical determinations if we wish to describe nature with the greatest accuracy and by means of the simplest laws. According to this theory, a different geometry must be used at each place in the world, a geometry that depends on the physical state (the gravitational potential) at that place. On the basis of Einstein's latest work it is likely that world space as a whole can best be viewed as endowed with approximately "spherical" properties (thus as finite, although of course also unbounded).

It cannot be emphasized too much that we are not *compelled* to conceive of space in accordance with a theory of this kind. No experience can prevent us from retaining Euclidean geometry if we insist on doing so. But then we do not obtain the simplest formulations of the laws of nature, and the system of physics as such becomes less satisfactory. Nevertheless, anyone who has been preoccupied with Einstein's theory and has come to know its inclusiveness, which simplifies the entire world picture so magnificently, will not doubt that the monopoly of Euclidean geometry in physics is at an end. The physical description of nature is not tied to any particular geometry and no intuition dictates that we must base such a description on the Euclidean axiom system as the only correct one, nor, of course, on any of the non-Euclidean systems either. We select — in the beginning instinctively, in more recent times deliberately — those axioms that lead to the simplest physical laws. In principle, however, we could have chosen other axioms if we were willing to pay the price of more complicated formulations of the laws of nature. Thus fundamentally the choice of axioms is left to our discretion.

And this means that they are *definitions*.

Our finding then is that geometry, not only as a pure conceptual science but also as the science of space, does not proceed from synthetic *a priori* propositions. Instead, it proceeds from conventions (see Part I, § 11), that is, from implicit definitions. To the extent that it moves about within just these definitions and the theorems that may be rigorously deduced from them, it is purely analytic in character and hence possesses absolute validity. But statements about the spatial relationships of reality do not belong to this pure geometry; rather they form part of its application to empirical material. They are judgments about the behavior of measuring rods and the locations of bodies. As such, they are synthetic in character but *a posteriori;* only experience can determine their validity. Einstein has formulated this insight in the now famous words: "In so far as the principles of geometry are valid, they do not refer to reality; in so far as they refer to reality, they are not strictly valid" (Geometrie und Erfahrung, pp. 3 ff.).

Geometrical space is a conceptual tool for designating the ordering of the real. There is no such thing as a pure intuition of space, and there are no *a priori* propositions about space.

Once we are clear about the validity of geometrical truths, it is an easy matter to assess the significance of arithmetic for the question we are examining. Do we perhaps find among the propositions of arithmetic the synthetic judgments *a priori* we vainly looked for in geometry?

Misled by the architectonics of his system, Kant thought that the intuition of time might play for arithmetic a role analogous to that played by the intuition of space for geometry. But he was quite right in not pursuing this idea any further, since it is of course wholly untenable. Counting, to be sure, takes time; but it would be a gross conflation of the psychological and epistemological viewpoints if one tried to derive from this fact a closer relation between time and the concept of number. *All* mental acts take place in time; but from this nothing can be inferred about *what* we think in these acts. The connection of number with the intuition of space is also only psychological, not logical. The fact that we illustrate arithmetical relationships by means of spatial objects (counting off points on a blackboard, or fingers on a hand) is of course quite immaterial so far as the validity of arithmetical propositions is concerned.

Of course, the epistemological status of arithmetic cannot be fully clarified at this point. Such a clarification can be had only within a more deeply probing philosophy of mathematics, to which I hope to contribute on another occasion. Here I add only a few words concerning the present state of affairs.

The proof cited earlier (§ 7), that pure geometry is analytic-deductive, that all of its theorems can be deduced from implicit definitions, was obtained by Hilbert on the assumption that arithmetic is a body of truths completely free of contradiction and thus consists only of analytic judgments about implicitly defined concepts. That all mathematical propositions can be deduced from a small number of axioms has been conclusively demonstrated by the recent work of Frege, Peano and others. But that these axioms may be conceived of as implicit definitions of the basic arithmetical concepts (in particular of *number)* can be proved only if arithmetic has been shown to be consistent. For judgments that contradict one another define nothing; they are empty verbal structures. In some brilliant new studies Hilbert, aided by his co-worker P. Bernays, has in essence succeeded in carrying through this proof, and thus the purely analytic character of arithmetical judgments has been assured. The validity of such judgments is not grounded in intuition. True, Hilbert's proof seems to appeal to intuition. But nonetheless no synthetic element is thereby introduced into mathematical judgments, since in his proof intuition appears not as a ground for validity but solely as a means of understanding. The role of intuition here is not epistemological, but psychological. However, we cannot now go into this matter in more detail.

In the case of the word 'geometry', we must clearly distinguish whether we denote by it the pure conceptual science or the science of space. It seems to me that there is no analogous distinction in the case of 'arithmetic'. It is true that we seem obliged to separate the purely formal (Hilbertian) concept of number — the essence of a number is simply that it satisfies certain axioms — and the "contentual" concept, according to which a number is conceived in terms of a quantity of objects (or better, with Russell, as a "class of classes"). The development of this second concept of number leads (along the path taken by Russell) to a theory of arithmetic that, despite its purely logical character, can still in virtue of its point of departure be termed a "realistic" one. Such a theory is related to Hilbert's theory as the science of space is related to purely formal, abstract geometry. Yet it is my belief that this difference is only apparent and that on a closer analysis (which, I must say, I have not yet succeeded in carrying through) the formal and the contentual concepts of number — the Hilbertian and the Russellian — will turn out to be identical.

Kant's doctrine that the validity of arithmetical propositions is grounded in intuition must in any case be rejected. No, even if there were synthetic judgments *a priori* in the science of numbers, their validity could be due not to a form of the intuition but at most to a form of *thought*. Just what that might mean we shall investigate in the following section.

But are there perhaps other judgments whose basis is to be sought in a pure intuition of time? The few fundamental propositions that Kant cites as issuing synthetically and *a priori* from the intuition of time (that time has only one dimension; that different times are not simultaneous but successive, that they are all parts of the same time) are meager enough in content. And the 28 principles that, according to Schopenhauer, can be set up regarding time represent simply an embroidering. As a matter of fact, the very same remarks can be made and the very same conclusions can be drawn about the intuition of time as about the intuition of space. As we know (see § 28), in the case of time too we must distinguish between intuitive time, concerning which empirical judgments may be made on the basis of psychological investigations, and mathematical or objective time. The latter, like space, is a conceptual construction, the fashioning of which is in turn governed by the principle that the laws of nature must assume the simplest comprehensive form possible. This view of time has been confirmed recently in natural science by the theory of relativity, which shows that the "evenly flowing" time of Newton can no longer be retained, that we must make use of different measures of time depending on the state of motion of the reference system with respect to which the processes of nature are described. Only in this way can we succeed in providing an explanation by means of a minimum number of concepts (see my paper, Die philosophische Bedeutung des Relativitätsprinzips, Zeitschrift für Philosophie, Vol. 159).

Thus, as in the case of geometry, the "science of time" that appears to lie at the base of physical knowledge is not a science of the intuitive, of the real. It is a conceptual tool; its fundamental principles are definitions, not synthetic judgments.

In saying this, we pronounce judgment on the Kantian doctrine of forms of the intuition. The question posed at the beginning of this section is answered in the negative: we have looked in vain for a pure intuition that might serve as the basis for empirical intuition by supplying it with its form and lawfulness. Space and time are not *a priori* forms of the intuition in the sense that they make possible synthetic judgments that are absolutely and universally valid. The basic spatial and temporal judgments of the exact sciences, whose synthetic *a priori* character Kant did not doubt, actually do not possess this character. And the suspicion that arose almost at the outset of our inquiry continues to grow: man is not in possession of any judgments of this kind and thus apodictically valid knowledge of reality is denied him altogether.

§ 39. Are There Pure Forms of Thought?

We come now to examine the last possibility that might still hold out some hope of an *a priori* knowledge of reality. Perhaps concepts can supply what intuition is unable to provide. Perhaps Kant is right when he says that our thought can make apodictically valid judgments about empirical reality because thought itself participates in the construction of empirical objects, because nothing can become an object for us without having been given its form by the *categories*.

Are there categories in this sense? Can concepts fulfill the function that Kant assigns to the pure concepts of the understanding? Is it meaningful to speak of *forms* of thought?

These questions can be decided only if we refer back to what was said earlier about the essential nature of concepts. As we saw, concepts are merely signs, which first obtain a meaning when they are correlated with objects. It would obviously be self-contradictory if we were to understand by *a priori* concepts those that are already supposed to have a meaning independently of all other concepts and of empirical objects. A claim that concepts might dwell *a priori* in the understanding seems to be as absurd as the view that certain things must necessarily be designated by a certain word of the language (a view that actually turned up among the Greeks in the early days of the philosophy of language). In fact, it is even more nonsensical; for a word as articulated possesses at least some concrete intuitive content, whereas a concept has no content of its own and hence is nothing at all until it designates something. Kant, indeed, should not have spoken of *a priori* concepts at all. Even under his own assumption the concept of the *a priori* is applicable, strictly speaking, only to *judgments*. The expression 'a priori concept' can be conceived of only as a verbal shorthand used to refer to the concepts that occur in *a priori* judgments. Indeed it is for that reason that Kant, as is well known, arrives at his twelve categories through a table of the twelve possible kinds of judgments.

We must bear in mind that because of the correlativity of concept and judgment, which came into view quite clearly in §§ 7—10, the logical meaning and function of concepts consists entirely in their being nodal points of judgments. A judgment serves to designate a set of facts; a set of facts always contains a relation. We might suppose that it is possible to speak meaningfully of forms of thought in so far as the forms of judgment of our understanding perhaps "anticipate" the real relations. But if, as we found, judgments are merely signs that are correlated with facts and cannot in any way repeat or portray them, this possibility disappears. For the form of a sign is wholly independent of what it designates; all that is involved is a reciprocal unique correlation, and such a correlation between facts and thought can be set up no matter what "form" thought may have. We can never guarantee that because thought has a certain form there exists *a priori* a unique correlation, any more than the possession of a certain lottery number guarantees that we win the lottery. The truth of a judgment, like the victory in the lottery, results from the presence of *two* factors that do not determine each other's internal structure but merely confront one another externally. This conclusion follows necessarily from the nature of knowing as designating, and of thinking as a combining of mere signs.

The products of thought that come closest in function to that of the Kantian "forms of thought" are conventions in the sense defined above (§ 11). But we already found at that time that conventions do not give rise to synthetic judgments about reality.

Thus as we have come to understand it, thought, with its judgments and concepts, possesses no form that it could impose upon reality. But suppose with Kant we accept such a possibility. Suppose we believe that there exists a very intimate relation between thinking and being by virtue of which that which is real first becomes an object for me through thinking and then naturally carries with it the traces of thought. In that case, by "concept" we obviously must understand something else, something *more* than a mere sign; we are then committed to the view that our judgments not merely are correlated with facts but in a certain sense *generate* them. This is not to say that thought is a cause producing reality — this would indeed be an absurd notion — but that only through thought does the real first become a "fact" for us.

This in rough outline is actually the view of Kant and his disciples. In Kant's opinion, concepts are realities in consciousness, as it were; along with intuitions, they are regarded by him as "representations" *(Vorstellungen)*. Hence they can fulfill functions quite different from those performed by mere signs. Only through concepts, Kant believes, is it possible "to know something as an object"; unless we presuppose the existence of concepts, "nothing can be an object of experience". Here Kant relies on a concept of knowledge that is entirely different from the one to which our investigations in Part One have led us. How Kant's concept differs from ours may be seen quite clearly in the following passage in which Riehl elucidates Kant's view (Der philosophische Kritizismus, 2nd edition, Volume I, p. 367): "There exists an original judgment which, in contrast to the derived judgment, does not compare objects but first provides a foundation for the representation of an object." Now an object is always a complex of relations. These relations, on Kant's theory, are not immediately given, but must be charged to the account of thought, judgments and concepts. According to the Criticist view, therefore, relations originate in judgments, whereas according to our concept of knowledge judgments are simply correlated with the relations, which exist outside of this correlation.

If we have succeeded through our previous efforts in establishing beyond any doubt the designating or semiotic character of thinking and knowing, then the Criticist concept of knowledge is thereby disposed of. All the possibilities contained in that concept, all the consequences that flow from it, must be recognized as untenable. On the basis of our earlier positive findings, we may therefore regard the whole question as settled against the Kantian philosophy.

We still need to add certain considerations, however, so as to forestall any complaint that we might have unwittingly rested our own inquiry on untenable assumptions. Kantians may say that our error lies in starting from "given" facts and objects that are supposed to confront thought as finished entities; for in truth facts and objects are never given to us without operations of thought.

We believe we have shown that an analysis of science and scientific procedure leads to no other concept of knowledge than the one we have developed here. Nevertheless, it will be instructive to reexamine the concept of knowledge offered by the Kantian school. We shall then come to understand in particular how it could ever have been put forward in the first place. More important than discovering an error is discovering the grounds for the error. Only then is our mind set fully at rest.

In the light of the foregoing, the problem may be expressed in the form of the question: May epistemology assume as given actual facts and objects that, logically speaking, are present *prior* to any thought and judgment? Or is it perhaps the case that what must count as real and as fact is not there in the beginning at all, but, as the ultimate goal of knowledge, can be established only through knowledge itself?

Even Kant conceded that at least a certain material is given to us prior to any shaping by the mind. According to him (Kritik der reinen Vernunft, Kehrbach edition, p. 107), "objects can of course appear to us without their necessarily having to be referred to functions of the understanding and thus without the understanding containing the conditions for them *a priori*", since "appearance can of course be given in intuition apart from functions of the understanding". At another place he says: "In the proof above, there was one portion alone from which I still could not abstract — that the manifold for intuition must be given prior to and independently of the synthesis of the understanding" (*ibid., p.* 688). This synthesis, this joining by means of judgments, is something that is added; it does not *have to be* added, however, since an intuition need not become knowledge.

In our times, certain of Kant's followers, banded together in the influential "Marburg School", have taken a direction that grants to pure thought an even more fundamental share in the occurring of experience and seeks to overcome the antithesis between thinking and pure intuition. They detect an inconsistency in the Kantian assumption that thinking finds already present in intuition a content independent of thought, and they offer in its place the striking formula: objects and facts are not "given" but "arrived at"; to attain facts and objects is the unending, never conclusively solved task of knowledge.

For purposes of evaluation, let me cite a few passages from PAUL NATORP's Die logischen Grundlagen der exakten Wissenschaften (Leipzig and Berlin 1910), one of the leading works of this school. These passages reflect the basic themes and ideas of the movement:

"All hope of ever reaching absolute facts in scientific knowledge disappears, but so does any need to reach them. For reality is never given; on the contrary, it is the eternal problem or task, and in actual experience admits of only relative solutions" (p. 94). "In each case, the 'facts' only answer questions set in advance by knowledge in conformity with its specific concept" (ibid.). "A fact in the absolute sense, however, is the last thing that knowledge has to reach but in truth never does reach; it is cognition's eternal X. This last thing has been made into a first, the X into a known quantity, the unattainable, eternally sought for into the given. Whence has come this strange pseudo-concept?" (p. 96).

The correct idea set forth here is that due to the infinite wealth of relations among objects it is impossible ever to know anything exhaustively. No process, historical or natural, can ever be so completely captured by concepts that all questions one could ask about it are answered. Every real object contains infinitely many details, stands in infinitely many relations to other objects. To designate it with absolute accuracy we would therefore need infinitely many or infinitely complicated concepts. We can determine an historical event first in its broad features and then in ever more exact detail down to the individual gestures and thoughts of the personalities involved. But a complete determination of the event and its causes still remains an unattainable goal that can only be approximated. We can ascertain the path of a planet with ever greater exactness, to which in principle there is no limit. But no matter how far we go, the degree of precision can always be improved upon, for the number of circumstances on which the path depends is endless. And this is true not only for individual cases in nature and in history, but also for theories. After we have broken matter down into molecules, molecules into atoms, atoms into electrons, the question could still arise of distinguishing parts within an electron, and the cognitive process advancing in this direction ought never be reckoned as absolutely completed. The question 'How then is matter constituted?' can never receive more than a provisional answer.

Is it therefore false and nonsensical to speak of facts that are absolutely certain *prior* to any scientific knowledge, and that can and must be accepted as the foundation of all thought and inquiry? Such a conclusion is most assuredly not justified. True, knowledge is by its very nature an unending process. Yet it is not absolute facts but absolute knowledge of the facts that stands as the unattainable goal of the process. Although the edifice of science is never completed, that edifice is not reality itself but a network of concepts. The network is woven ever more densely so that it clings to reality ever more closely. But it never fits each tiniest contour perfectly without crease or wrinkle; it remains a garment only draped around reality.

Fundamentally, philosophers of the Neo-Kantian school still commit the error of taking the conceptual wrapping for reality itself. On their view, the world itself is found in scientific knowledge, whereas in truth scientific knowledge is only a conceptual sign system. There is no doubt that a strong, if concealed, motivation of this whole school of thought is the wish to have or "grasp" reality itself in knowledge. The notion that a system of science is only to be correlated with reality is felt to be unsatisfactory. And so they persuade themselves that the framework of concepts itself belongs to reality and forms part of its structure. They slip back into the concept of knowledge as intuition, according to which the relationship between knowing and the object known is something more intimate than that of mere correlation (see above, § 12). What we actually have here is a view characteristic of the doctrine of intuitive knowledge, namely, that mere representing amounts to knowledge. Thus in speaking of "representations", Natorp says: "They are in any event complete elements with a 'fixed content' . . . and thus constitute primitive knowledge" (*ibid.*, p. 41). Of course the world with which the system of scientific concepts is correlated is not "given" to us. The facts and objects that we designate by means of historical and natural science concepts are not *experienced;* we are not *directly acquainted* with them. On the contrary, we are referred to them only indirectly. Whatever knowledge of them we come to possess is just exactly the network of concepts with which we drape reality in the course of knowing it. This circumstance provides further motivation for the Neo-Kantian mode of thought: Neo-Kantianism, like all idealistic systems, demands of the real that it be something with which we are somehow *directly acquainted,* and consequently regards the conceptual sign system that represents extra-mental reality to our mind as a component part of reality itself[45]. But for us, who have lost the fear of a reality that is not given, that is not known by acquaintance, such motivation is altogether absent. We make a sharp distinction between the scientific world picture and the world itself, and we do not succumb to the temptation to confuse the one with the other.

It will of course be denied that what is involved here is a confusion. We can prove rigorously, so it is held, that by real facts we can understand nothing other than determinations of thought, that facts cannot be conceived of as something confronting thought independently. "It is not true that a fact ... as though it were something preestablished independently ... furnishes the particular combination of thought determinations that seeks to express the content of the fact. Rather, it is the combination of thought determinations that furnishes, indeed *is,* the fact, and the fact is not more firmly fixed than is this combination of thought determinations" (p. 95).

Now the proofs available for this thesis are the same as those drawn upon to establish any idealistic system and are subject to the same objections. "Thinking is simply positing that something exists, and what this something may otherwise be or may have been is a question that has no specifiable sense" (p. 48). This formulation is not an especially happy one (the definition of 'thinking' presupposed here ought perhaps be rejected). But we can appreciate the idea that emerges from this passage. For we ourselves were obliged to state

---

45 The same motivation, it seems to me, is operative in the account given by the Neo-Kantian A. GÖRLAND in his work Die Hypothese (Göttingen 1911). According to him, we must regard the content of natural science (which in the final analysis is built up out of hypotheses — see below, § 41) as either a reality or else a fiction. The latter view he rejects in these words: "... I believe we must seek to purify hypotheses from any suspicion whatsoever of being fictitious, that is, fabricated. For I think it shameful to maintain that in his work a scientist resorts in any way to fictions" (p. 38). The author therefore concludes that hypotheses are "first and foremost processes of *realization*" (p. 43). It is in this way that reality supposedly is created through thought. Görland finds it "downright intolerable", for example, to call the auxiliary physical concept of a "rigid measuring rod" a fiction (p. 38). But anyone who, with us, views the conceptual structures of science not as reality itself but only as signs for reality, can find nothing objectionable in regarding rigid rods as fictions.

earlier (§ 22) that any answer — which of course must always be a *judgment* — to the question of the nature of being can represent only a new *designating* of what is. It can never give the essence of that which is designated. To demand an answer that would supply this essence would of course be nonsense. But from this, the logical idealist infers that it is thought that determines being. The same notion has been formulated in other terms by HEINRICH RICKERT who (in Gegenstand und Erkenntnis) states that in order to know what is, one must already have *made a judgment* that it exists. How else would one know it? Hence thinking always comes first under any circumstances. Thinking cannot be governed by being. On the contrary, what is there is always determined by what I have been obliged to judge. The actual existence of a red something that I am looking at, for example, is determined by the fact that I experience the following compulsion: I cannot judge other than that it is. The necessary character of a judgment, the "transcendental ought", determines being, since being is first assured through the necessary character of judging. No other ground for being can be given.

This reasoning is fallacious. It rests on an equivocation on the word 'know' *(Wissen)*[46]. 'Wissen' may designate either knowledge *of* something *(Wissen um etwas)* and thus a mere being acquainted with, or knowledge *about* something *(Wissen über etwas)* and thus cognition. Only in the second sense does knowing presuppose judging, hence thinking; but in the first sense, knowing is an absolute datum of consciousness, an absolute fact that rests on itself. In intuitive experiences or immediate data of consciousness (pure sensations, for instance) we find pure facts that are independent of any thinking — unless one insists on *calling* the process of sensation itself a thought process, in which event any further discussion would be useless. We also know where the error lies in the argument by which the logical idealist seeks to prove that pure perception is a thought process. "What distinguishes perception from a mere determination of thought? Definitely nothing contentual. For whatever we might affirm as the content of a given perception is, as the content of a statement, necessarily a determination of thought ..." (NATORP, *ibid.*, p. 95). But what is affirmed in a judgment is not

---

46 For a detailed critique of Rickert's arguments, see my paper on the nature of truth in the Vierteljahrsschrift für wissenschaftliche Philosophie, Volume 34, pp. 398 ff.

"contained" in the judgment, as though knowledge took hold of and absorbed the real. It is only correlated with the judgment. The statement, as such, independently of what it designates, has no content and is merely empty sound. A sensation of red is simply a given fact. But to utter the judgment "This is red" of course presupposes a cognitive act; for the experienced color must then be re-cognized as belonging to the class of hues designated by the word 'red'. Thus a judgment can come only after still further experiences have been added to the original fact, the sensation of red.

Hence it won't do at all to attribute to thought any part in the origin of a sensation. Sensations are described by the Neo-Kantian school as mere somethings that, prior to thinking, are not at all determined. "To think is in general to determine", says Natorp (p. 38). This definition is unsatisfactory enough, since 'determine' is an ambiguous word. (In another passage — p. 67 — he says that "to think is in general to relate", a formulation that one is more inclined to let pass.) But under no circumstances can we infer from this definition that there is no determinateness without and prior to thinking. In our view, facts stand fixed even without being captured by concepts. Anyone who supposes that determination must signify determination by means of concepts assumes what is to be proved, and locates in a state of affairs itself that which we use in describing the state of affairs. It is quite impossible to demonstrate that there is no determination, no fact, no given that has not first become such through thought. All apparent proofs of this thesis are circular.

Hence we must conclude that there are *no* pure forms of thought in the Neo-Kantian logical idealist sense of forms of reality in general.

§ 40. On Categories

Forms of thought, if we may speak of them at all, could have only one function: to impart form to a material already at hand, given through intuition but in a sense still formless, and thereby to produce in the material the relations that make knowledge of it possible. This, as we have said, was the view held by Kant himself. He called the material the *"manifold of intuition"*, and according to him the relations were instituted by the understanding which brought about a "synthetic unity" in the manifold, that is, drew the manifold together into the unity of consciousness. On occasion, he thought of "imagination" as being interposed between intuition and understanding. Imagination was supposed to create the synthesis of the manifold, but not to yield any knowledge. Knowledge first came about through the understanding, which gave unity to the synthesis by means of the pure concepts of the understanding.

We need not comment here on the doctrine of the imagination. We need only ask whether it is true that the relations on which knowledge rests are already found in the material given intuitively or whether they are first called into being by judgments, by certain functions of thought peculiar to consciousness. The question thus is whether or not there are categories in the Kantian sense.

In order to achieve clarity here we must return to the concept of "relation", heretofore touched on only fleetingly (§§ 8, 9). Earlier we viewed a relation as an object which, like any other object, can be designated by a concept (in contradistinction to a judgment, the function of which is to designate the *existence,* the presence of a relation). Were we mistaken in believing that a relation may be present even without the concept and hence is not merely contained *in it?*

A moment's reflection is enough to arouse misgivings about settling in either way the question of whether relations are created by our consciousness or whether they are only perceived. The correct course, rather, is to distinguish between two different species of relations. Suppose I am writting. I see the thumb of my right hand to the left of my index finger. The spatial relationship of the two fingers is given and contained in this perception in the same way and in the same sense as the skin color of my hand. Color and intuitive spatiality are both qualitative data and stand on one and the same level with respect to their being given by the senses. The color elements, for example, have inseparably connected with them not only intensity but also spatial relationships. These latter are perceived just like the elements; an experience of a "Gestalt-quality" is generated, and on that basis we can simply correlate concepts with the relationships.

Thus spatial relations are just as certainly prior to thought as are qualities of sensations. Judgments about spatial relationships designate something we come upon. The sets of facts they designate contain at least some features that do not first come into being through judgments but are logically independent of them. And pre-

cisely the same thing has to be said of *temporal* relations. The qualitative experience of the duration, simultaneity and succession of
elements of consciousness is an intuitive datum that is found there
in the same sense as are the elements themselves. To be judged as
succession or simultaneity, the temporal relationship must be apperceived. Thus judgment always follows later, both logically and psychologically. The temporality of all processes is something given
directly and intuitively that can thereafter be designated by concepts
and that provides the experiential foundation for any knowledge
of temporal relationships. There is an immediate difference for experience between four-quarter time and six-eighth time, a difference
that is likewise to be conceived of as a difference in Gestalt-quality.

Unlike spatiality, temporality has the special feature that it is
not bound to a particular sensory domain. Thus temporality is not
one thing for sensations of touch and another for visual perceptions
or for feelings. On the contrary, it is a facet or aspect that is present
in *all* experiences in the same manner, in sense perceptions as well
as in various non-intuitive acts or in emotions. While we can still
say of spatial relationships that they are directly "perceived" and
can specify the sense organs through which this happens, we cannot
speak this way about temporal relations, especially since we have
already had to reject as unworkable the notion of an "inner perception" (see above, § 20). There is no organ for time perception; such
perception requires no mediating act. Temporality is a general property of all contents of consciousness and is simply experienced.

But we must also recognize the existence of a second species of
relations [47]. These are like temporal relations in that we cannot speak
of their being perceived through any sense organ, whereas the perception, say, of colors or sounds is tied to a specific organ. But they
differ from spatial and temporal relations in that they do not seem
to be directly apprehended in the same sense. When I say that the
carpet pattern in my room and the rug pattern in the room of a
friend are *similar* or that a color and a sound are *different*, I express
relations. But it seems as though these relations actually have existence only through and in the judgment. Obviously the difference
between two sensations and the similarity between two patterns are

---

47 This distinction between two kinds of relations is also found in
LEIBNIZ (Nouveaux essais). The first type he calls *rélations de concours*
and the second *rélations de comparaison*.

not really at hand in the same sense as the individual colors in the perception of the pattern itself or the spatial juxtaposition of the colors. We are loath to conceive the similarity between Caesar and Napoleon as a real relationship between the two generals existing beyond space and time. Rather, such relationships appear to be generated first by the judging consciousness.

This odd state of affairs was already recognized in ancient times in the psychology developed by Plato. He held that relations are not apprehended through sense perception, but are formed by the soul itself (see ERNST CASSIRER, Substanzbegriff und Funktionsbegriff, pp. 434 ff.). Whether Plato's notion is to be understood in a way that calls Kant to mind is something that need not be decided here.

In any event, the concept of difference of which we have been speaking can be included in the Kantian table of categories. For it is equivalent to the concept of negation, which Kant reckons among the categories (see § 10). On the other hand, similarity and identity are not to be found there. Again, other concepts of relations that certainly belong to the second class of relations appear correctly in Kant's table. If on one occasion I treat a house as a single object (in a lease, for example) and on another as something constructed out of a set of bricks (in a ground plan, say), I have thus correlated with one and the same thing first the concept of unity and then the concept of multiplicity. Both procedures are equally justified, and which mode of designation I choose depends on my purposes. Neither of the two conceptions is immediately present, neither is given by the nature of the object. According to this, it is possible to believe that Kant was right in viewing the concepts of unity and multiplicity as forms of thought in his sense. And the same seems to hold for those concepts that in Kant's account represent what are undoubtedly the most important categories, namely, causality and substantiality. For I never directly perceive that one occurrence is the cause of another occurrence; at most I perceive that it regularly precedes it. Similarly, the relationship between substance and accident or between thing and property is never something we simply come upon; at most what we experience is a spatio-temporal coincidence of characteristics (see § 10). Only when these characteristics are gathered together in thought in a certain way do we obtain a complex of "properties" that can be designated by the concept of thing or substance. And to convert a mere succession of processes into a causal dependency likewise requires that thought add something, a special bond that, so it seems, is first created by a judgment.

For the present, we omit discussion of the other Kantian categories, since for the basic issue it is inessential whether we end up with the Kantian table itself or with some other. The only question is whether there are any such things as concepts of the understanding in his sense. So we ask at once: Do the relations belonging to the second species actually play the role that Kant assigns to the categories? Are they combinations that we set up through our judgments (combinations that we *must* set up if we wish to judge at all) and through which for us reality first obtains its form, a form that can then be asserted of reality with certainty and absolute validity?

Let us consider briefly the basic ideas in the proof that Kant offers for his view.

In his opinion, a "combining" or "joining" can take place only through the *understanding*. A manifold can be given through the senses; but it remains of necessity uncombined until thinking has taken possession of it (Kritik der reinen Vernunft, 2nd edition, § 15, B 129—131). Combination means the gathering together (synthesis) of a manifold into a *unity*. Such a synthesis is possible because the given intuitive elements are given to one and the same self. It is the *unity of consciousness,* the "synthetic unity of apperception", that joins them (*ibid.,* § 16). Kant calls *object* that "in the concept of which the manifold of a given intuition is united". Thus in order for something to become an object for me, it must be subject to the laws of the unity of consciousness. Now according to Kant, knowledge consists "in the definite relation of given representations to an object". Hence the unity of consciousness makes knowledge of the object possible and it is to this unity that knowledge owes its validity (*ibid.,* § 17). "But that act of the understanding through which the manifold of given representations ... is brought under one apperception [that is, embraced in the unity of consciousness] is the logical function of judgments." These functions are the categories, and "thus the manifold in a given intuition is necessarily subject to the categories" (*ibid.,* § 20). Accordingly the presupposition, under which for Kant synthetic judgments *a priori* about reality are possible, is fulfilled.

The heart of this proof is the appeal to the fact of the unity of consciousness.

Earlier we ourselves were obliged to point out this peculiar fact and make use of it to guarantee the strict validity of certain judgments. But these were the *analytic* judgments (see above, § 17). When this class of judgments was threatened by radical skepticism, we were able to ward off the attack by pointing to the unity of consciousness and exploiting the full weight of this fact. Can we expect the same help from it in connection with the incomparably more arduous task of providing an absolute guarantee for synthetic judgments about reality? This would indeed seem to exceed its powers, already taxed to the limit on that earlier occasion.

Actually, if the other assumptions on which Kant's reasoning must rest do not hold, the fact of the unity of consciousness does not prove anything so far as our question is concerned. And these assumptions are truly in a bad way.

For one thing, the claim that all joining or uniting in consciousness is brought about through quite definite *logical* operations peculiar to the understanding already contains in hidden form the presupposition that we do possess synthetic judgments *a priori*. This is also evident in the derivation, given later by Kant, of the individual basic principles that he takes to be synthetic *a priori*. But we need not go into that any further. For, as we have repeatedly emphasized, Kant did make just this presupposition, and his entire deduction was intended only to render the *possibility* of synthetic *a priori* knowledge intelligible, that is, to establish this possibility by the fact of scientific *experience*. But that is of no service to us and hence for us nothing has been proved.

Furthermore, what of the startingpoint of the whole argument? What of the claim that combination takes place only through the understanding, or, as we would express it, that there are no relations other than those created by thought? The sole ground that KANT can offer for this claim is that combining "is a spontaneous act of the faculty of representation" (Kritik der reinen Vernunft, 2nd edition, § 15). Nothing, of course, can be done with such a notion. It seems to be quite dogmatic. How are we to know that what is involved here is a spontaneous act of the understanding?

The introduction of the antithesis between spontaneity and receptivity — in modern terms, between activity and passivity — is entirely inappropriate at this point. This antithesis has an immediately intelligible sense initially only in its practical significance, in its application to the volitional processes of life. It is not suitable for giving an account of the fundamental epistemological situation with which we are concerned here. (See, too, the chapter on activity and passivity in BERTHOLD KERN's Weltanschauungen und Welterkenntnis, 1911.) In the discussion of these basic questions, the world of the given, for the epistemologist no less than for the physicist, is a continuous stream in which the distinction between the passively received and the actively added has, to begin with, no meaning. Such a distinction can be made only at a wholly different level of consideration by means of a special interpretation. Only if, with Kant, we view the understanding and sensibility as primordial "faculties" can we regard that difference as fundamental. But this is out of the question in the light of our present day knowledge of psychology.

Once we are convinced that a consideration of the Kantian philosophy does not help us reach a decision, we may then search for it along a direct path, undisturbed by Criticist misgivings.

Our examination of the two kinds of relations has shown in what sense it might still seem possible to make the understanding (thinking and judging) responsible for the occurrence of relations in the stream of consciousness. For we saw that relations of the second kind — identity, similarity, and the like — are not something encountered *realiter* in quite the same way as the sensuously perceived with its accompanying spatio-temporal relationships. Hence it was bound to seem as though this second species of relation was itself created by the very act of judging and not in any sense "encountered". A closer analysis, however, shows that this is not the case.

The difference we found between the two species of relations may be most appropriately formulated as follows: relations of the second kind (the category kind) are not to be understood as something just as *objectively* present as spatio-temporal relations. The (metaphysical) question may then be raised as to whether the former exist outside of consciousness or whether they are purely subjective. But that is not the point here. We are asking something else; our inquiry is about a difference that must already show itself within the sphere of the subjective. These two questions can easily be conflated and are often confused; for if relations indeed possessed the same objectivity as, say, the physical bodies of the external world, they would presumably give rise to immediate perceptual experiences just as bodies do.

But no matter what holds with regard to the objectivity of relations — and even if they lack objectivity — judgments about relations of the second kind can certainly designate facts that are simply encountered. The difference is that these facts are subjective; they are states of consciousness, results for the most part of such mental processes as acts of comparison, and it may still be uncertain whether objective facts correspond to them in any way. The similarity between Caesar and Napoleon is something less independent, more shadowy, than the two persons themselves or their temporal succession. The difference between a melody heard at the moment and one heard years ago is not something that now exists objectively in the same way as do the notes of the melody itself just being played. But there is no doubt that the *experience* in which the similarity or the difference is established is really present in consciousness. The occurrence of the experience of similarity is a fact: it is encountered just as any other fact is, and can then be designated by a judgment. Thus the judgment follows afterward; and there can be no question of its having to precede that experience temporally or logically, or of its containing that experience.

To be sure, experiences of such relations never occur except in connection with other contents of consciousness. They do not appear suddenly, unprepared for, like a sensation of sound, for example. To use a current expression, they are "founded" *("fundierte")* experiences: a relation does indeed presuppose terms between which it holds. But once these experiences of relations are present, they are simply encountered; they do not owe their existence to any "thinking" in our sense. This is a truth that Stumpf expressed (albeit in a terminology that deviates widely from ours) in the following passage from his paper on appearances and mental functions, often cited above: "Relationships between appearances are given us in and with any two appearances; they are not inserted by us, but are perceived in and with the appearances. Relationships belong to the material of the intellectual functions; they themselves are neither functions nor the products of functions."

Thus our examination of relations does not compel us to surrender the concept of "thinking" we have adhered to so far. We may continue to conceive of it as a mere correlating of judgments with facts. Thinking is neither a creating of facts nor the imparting

of form to a formless stuff. In every case, the relation that a judgment designates is given in consciousness, even if mostly as a result
of special mental processes. These latter are not to be designated
as *thinking* in our sense, but are more akin to processes of association.

When any two data of consciousness are given, the processes
that establish a relation between them may either take place in
such and such a manner, or else be absent altogether, depending on
the accidental circumstances. For these processes are part of the
natural world and their course depends on a whole series of empirical factors. But if this is the way things are, then it is evident that
a foundation for the *a priori* validity of synthetic judgments can
never be provided by the combining or connecting processes of consciousness. For these are changing natural processes, which do not
necessarily belong to the essence of consciousness, do not constitute
its unity. Consequently they lie outside the sphere of epistemology;
knowledge about their number and kind is given by psychological
analysis. (Such an analysis has been carried out in exemplary fashion
by ALFRED BRUNSWIG in his Das Verlgeichen und die Relations-
erkenntnis.)

Our finding is confirmed if we turn out attention once more
toward the relation concepts that are meant to play the role, in the
Criticist philosophy, of categories on which knowledge is grounded.

Whether we conceive a complex of given objects as a unity,
a plurality, or a totality (these are the first three Kantian categories)
will certainly be determined by fortuitous psychological conditions.
But once units are fixed and the real objects thus made countable,
the latter are subject to the concept of number; and the laws of
number — arithmetic as a whole — must be valid for them. It might
then be thought that the concept of plurality is the source of these
laws. But we know that the laws are purely analytic judgments.
Hence the validity of arithmetical judgments (see the discussion in
§ 36) offers no problem whatever so long as the premises hold for
reality. These premises come into being simply through counting
units of the real, and thus, by what has just been said, depend on
certain stipulations conditioned by empirical aims and circumstances.
Their validity is that of *conventions* and is thus grounded solely in
arbitrary determinations, such as measuring systems and the like.

They never give rise to new knowledge. Hence unity, plurality and totality, and numbers in general, are not "categories" in the sense in question.

A similar conclusion holds for the next three entries in the Kantian table of pure concepts of the understanding: reality, negation, limitation. As far as *reality* is concerned, it reappears in the table under the name of 'existence'. There is no difficulty in establishing that to count this concept as one of the categories is hardly compatible with the premises of the Kantian system; moreover for us, on the basis of our earlier discussion (III A and § 39), it is quite out of the question to characterize existence or reality as a form of thought that might give rise to synthetic judgments *a priori*.

It is the same with the concepts of negation and limitation. They too never lead to synthetic propositions, to new knowledge, and it is incorrect for them to appear in this table of categories. The *a priori* principles that Kant regards as issuing from the table — the so-called anticipations of perception — are in part mere definitions (for example, of the concepts of intensity and the like) and in part propositions of very doubtful validity. For the separation of the intensity of a sensation from its quality, which Kant always presupposes in the "anticipations of perception", is not something that can be carried out neatly for all the sensory domains.

We come now to the most important categories, those of substantiality and causality. (The third member of the group — interaction — will need no separate treatment.)

Both in everyday life and in scientific thinking, the concept of substance undoubtedly plays a great role. We speak of matter and its various states, of energy and its changing forms, of bodies and their varying properties. Basic in each case is the notion of a constant something within which the changes proceed but which itself does not change. The principle that in all change there is present an enduring constant is certainly a synthetic judgment; in Kant's view, it is obtained *a priori* from the application of the category of substance to the given. Is this its true source?

We said before that substances are never perceived. At most we perceive coincidences of qualities, or characteristics, or properties, or whatever we may call them. And something must be added to them before the complex of data that belong together can be designated by the concept of substance. There is no doubt that what is added is the associative connection in our consciousness of individual characteristics, thanks to which they, for our experience, henceforth belong together: when one is given there is bound up with it the expectation that the others also will be given. Suppose I am looking at a piece of wax; that is, suppose certain visual perceptions of a yellow color are present. By virtue of previously formed associations I expect that the sensations will vary in a certain way with changes in the external circumstances (the location, lighting, and the like). If I stretch out my hand, I expect certain tactile sensations (the feel of something smooth). If I set the wax near the fire, I expect certain transformations to take place during which instead of the firm body something fluid will appear. And each time my expectations will be fulfilled. Yet I can designate all these complexes with the same concept and the same name, 'wax', since their spatio-temporal connection is continuously preserved. Now everything is at hand that makes possible the use of the concept of substance as applied in everyday life. Nothing further is needed, no new act of thought or of the understanding, to allow the idea of a physical object to be formed.

True, the metaphysical concept of substance contains more, namely, the notion of a bearer different from and underlying the changing properties it bears. But it is just this notion that we long ago recognized as incorrect (see above, end of § 26 A 2). It is most certainly not a category that can constitute objects and provide a foundation for knowledge.

The scientific concept of matter refines and develops the vulgar metaphysical idea of substance in that it replaces an associative connection of properties by a law-like connection of qualities. But this scientific concept also offers no possibility of establishing *a priori* the synthetic proposition of the permanence of substance. KANT expresses the proposition in these words (Kritik der reinen Vernunft, Kehrbach edition, pp. 176 ff., A 184): "In all changes in the world, substance remains and only the accidents change." He believes that not only philosophers, but also ordinary persons, have in all ages assumed this proposition and will always accept it as indubitable. Now so far as this last state of affairs is correct, it admits of a psychological explanation; but it surely does not obtain universally. Even for the ordinary mind there is no necessity to conceive all that happens in the world as a change and alteration of something constant. The belief in an absolute coming to be or passing away has also existed, and remains admissible. Kant's demonstration that an absolute coming to be or passing away can never be the object of a possible experience is not cogent.

In modern science, indeed, the notion of substance has lost all ground. Psychology took the lead when it ceased to consider the data of consciousness as accidents of a substantial soul; by "soul" it now understood only the complex of mental qualities, which come and go. Today natural science too has been compelled by certain empirical data to conceive of its substance, matter, as an association of qualities that change with law-like regularity. (See the author's Naturphilosophie, Berlin 1925). Even the principle of the constancy of mass has, on empirical grounds, been abandoned. According to the "energeticist" conception of nature, constant energy is now to play the role formerly assumed by the old substance, so that all that happens in the world is to be regarded as no more than changes in the forms of energy. But this theory is to be viewed as only a possible, not a necessary, kind of description of nature. And it has by no means as great a following among scientists as might appear from the frequency with which this outlook is discussed in philosophical and popular literature. Moreover, no thoughtful scientist would wish to declare it absolutely impossible for future experience to show that even the principle of the conservation of energy is valid only to within some degree of approximation.

The only thing that science seeks to retain as absolutely immutable — and indeed *must* retain if it is to gain any knowledge at all — are *laws*. The finding again of the same in what is different, which constitutes scientific knowledge, turns out in the final analysis to be a finding again of the same *laws*. The immutability of substance has been dissolved into the constancy of the law-like regularity of relationships.

There are then no synthetic judgments *a priori* about substance, and the concept of substance is not a category in the sense of the transcendental philosophy.

We have thus been led back to the concept of law as the ultimate *terra firma*. This finding might engender the hope that here at last we have the desired "category" and that the law-like regularity of the world is assertable of the world *a priori*. We would then have the category of *causality*, for that is what the notion of law

obviously comes to. The assertion of the principle of causality —
that every event has a cause from which it necessarily follows — is
identical with the assertion that law-like regularity pervades all that
happens. For when I say that some particular process A must have
preceded another process B, I assume that there is a rule that specifies which B belongs with a particular A. If there were no such rule,
then B would not be determined at all. The rules are called laws of
nature; thus the law of causality signifies simply that all that happens is governed by laws.

To investigate the character of the assertion of causality thus
amounts to testing the validity of the proposition "All processes in
the universe take place according to law." And the investigation
must, as in all similar cases, answer the question whether this proposition is a synthetic judgment *a priori* or a convention or a hypothesis advanced on the basis of experience. The natural place for
an exhaustive treatment of this question is the philosophy of science,
and we cannot undertake it here. (For the present, the reader may
be referred to the author's paper, Naturphilosophische Betrachtungen
über das Kausalprinzip, in: Die Naturwissenschaften, Volume 8,
p. 461, 1920). It should be enough if we call attention to a few
critical aspects.

If there were any justified doubt in science or everyday life
about the unlimited general validity of the causal principle, then
of the three possibilities mentioned above, the first two — that the
causal principle is either a synthetic judgment *a priori* or a convention — would be immediately eliminated. For then the principle
would not possess *a priori* validity. Now there are in fact experimental data in modern physics that raise a serious question for the
scientist as to whether the assumption of a causal course for intra-
atomic processes should still be maintained. This is not to say that
a breakdown of causality, an absence of law in the smallest domains
of nature, has already been made probable in any way; nor do I
believe that it is the case. But the mere fact that certain experiments
invite us to consider the possibility already shows that the principle
of causality is to be regarded as an empirical proposition. To be
sure, this reference to the present state of physics can be viewed
only as a useful indication and not as an absolutely decisive factor.
A philosopher can always maintain that the physicist has come to
his doubts only through error and misunderstanding. Yet the history

of thought does teach us that philosophy is ill-advised to ignore voices coming over to it from research in the sciences.

The theory that the principle of causality is a convention has found its heralds precisely among thinkers with a natural science orientation (Philipp Frank, Hugo Dingler). Meanwhile, however, it has become quite clear that this conception is untenable. Of course causation can be defined in such a way that the principle actually does become a convention. But then the question is whether the concept thus defined is really the one with which science works and whether it may be used to describe what occurs. The answer is most assuredly in the negative. This follows at once from the situation in modern physics, referred to just above, and is confirmed by a thoroughgoing analysis of the content of the assertion of causality.

For Kant's theory of causality, the decisive element was the knowledge (brought into such great prominence by Hume) that actual causation — the following of one process *out of* another, the bond between cause and effect — is as little an object of perception as substantiality. What we experience is only temporal succession. This made it possible for Kant to claim that causality is a root concept first introduced into the appearances and imprinted upon them by reason. But an unbiased analysis of the idea of cause and of its role in scientific thought shows that the notion of a "bond" between cause and effect, a foundation for which Hume had already sought in vain, does not form an integral part of that idea. Rather, its content is exhausted in the concept of a certain regular sequence of events (where of course the concept of the regularity of a sequence requires the most exact refinement). And with this the Kantian motivation for conceiving of causality as a category, in his sense, falls by the wayside.

There is no need for the notion that processes follow not only after one another but through or out of one another, that some real coercive power stands over or in them binding them together and making one of them of necessity issue forth from another. As to why this notion in fact crops up we can seek only psychological explanations. For the modern scientist, a law of nature is not some real power, but only a rule of succession. It does not tell things how they must behave; it is only an expression for the way they do behave.

We do not know *a priori* whether a state *A* that has never before been observed without being followed by another state *B* will, when it reappears at any future time, draw *B* along with it. But we expect it to. In other words, we believe in the principle of causality, but its validity is not established *a priori* for our thought. Kant's attempt to prove the law of causality — his claim that if the law were not valid, experience would not be possible — contains a kernel of truth. But, as we suggested earlier by way of anticipation, it is of no advantage to us. For we have no guarantee that we possess any such thing as "experience" in the sense that must be presupposed here. We shall return to this matter in the next section.

Having seen that we cannot find in causality a "form of thought" in the desired sense, we turn now to the last three Kantian categories — existence, possibility, necessity. The first of these has been disposed of as far as we are concerned by earlier considerations. What remains is for us to examine the concepts of the possible and the necessary in connection with our problem.

If we take these two concepts in the sense stamped upon them by their origin in everyday life, we recognize at once that they are only signs for subjective states in the consciousness of the person who judges. In the final analysis, problematic and apodictic judgments express certain mental states of affairs and not a relation between the objects with which the judgment at first glance appears to deal. The problematic judgment "*S* can be *P*" designates a state of uncertainty on the part of the person who judges; the apodictic judgment "*S* must be *P*" a state of certainty. The feelings of uncertainty or certainty, of not knowing or knowing, are present in consciousness and provide the basis for the application of the two concepts.

The word 'necessity', like its opposite 'freedom', signifies a thoroughly anthropomorphic concept and presupposes the experience of *coercion*. We call human behavior *free* when it proceeds from motives in a normal way, without being inhibited by obstacles that lie outside the nature of the person in question. Otherwise, if prison walls or chains or threats determine the behavior, the latter is said to be *coerced*. And it is this feeling of not being able to do anything else that is the source of the concept of necessity. In fact, the word 'necessity' (like the word 'purpose') has an immediate sense only when applied to the behavior of willing beings; beyond that, it ought not appear in any rigorous theory. Viewed objectively, a happening either takes place or does not take place: the addition of the word 'necessary' is actually meaningless. It is as if we wanted to ask whether the moon moves around the earth easily or with difficulty. These are inadmissible carryovers of concepts that have a specifiable sense only in the sphere of the emotions.

The situation is quite similar with respect to "possibility". Just as existence cannot be distinguished at all from necessary existence, just as the necessary does not possess a higher degree of reality than the simple real, so the possible, taken in the strictest sense, cannot be distinguished from the actual. What is not real is basically not possible either. Since the conditions for its appearance are not fulfilled in the world of facts, the unreal becomes in fact *im*possible. We may designate an unreal event as possible only so long as we do not know whether the causes leading to its occurrence are present in nature. If they are, then it is real; if they are not present, then it is not real. There is no room for a third alternative. (Here we do not distinguish between the presently real on the one hand and a past or future real on the other; if anyone wishes to designate the latter as possible, there is no objection, but then the word has forfeited its specific meaning.) The statement "This event is possible" is thus not a judgment about objective happenings; rather, it designates only the state of uncertainty in our knowledge of the relationships that condition the event. In other words, the problematic judgment "S may be P" is equivalent to the categorical judgment "Q is R", where the concepts Q and R refer to a certain mental state of the person who judges.

Besides this original sense of the word 'possibility', we can of course by definition decide upon another sense for special purposes. And this has been done by redefining 'possible' as 'compatible with the laws of nature'. What happens in the world is determined not alone by the laws that govern it but also by the states present in it at the time. (Kant calls the former the formal conditions and the latter the material conditions. See above, § 23, near the end. In theoretical physics, the first appear as differential equations and the second as initial and boundary conditions.) Now since what is factually present is infinite in its multiplicity, we can never know it with any completeness; at most we can know the laws that govern it. Hence we feel certain that a particular event will never occur only if it contravenes the laws of nature. If, however, it is compatible with them, we still never know precisely whether the material conditions for its occurrence will ever be fulfilled, whether it will ever be real. We know for sure only that the laws do not rule it out. An uncertainty remains, and it is thus easy to see how one arrives at the second concept of the possible from the first. In the case of the second concept, the state of affairs that the judgment designates (for instance, "The war *may* last 100 years") is not the subjective state of uncertainty but the objective fact that the concept of the judged event does not run counter to the concepts of the laws of nature. To this objective fact, however, we can correlate a categorical judgment. Thus in this case too the problematic judgment reduces to a categorical one.

Similarly, the apodictic judgment "S must be P" is either simply identical with the categorical judgment "S is P" or else it designates a feeling of mental compulsion to judge, that is, a subjective conviction of the truth of the judgment. Obviously, this set of facts also can be expressed merely by a new categorical judgment.

Thus neither necessity nor possibility are forms of thought; they are but signs for certain states of affairs.

With this we conclude our review of knowledge-creating categories, a review that could only serve to reinforce a finding already obtained. Many attempts have been made to increase the total number of categories and to add various complicated concepts. But we need not go into these extensions once we have recognized that the general direction in which they lead is wrong. The end result has been this: the relation with which we have to do in a judgment is in no sense ever generated by the judgment. No matter what sort it is, the relation is always prior, logically and psychologically, to the act of thought.

Thus relations are not forms of thought but must be regarded as *forms of the given*. In this respect, they are like the spatiality and temporality of our intuition. Even followers of the Kantian trend of thought have on occasion conceded that the given is encountered already endowed with form. Thus we read in F. MÜNCH (Erlebnis und Geltung, 1913, p. 51): "Positivism is quite right when it claims that even in the phenomenal world forms are 'encountered': space and time, substance too in the sense of relatively constant coexistence, causality in the sense of relatively constant succession. But positivism is vastly in error when it takes these 'coordination forms' to be categories, when it holds as identical these two concepts that logically must be strictly distinguished." We agree, but we add that by the same token no categories are needed. Thought does not dissolve into various categorial functions; on the contrary, in our view "thinking" signifies only one function, that of *correlating*.

The correlating of two objects with one another, the relating of one to the other, is in fact a fundamental act of consciousness not reducible to anything else. It is a simple ultimate that can only be stated, a limit and a basis, which every epistemologist must finally press toward. This is confirmed for us by the example, among others, of Richard Dedekind, the brilliant investigator of the concept of number. He found that his study led him to the "ability of the mind to relate things to things, to let one thing correspond to another — without which ability thinking is not possible at all" (Was sind und was sollen die Zahlen?, 3rd edition, p. VIII).

In thinking, there is basically no other relation than that of correlation. The other relations spoken of in philosophy, science and everyday life are, so far as thinking is concerned, only *objects*. They belong to the material that is given to thought just as much as do things or properties or sensations.

For this reason we must also regard as erroneous the view that in logic and the theory of knowledge various *kinds* of judgments are advanced and coordinated. Essentially, and in the nature of the case, every judgment is categorical. And if outwardly it is not clothed in categorical garb, it can still always be converted into a judgment in categorical form through purely linguistic reformulations. This point has already been established for problematic and apodictic judgments, but it also holds for the others. An example will serve as corroboration. The *hypothetical* judgment "If A is, so is B" may be transformed naturally and without difficulty into the categorical judgment "A is the ground (or the cause) of B" or "B is the consequence (or the effect) of A". It then becomes clear that relations are not forms of judgment but objects of the act of judging. Since in many cases the content of statements can be rendered most conveniently by certain linguistic forms of sentences, the erroneous belief arises that what is involved are not different thought contents but different thought forms. In truth, however, what distinguishes the individual "kinds of judgments" from one another is to be found not in the judgments themselves but in the objects judged.

There is only one kind of judgment, the categorical. And there is only one kind of thought relation, that of correlation or designation.

We see then that from whatever angle we approach our problem, we always arrive at the same result. Thinking does not create the relations of reality; it has no form that it might imprint on reality. And reality permits no forms to be imprinted upon itself, because it already possesses form. Moreover, since there is no pure intuition that prescribes strict laws for reality (see § 38), we then have the following result: reality does not obtain form and regularity first from consciousness; on the contrary, consciousness is only a section cut out of reality. Now the last and sole possibility of strict, universally valid knowledge of reality lay in consciousness dictating to nature the laws of nature. Since this possibility has vanished, we are bereft of any hope of arriving at absolute certainty in the knowledge of reality. Apodictic truths about reality go beyond the power of the human faculty of cognition and are not accessible to it. There are no synthetic judgments *a priori*[48].

§ 41. On Inductive Knowledge

The question of the validity of knowledge of reality has found, in the pages above, a perhaps unwanted but not unexpected answer. The more familiar we grew with the wellsprings of human cognition the clearer it became that all synthetic judgments are *a posteriori* in both origin and validity.

The acts of finding-again, on which these judgments are grounded, are individual instances of experiences, and the knowledge thus obtained is, to begin with, valid only for the individual instances. But to live, to act and to carry on science we need general propositions, premises universally valid for reality, from which we can infer

---

48 HANS REICHENBACH, in his little book Relativitätstheorie und Erkenntnis a priori, has expressed the opinion (which he must surely no longer hold) that my theory of the uniqueness of correlation in knowing is basically also a synthetic judgment *a priori* and that I have thus unwittingly taken over the erroneous portion of the Kantian philosophy. This view is of course quite wrong, since my account of knowledge and truth by means of the concept of correlation is simply a *definition* and thus most certainly a purely analytic judgment.

conclusions that hold also for instances remote in time and space. It avails me nothing to know that the bread I eat has always nourished and agreed with me, if I do not also know that the bread I am going to eat tomorrow will possess the same properties and that it will also provide nutrition for others with whom I share it. That I am justified in assuming this no one will doubt. We never hesitate to make statements about real processes with which we are not directly acquainted because they lie in the future or far away; and our life depends at every moment on the validity of these statements.

Yet the result of our deliberations just above was precisely that we may not claim absolute validity for such statements. Thus there is a problem here, and its solution requires an answer to the following questions:

First, how do we come to carry over propositions about perceived instances to instances not perceived? How do we come to apply judgments that fit events experienced earlier to events not yet experienced?

Second, what kind of *validity* do we claim for propositions of this sort since we cannot assert their absolute validity?

Third, with what *justification* do we make this claim?

These three questions constitute the problem of *induction*. For this is the name given to extending a proposition from known instances to unknown ones, carrying over a truth from a few cases to many, or, as it is usually described, inferring the general from the particular.

1.

We must be clear about what answers to these questions can be obtained on the basis of our present viewpoint. Only then may we count the range of our considerations as more or less complete. We take up the questions in the order listed, and begin by tracing the path along which, starting from knowledge of particulars, we arrive at general propositions.

What powers extend our knowledge of past and present facts over to the remote and the future? That they are not the powers of thought, of reason, we know from previous considerations. The inferences of the understanding are by their very nature analytic; they only develop particular truths from the general truths in which they are already contained. Nor can thinking provide more than this.

It only gives order and connection to knowledge already gained by means of deductive inferences (§ 15); it does not create any knowledge (§§ 39, 40). On the other hand, induction *does* yield knowledge in the highest degree; it is through induction that we obtain the content of all our sciences of reality. Yet induction cannot be explained by experience any more than by thought, since it extends our knowledge to cases of which we have as yet *no* experience, to wit, cases that are temporally and spatially distant.

I believe that there is only one answer to the question of the actual origin of inductively obtained propositions and that philosophy has long been in possession of it, thanks above all to Hume.

The question, as is evident from its formulation, is psychological in nature. Our ability to take knowledge gained from certain cases and apply it to other cases must be grounded in certain factual characteristics of our mental life. If in every investigation of some object A we have found the object B again in it, we expect that *wherever* the concept A is applicable the concept B may also be used to designate the same object and will thus lead immediately to a unique correlation. For example, I have often observed that paper bursts into flames when I throw it on the fire. And I am convinced that the letter I am holding in my hand will burn up forthwith if I toss it into the fireplace, even though today is the first time I have ever seen this letter and these logs. Special circumstances aside, I regard the judgment "Paper is combustible" as generally valid. Again, I have never seen my window decked out with frost except when the temperature outside is quite low; hence whenever the window panes are covered with beautiful crystals, I may definitely expect to have a feeling of intense cold when I leave the house. The proposition that ice can exist only in the cold I have obtained through induction.

If we ask to which human capability we owe knowledge of this sort, we can find no other psychological basis than *habituation*. And habituation in turn rests entirely on processes of association. The image of burning has been firmly tied to the combination of the ideas of paper and fire, and the image of cold to the appearance of frost. I am equipped by nature with an association mechanism that allows me without further ado to expect the second term as soon as the first appears, assuming that I have experienced the union of the two often enough. This is a biologically favorable arrangement; man could not live without it, since then he would not be capable of life-preserving behavior.

The objection has often been raised that belief in the universal validity of a proposition frequently grows out of a single observation, that is, where there has been no opportunity to establish a strong association and develop an habituation. When a scientist describes the properties of a mechanical compound he has just discovered, he does not doubt that a compound produced in the same manner by anyone else anywhere will possess exactly the same properties, even though there is at the outset only a single observation on which he bases his judgment. It is perfectly true that in such a case the assumption of universal validity does not rest on associations formed on the occasion of that single instance. Yet in the final analysis the assumption still rests on associative habituation. That is, it rests on the fact that a very great number of *other* items of knowledge have preceded it. A great deal of experience has been gathered about the behavior of chemical compounds, about the factors on which that behavior usually depends and about those that do *not* matter. Had such thousand-fold experience *not* taken place, we could not in fact draw that inductive inference. We would not know whether the properties of the substance might depend on, say, the form of the container in which it is stored, or the age of the experimenter, or the location of the planets, or the like. In brief, the induction does not rest on the single observation alone, but presupposes a great mass of additional knowledge, which ultimately is always the result of an accumulation of similar experiences and thus the product of association, of habituation. Through this habituation a vast complex of expectations or rules is imprinted on our consciousness, a complex that pervades our entire life and thought. New individual cases are fitted into this context of habituation; it is not necessary to provide a new foundation each time through special processes of associative training.

If we are properly attentive to these circumstances, we may easily refute all objections against an associative foundation for induction. In a world in which similar experiences did not recur uniformly time after time and in which there was no opportunity for habituation and training, inductive knowledge would not come into being. Indeed, the cognitive process has evolved from processes that originally were of immediate biological utility (see above, § 13). It presupposes an adaptation to environmental circumstances that can take place only if these circumstances are so constant that habit formation becomes possible both for individuals and for the species.

Clearly, it is impossible to find any other reason for the naive belief in the universal validity of synthetic propositions. Naturally, this belief is not an *insight;* an insight would presuppose that the belief is *justified,* and whether and how such a justification can be given is the very difficult third question with which we shall shortly be concerned.

The striking thing about the answer we have found to the first question of induction is that it refers us to the very same processes recognized in preceding sections as the subjective roots of the notion of causality. Here is revealed the interconnection between the problem of causality and that of induction. In fact, they are not solvable independently of one another; the one is embraced in the other. This general connection of habituation of which we have been talking — and on the assumption of which even a single case can under certain circumstances suffice to establish an inductive proposition — is nothing other than the causal connection, or rather its subjective mirror image. The causal principle (see above, § 40) is merely a summary expression for the pervasive existence of individual law-like regularities. It is obtained by induction from the totality of observed laws, but naturally it cannot replace them. For even if the causal principle is accepted as valid, it remains the business of induction to ascertain which individual laws govern nature and thus which processes belong together as causes and effects.

The general connection of habituation, which provides the background for individual inductions and puts an end to their isolation and self-dependency, has thus turned out to be the causal nexus. The meshing of all our experiences, which is conditioned by the causal nexus, also prevents us from blindly regarding *anything* that in any way follows anything else as causally connected to that something else. The objection made often and quite early against the empiricist theory of cause — that, for example, the regular sequence of day and night still does not lead to the one being declared the cause of the other — is thus disposed of immediately. We soon find that the concepts of cause and effect are applicable only to processes, not to things. When, for example, we say that a chemical compound always has the same properties (this was the illustration we used of an induction based on one observation) what we mean is that chemical interactions carried out with the substance always have the same sequence of processes as their effect. Day and night, however, are not processes of nature in the scientific sense.

Thus from every side we find confirmation that the same, identical process — association — furnishes the subjective occasion both for the formation of the idea of causality and for the belief in universally valid propositions about reality.

2.

The first question raised by the induction problem — how we in fact arrive at generally valid synthetic judgments — may be counted as answered through this reference to psychological and biological processes. We now turn to the second and more difficult question: What kind of validity do such judgments have for us in view of the fact that they are not valid absolutely and beyond all doubt?

How can we speak at all about different kinds of validity? A judgment either designates some fact uniquely or it does not, and is thus either valid or not. Hence it appears nonsensical to distinguish various kinds or degrees of validity.

It is customary to say that inductively obtained propositions do not bear the character of certainty; they possess only *probable* validity. But what does this mean?

When I say "*A* is probably *B*" (for example, chemical forces are probably electrical in nature), I do not thereby intend to correlate the concepts *A* and *B* definitively with the same object, that is, to designate the object *B* as always surely to be found again in *A*. Rather, the correlation of *B* with the actual object is tentative, one that I *hope* will be unique. In other words, the proposition "*A* is *B*" represents an *hypothesis*.

All knowledge of reality consists, strictly speaking, of hypotheses. No scientific truth, whether it belongs to history or to the most exact of investigations into nature, is an exception. No scientific truth is in principle secure against the danger that at some time it may be refuted and thus become invalid. Although there are innumerable truths about the real world that no one who is acquainted with them can doubt, still none of them can be completely stripped of their hypothetical character.

But these things are all very familiar. Modern philosophy and science have long since become accustomed to claiming only probability for knowledge of reality. And with this they can rest content, knowing that in everyday life — where the stakes are happiness and misery, existence and death — we accept as secure bases for action judgments that have a lower degree of probability than science is able to attain for its own judgments.

In other words, as everyone knows, we distinguish higher and lower degrees of probability. Our judgments may be more or less hypothetical. From a subjective point of view, and as a psychological fact, this situation is not difficult to understand. It can easily be explained in conjunction with analogous considerations set forth in the preceding section. When we assert something with great certainty, our conscious disposition is quite different than when we utter only a vague surmise. The greater or lesser probability of the validity of a proposition is something we experience in a specific way. This conscious state of certainty or doubt may be characterized as a feeling, or in any other manner. It is in any event a reality with which everyone is acquainted and which everyone has experienced for himself any number of times when he has thought about reality. It determines and measures for the judging subject the amount of validity a proposition has. And if asserting a certain probability for the validity of a judgment meant nothing more than affirming the presence of that subjective state of certainty or uncertainty, then our second question about induction would now be disposed of.

But this is not the case. There is no doubt that probabilistic statements lay claim to an objective meaning beyond the subjective sense. When we say "A is probably B", the sense of the assertion consists not simply in our wishing to affirm that we have within us a certain feeling; our intention is to say something about the behavior of objective reality. We are not stating flatly that the designation of object A by concept B leads to uniqueness, but we also are not asserting that this is *not* the case. Nor are we saying merely that we know nothing as to whether the one or the other is correct. Apparently what is involved is a mean between contradictory opposites, a third something besides affirmation and denial. No wonder this strange situation challenges logicians of probability to ever renewed efforts.

What objective sense does it make to ascribe probable validity to a proposition? In studying this question, one usually begins with a consideration of the mathematical concept of probability. And that indeed is where one might first expect illumination, since a rigorous formulation is already to be found there. But it should not be forgotten that the philosophical problem lies not in the mathematical definition of probability but solely in the application of the concept to reality. Our interest is only in the latter.

The probability of throwing a six with an ordinary die is, as we know, one-sixth. For a given throw, any one of the six sides of the die may be face upward (there are six "possible" cases) and just one of these sides has the desired six pips (there is one "favorable" case). And in mathematics the probability of an event is defined as the number of favorable cases divided by the number of possible ones. It is assumed that all cases are "equally possible"; but what is to be understood by that and how it is to be determined is not of concern to the calculus of probability itself. Yet it is precisely this that is the one important thing for us. Thus if we ask: What does it mean to say that the probability of an event is $1/6$, we are not satisfied by a reference to the quotient of favorable cases over possible cases. What we want to know is to what facts of reality can the concept be applied.

It has occasionally been held that numerical probability in this case is nothing more than a measure of the confidence with which a dice player expects a six to turn up. But clearly this interpretation is incorrect. For a player's hope of winning depends on his accidental mood, his frame of mind, his feelings and his knowledge. Thus hope varies, whereas the objective probability remains $1/6$. Hence that fraction cannot be a measure of his *actual* expectation, but at most of his *justified* expectation. With what *right* he expects a particular result from the game depends entirely on objective conditions. There is no question that the numerical probability has a thoroughly objective meaning. But what is it?

Once the theory of subjective expectation is abandoned, the probability proposition in our example is usually interpreted to mean that in a lengthy series of throws, the greater the total number of throws the closer the number of sixes comes to $1/6$ of the total number of throws. But the precise meaning of the proposition cannot lie in this formulation. For this statement itself is valid not strictly, but only with a certain probability, and this probability may be specified numerically.

That the number of sixes among n throws deviates the less from $n/6$ the greater the number n cannot be asserted with certainty for a finite n. It is only probable. It is said to be valid for "large" numbers; but since "large" is a relative concept, this is not a rigorous statement. For example, it may happen accidentally that six turns up exactly ten times in the first 60 throws, but less and less often in the next thousand, so that the average frequency of its occurrence diverges from the fraction $n/6$ instead of approaching it. No matter how large we take n, there is always a finite probability that a six will *not turn up at all* among the throws; that probability is $(5/6)^n$. Regardless of how one twists or turns, it is impossible to specify in this manner the exact meaning that a probabilistic statement has for reality. Whatever formulation one chooses, the statement has only a probable validity. An assertion about reality based on probability considerations has strict validity only when we pass to the limit of infinitely many cases; only with the aid of a limiting process can we specify exactly the meaning of a probabilistic statement about reality. But since in reality infinitely many cases are never given, this does not help. In other words, the concept of probability cannot be reduced to that of truth so long as one regards the matter or substance of the judgment to be the unknown sets of facts mentioned explicitly in the "probabilistic" judgment. It is simply not possible to make statements about the unknown as if it were known.

It must therefore be conceded that the concept of probability in its application to the real world still holds many profound mysteries. And until these are solved the problem of the kind of validity possessed by propositions obtained through induction is not definitively mastered. But since *all* universal judgments about reality are obtained through induction, the fundamental importance of the problem is thus apparent. Perhaps the concept of probability is an ultimate, not further analyzable — something to be accepted as an elementary means of describing the world. Yet, clearly, only in case of direst necessity could a philosopher decide to set over against, say, categorical judgments a special, not further reducible class of probabilistic judgments.

An exact study of the alternatives that present themselves and thus a solution to the problem of induction is possible only where the concepts involved have obtained a sufficiently sharp clarification, that is, in the domain of the natural sciences. The inquiry must be conducted with the methods of the philosophy of science; it cannot be carried any further at this point.

Just one thing must be noted. No matter how the validity for reality of probabilistic propositions may be formulated, it is in any event as accessible to testing by experience (in turn, with probability) as any other hypothesis. Whether the laws of the calculus of probability hold for the behavior of nature can certainly be decided (with probability) by observation. Thus in any case their validity is not *a priori*.

3.

While we now know how we come to set up inductive propositions and what kind of validity we claim for them, we still know nothing about whether this claim is justified. The third question raised by the problem of induction is directed to precisely this *quaestio juris*. It therefore requires new considerations from an entirely different viewpoint.

The opinion has often been advanced that in order to establish the validity of inductively obtained judgments nothing further is needed than the principle of causality. That is to say, with the aid of this principle any inductive inference may be reduced to a syllogism as follows: Observation shows that A was the antecedent of C; since according to the causal principle the same antecedent is always attended by the same consequent, it thus follows that C will also be the consequent of A in any future and anywhere. With this, the universal validity of the connection between A and C is expressed and the transition from the known to the unknown is carried out in a logically unassailable form.

Now this view would be quite correct if exactly the same process always reappeared as the antecedent. But, strictly speaking, this is not the case. Each cause, again strictly speaking, is infinitely complicated. It never happens in nature that in the case of two events exactly the same circumstances recur to within the most minute detail; there are only similarities, never perfect identities (and if there were, they still could not be established with certainty). But expressed in the form that *similar* effects follow upon *similar* causes, the causal principle certainly does not always hold. For, as we know, very small differences in the cause may at times be attended by the greatest of differences in the effect. There are some circumstances that matter and others that do not. To separate the latter from the former and to find out which circumstances are the conditioning ones, the causes, is precisely the task of induction. The procedure to be applied is exemplified (if not in quite the most perfect way) in Mill's famous four methods of induction. It is only through some procedure of this sort that we determine the A that is to appear as subject in the minor premiss "A is the antecedent of C" of the above inference. The minor premiss thus does not designate, say, a simple fact of observation. Moreover, the strict principle of causality is of no assistance in deriving this premiss logically from the observations; for it holds exactly only with respect to the total causes, and we can never be sure that we have found all the essential circumstances and have united them in the concept A. There are infinitely many circumstances that might possibly enter into consideration as the cause, since, theoretically, every process in the universe could make a contribution.

We must therefore conclude that even if it were possible for us in some fashion to guarantee the validity of the causal principle, this would in no way prove that the individual inductions are justified. The validity of the causal principle, although indeed a necessary condition for the inductive procedure, is not a sufficient one.

That causality and hence inductive inference cannot be established by a rational proof was perceived quite early with the aid of an empiricist line of argument. Still, people consoled themselves that the validity and trustworthiness of such inferences are guaranteed by *experience*. But then Hume showed that under no circumstances is experience capable of discharging the responsibility with which it had been burdened. Let us imagine how someone might try to prove that the belief in causality is justified by experience. If observation has shown that A and B often occur together, then I expect, without having a logical right to do so, that this will also be the case in the future. Further observation then teaches me that in all cases A never occurs without being tied to B. Thus my expectation has been confirmed. Perception has shown that my doubt in the validity of the inference from earlier instances to later ones was unnecessary. And this, so it is said, provides the justification for my expectation, for the belief in the causal principle.

It was Hume who most clearly demonstrated that this argument is circular. If observation confirms a proposition obtained by induction, this indeed proves that my expectation was justified, that the inference from the earlier to the later was correct. But it proves the validity of the inference only for the factually confirmed cases. When I look upon previous fulfillment of my expectation as a warrant for its being confirmed again in the future, I already presuppose the proposition that I wish to prove. Observation does teach me the admissibility of carrying over a proposition from earlier known cases to later ones that in the meantime have likewise become known; but it does not instruct me in the least about the validity of cases that have not yet been perceived. It cannot erect a bridge from past observations to future ones, and this is the whole point to induction. The entire argument has not resolved the question; it has only deferred it.

This is the import of the skeptical objections put forward by Hume. These show most rigorously that experience not only fails to provide a conclusive proof of the validity of the causal principle for the future, it does not provide any proof at all. Learning from experience means utilizing perceptions, inferring what is to come and what is past, and this is possible only with the aid of the causal principle. This principle is thus always presupposed by experience and cannot first be established through it.

Thus neither through experience nor through reason is a proof to be had. That Hume's objections are convincing cannot be doubted. And so Kant sought, as we know, a deduction neither from reason nor from experience, but from the "possibility of experience". We have criticized these efforts in the preceding two sections and have found them to be wholly inadequate. We said that nevertheless we find in Kant the kernel of a correct thought. And the attempts on the part of modern thinkers to construct a foundation move in this same direction, although these thinkers have learned from his mistakes. BENNO ERDMANN seeks to prove that human thought would not be possible at all if the causal principle and induction possessed no validity (Über Inhalt und Geltung des Kausalgesetzes, Halle 1905). S. BECHER limits this assertion to *scientific* thought (Erkenntnistheoretische Untersuchungen zu Stuart Mills Theorie der Kausalität, Halle 1906).

In the case of these and similar attempts at a foundation (other kinds need not be considered today in serious epistemological inquiries), the strict validity of the causal principle and of hypothetical, inductively obtained truths figures as a *postulate*. What is shown is that unless the principle is valid, there would be no point at all in making reality the object of thinking, that it would be meaningless to strive for knowledge and to carry on science. But anyone who asks about causality, induction and the like is looking for knowledge of reality. And so he is told: you must either renounce altogether any reflection on things and any discussion with us, or else you must recognize the validity of these principles. Without them, the very possibility of research and inquiry is eliminated.

This is certainly true, and no one is likely to commit himself to proving more than this. But we want to be quite clear about the true import of these ideas and to account for the special character of this mode of providing a foundation. The mode is not a logical one. A "postulate" is something completely foreign to thought. Science has to do only with facts, not demands or wishes. Thus if we accept the validity of a general principle without in the least being able to prove it, then what is involved is not a theoretical requirement but a practical act. Theoretically, so far as providing a foundation is concerned, it is of no use to me to know that without the causal principle no learning from experience would be possible nor any thinking, whether in everyday life or in science. For why should there be human thinking at all? Why must knowledge be possible? Obviously something of the sort has existed up to now, but from this fact we cannot infer anything!

The drive for knowledge initially has biological roots (see § 13). Man himself is a part of reality, and if he pursues the sciences of that reality he will find himself directed toward real connections that bind him to reality. And these in the final analysis are practical in nature. Only through his feelings and drives does he react to the influence of the external world; otherwise he would never strive to know.

For the sake of living, there must be learning from experience. Man needs it for existence, and if not for science then for the possibility of science. The world must be knowable for man if he is to be able to live in it. Man stands in a much closer relationship to reality in ordinary life than he does in the sciences. The philosophical questions about the existence of an external world, about the boundary between subjectivity and objectivity, and the like, do not exist at all from the standpoint of life in general. What philosophy with great effort has first separated, and then with greater effort put together again in suitable fashion, is for ordinary life an undivided unity. Between myself and the external world, between past and future, there does not exist that gulf which the philosopher discovers and then struggles to bridge over. It is for this reason that life also easily masters the transition between subjective and objective validity and probability, on which logical thought comes to grief. Consciousness is adapted to the world; its subjective expectations are generated by objective processes, and coincide with these processes precisely because they are so adapted.

Accordingly, the practical justification of the causal principle — a theoretical one is not possible — lies in the fact that our first and third questions about induction merge with one another, no matter how sharply they are to be separated theoretically. The question of how I come to believe in the causal principle and the question of what is the guarantee of its validity have a common answer. The practical belief in the principle arises through association, through an instinct that at every instant pervades life in its everyday activity, dominates and preserves it. The results of this fundamental life function are valid for living. As far as action is concerned, there is no other kind of validity. And the conduct of science is also an activity. Because the world is constructed in accordance with the causal principle, all life in this world must be subject to that instinct.

The surety is an absolute one. For the belief that everything that happens has a cause is contained implicitly in every conscious action with absolutely no exception. The concept of acting, of goal-setting, contains the concept of the causal determination of all real processes. Doubt as to the validity of the causal principle comes only as the consequence of reflection (which is also required if the principle is to be put forward explicitly at all). This doubt is therefore theoretical in nature. The case here is similar to that involved in the question of the so-called freedom of the will. This problem also is merely a theoretical, philosophical one, to which the non-philosopher as well is of course easily led by a minimum of reflection. Under all circumstances, the practical affairs of life presuppose a thoroughgoing causal determinacy for every action, a fact that is first revealed, to be sure, by philosophical thinking.

On the other hand, belief in the validity of any particular, inductively obtained truth is, also speaking practically, not absolute and inescapable. What is absolute and inescapable, however, is belief in the probability of such a truth. In other words, with respect to empirical propositions we behave without exception as if from among the truth conditions of these propositions a certain portion is fulfilled, the size of which portion corresponds to the degree of the probability. The absolute practical assurance of the probable validity of universal empirical judgments is not something special over and above the precise validity of the causal principle; rather, the two coincide fully so far as ordinary life is concerned.

We do of course establish that the causal principle does not suffice for the theoretical, logical grounding of the validity of induction, but that on the contrary other presuppositions must also be fulfilled. In order for inductive inferences to be drawn, not only must every effect in the universe be conditioned by sufficient causes, but also the causes must admit of being discovered and separated from one another. For this, however, it is necessary, first, that a certain uniformity exist in nature, a recurrence of similar circumstances; second, that the greatest possible variety of material conditions prevail (what EDGAR ZILSEL in his book, Das Anwendungsproblem, calls "general diversity"); and third, that it be possible to separate important circumstances from unimportant ones so that causes may be isolated. The complete analysis of these conditions of induction and the searching out of any that may be lacking is a special task of logic which cannot be undertaken here. It is of course totally impossible to prove that the structure of the world fulfills these presuppositions. But the complete practical guarantee for this lies in the fact of life's everyday activies. If these presuppositions were not fulfilled, there would be no instinct or habituation, which first makes all activity possible; there would be no harmony between the world and our actions. Thus, as far as life is concerned, whatever belongs to its own foundations possesses validity for it. Here we need only repeat what was said about the practical validity of the causal principle. The principle itself always plays its role in life only implicitly, clothed in the form of specific empirical propositions. These propositions alone are of immediate interest for life, and it is they that first yield, through inductive generalization, the result that every happening is causally conditioned. Psychologically, the more specific always precedes the more general, whereas in logical deduction the relationship is the converse.

The point of view we arrive at through considerations such as these is basically Hume's. I do not believe that it is possible to move essentially beyond him. Hence it seems to me that there is a more rewarding task than renewing attempts to refute this viewpoint. It is to do everything possible to reconcile the difference between Hume and those who oppose him, and to understand clearly that the position we have reached does not signify the sort of skeptical renunciation with which our theoretical needs could not be satisfied at any price.

It is of course true that the theoretical insight demanded by the understanding can never be supplanted by any practical postulate (or guarantee). But what life *requires* is merely the latter, and one must be careful not to mistake the practical requirements of life for logical requirements, for cognitive postulates. If there were no validity to empirical judgments, life and science would be put in question. But obviously the possibility of science itself is not in turn a scientific requirement; on the contrary, it is a practical one. Knowledge consists in a unique designation of the world with the aid of a minimum number of concepts, and it is made possible by the fact that real things can be reduced to one another by finding the one in the other. Knowledge demands that the reduction of concepts to one another be carried as far as possible. But *that* such a reduction should be possible, that the world in all its regions, in the past and in the future, should turn out to be equally accessible to our knowledge is a wish, and its fulfillment or non-fulfillment is something for theoretical science simply to record. For life, however, it is something on which being or not-being depends. But life does exist. The correct element in the Kantian notion that the validity of general propositions can be proved from the possibility of experience is preserved if we take the concept of experience in the sufficiently general sense of practical activity, and understand by proof not a logical deduction but a practical justification.

Knowledge would not be possible if there were no *samenesses*. Through them alone are we able to find again the one in the other and to describe the multiform world with the aid of a very few concepts. It will be asked: How is it possible to designate the entire world in its endless abundance of forms by means of a simple, perspicuous conceptual system built up out of a few elements, and to bring it so to speak under one formula? We may answer without hesitation: Because the world itself is a unified whole, because everywhere within it the same is found in the different. In this sense reality is wholly rational, that is, it is objectively so constituted that a small number of concepts are enough to designate it uniquely. Thus it is not our consciousness that first makes the world knowable. By reducing the number of conceptual signs to a minimum, we conform to the true essence and law of reality. It is for just this reason that this reduction is *knowledge* of the world.

The actual obtaining of knowledge of reality is the task of the individual sciences. The theory of knowledge need consider only the principles and conditions for solving this task. This is a work of pure criticism, which, in comparison with the accomplishments of the sciences, may seem less rewarding. But the criticism is not destructive. For it cannot do away with or overturn or change anything that the sciences have once actually made their own. Rather, that criticism aims only at correctly interpreting the achievements of the sciences, at discovering their deepest significance. Such an interpretation, indeed, is the ultimate, supreme task of scholarship, and will ever remain so.

Index of Names

Subject Index